PRINCIPLES AND HERESIES

Principles and Heresies

Frank S. Meyer and the Shaping of the American Conservative Movement

KEVIN J. SMANT

ISI Books • Wilmington, Delaware
2002

Cataloging-in-Publication Data:

    Smant, Kevin J.
        Principles and heresies : Frank S. Meyer and the American conservative
    movement / Kevin J. Smant — 1st ed. — Wilmington, DE : ISI Books,
    2002.

    p. ; cm.

    ISBN 1-882926-72-2

    1. Meyer, Frank S. 2. Conservatism—United States 3. United States—
Politics and government—1945-1989 I. Title II. Frank S. Meyer and the American conservative movement

JC573 .S63 2002   2001097018
320.52/0973—dc21   CIP

Interior book design by Claudia L. Henrie

Published in the United States by:
ISI Books
Post Office Box 4431
Wilmington, DE 19807-0431

Manufactured in the United States of America

*T*o all who over this past decade helped me write this, even if they didn't know how much they were helping me: to my family, who always encouraged me. To Lauren, who never let me stay down, kept me going, and would never let a friendship die. To Renee, who understands me as few persons can, whose encouragement meant a great deal, too. To all my teaching colleagues at IUSB—thanks for your help and advice. To Michael, and Bruce; to Maureen, and Jackie; to Shirley and Betty; to Jenny and Patty; to Penny; and to Theresa, who always stuck by me. You were my friends, my counselors, my confidantes. You cared about me, and I you. I couldn't have done it without you.

~ Contents ~

~ *Chronology* ~

1909:   Frank Straus Meyer is born on May 9 in Newark, New Jersey.

1926:   Meyer enrolls in Princeton University.

1928:   Meyer withdraws from Princeton due to ill health.

1929:   Beginning of the Great Depression.

1930:   Meyer arrives in England, studying privately for a year with tutors.

1931:   Meyer enters Oxford University.

        Meyer joins the British Communist Party.

1932:   Meyer enters the London School of Economics.

1933:   As an avowed communist, Meyer is elected president of the LSE Student Union.

1934:   Meyer is expelled from the LSE for, in violation of school policy, distributing communist literature.

1935:   The Communist Party reassigns Meyer to the Chicago area.

        Meyer enrolls as a graduate student at the University of Chicago.

1938:   The American Communist Party appoints Meyer as its educational director for the Illinois–Indiana district.

1939:   Nazi Germany and the Soviet Union sign Non-Aggression Pact.

        Germany attacks Poland. World War II begins in Europe.

        Because of the USSR's alliance with Germany, Meyer and other American communists oppose American entry into the war.

1940:   Meyer marries Elsie Bown.

1941:   Nazi Germany attacks the Soviet Union.

        Meyer and other American communists urge American entry into the war on the side of the Soviet Union.

        Japan bombs Pearl Harbor.

The United States declares war on both Germany and Japan.

1942: The Communist Party gives Meyer permission to join the U.S. Army.

Meyer is inducted into Officer's Training School as a volunteer officer candidate.

1943: Meyer is discharged from the army for medical reasons.

Meyer writes letter to American Communist Party head Earl Browder that is critical of the party's positions.

1944: Browder announces new, moderate Communist Party line.

Meyer attends CPUSA annual convention.

Meyer and wife Elsie buy home in Woodstock, New York.

A son, John, is born to the Meyers on December 31.

1945: Meyer teaches at Communist Party's Jefferson School in New York City.

Earl Browder is removed as head of CPUSA.

Meyer cuts ties with Communist Party in fall.

1947: "Cold War" begins between United States and Soviet Union.

1949: Meyer cooperates with Federal Bureau of Investigation and describes what he knows of Communist Party activity in the United States.

Meyer testifies against Communist Party members in trials in New York state under the Smith Act.

1952: Meyer becomes contributor to conservative magazine the *Freeman*.

Meyer becomes lead book reviewer for conservative magazine *American Mercury*.

The Meyers' second son Gene is born on June 27.

1955: Meyer joins *National Review* magazine as "contributor."

1956: Meyer begins writing monthly column, "Principles and Heresies," in *NR*.

1957: Meyer becomes editor of book review section in *NR*, soon to be called "Books, Arts, and Manners."

1960: Meyer becomes adviser to conservative youth organization Young Americans for Freedom.

Meyer and *NR* decline to endorse Richard Nixon in his presidential campaign against John F. Kennedy.

NR holds fifth anniversary dinner in New York City. Meyer is one of the featured speakers.

1961: Meyer's first book, *The Moulding of Communists,* is published.

Meyer joins the organizing committee of the New York State Conservative Party. He later becomes member of its executive committee and party's chief spokesman on foreign policy.

1962: Meyer begins publishing a quarterly conservative academic newsletter titled the *Exchange.*

Meyer's *In Defense of Freedom: A Conservative Credo* is published.

1964: Conservative U.S. Senator, *National Review* supporter, and Meyer acquaintance Barry Goldwater receives the Republican Party's presidential nomination.

Goldwater is defeated in November in a landslide by Democrat Lyndon B. Johnson.

Meyer's third book, an edited collection of essays, is published under the title *What Is Conservatism?*

The American Conservative Union is formed. Meyer joins its board of directors and later serves as its treasurer.

1965: Meyer becomes adviser to conservative academic organization The Philadelphia Society.

Special issue of *National Review* expels John Birch Society from responsible conservative movement. Meyer writes special "Principles and Heresies" column in support of the magazine's stand.

NR holds large tenth anniversary celebration in New York City. Meyer is one of the featured speakers.

1968:   *National Review,* after remaining neutral during the primary season, endorses Richard Nixon for president, with Meyer's support.

NR strongly opposes George Wallace's bid for the presidency and conservative support. Meyer strongly supports magazine's stand.

Meyer's fourth book, an edited collection of his columns and essays, is published and titled *The Conservative Mainstream.*

1969:   Richard Nixon is inaugurated as president of the United States.

1970:   Conservative Party candidate James L. Buckley wins election as U.S. Senator from the state of New York. Meyer is a close behind-the-scenes adviser.

1971:   President Nixon announces new domestic spending plans, arms control negotiations with the Soviet Union, and a coming visit to communist China.

Meyer increases his criticisms of Nixon in his "Principles and Heresies" column and within the American Conservative Union.

Conservative leaders, including Meyer and others from *National Review,* meet in New York City and announce a "suspension of support" of the Nixon administration.

1972:   Meyer dies of cancer in Woodstock, New York, on April 1.

1973:   Meyer's final book, an edited collection of verse, is published and titled *Breathes There the Man: Ballads and Poems of the English-Speaking Peoples.*

– *Foreword* –

T HE RISE OF AMERICAN conservatism in the second half of the
twentieth century has become, it seems, a popular academic topic.
That this should be the case is in one sense encouraging (and long
overdue), but in another problematic.

Behind this surprising scholarly trend are certain political facts of record.
It's obvious now to all observers that there has been a general rightward drift
in our elections, extending over several decades. In nine presidential contests
since 1968—four years after the defeat of Barry Goldwater allegedly ended
conservatism forever—six have been won by Republican candidates, all running to greater or lesser degree on conservative themes and values. And, almost as telling, the three elections that went the other way were won by
Southern Democratic candidates perched—albeit in rather shaky fashion—to
the right of their party's usual stance on issues.

In the middle of this historical cycle, moreover, towers the dominant
figure of Ronald Reagan, the most conservative of the successful GOP contenders, and also the most politically potent. In retrospect it's fairly plain, even
to those who didn't like him, that Reagan and whatever it was he represented
were major causative factors in remaking the political landscape. So, from the
standpoint of understanding what has been going on in U.S. elections for
better than a generation, maybe it's time to forgo the usual focus on New Left

upheaval, flower children, and getting stoned at Woodstock and look at what was happening elsewhere. Hence a considerable spate of books about the conservative movement of the '60s.

Here, unfortunately, is where the problematic part comes in. In the prevailing academic culture, and the media world that is its offshoot, "conservative" is a term of loathing. The folks who hold forth in these precincts are generally of the Left persuasion. They don't like conservatism, have spent many years abusing it, and have stayed as far from it as possible. Accordingly, they don't know much about it. The result is that would-be historians from this sector are so far beyond the loop they have a hard time figuring anything out, even when they really want to.

One thinks of a recent book about these matters which, despite commendably diligent sleuthing, wanders down some curious by-ways. The opening passages of this work (and some later ones as well) would lead the unwary to believe the birth of the modern conservative movement was somehow linked to the political fortunes of—Orval Faubus! (For those who have forgotten, or never knew, Faubus was the liberal-*cum*-segregationist Democratic governor of Arkansas who in the late 1950s sought to block the integration of Little Rock High School—an episode handled, in proper context, in the present volume.)

Now it is a fact that Orval Faubus was a kind of precursor to George Wallace, whose maverick presidential candidacy helped shatter the Democratic coalition in 1968, and was seen in like manner in the '50s by people who wished that coalition ill. However, as somebody who was around back then, I can testify that advancing the exiguous presidential hopes of Orval Faubus was never once mentioned in my presence. Nor was it discernible, then or later, that anyone in the conservative movement seriously thought he should be lifted to the White House. The emphasis given this fey notion could hardly be more misleading as to what was actually going on.

A further problem with histories of this sort, born also from lack of firsthand knowledge, is that they tend to focus on political players and their visible public actions, and to slight or ignore the seismic working of ideas beneath the surface. This is always the wrong way to do it, but in the case of the modern conservative movement is more egregiously wrong than ever. For the thing that was most distinctive about conservative standard-bearers

Goldwater and Reagan and the political forces they represented was that they were first, last, and always about ideas and principles. To miss this is to miss the very essence of the story.

At this level, if anything, the problem of historical ignorance is even worse, since so many important people and developments in the growth of the conservative intellectual project were unfamiliar to outsiders, and especially to academic-media types who were not only distant from the scene but could scarcely imagine its existence. These were gentry, after all, who dismissed the whole conservative enterprise as a joke (or fascist *putsch*), said conservatives had no ideas to speak of, lampooned them as knuckle-dragging bigots. Needless to remark, that view of the political Right is not conducive to deep inquiry about its philosophic basis.

Thus one can scan any number of books about the Goldwater-Reagan epoch and find but fleeting mention, if any, of such as Richard Weaver, Russell Kirk, or Frank S. Meyer, the worthy subject of this volume. To read some of these alleged histories, one would have no idea of the prodigious intellectual effort put forward by these scholars, or by numerous others like them. It was all supposedly a revolt of the rednecks, perhaps a psychiatric problem, or possibly the effect of sunspots. That there was a substantial body of conservative thought—and a lot of fierce internal debate about it—is something that could not be deduced from many treatments of the era.

In the true history of the matter, few individuals are as important as Frank Meyer. Frank was a central and—despite his polemical battles on many fronts—unifying figure. He was unifying first of all because he looked past the sectarian quarrels that troubled the dawning conservative movement to the coherence of the larger effort. In that day, as to some extent in this, the principal philosophical divide was between traditionalists and libertarians— each stressing an aspect of the rightward outlook in opposition to the other. On the one hand, order, virtue, and religion, to the apparent neglect of personal freedom; on the other, free markets, limited government, and personal liberty, to the apparent exclusion of tradition and religion.

In the late '50s and early '60s, these issues were hammered out at length in books, articles, speeches, and debates in many intellectual synods. In that process, nobody wielded a weightier hammer than did Frank Meyer, who grasped and preached the seminal truth that the disagreements being aired were the result of inadequate vision and ignorance of the cultural record. As Frank saw it, the traditionalist and libertarian emphases in the Western ethos were properly seen as complementary, not conflicting—hemispheres that needed to be put together to make the object whole. This despite the fact that the sectarians were unquestionably at swords' points and often unwilling to see the unity Frank expounded.

In essence, Frank argued that religious and traditional precepts were needed to undergird a regime of freedom, which could not subsist on the relativist-materialist premises of modern thought—premises that, pushed to their logical outcome, bred all the despotic horrors of the century. Conversely, liberty was integrally linked to our religion because it was the ground of ethical choice and because it was itself a unique by-product of Western faith. In time, as noted in this study, his view of the subject would be accepted as a consensus on the Right, especially for the rising generation.

Translated into practical terms, Frank was saying that the conservative movement *was* a movement, not a hodge-podge of conflicting factions, as its critics, and some of its asserted friends, contended. And as a movement it could go forth in full battle armor to smite the liberal-Left behemoth, with traditionalist and libertarian forces marching together in common phalanx. (It is noteworthy and instructive that the liberal-Left has long been and remains today the polar opposite of both the traditionalist and libertarian positions— relativist-permissive on value questions, coercive on all others. For some reason, nobody ever saw any terrible contradiction in that particular mix of features.)

As the above suggests, Frank's argument on this score was not simply a conjuring with abstractions, though he certainly did his share of that, and did it very ably. Much more to the point, it was grounded in the realities of Western history, the history of the United States itself, and the convictions of rank-and-file Americans who never for a moment thought there was some kind of ghastly conflict between their faith and their political-economic freedoms. The existence of this awful dilemma could occur only to cloistered ideologists, not to everyday real people. (Mostly it occurs to secularists who have misread the nation's founding, in which the concept of religious virtue as the only possible basis for political freedom was routinely and explicitly stated.)

So Frank was unifying in this way as well—linking the philosophical effort to the history, beliefs, and common aspirations of the great American public. This impulse to join the theory with the practice was inveterate with him, and was expressed as well by his many involvements in the political arena, his unceasing attempt to bring principle to bear on current issues, and his yen for networking and organizing with all manner of conservative groups and causes. These facets of his career are set forth in admirable detail by Professor Smant in many absorbing recollections and vignettes. As the author has chronicled these so well—and as most of the intramural disputes recounted occurred in New York while I was safely (and thankfully) away in Indiana— I won't presume to comment on such topics. I would like, however, to offer a couple of final thoughts in defense of Frank's position, as I understood and shared it.

That Frank quite openly sought and helped to achieve a unification of conservative discourse and political effort is sometimes put down to his discredit—as an attempt to paper over disagreements for the sake of coalition building. Specifically, his linking of freedom and tradition, commonly called "fusionism" (a term I personally reject), is often seen as a weird amalgam of warring tenets—a kind of philosophical muddling through to get everyone more or less together. From the record, and from innumerable talks with Frank (usually at about three in the morning), I think nothing could be further from the truth than these invidious descriptions.

Far from fudging issues to get agreement, Frank was often in conflict with both traditionalists and libertarians—not to mention the smiting of liberals—which as an experienced and skilled debater he never minded in the slightest. The unity that he envisioned was based on clarity, not muddle. His object in all cases was to get matters plainly sorted out, and to state with utmost rigor the true position as he saw it: namely, the necessary and indissoluble linkage, conceptually and in the history of our culture, of religious faith and Western freedom. I think he succeeded in this, a task of immense importance—and one for which he should be greatly honored. Read on, and make the acquaintance of Frank S. Meyer. You'll find him a person well worth knowing.

— M. Stanton Evans

~ *Preface* ~

THERE HAS BEEN A SLOW BUT STEADY growth of interest in the recent history of the United States (which is usually defined as the study of any part of U.S. history after 1945), and in the place of American conservatism within that history. John P. Diggins's 1975 book *Up from Communism* surveyed the movement of several prominent conservative intellectuals from communism to conservatism. George H. Nash's *Conservative Intellectual Movement in America* examined the rise of conservative intellectual thought generally in America since 1945. John Judis's *William F. Buckley Jr.: Patron Saint of the Conservatives* is the best treatment yet of the life of the man who has done the most to popularize conservative ideas, and of the rise of *National Review*. Lee Edwards, Robert Goldberg, and recently Rick Perlstein have penned interesting biographies of Barry Goldwater. The well-known British author and historian Godfrey Hodgson has also published an account of the rise of conservatism since World War II, titled *The World Turned Right Side Up*.

All of these books at least mention the conservative intellectual and political activist Frank Meyer, and in some cases give him as full and fair treatment as space allowed. All acknowledge Meyer's contribution to the growth of the American Right. But there has as yet been no full-length biography of this man. No work has appeared which fully explores his immersion in the world of communism and

his move away from it, examines his ideas and their impact upon the conservative movement, more fully seeks to explain the roots of Reaganism in the
early conservative movement, or details Meyer's involvement in the growth of
conservative politics in the crucial years of the 1950s and 1960s. I hope this
book fills that void.

To fully understand the political developments of the times in which we
live, we must understand the history of modern American conservatism. As
George Nash writes in the preface to the most recent edition of his history of
the American Right, conservatism "has not faded into quaint irrelevance. It
has not become history. To the contrary, in the years since 1976 it has *made*
history and is still making history—to the point that, for adherents and de-
tractors alike, it is more relevant to our nation's life than ever before."[1]

FRANK S. MEYER (1909–1972) was a crucial figure in the birth and growth of the
post–World War II American conservative movement. His importance lies in
several areas. He was once a communist who served as a key functionary for the
American Communist Party in the Illinois-Indiana region during the 1930s and
early 1940s. His eventual rejection of Marxism, along with his embrace of
free-market ideology, serves as a particularly dramatic instance of one of the
twentieth century's most prominent intellectual trends: the movement of a
number of serious thinkers from Left to Right.

Meyer went on to become an influential conservative intellectual,
authoring in the 1950s and 1960s several seminal books. These volumes laid
an important intellectual foundation for the American Right, making it possible for conservatives to maintain that theirs was a coherent worldview. For
example, *In Defense of Freedom*, published in 1962, put forth a powerful case for
the primacy of the individual person, and for the morality and the efficacy of
the free market. Even more importantly, Meyer in that work convincingly
articulated his synthetic conservative philosophy, which became known as
"fusionism." This philosophy was an attempt to construct a marriage between
libertarian and traditionalist conservatives. Meyer argued that both camps had
things in common, and that for their thought to be complete each must accept
crucial points made by the other. Traditionalists had to realize that truth and
morality must be accepted voluntarily, that their acceptance cannot be coerced. Libertarians needed to comprehend that freedom without order, lib-

erty without transcendent value, must degenerate into meaningless libertinism, into anarchy. By the late 1960s, Meyer's "fusionism" was widely accepted in conservative circles, and historians of conservatism credit him with helping to unify the conservative intellectual movement. In fact, when Ronald Reagan spoke on the meaning of conservatism before the National Conservative Political Action Conference in 1981, he lauded Frank Meyer for his pivotal role in shaping contemporary conservative ideas.

From 1956 until his death in 1972, Meyer was a senior editor at William F. Buckley Jr.'s *National Review*. Meyer played a crucial role in the internal political and policy debates within *NR* during those years, and Buckley consistently sought out his advice and counsel. Meyer also wrote a regular column for the magazine, titled "Principles and Heresies," and edited *NR*'s book section. In seeking out book reviewers and discussing their work and ideas, Meyer built up a huge list of contacts within the conservative movement, thus making his name and his ideas known to nearly every active conservative thinker.

Meyer was also a political activist and an important player in the growth of the conservative political movement. He knew and corresponded with Barry Goldwater. He was a founding member of, and a senior adviser to, the New York State Conservative Party. He regularly advised the Young Americans for Freedom organization. He was on the board of directors of the American Conservative Union. Meyer was particularly active within the conservative movement during the important Nixon years. Many on the Right believed that Richard Nixon's presidency would fundamentally shift American foreign and domestic policies in a conservative direction. This did not happen, and Frank Meyer was intimately involved in the attempts of some on the Right to mount opposition to Nixon's policies. Conservatives faced a fundamental dilemma here. One of their own, they thought, was in the White House. Yet would it be possible to effectively oppose him if his actions departed from conservative principles? Conservatives had achieved greater access to power; but would this always be a blessing? Or would the victory of 1968 simply create new frustrations, as sometimes happens to anti-establishment movements which finally gain access to the corridors of power? Those on the Right opposing Nixon between 1969 and 1972 would not find much success. Yet from them would emerge a remnant that was instrumental in providing support for the Reagan candidacies of 1976 and 1980.

In sum, Frank Meyer was instrumental in the creation of the energetic and influential conservative political network (or "counter-establishment," as some have called it) that came to full flower in the election of Ronald Reagan in 1980 and in the Republican takeover of the House of Representatives in 1994. The 1950s, 1960s, and early 1970s were crucial years for the growth of the American conservative movement, and a study of the life of Frank S. Meyer illuminates the ideas and the changing politics of that era as few studies could.

NO SCHOLAR WORKS ALONE. In completing this work, I am indebted to the staffs of the Library of Congress in Washington, D.C., the Hoover Institution at Stanford University, and the Yale University Archives. I wish to thank Indiana University South Bend for the research support it afforded me. I owe a special debt of gratitude to the Bradley Foundation of Milwaukee, Wisconsin, and the research grant it provided me. Without its support, this study may never have been completed. I must thank William Rusher, Priscilla Buckley, William F. Buckley Jr., and William F. Rickenbacker—*NR* veterans all, who offered me their advice and memories, and thus helped make this biography what it is. My thanks go to both John and Eugene Meyer, who allowed me to interview them about their father and shared their recollections with me. And I want to offer my most effusive, special, and sincere thanks to Betsy Cotter, Maureen Kennedy, and the rest of the staff of the Interlibrary Loan Department at the Indiana University South Bend library. I owe all of you big time. Thanks for fulfilling all of my endless requests.

The Communist

FRANK STRAUS MEYER WAS BORN ON May 9, 1909, in the industrial city of Newark, New Jersey. His parents, Jack F. and Helene (Straus) Meyer, were part of a well-known, comfortable Reformed Jewish clan. Through various business enterprises, they were able to send their son to the finest schools and, eventually, leave him a significant inheritance. There is little evidence that young Frank's family, or his childhood in Newark, influenced his political development in any profound way.

In fact, little is known about Meyer's youth. He spoke little about it in later years, and when he did mention his early days he left his later friends and family with the impression that it was not a happy time. Rather sickly, and an only child, he was indoors a great deal. His parents may have been overprotective, and he chafed at their restrictions. By the time his teen years arrived, he had begun to turn to intellectual pursuits. He found friends who shared his interest in books and ideas, and he began to frequent the smoky bars and coffeehouses in Newark which catered to men and women like himself. Eugene O'Neill Jr., the son of the great playwright, became a close friend in this period. Meyer began to search, to question; he developed keen interests in history and politics, and apparently fancied himself a progressive, tacking up a poster of Woodrow Wilson on his bedroom door. He also began to doubt his Jewish faith. His parents evidently thought him rebellious and his bookish ways frivolous. He did well enough in school, though, attending Newark Academy during his teen years, and when he was seventeen his parents sent him off to Princeton University with high hopes. But he remained unwell, unable to function fully in New Jersey's climate and amid all of the academic pressure at Princeton. How he envied those that could—such as James Burnham, who when Meyer arrived at Princeton was about to graduate with honors and used to hold forth at dinnertime before tables full of admiring undergraduates. (Burnham would later become one of America's leading anticommunist authors, and a fellow senior editor with Meyer at *National Review*.) Meyer coveted such popularity and intellectual dexterity. But nothing was to be done about it; in 1928 he withdrew from the school, never to return.[1]

At first his parents were unsure what to do with their sickly young son. But, after some time at home, his health improved, and his parents decided to send him to England to further his education. There he could study the classics, English literature, and economics, in which Meyer had shown some interest. So, his parents sent him off again, hoping that he would finally mature and become more independent, little realizing that, in the process, he would enter a movement that would not allow him to return "home" again.[2]

The world was changing, and Meyer must have been aware of it even before he left home. The United States by the late 1920s was a growing, industrialized nation, as evidenced in Newark by the factories, the wealth of those who owned them, and the poverty of some of those who worked in them. He must have been aware, too, that many American intellectuals were vastly dissatisfied with their country. Before World War I, an era of much hope and faith in mankind, many believed that civilization's progress would march on into the foreseeable future. After all, was not man making life easier with the invention of new machines and new technologies? Were not many diseases being slowly controlled and eliminated?

But, as Meyer surely knew from his long discussions in Newark's smoke-filled intellectual hangouts, those beliefs had disintegrated in the wake of the cataclysm of World War I. Millions of idealistic young men had marched off to war, believing they were going to battle for the forces of progress and right. Instead, they tasted blood and met terrible slaughter. And for what? Was the world of the 1920s, with its commercialism and materialism, really changed for the better? Did anyone really think that permanent peace had arrived? No wonder many disillusioned American intellectuals, alienated from their country and their times, lived as expatriates in Europe and relentlessly criticized American society.[3]

And now, as Meyer sailed to England in the summer of 1930, the world faced a new crisis. A terrible economic depression had fallen upon the United States, set into motion by the stock market crash of October 1929. Unemployment had begun to rise and families were becoming trapped in joblessness and poverty. And this when respect for business had been at its zenith, when President Herbert Hoover had assured voters that there would be prosperity for all. Now American capitalism had seemingly collapsed, with no cure in sight. Writers such as Edmund Wilson were calling the 1920s "the stupid, gigantic fraud."[4]

Naturally, all of these changes, and the new intellectual currents they brought with them, affected Meyer. Indeed, the Depression had touched him personally. His father's business was practically destroyed, and Jack Meyer died in 1930, a beaten, broken man. Still, Meyer remained in school in England. There seemed nothing else for him to do.

His time there began quietly enough. As his parents had arranged, he "studied privately" for a year with various tutors and instructors, then entered Oxford University, seeking a B.A. from Balliol College. Clearly he hungered to find an anchor in this changing, Depression-wracked world. His later contemporaries remembered him as the kind of man who constantly sought out the fundamental principles that shaped the world, who needed to understand society and its workings. For Meyer, that way of thinking began in earnest in Oxford. On the one hand, in the radical atmosphere of Oxford, Meyer first seriously read the works of Karl Marx, and was fascinated with their implications for society and economics. Yet at the same time, he had a brief fling with Catholicism, studying Catholic theology and history under the tutelage of Balliol's Martin D'Arcy. But the fact of the Depression remained, and the power of Marx's writings took hold. Meyer soon left D'Arcy's Catholicism behind and joined the British Communist Party.[5]

Why did Frank Meyer—born into a relatively wealthy family—take such a radical step? Meyer himself later indicated that the reason lay in the accumulated weight of intellectual developments such as the "disillusion" following World

War I and the "shock" of the Depression. Moreover, he had at first joined the British Labour Party, but he soon became frustrated at its "slowness" and "reformism." The young Meyer felt that the crisis demanded fundamental societal change, not halfway measures and incremental reforms.[6]

Joining the Communist Party was to Meyer the logical result of the Depression and the need for fundamental change. For an intellectual such as Meyer, alienated from the world of business and finance, Marxism provided all the answers. It offered a moral vision of a world run by the working class in which each person would contribute to society according to his ability and be rewarded according to his needs. In a poverty-stricken world seemingly divided between the fabulously wealthy and the wretched poor, this vision of justice and equality was extremely powerful.

But Marxism was more than just moral philosophy. It claimed to be a scientific theory of history and economics based upon fact and analysis. Society would be scientifically reconstructed after the inevitable working-class revolt, and the new "dictatorship of the proletariat" would see that it ran efficiently, as well as morally.

The power that Marxism exerted over new converts was striking. Suddenly a comprehensive theory and framework through which to see the world existed; suddenly every question had an answer, every problem a solution. You knew where history was going, and only had to wait for capitalism's "contradictions" inevitably to destroy it. The British writer Arthur Koestler, himself a member of the Communist Party for several years, called this "seeing the light." The light "seems to pour from all directions across the skull; the whole universe falls into pattern like the stray pieces of a jigsaw puzzle assembled by magic at one stroke. . . . [D]oubts and concerns are a matter of the tortured past. . . ." Communism provided Frank Meyer with the total, metaphysical philosophy of life for which he had hungered. Thus he joined the British Communist Party in 1931, and it would be a central part of his life for the next fourteen years.[7]

Meyer quickly plunged into Party work. He remained at Oxford, and managed to complete his B.A. from Balliol College in 1932. But he was clearly a Party member first; everything else was secondary. Initially, Meyer merely led a small CP "cell" at Oxford, a small number of students with the innocuous name of the "October Club."

But in 1932 Meyer, with the Party's encouragement, decided to enter the London School of Economics. In the following two years, however, he made little progress toward an advanced degree. Instead, he focused on recruiting and organizing students into the communist movement. He held meetings, passed out Party literature, and organized separate student cells in Oxford, Cambridge, and London. Within two years he had recruited roughly five hundred students, so impressing the leaders of the British CP that they had him instruct youth leaders of the Chinese and Indian Communist Parties as well.

Meyer became an important and recognized figure within the Communist Party. In 1933 he was elected president of the student union at the London School, running as an avowed communist on a "united front" platform. This eventually landed Meyer in the middle of controversy. In the 1930s, the London School of Economics was a quiet, studious campus consisting of approximately three thousand students and run by a British aristocrat named Lord William Henry Beveridge.

Meyer, of course, believed it his duty to raise the "revolutionary consciousness" of the place, and especially to introduce communist ideas there. Thus, he and a small cadre of students attempted to distribute CP literature on the campus, even though specifically prohibited from doing so by the school's administration. By 1934 Lord Beveridge had finally had enough. "Six or seven students," wrote Beveridge later, still aghast, "led by a very red politician from America, having produced or acquired a pamphlet called the *Student Vanguard,* insisted on selling it in the School even after they had been forbidden to do so. . . . [T]he Emergency Committee after full consideration felt [this student] to be better suited to the United States than to the School. . . ."[8]

Meyer had been kicked out of the school, and would have to leave Britain. Even so, before he left he led Communist Party student delegations to several international anti-war and antifascist youth conferences in places such as Paris and Amsterdam. At the Party's behest, Meyer tried to organize within the London proletariat, too, hoping to make headway in the London Busmen's Organization and within the Railway Workers' Union. In 1934 he officially joined the Party's higher echelons; he was appointed to the British CP's Central Committee, one of its highest decision-making bodies.[9]

In that same year, however, Meyer's life changed. As a result of his expulsion from the London School of Economics, the Party decided to reassign him, to transfer him back to the United States to work with the American Communist Party. It must have been difficult for Meyer to leave Great Britain and his many friends in the communist movement. His British comrades clearly respected him, too, having heaped more and more responsibilities on him. But the Party wanted to expand its base of support in the United States. After all, America now had a sizable industrial proletariat, hit hard by the Great Depression. According to Marxist theory, it should be ripe for a workers' revolution. Communists needed to be more active there, especially among American students. That was where Meyer would come in. He was now a hardened, battle-tested member of the CP elite; he knew the Leninist rules of "democratic centralism" and "Party discipline." The Communist Party was the voice of the working class. Its decisions were always right. Of course he would go.[10]

Upon arriving in America late in 1934, Meyer bounced around for a time. He was helped, though, by a letter of introduction from Harry Pollitt, general secretary of the British Communist Party. At first the Party had him instruct the American Young Communist League in organizational and recruitment methods; later, they sent him to Canada to attend the founding sessions of the Canadian Students League and Antiwar Congress, a communist "front" organization. Eventually, in 1935 he was assigned to what would be his home for the next seven years: Chicago, Illinois.[11]

At first, his superiors envisioned him repeating the successes he had enjoyed in Great Britain. He kept his scholarly cover, enrolling as a graduate student (this time in anthropology) at the University of Chicago. He worked with the local branches of the Young Communist League and the American League Against War and Fascism. The latter was a communist-dominated organization that recruited liberals and socialists into a "united front" against fascism and Nazism. This was a radical departure for American Communists. In the past, the American CP had been a tiny, faction-ridden sect, which, taking its orders from Moscow, seemed to do everything it could to stay that way. The Party had endorsed bizarre ideas, such as that American blacks in the South form an independent nation, and it had fiercely denounced liberals, socialists, and New Deal Democrats as "social fascists" who were surreptitiously leading America to dictatorship.

But all of that abruptly changed in 1935 when Moscow ordered a shift in tactics. Now American Communists followed a "popular front" line; they professed friendship for liberals and socialists, sought to include them in their organizations and activities, and instead of talking only about Leninist theory and Bolshevik Russia, focused on their roots in America's radical and populist past. Yes, they were Americans too, and proud of it. The writer Saul Bellow, who moved in radical circles in the 1930s, recalled that this period was a "bonanza" for the American CP: "The Party was freed from its foreign-sounding jargon and began instead to speak the language of Wobblies and working stiffs. Embracing native populism, it sang folk songs and played guitars. Not Lenin and Stalin but Jefferson and Lincoln sat at the center of the new pantheon. . . . [T]he CP learned for the first time how heady it was to be in the mainstream of national life."[12]

It was exciting for Meyer, too. In his first eighteen months in Chicago, he spent most of his time trying to recruit cell members at the University of Chicago. Edward Shils, a graduate student and acquaintance of Meyer in those years, described him as "by nature a mischief-maker, . . . a demonic figure with flashing black eyes, a mop of black hair on his head before it became the fashion, shabby in dress, eloquent, voluble, excitable." He took classes, but even then he "frequently interrupted [the instructor's] fluent if not very solid discourses with Marxist corrections, supplements, and reinterpretations."[13]

Everyone could see what Meyer was up to—"he certainly had no interest in learning anthropology," Shils wrote—and he made little headway among Chicago's graduate students. So the CP shifted him over to full-time Party work in Chicago, instructing him to organize and agitate among the Chicago "masses" and build a Communist Party infrastructure in the city.

As before, Meyer's work impressed his superiors, and he quickly began to rise within the local Party hierarchy. At first he was assigned to Chicago's South Side, an area increasingly populated by blacks. Working under local section organizer Harry Haywood, Meyer soon rose to the rank of "educational director" of the area, and by 1938 the Party had put him in charge of educational activities in the entire Illinois-Indiana district. He also became the director of the Chicago Workers' School, one of the few visible Communist Party training and educational facilities in the country. Meyer later testified that "I was responsible for all inner education, agitation, and propaganda, public meetings, [and] printed matter."[14]

This life was different from what Meyer had known before. The life of a local Communist Party functionary in the late 1930s was a grinding, ceaseless struggle. It was a life of weekly two- or three-hour cell meetings, during which local leaders such as Meyer announced the latest political and organizational directives from Party headquarters and exhorted weary comrades to recruit more members and contribute more in dues. In every election year, Meyer would "agitate" and distribute literature for the Party's candidates in the (mostly vain) hope that the CP would break through and become a significant force in American political life. Occasionally, Meyer would hold an "open forum," to which the general public would be invited and in which perhaps a high Party official from out of town would speak and informational materials would be handed out. At times, to support himself and to contribute more to Party coffers, Meyer would take a regular daytime job and fulfill his political duties at night. He often crawled into bed, exhausted, in the wee hours of the morning.[15]

It was hard in other ways, too. Despite all efforts, the Party made little headway in entering the American political mainstream. Its electoral totals remained low, and at times Meyer and his comrades faced physical danger. Armed mobs broke up Party meetings in Indiana and Illinois in this period with many injuries and arrests (of the communists, not their attackers). In 1940, Congress passed the Smith Act, which not only authorized the deportation of "aliens" belonging to "revolutionary groups," but also made it a crime to advocate the necessity or desirability of overthrowing the government. Earl Browder, the spare, mustachioed head of the American Communist Party, himself spent several years in prison for violating the Smith Act's provisions.[16]

And one never knew when a Party political or tactical "line" would change. In Meyer's time, the CP pursued for some time its "popular front" strategy; then, after the Soviet Union's nonaggression pact with Nazi Germany in 1939, the Party hastily silenced its attacks against Adolf Hitler and began to savagely assail President Roosevelt's attempts to aid Great Britain against the Nazis in the first years of World War II. Of a sudden, Soviet officials, such as Foreign Minister Vyacheslav Molotov, routinely made astonishing statements, such as that fascism had always been "just a matter of taste." American CP members also found themselves defending the confusing, at times fantastic, Moscow Trials, in which many heroes of the original Bolshevik Revolution were convicted of the most heinous alleged acts of treason against the Soviet state. Even Leon Trotsky was judged *in absentia,* which split the American radical Left into "Trotskyist" and "Stalinist" factions. Meyer and his comrades, though often bewildered, confused, and ridiculed, dutifully followed their Party's instructions and mouthed each new "line."[17]

Yet what most impressed Meyer during those years was not the nuts-and-bolts Party work, the late nights, or the sudden shifts in the Party line. Instead, he remembered that the commitment to the Party had to be "total," that it took over a member's life until the Party was all he had. This could especially be seen in the CP's never-ending drive for ideological purity among its members—a part of Party life that Meyer insisted was crucial.

To be a communist, Meyer later wrote, meant more than simply joining the Communist Party and taking part in its activities. It also required absorbing the Marxist ideology and "ethos" into your very personality. One had to eliminate all capitalist and "bourgeois" thoughts and impulses from his view of history, of current events, of society in general—even his personal life came under scrutiny. After all, "bourgeois" tendencies could arise from contact with one's family, the books one read, even from vacations. A Party member was always a communist, and was expected, in all situations, to think and act like one—that is, always to think politically, to spread Party influence, to promote the coming of the "revolution." Thus, not surprisingly, Meyer's friends tended to be communists. He could relax with them, let his guard down, and not worry about the "consciousness of always having another motive other than the surface one." Meyer's old life and family ties in New Jersey seemed far, far away, which gave him a "half-pleasurable, half-frightening sensation of bridge after bridge being burned" behind him.[18]

Nearly everyone had times of weakness when "deviationist" thoughts entered his mind. But the Party worked strenuously to stamp these out, and Meyer, as a communist educator and propagandist, was deeply involved in such efforts. He participated in lengthy "struggle" sessions with Party comrades suspected of harboring bourgeois ideas, in which the offender was argued against, bullied, and cajoled to recant. Occasionally this meant that important cadres such as Meyer were involved in the most painful intimate details of CP members' lives. *Anything* that could reduce a member's effectiveness on behalf of the CP was relevant to Party leaders.

On one occasion, for example, Meyer was ordered to tell a member of the Communist Party, who happened to be a practicing homosexual, to alter his sexual lifestyle. Local Party leaders cared little about the man's sexual behavior; rather, they feared that his homosexuality would be discovered and that the resultant scandal would discredit the Party.

Party officials gave Meyer the task of "transmitting" the Party's decision on the matter. "My discussion with him was in no way hostile or brutal," Meyer recalled, "[but] it was sharp and direct." The man's homosexuality was simply "politically impermissible," Meyer told him, and he must renounce all homosexual practices within two days or lose his Party membership. Within forty-eight hours the man accepted the Party's directive, and, amazingly, soon completely changed his lifestyle—he married and raised two children. Belonging to the Party was that important.[19]

Meyer sometimes had to watch grimly as comrades who refused to disavow heretical beliefs were put on "trial" and forced to answer numerous "charges." If found guilty, the offender was expelled from the CP; occasionally, he confessed to his "errors"—but was expelled anyway. The process made even longtime Party members, such as Meyer, continually question themselves, worrying that they too were becoming "pseudo-bourgeois." Seeing to it that your "total personality" was "remoulded," as Meyer put it, was a full-time job.[20]

Given all of this, why did Meyer, and so many like him, remain in the Party? How could they rationalize its dictatorial ways, its sudden political shifts, its trials, its banishment of "heretical" members? This is a difficult question, which many ex-communists struggled years later to answer. Part of the explanation lay in communist ideology. Members of the movement had been told, and fully believed, that they were the "chosen." Communists, in an era of severe economic hardships, had a blueprint for what should be done. Ex-communist Granville Hicks later stressed that, in a time when others "were questioning and criticizing, we were acting." Besides, as far as they knew, communism worked. Party members were told over and over about the great things being achieved in the Soviet Union—wiping out illiteracy, building new factories, and setting new production records. Any contrary information was simply ascribed to a lying "capitalist press" or to "anti-Soviet prejudice."[21]

Moreover, by the late 1930s Meyer had spent a great deal of time and energy within the communist movement. "In general," Meyer later wrote of the typical communist, "the longer he remains, the longer his original motivations become corrupted, the more deeply indoctrinated he becomes in Communist ideology and practice, and the more difficult it becomes to break with the movement." Leaving the movement himself was simply unthinkable.[22]

Thus Meyer's involvement was too deep, his ideological convictions still too strong, for him to break. The mental "high" he felt when he came fully to accept the validity of Marxist-Leninist theory "was not a feeling of dogmatic certainty, in the sense that I felt I knew the answers to every possible question," he wrote later. "Rather, it was the vision of the correlation of all aspects of experience, each with each, the certainty that an answer could be found to every meaningful question and that everything which did not fit could be dismissed as meaningless, unreal." Few who still accepted communism's basic assumptions, and who had tasted the excitement of being at the center of "history," could bear to give that up. Leaving the Party "is not simply a question of friends, associates, habits," Meyer wrote, " . . . [but entails] the loss of a way of thinking which makes it comparatively easy to find answers to everything: the simple moral problems of everyday life; how to vote in a trade-union meeting; what to think about the latest newspaper headline. Life for the Communist contains no mystery, and the fight back to the acceptance of the glorious human fate of living with mystery is difficult indeed."[23]

Besides, Meyer did not endure these years alone. Early in 1940, still working for the Party in the Chicago area, he met a young woman named Elsie Bown. She was a Radcliffe graduate and a Communist Party member who had joined in 1935, while she was still in college. She had married a fellow Marxist just after graduation; her parents had strenuously objected to her plans—which, she would say in later years, only made her more determined to go through with them. She became deeply involved in agitating for the Party among the American working class; at one point, she traveled to Flint, Michigan, to take part in the sit-down strikes then occurring in the automobile factories. Later she and her husband settled in St. Louis, Missouri. But their marriage went sour, and Elsie wound up gravitating to Chicago, where she soon made contact with the local Communist Party branch. She took a Party class at the Workers' School, taught by the now thirty-one-year-old Meyer. She began staying after class, to discuss and debate Marxist theory with him, for she was fascinated with his ideas and his style. Soon they began seeing each other, even though officially the Party frowned on such relationships. Within a few months Bown divorced her husband, moved to Chicago permanently, and became Elsie Meyer. Naturally she also willingly accepted Meyer's work, helping her husband with his late-night CP assignments. They even tested each other ideologically, making sure that neither of them slipped into bourgeois "errors." "Frank was terrible," Elsie would say in later years. "He was always telling me I was subjective." "Well, you *were,* dammit," Meyer would reply.[24]

MEYER AND HIS COMRADES soldiered on into the early 1940s, denouncing the new world conflict as an "imperialist war" and completely muting any criticism of Nazi Germany—and thereby losing members and influence. But then in the summer of 1941 came the sudden, shocking German invasion of the Soviet Union. While many communists worried about the USSR's steadily worsening military situation, there was also a feeling of "relief—even exultation." The Party's political line shifted once again, back to its previous anti-Nazi, pro-Soviet stance. Now American communists urged the Roosevelt administration to give Stalin's USSR all possible military aid, and even demanded that the U.S. enter the war—positions much more in line with American public opinion.[25]

When the war came, Meyer was bogged down in Party "organizational work" in Chicago. But he soon told his superiors that he wanted to join the U.S. army. He wanted to defeat the forces of Nazism and help the Soviet Union—communists had been propagandizing about this (off and on) for years. But he was also motivated by patriotism and a desire to serve his country—a service in which he would take considerable pride for the rest of his life.[26]

Meyer's plans met significant opposition from the Party hierarchy. His organizational and recruiting skills were too valuable to lose, and who knew what would become of him, exposed to the alien culture of the U.S. army? It took "several months of argument" to secure Party approval, Meyer later recalled, but eventually he received it. To guarantee his acceptance in the army, he formally ended his membership in the Communist Party—but with every intention of resuming it when he got out. In October 1942 Meyer was inducted into Officer's Training School as a volunteer officer candidate.[27]

The next three years were perhaps the most important in Meyer's life. But not because of his career in the army. For within four months he washed out of the service. He had, it turned out, severe problems with his feet. No matter how hard he tried, he simply could not complete the obstacle course, which was required of every graduate of basic training. The army discharged him in February 1943. Meyer immediately underwent surgery on both of his feet, which left him effectively immobilized for the next eighteen months. This gave him plenty of time to *think,* and he knew that he had much to think about.[28]

The truth was that, although communists like himself were not supposed to have doubts, Meyer had felt some misgivings about his beliefs and his Party. For example, he had heard some negative things about life in the Soviet Union. Meyer talked, occasionally, with students at the American Lenin School or with Communist International "reps" back from Stalin's Russia. They told him of serious "difficulties" there, that quite simply it was not a "workers' paradise." He also had a difficult time accepting the Soviet Union's pact with Hitlerite Germany in August 1939, and had an even harder time with the subsequent Soviet invasion and partition of Poland. Edward Shils saw him standing on a street corner in Chicago in mid-September 1939; he looked so "despondent" that Shils told an acquaintance, "I thought that Frank Meyer was reaching the end of his Communist tether."[29]

But he had not reached the breaking point, not yet. And when Germany invaded Russia and America entered the war, Meyer had a renewed sense of dedication. But his physical problems changed everything. Fortunately his drill instructor took pity on him during the month in which Meyer was in a kind of limbo, waiting for the army to decide what to do with him. His instructor gave him free time, which Meyer used to escape to the camp library. There he began his intellectual odyssey away from Marxism. He read everything about American history that he could find, focusing especially on the *Federalist Papers.* He found himself in agreement with some of the arguments of James Madison and Alexander Hamilton, and he gained a new appreciation of America's heritage of limited government and the separation of powers. Yet he was supposed to be a communist, supposed to banish un-Marxian notions of "nationalism" and dismiss Madison and Hamilton as simply defending the interests of their class. What was happening to him?[30]

Perhaps in an attempt to flesh out the changes that were occurring in his thinking, late in 1943 Meyer took a big step: he wrote a long letter to the leader of the American Communist Party, Earl Browder, discussing his concerns about communism's future in the United States and urging Browder to initiate some fundamental changes. Yes, he felt some "trepidation" in writing to the head of the CP, Meyer began; his time in the army, and his recovery from his operations, had kept him away from "the hard facts" of day-to-day Party life for some time. "But it is exactly the rather rude immersion among the American people in the most undifferentiated sense, which my Army career represented," he added, "which made me think very hard about problems of our Party . . . which personally, at least, I feel I had faced rather abstractly before."

Meyer told Browder that American communists had not been self-critical enough, had not "overhauled" their existing theory in the face of changing experience. The Party needed to enter into a period of necessary "theoretical development." For example, Meyer had greatly modified his view of capitalism—communist references to capitalism as being always "imperialistic" were incorrect. American capital after World War II could be a real aid to economic development in places such as Latin America, China, and the Middle East, and need not lead to "exploitation."

Furthermore, Meyer believed that, while it was certainly possible that the postwar years would see a "gradual transition to socialism," it was more likely that state control of the economy would coexist with private ownership for some time to come. "I don't mean class peace," Meyer hastened to add, "which is of course impossible in a class society." But he did foresee "a very different form of class struggle," one that might repeat "on a higher level" the "people's liberation movement of Marx's time, with the same passing over into socialism which he saw possible then." In short, Meyer wanted a more democratic Communist Party, in order to garner wider popular support than did the Party's current "apocalyptic" revolutionary platform.

He also addressed the question of the Party's organization. If the Communist Party was to become "democratic" and "gradualist," it must also give up its "Bolshevik" structure. Drawing on his recent readings in American history, Meyer urged the creation of a party "something like that described in the Communist Manifesto—and incidentally, something like that which Jefferson and Jackson led. Isn't the Leninist party designed for an immediate sharp and final struggle? Is it possible to build a mass Marxist party to meet the challenge that lies in front of us today on such a basis?" Meyer argued that the typical American worker simply could not spare the time for such a struggle, and the Party "actives" (such as himself) wasted their time in an endless "inner round" of CP activities. Instead, he wanted a more flexible, less demanding Party, in which "the one main task of every party member is to think and act where he lives, works, plays, participates in the life of his community, as a communist."

In sum, wrote Meyer, the Communist Party should stress its new goal as the building of a "people's America," and it must stress its roots in the American tradition "as a natural, integral outgrowth of our whole past history, and presented in terms of our tradition. And this will only come about when our leaders from top to bottom are as familiar with the struggles of Jefferson and Jackson and Lincoln, and what we have inherited from these struggles, as they are with 1848, 1902, 1917."[31]

Frank Meyer was a man in transition. He still clung to his communist faith, still belongd to a Party that slavishly followed directives from Moscow and emphasized its international character. But Meyer was now focusing on *American* traditions and roots—and saw them as his own. Yet he was not prepared to break. He did not yet dare criticize the Soviet Union publicly, although surely he had doubts about its economic and human rights record. And he still accepted certain fundamental Marxist tenets, such as the inevitability of class struggle. Besides, Earl Browder and the CP appeared to be moving in exactly the direction Meyer advised (although no evidence suggests that Browder did so in response to Meyer's letter). In 1944 Browder announced that he was dissolving the old Communist Party organization, and replacing it with a "voluntary" grouping to be called the "Communist Political Association." Furthermore, Browder and other communist leaders stated publicly their new belief that free enterprise would be useful in creating a prosperous postwar world.[32]

"[I] perhaps might have moved still further away from the party during the 1943–44 period," Meyer remembered, "had it not been that the Browder position seemed to be just what I wanted, and I remained in for a couple of more years, and became rather enthusiastic about it." He even attended the Party's annual convention in Chicago in 1944, watching happily as the shift was made.

But there was a further problem—the Party could not figure out how to use him. After his operations, Party leaders tried to infiltrate him into government service in Washington, D.C. Meyer went to the capital in early 1944 and met a Communist Party contact there, who attempted to get him attached to the staff of Congresswoman Helen Gahagan Douglas of California. But the attempt failed. And so he went back to New York City, where through the end of 1945 he did some writing for the *New Masses* (a communist literary magazine) and taught at the CP's Jefferson School.[33]

But his relationship with the Party during this period was at best uneasy, and in fact steadily deteriorating. This was why the Party had shunted him to the Jefferson School in the first place; everyone in Party circles knew that being assigned to teach there meant you were being shuffled outside of the main centers of CP decision-making authority, that you were now one of the CP's "lesser intelligentsia." Soon Earl Browder himself was gone as head of the CP, forced out in the wake of criticisms of his moderate line enunciated by Jacques Duclos in a French communist journal. But everyone knew the judgment upon Browder was actually Stalin's.[34]

Meyer continued to harbor his own doubts and criticisms of the Party. He had occasionally voiced them to his wife during these years; at first Elsie, dutiful and long-standing member of the Party that she was, had defended the CP and tried to quiet her husband's qualms. But as time went on, it was she who first saw both the logic and the truth of what Meyer was saying, and first voiced what both of them surely knew: that if his doubts about the Party were true, both of them must break with communism. For some time Meyer had resisted his wife's logic. But as he later wrote, it was inevitable that such questions would have a corrosive effect upon his beliefs. For "if ever a trained and developed cadre Communist allows himself fully and deeply to acknowledge any reality independent of the Communist cosmos—a fact, an idea, an aspect of an order of being—the whole tense, complex structure is in imminent danger of shattering into bits."

Now, Earl Browder had been removed as head of the American CP, and as 1945 moved along it was clear that communists everywhere were retreating into a Stalinist shell. But Meyer, as his 1943 letter to Browder demonstrated, could no longer be a Stalinist. He no longer accepted the Stalinist denunciation of capitalism, nor a Moscow-dictated Party line. He was starting to rebel against his past in its entirety—and especially against communist morality. He now knew, as he wrote later, that he had belonged "to a disciplined revolutionary organization, all of whose activities are subordinated to a single goal— not to a liberal organization for doing good." In other words, communists believed that the end justified the means, and Meyer no longer accepted that. He was sick of the endless discipline, too. He later told a friend that he finally realized the Party had been trying to "regiment" him, but given that he no longer accepted the fundamentals of Marxism, why should he submit? No, the more reading Meyer did, the more convinced he became of the value of individual freedom. As he later wrote:

> The Hellenaic and Hebraic traditions of the dignity of the individual man, fused by Christianity in the self-sacrifice of a divine Person, imbue the deep consciousness of the West with that view of the human person as ultimately sacred. . . . The whole of Communist teaching, however, drives toward the acceptance of the revolution as the end to which all things and all persons must be strictly subordinated as means. . . . The good or evil in any situation is determined by whether it helps the revolution or impedes it. Sooner or later, these opposing outlooks come seriously to grips. Throughout the Communist's rank-and-file experience, the development of such a crisis is adumbrated in smaller ways. But the crisis itself and its resolution will decide whether he leaves the Party, or remains in a suspended rank-and-file position, or moves to the cadre.[35]

Perhaps one of the most crucial moments in Meyer's developing break with communism occurred in the summer of 1945. Meyer was still teaching at the Jefferson School in New York City, and in the wake of the Duclos letter, and the fear and confusion it had sowed, the Party set up a meeting at the school to explain and discuss the CP's new anti-Browder line. Over forty employees attended amid an atmosphere of tension and foreboding.

Holding the floor for most of the meeting was perhaps New York City's leading Marxist-Leninist ideologist, Jacob Stachel. What he said that evening shocked Meyer. The American Communist Party had, during the years of "Browderism," sunk into a "swamp of revisionism," Stachel asserted. Luckily the Duclos letter had shocked them out of it. The Party had been on the wrong path; continuing such policies would have led to the "liquidation" of the entire American Communist Party.

Stachel especially condemned the idea of American "exceptionalism,"

and he attacked the Party's recent friendliness toward the Roosevelt administration as having "dampened" its understanding of the class struggle in
America. He hoped, then, that all Party members would unite around this
new understanding of the CP's position in America, and he stressed that
the Party's Central Committee was now unanimous in denouncing
"Browderism."

In the discussion that followed, Frank Meyer was one of the few to
disagree. The Duclos line, he said, was one which "in the circumstances of
[the] postwar [period], after the democratic peoples of the world had already
spilt their blood in a struggle against tyranny, was one that was bound to lead
inevitably to a war between the United States and the Soviet Union, a war for
which the communists themselves would be responsible if that line became
the line of the international communist movement; that peace was possible
and that all democratic and progressive people should attempt in every possible way to create a peaceful world."

It was an eloquent statement, and much of it was borne out by later
events. But at the Jefferson School in 1945, Meyer's views were heresy. Stachel
rebuked him sharply, calling Meyer's remarks "provocative," but did little to
refute them. Instead, Meyer was simply ignored. Later, he wrote a letter to the
CP's official newspaper, the *Daily Worker,* in defense of Browder. But his letter
was never published, and when he called to complain, he was told that
Browder could speak for himself.[36]

Frank Meyer was finally having his crisis, and he made his decision. In his
case, there were no truly dramatic showdowns or theatrical confrontations. He
simply began to drift away from the Party. The CP did not argue. The final
class taught by Meyer ended at the Jefferson School in the fall of 1945, "and
then we just let it go."[37]

Now came the task of putting his life back together, and deciding on a new
career. He had no idea how he would go about doing either. All he knew, as he
told ex-radical Eliseo Vivas, was that during the war he "had time to grasp the
true value of the world [the communists] had been trying to destroy, and from
now on [he] would try to save."[38]

Transition

THE YEARS FOLLOWING Frank Meyer's break with American communism were extremely difficult for Elsie and him. Party work had been Meyer's life for nearly fourteen years. And although the CP had not attempted to thwart his decision to break, it did pressure his wife to divorce him. This gambit failed, of course; Meyer had told his wife of his doubts about the Party all along, and Elsie had grasped the logic before her husband. Frank had been the first to break, but his wife stood by him, as she would until the end of his life.[1]

Meyer knew almost no one outside the communist movement, and he feared venturing out anew into the mainstream of American life. There was also the danger of assassination. Meyer had broken with a movement still in the grip of Stalinism, well known for the "liquidation" of its enemies. Many communists who left the movement in these years feared for their lives; Whittaker Chambers hid in Florida for several months after his break.[2]

The Meyers managed to pool their resources (Frank received over $600 per month from the rent paid on a family-owned building in Newark, his inheritance from his parents) to purchase a comfortable house hidden away in the Catskill Mountains near Woodstock, New York. This originally appeared to be a mistake. The Meyers first settled in the area in 1944, when they were still members of the Party, because Woodstock was known to be (relatively speaking) a hotbed of communism; several Party members lived nearby. And so when Meyer broke with the CP, his isolation became even greater, for some of his neighbors ostracized the family. Still, they came to love their house and the area, and there simply wasn't enough money to move again.

So they stayed, and for several years they eked out a meager existence. Still in fear of assassination from avenging communists, Meyer took to sleeping with a loaded rifle next to the bed. Their fears often meant that sleep would not come. Both of them took to staying up later and later at night, until their lives were completely upside-down—they slept almost all day, and stayed up reading and working through the night. This would be Frank Meyer's pattern for the rest of his days, and he became notorious for it among his many friends and contacts. He seldom arose before 5 P.M., and he looked askance at his wife's penchant for occasionally working outside in her garden during the day; to Meyer, "all good things got done at night." Some years later, he called *National Review* managing editor Priscilla Buckley at noon, an unheard-of time for him. How come? she asked. "I have insomnia," Meyer replied.[3]

The Meyers constantly worried about money. Frank had almost no contacts or marketable skills and was consequently unable to get work. They lived on their monthly inheritance check and on Elsie's remarkable skill at growing vegetables. Nor was it just the two of them any longer. The Meyers would raise two sons: John, born on December 31, 1944, and Eugene, on June 27, 1952. Yet despite the difficulties, this period allowed Meyer to think, and especially to read; and hence his thought continued to evolve—until he found that he was ready to join a new movement.[4]

HE LEFT COMMUNISM, Meyer later recalled, because holding to the Marxist creed meant acquiring a slowly expanding core of assumptions and suppositions, all dependent on each other. "It is like a balloon," he later testified, "that if you prick it in one spot, the whole thing will blow up; and for a series of reasons . . . in the later years of the war doubts began to enter my mind. The process then was for me . . . one of a terrific effort to sew up the doubts; and once you start trying to do that, the doubts begin to sprout up all over the place until events, your own activities and so on, bring you to break your formal connection with the communist movement."[5]

But Meyer still had doubts, plenty of them. What was his position on the state's proper role in the economy? On America's stance toward the Soviet Union? On his former communist comrades? Would he cooperate with the authorities? For that matter, would Meyer ever become actively involved in politics again? At first he did not know. But shortly after the end of the war and his move to Woodstock, Meyer read two books that deeply influenced how he would answer such questions.

The first was a small, thin volume originally published by the University of Chicago Press in 1944. It was called *The Road to Serfdom* and was written by Friedrich von Hayek. Hayek was a bespectacled, gray-haired, grave-looking man, an Austrian economist who had escaped Hitler by becoming a British subject in 1938. But despite his good fortune, he looked with horror upon the increasing centralization of government in Britain and elsewhere during World War II. In this book, he argued a simple thesis: that state planning must, by its very nature, lead to totalitarianism.

Why? Because, argued Hayek, history had shown that all attempts at socialistic redistribution of material wealth must involve coercion. Look at Nazism and Soviet communism, which promised redistributionist utopias but instead succumbed to mass terror. In addition, Hayek felt that such utopian dreams were unrealizable in any case. The economic life of a modern nation involved so many facts and transactions that it was impossible for any planner to be familiar with them all and thus come up with an intelligible "plan." Only competition, in which each economic agent applied the knowledge that he alone could know, produced rational price and supply levels.

Furthermore, Hayek insisted, in a democracy there was no way to secure the agreement of all to a single plan, much less to the morality behind such a plan. Individual rights were bound to be ignored and trampled upon. Yet a planned economy rationalized such actions, since planners were by definition working toward moral ends and could not be held back by a few malcontents. Yes, power would now be in the hands of planners and bureaucrats—who would surely misuse and abuse it. They would favor one person or group over another and inevitably force dissenters to conform to the plan.

Hayek argued that the rise of relativist thought, and the erosion of standards of morality and truth, would make such dire predictions seem mild. If "the state" became most important, or if "ends" such as the elimination of poverty became supreme, then it became easy to sanction questionable actions done for a greater good. In such a climate, the freedom of the individual can quickly disappear—as in the worlds of Nazism, fascism, and communism.[6]

Hayek's book hit Meyer with incredible force. He would later write that he "owed so much personally" to Hayek, because he had read his book "at a crucial moment in my life and [it] played a decisive part in helping me free myself from Marxist ideology." In truth, Meyer had already begun this process himself. Living in his mountain hideaway not only protected him from assassins, but also allowed him to assert his individuality. He defied society and ignored the state, living his life at night despite common practice, and living on garden vegetables, not government welfare. Hayek gave these impulses more concrete form. Meyer now realized that communism, or any such all-encompassing ideology, must lead to planning, which in turn must lead to violations of individual rights. That was what had bothered him about Marxism all along—that an individual became subsumed under the Party's "plan" for society. Dissenters were simply crushed. Meanwhile, the rise of relativist thought rationalized it all—it excused the use of any means to achieve a moral end. Meyer now really understood, could really verbalize, just why communism was wrong.[7]

Soon Meyer was intently studying another book, again by an academic at the University of Chicago. This one was by Richard M. Weaver, an unknown English professor and one-time member of Norman Thomas's Socialist Party, and whose contemplation of the horror and destruction of World War II raised serious doubts in his mind about the future of the West. As a result, Weaver wrote *Ideas Have Consequences,* first published in 1948. His thesis was that the decline in Western civilization that had resulted in World War II began in the fourteenth century with the nominalism of William of Occam. Nominalism led man to abandon his belief in absolutes, in the idea that a truth exists which is higher than man. This eventually resulted in the twentieth century's denial of original sin, which was replaced by a mistaken trust in the innate goodness of man. It led to materialism and rationalism—the doctrines that man could find true happiness in material things and that all problems were soluble by man's reason. Inexorably, Nazism, communism, and war resulted; unless man again learned to tap his spiritual roots, realized that he was imperfect, and thus began to restrain himself, such disasters would continue.

In elucidating his thesis, Weaver touched on a number of different topics:

the "decadence" of mass culture, as seen in such things as modern art; the decline of language and of the study of semantics; and the nature of modern war. Two points, however, had an especially "great influence" on Meyer. First, Weaver affirmed the existence of a "transcendent" and a "real"; he affirmed that there *were* universals. To Meyer, Weaver promised that belief in a world of "metaphysical certitude" would comfort those made "seasick" by "the truth-denying doctrines of the relativists." And Meyer was convinced that "truth-denying doctrines" were at the heart of the failure of communism.

Meyer was also struck by Weaver's defense of private property. Weaver argued that it made man's very existence possible, for it promoted virtue. Virtue was impossible without the concept of volition, and private property was the bulwark of freedom and of choice. It "makes [man's] virtue an active principle, breathing and exercising it," Weaver wrote. It was one of man's "inviolable rights," helping to set limits beyond which governments or electoral majorities might not go. To Meyer, Weaver's book was a benchmark for his later thought. It welded two ideas—tradition and liberty—and showed how, together, they could serve as the foundation for a new kind of thinking. Private property—economic freedom in general—was an essential part of man's freedom. Yet economics was not enough; Meyer's communist experience convinced him of that. Instead, his reading taught him that a belief in the normative validity of traditional values was crucial in protecting mankind from pernicious doctrines such as communism or Nazism. He would develop this thought further in the years ahead.[8]

THE HAYEK AND WEAVER books came, as Meyer said, at a crucial time in his life. He now began to form his political philosophy, although not without some hesitation. Meyer began to make new friends and with them he indulged his habit of developing his ideas through long argument and discussion. His old boyhood friend, Eugene O'Neill Jr., lived just down the road, and the two renewed their friendship. O'Neill was a former professor of classics at Yale who had abruptly left his teaching position, had dabbled in radio and show business, and currently led a rather aimless, unemployed existence filled with regrets and heavy drinking. But he and Meyer got along famously and spent many nights in the late 1940s loudly debating politics, art, or religion. Meyer's friend Garry Wills reported Meyer telling him that "Gene was a natural actor who shunned the theater in flight from the ghosts of his father and grandfather." According to Wills, O'Neill "and Frank divided up all the parts of a Shakespeare play and declaimed them at each other through the night." Indeed, Meyer's second son, Eugene, was named for his friend.

Their friendship, however, would end in tragedy. In 1950, Elsie and son John found O'Neill's body, naked, at the foot of a staircase in his home. "He had spent a long night of poetry and memories with Frank, went back to his home and brooded for hours, then opened his wrists in a hot tub," Wills remembered, "and [he] trailed blood around the house arguing with death."[9]

His talks with Eugene O'Neill Jr. had played a large role in Meyer's re-evaluation of his former worldview, and by 1950 his views had begun to change markedly. At first Meyer refused to cooperate with the government and testify against his former communist comrades. "As my wife and I later put it," he said, "we are not anticommunist, we are just noncommunist. . . . [L]arge amounts of prejudices that have been instilled all your life against investigating agencies remain. One feels that, well, this is not the way to fight them, and one thinks it can be fought only in the labor movement or only by intellectual methods."

But by this time the world situation had decisively changed. The Soviet Union had begun to impose what Winston Churchill later called an "Iron Curtain" across much of Eastern Europe. Nations such as Poland, Hungary, and Czechoslovakia had Soviet-style, dictatorial regimes thrust upon them through violence and intimidation, and there were real fears that other countries threatened by instability and civil war, such as Greece and Turkey, would be swallowed up by the Soviet bloc. Meanwhile, in the United States, sensational accusations of Soviet spy networks operating in the nation's capital abounded, including charges made by a rumpled, pipe-smoking man named Whittaker Chambers against a former key official in the Roosevelt administration's state department, Alger Hiss. To many, it appeared that the Soviet Union was out to dominate the entire world and would stop at nothing to subvert its main capitalist enemy, the United States.[10]

In the wake of this growing "Cold War," and given that he understood the Stalinist mentality and the reality of communist espionage against the United States, Meyer increasingly supported the anticommunist policies of the Truman administration—including increases in defense spending and containment of the USSR's expansionism. He supported Truman's reelection bid in 1948,

deplored the candidacy of fellow-traveling Henry Wallace, and began opening up to the authorities. In 1949 he testified in several New York state pros-
ecutions of communists under the Smith Act, and he spent a great deal of time
with the FBI. Later on he traveled to Washington, D.C., to tell about Communist Party organizational and underground tactics, and named names. Occasionally the FBI interviewed him in Woodstock—gray-suited, anonymous
figures, ensconcing themselves in Meyer's study, questioning him for hours.
But Meyer didn't mind; he had not only broken with communism, but had
resolved to fight it. Testifying was a moral duty.[11]

Such actions by Meyer and other ex-communists enraged their former
communist associates. Earl Browder complained that the writings of former
communists and their "breast-beating confessions of sin" were "so stale and boring to the point of nausea." Another ex-communist, George Charney, fiercely
castigated those who cooperated with the authorities against the CP. Charney
argued that an ex-communist's "hatred of the Party," however he and others
might justify it, became part of a larger hatred that sought to engulf more than
the Party. None of these men really understood the internal struggles of men
such as Frank Meyer.[12]

But Meyer's political evolution had not ended. In 1948 he was a Truman
Democrat, supporting the administration's New Dealism at home and its anti-
Soviet "containment" policy abroad. But certain things continued to trouble
him. For one thing, Meyer was uncomfortable with those in the Democratic
Party who called themselves "liberals." His reading convinced him that too many
liberals were relativists who denied the existence of good and evil, right and
wrong. This encouraged attitudes fertile for the growth of communism, such as
utopianism and the belief that the end justifies the means. Yes, many liberals
professed to be anticommunist. But, to Meyer, that anticommunism was weak. It
had, for example, allowed China to fall to Mao's communist guerrilla army.
Liberals also continued to support the expansion of the welfare state. Meyer at
first accepted the New Deal. Through 1948 he still considered himself a man of
the Left. But soon the logic of Hayek's analysis of the welfare state led Meyer to
denounce even the New Deal as leading to "collectivism," and eventually to a
totalitarian state.[13]

By the early 1950s, other writers appeared who shared many of Meyer's
ideas. John Chamberlain and Henry Hazlitt joined Friedrich von Hayek in

making the case for free markets. James Burnham wrote a series of books outlining in the strongest language the nature of the Soviet Union's threat to American security, and urging the liberation of Eastern Europe. And Russell Kirk joined Richard Weaver in rejecting philosophical relativism and calling for a return to tradition and absolute values. There were even a few "little magazines," such as the *Freeman* and the *American Mercury,* that published these writers and stressed anticommunism. Some saw all of this as the beginning of a serious trend in American thought and politics, calling it a "new conservatism." So was Meyer a conservative, too?[14]

He certainly appeared to be. He began to contact conservative authors and journalists, hoping to become active in the movement. Some time in 1950 Meyer phoned Ralph de Toledano, whom he had never met, and introduced himself. Toledano, a journalist, wrote on national political affairs for *Newsweek* magazine. He had written widely on liberalism and communism, and had close knowledge of CP operations and internal battles (though he himself had never been a communist). Toledano had lately published *Seeds of Treason,* a controversial but widely respected work on the Hiss-Chambers case that delighted conservatives with its conclusion that Hiss was guilty. Meyer, Toledano said, "wanted to get to know me because of my knowledge of [Communist] Party operations and my war on liberalism—as well as my position as a *Newsweek* editor covering big-time politics. But he also wanted an entry-point into anticommunist and conservative circles."[15]

The two men quickly became friends; Meyer began to travel to New York City to visit Toledano and his wife Nora, staying overnight in their apartment. The three of them would have dinner, and then sit in the living room for hours, discussing anything and everything into the wee hours—religion, politics, philosophy—all accompanied by a bottle of Scotch. But their relationship was a complicated one. Meyer "was a little dubious of my intellectual training, since I had merely the requisite four years of college and was a professional journalist. I played up to that whimsy of his by sometimes saying, 'But of course I'm not an intellectual,'" Toledano remembered. Toledano, however, explained to Meyer the current American political scene, and gave him insights into various of its major players. Toledano knew Richard Nixon well, which naturally piqued Meyer's interest, and he was a close friend of Whittaker Chambers, whom Meyer passionately wanted to meet. Soon Toledano introduced him to Chambers, though Chambers "was at first suspicious of Frank as one more ex-Communist who did not really know what the battle was all about." But soon the two men—and their families—became friends, and the Meyers would drive down to the Chambers farm in Westminster, Maryland, for overnight stays.[16]

All of this was very important for Meyer. He was making crucial contacts within the conservative movement, as well as with important people. It was also vital for his intellectual and philosophical development. He had broken with communism politically; but mentally he continued to have to reorient his thinking and outlook, to understand reality as it was—not as the fog of communist propaganda portrayed it. Meyer of course could be a source of knowledge for conservatives as well. "I could talk about a conversation with Kerensky, of the great and near-great—people I knew either as a participant in the anticommunist wars or in my capacity as a newspaperman," Toledano recalled. "On his side, he supplied me with valuable academic background and insights."[17]

Meyer soon began to put all these contacts to use. By 1952, using his past writing experiences and relying upon Toledano's vast conservative influence and connections, he began to write book reviews and an occasional article for both the *Freeman* and the *American Mercury.* For a time, he was the *Mercury*'s lead book reviewer, writing and editing the entire review column. In one issue Meyer reviewed no fewer than eighteen new releases. He also made further contacts with the growing conservative community, phoning John Chamberlain of the *Freeman* and William F. Buckley Jr. (who for a time worked at the *Mercury*).[18]

Meyer's writings were the definitive sign that he had joined the conservative movement. Running through them in the early 1950s were all of the pieces of the new conservatism: a devotion to individualism, a fierce anticommunism, and a belief in the necessity of absolutes and tradition. Anger against government encroachments upon individual freedom dominated his writings. Liberals appeared "not at all terrified by the galloping strides of state power, as bastion after bastion of private property is destroyed." Excessive taxation and government power, Meyer argued, was out of step with the Western tradition, and "the essence of that spirit is the value of individual man."[19]

This was radical talk for a one-time communist. But Meyer was so determined never to let *anyone* "regiment" him again that he moved to an opposite extreme. Convinced that his communist past was terribly wrong, he felt that he must completely repudiate his past, that he must "unremittingly trace his errors to their sources."

This explains why Meyer turned so ferociously against American liberalism. Liberals had not understood the errors of their past, had not disavowed their tragic mistakes. Indeed, many of them, though former communists like himself, still claimed that Marxists were "idealistic" and strove only to do good. Meyer claimed that there were two kinds of ex-communists—"those who do and those who do not face the full horror of what they worked for." Liberals moreover still "believe in the supremacy of society over man, of the state over the citizen; they have worked for planning and control for human welfare, as ends superior to the freedom of the individual." This "collectivist," socialist program had come to dominate America so slowly that the great mass of citizens did not realize it.

Could liberals and socialists not understand, Meyer asked, that such ideas were fertile ground for the growth of communism? Communists too planned to use the state to improve man's lot; but they took such principles to their logical conclusion and subordinated everything to their goal. Liberals were manipulated by the communists, but failed to see it. Adlai Stevenson, who twice ran unsuccessfully for president against Dwight Eisenhower, was a good example. "Mr. Welfare State," Meyer wrote of him, said that all citizens had a right to an education and a job. Well, such guarantees were not in the U.S. Constitution. But they *were* in the Soviet Constitution. Meyer was not calling Stevenson a communist, and even accepted Stevenson's claim to be an anticommunist. "But this is the hallmark of the generation of the New Deal," Meyer continued. "They are horrified by the tyranny and violence of Soviet society, but they scornfully reject the only safeguards which can prevent such tyranny." Government intervention in the economy must lead to totalitarianism, he insisted; even attempts to guarantee "equality of opportunity" were doomed to fail, for then the state must logically intervene to prevent any individual from receiving a large inheritance, or a superior private education. The American tradition of Hamilton, Madison, and the *Federalist Papers* was one of limited government. The failure of American liberals to grasp this point, Meyer concluded, put them in "radical opposition" to that tradition.[20]

Meyer had declared an unconditional lifelong war upon the state, and also upon liberals, for they refused to see communism as evil. He fought "collectivism" wherever he found it. And one of his favorite targets was America's educational system.

Education in America was in a state of decline, Meyer wrote. High school graduates had little learning or sense of values. He blamed this on the influence of the philosopher John Dewey and his school of "instrumentalism." The focus was no longer on trasmitting "the culture and tradition of the civilization," on the idea that truth and absolutes exist, or that ultimate value resides in the individual. No, Deweyites consciously eliminated such ideas. They were relativists, who believed that children could only learn through "experience." Nothing must be "imposed" upon them. But since teachers must say something, Meyer observed, they filled the students with the "fashionable collectivism" of the day.

Meyer traced all of this back to the "invasion of the field of education by public tax-supported authority"; this was "the first great breach in the concept of a government limited in its powers to the maintenance of internal and external order, the concept upon which our Republic was founded." State control must always breed "collectivism," which in erasing competition breeds "mediocrity." "The state's leveling effort to assure that no unworthy son of a wealthy father shall receive an education he does not deserve," Meyer marveled, "has made it certain that no one, rich or poor, shall receive an education pitched above the dead level of the mediocre." Meyer's only hope for good schooling lay in "the remaining vestiges of home influence and the providential survival of a few good teachers." He practiced what he preached. Both of Meyer's sons, John and Eugene, received all of their primary instruction at home.[21]

Meyer even opposed excessive American involvement with the United Nations on individualist grounds. He felt that a heavy U.S. obligation towards the UN would lead to "world federalism," or in other words world government. "Is there any reason to doubt that a world state, federal or otherwise, which possessed a monopoly of armed force would corrupt those who held so magnified a power, and become an enslaving monstrosity more terrible than any even this fearful century has so far seen?"[22]

Did his criticism of the United Nations mean that Meyer was an "isolationist," a pejorative liberal term? Meyer emphatically denied it. He called himself a "nationalist," who believed in basing American foreign policy "in terms

of American national interest," such as fighting communism. "Internationalism" did not help win this fight, but only meant throwing away billions of
dollars in worthless, bureaucrat-fattening foreign aid. American aid should be
used only to defend the United States directly or to arm our close allies.
Windy notions such as "international cooperation" distracted and "demoralized" people. The Cold War struggle could result in a U.S. victory or a Soviet
victory—nothing else.[23]

Clearly, Meyer's individualism made him a hard-line anticommunist, one
who rejected Marxism on moral grounds. Communism, he wrote, considered
the individual responsible to a collective; in such a system, a limb could be cut
off to benefit the whole. This is "the direct opposite of the Christian and Western faith in the individual. . . . Between these two concepts there can be no
compromise."[24]

We must recognize, he wrote, "that we are involved in a desperate struggle
for survival against an enemy whose only aim is total world power." Since the
United States was involved in a de facto war with the Soviet Union, nothing
less than victory would do. Therefore Meyer endorsed the idea, explicated by
James Burnham and others, of seeking the "liberation" of Eastern Europe
from Soviet control.[25]

Meyer had come to believe that the "containment" policy, as practiced
by Presidents Truman and Eisenhower, was woefully inadequate. That policy
expected the USSR's own weaknesses to destroy it. But "after thirty years of
shifts and turns, atrocities and purges, all conducted in the name of progress,
it is perhaps wishful thinking to hope that the new doctrines have within
themselves a contradiction that will tear the Communist system apart," he
wrote. The policies of Dwight Eisenhower greatly disappointed him. At home,
Eisenhower retreated from cutting the budget in the face of protests by liberal
interest groups. Abroad, the administration embraced "peace" as the primary
objective, which became "peace at any price." Secretary of State John Foster
Dulles was saying that the USSR should not be surrounded by "hostile"
peoples. But, wrote Meyer, if our goal was to win, then we should seek to
surround the Soviets with as many hostile peoples as possible!

Eisenhower, Meyer concluded in 1954, had failed to reverse "the disastrous policies of the last twenty years," and conservatives must either form a
third-party movement allied with Southern Democrats, or somehow take the

Republican Party back. In his anticommunism and in his rejection of Eisenhower, Meyer was perfectly in tune with other conservatives, such as Burnham—with whom he would have so many differences later.[26]

To many, though, this welding of free-market individualism with an anti-communist foreign policy seemed contradictory. After all, how could conservatives so opposed to the state be in favor of the huge amount of tax dollars spent on defense? Conservatives attempted to address this question. William F. Buckley Jr., writing in the *Freeman* in the summer of 1954, admitted the seeming "inconsistency." But he argued that those worried about such philosophical fine points underestimated the Soviet threat. Everything said and done by the USSR showed that the battle between communism and capitalism would be played to the finish—with a real possibility of war. And this was the key point: only the *state* could carry on a war. Only it had the resources to conscript an army, and to pay for it. Everyone on the Right could agree that using the state for the purposes of self-defense was a legitimate function. Once the conflict with the Soviet Union was won, the size of the state could be reduced. But the Cold War, Buckley concluded, must be won.[27]

By 1955, THEN, MEYER was a conservative. What expanded his role within conservatism, ironically, was his attack upon the much-celebrated "new conservatives."

Meyer had been observing the rise of the new conservatism for some time. When Peter Viereck's *Shame and Glory of the Intellectuals* came out in 1953, Meyer reviewed it for the *American Mercury*. Viereck was a poet and professor of history at Mount Holyoke College, a handsome, casually dressed man whose face sported a perpetual salt-and-pepper stubble of a beard. The son of a German-American defender of the Kaiser in World War I, Viereck had rebelled against his father and become an early conservative pioneer, denouncing both communism and Nazism. Meyer wrote that Viereck said many useful things, especially in his denunciations of intellectuals who had been "fellow-travelers" of communism. But he also supported a New Deal-style "mixed economy," which Meyer was quick to denounce. "There is no middle-ground in a modern industrial society between the separation of powers which capitalism has created and the road to centralization and tyranny which socialism envisages," Meyer wrote. "A 'mixed economy' . . . is bound to grow steadily at the expense of the privately owned sector of the economy until the 'mixed economy' flowers as a full-fledged socialist economy." Again, Meyer was drawing upon Friedrich von Hayek. But Viereck rejected Hayek, denouncing nineteenth-century classical liberalism as irrelevant to the present age. Thus, to Meyer, Viereck did not belong in the conservative movement. Classical liberals, wrote Meyer, were true liberals; they "were believers in liberty. And so are all genuine conservatives."[28]

Despite Meyer's criticism of Viereck, by late 1955 intellectual circles were even more agog over the new conservatives—this time in the person of Russell Kirk. Kirk was a bespectacled, serious, romantic traditionalist who taught for a time at Michigan State University and then settled in an isolated manse in Mecosta, Michigan. His book, eventually titled *The Conservative Mind* and published in 1953 by the fledgling, Right-leaning publishing house of Henry Regnery in Chicago, received a tremendous response. It was reviewed, mostly favorably, by over fifty serious intellectual journals, and Kirk received generous profiles in *Time* and *Newsweek*. The book was actually a lengthy (over 450 pages) compendium of liberal and modern sins, coupled with one of the first attempts to define modern conservatism. Kirk enumerated six conservative "canons" that together centered on the approval of traditional values and customs, the importance of private property, and hostility toward rapid change and reform. Naturally, Frank Chodorov, the editor of the *Freeman,* wanted his journal to address this entire "new conservative" phenomenon, especially since it was short on specifics (and short on criticism of twentieth-century statism). And so he assigned Meyer to review three books of this kind: works by Clinton Rossiter, Robert Nisbet, and Kirk.[29]

Meyer focused almost his entire review upon Russell Kirk. Yes, Meyer began, Kirk and others like him were critical of collectivism. The problem lay in that their critiques and skepticisms were just that: they were simply part of an attitude, a persuasion. They had no firm "body of principles" upon which to base their attack upon modern liberalism.

To Meyer, such "principles" were crucial. The fundamental political issues of the day were defined by the struggle between a free economy and statism, between individualism and collectivism. "This is not a problem of tone nor attitude, not a difference between the conservative and the radical temperament; *it is a difference of principle,"* Meyer wrote.[30] And what principles did Kirk espouse? Did he assert that all value resides in the individual person, that there must be clear, constitutional checks on governmental power? No; while Kirk criticized the New Deal's concentration of authority in the hands of the state, nowhere did he say what standards or principles should be used to judge this. In sum, Meyer argued, Kirk and his ilk put too much weight on tradition alone. Such a position leads, in the end, simply to acceptance of whatever *is*. This could easily be co-opted and used to create a powerful, centralized state. No wonder many modern liberals applauded Kirk's book. "The New Conservatism, stripped of its pretensions," Meyer concluded grimly, "is, sad to say, but another guise for the collectivist spirit of the age."[31]

The reaction to Meyer's review among the *Freeman*'s conservative readership was considerable, with opinion fairly evenly split. But one letter stood out from the rest; Chodorov was so impressed with it that he sent it on to Meyer. The letter was from Robert J. Needles of St. Petersburg, Florida. Needles was an articulate, well-read, and somewhat cranky medical internist who wrote countless lengthy letters to magazines and newspapers giving his opinions on matters great and small. He was also an impassioned conservative admirer of Russell Kirk. And so his letter was a two-fisted defense of Kirk, denouncing Meyer's "sickening attack."

But the thrust of what he wrote was directed at what he feared Meyer's attack on Kirk would do to the conservative movement as a whole:

> We are the great conservative mass of citizens who have been dwelling in cyclone shelters for the past twenty years. We see in Dr. Kirk the most articulate, believable, and historically most unassailable of those opposed to the welfare state. Now . . . those who might be easily in Mr. Kirk's camp, and he perhaps in theirs, are about to tear him apart because of some egotistical difference of opinion. . . . These splinter writers if allowed to carry on will wreck us. Conservatism needs a structure and a home. My concept of a home is a place which may not be so orderly but is secure and comfortable, and gives us a feeling of pride in its impregnability. . . . Mr. Meyer and his colleagues . . . are encouraged to dynamite the home of the conservatives.[32]

This letter affected Meyer deeply—he even sent a copy to his friend William F. Buckley Jr. It was not that he accepted Needles's criticism. But what about Needles's point concerning the need to build a conservative "home"? Had a coherent body of conservative beliefs—had a conservative *philosophy*—been constructed? Had it even been started? No, it had not, and in fact he had told Chodorov, even before his review of Kirk, that he intended to write his own book on the subject. He would continue the process of defining American conservatism for the rest of his life.[33]

Meanwhile, Meyer had become rather good friends with the young Buckley. Buckley had noticed Meyer's work in both the *Freeman* and the *Mercury,* had contacted him, and the two became "phone-mates, as was his habit," as Buckley recalled. The telephone had become Meyer's main link to his growing list of conservative friends and acquaintances, especially since Meyer continued to spend most of his time at his mountain hideaway in the Catskills. For his friends, it was difficult, and Meyer knew it; his phone conversations usually occurred late at night and could go on for hours. "I enjoyed talking to you the other evening," Meyer wrote Buckley in the summer of 1955. "I trust you are not sufficiently Puritan—or should I say Jansenist?—to be shocked by my phoning habits. After books and drink, phoning is my main luxury."[34]

Very little bothered Buckley. In fact, aided by his associate William S. Schlamm, he was in the process of beginning a new conservative weekly magazine of opinion, and he needed and wanted the help of every thinking conservative he could find. Sometime that summer, Buckley asked Meyer if he would like to contribute to the magazine, which would eventually be named *National Review.* Meyer enthusiastically agreed.

A National Review *Conservative*

NATIONAL REVIEW WAS the brainchild of two very different men. William S. Schlamm was an energetic and voluble Viennese expatriate who had been briefly drawn to the communist movement in Europe in the 1930s. He only narrowly escaped Hitler, and he saw the carnage of World War II at close range. After coming to America, he wrote for *Time* magazine and was briefly an adviser to Henry Luce. His real passion, though, became the growing American conservative intellectual movement. Liberalism dominated American thought and action, in Schlamm's view, but without the least understanding of communism or how to fight it. American conservatism must challenge the reigning liberal intellectual establishment. At first, Schlamm hoped that Luce would provide the vehicle for such a challenge by financing Schlamm's plan for a conservative monthly magazine of culture. But the plans fell through, perhaps because Schlamm was not all that he seemed. He was never a deep or original thinker. An acquaintance, the journalist Ralph de Toledano, remembered him as "a political *flaneur* and bistro Bolshevik who could not have explained Marx's theory of surplus value if his life depended on it. . . ."[1]

But Schlamm did have passion, and he did have an important idea. He found what he was looking for in William F. Buckley Jr. Buckley was one of ten children born to a conservative Texas oilman and his wife, who eventually settled in Connecticut. He raised his children in his own image, teaching them to cherish their Catholic faith, to revere order and traditional values, and to believe in the benefits of free-market capitalism. After an energetic childhood filled with private tutoring, foreign travel, rollicking fun with his brothers and sisters, and service in the army during World War II, Buckley enrolled as a student at Yale University in 1946.

There his life began to change. In one sense, Buckley reveled in his Yale surroundings. He did well in his studies and earned the coveted post of chairman of the *Yale Daily News*. He was a well-known figure on campus. But he became deeply disillusioned with what he saw as the prevailing liberalism at Yale, and hence in the student newspaper he flayed what he saw as the dominant agnosticism, collectivism, and anti-anticommunism among Yale students and faculty. Upon graduation in 1951, Buckley wrote a book called *God and Man at Yale* that laid out his searing intellectual indictment of his alma mater. And to almost everyone's surprise, the book caused a sensation. Henry Regnery, its publisher, ordered several additional printings, and Buckley garnered national media attention. It was the first time in memory that an openly conservative book had received such notice.

Buckley thereafter served briefly in the Central Intelligence Agency, but like Schlamm he was more interested in participating in the burgeoning conservative movement. After all, *God and Man at Yale* contained all three pieces of the emerging conservative synthesis: individual freedom, tradition, and anticommunism. And so Buckley began to work within the movement. He wrote occasionally for the *Freeman* and the *American Mercury*, and in 1954 he and his fellow Yale alum L. Brent Bozell penned a book-length defense of Senator Joseph McCarthy titled *McCarthy and His Enemies*. But Buckley remained unsatisfied. No avowedly conservative forum existed within the print media. The *Mercury* had come under new ownership, turning thereafter in a viciously anti-Semitic direction; meanwhile, the *Freeman* had become a monthly concerned almost exclusively with libertarian economics.

Buckley therefore soon found that he shared Schlamm's view that liberalism's dominance over American culture had to be challenged (in the mid-1950s Buckley calculated that liberals controlled no fewer than eight journals of opinion, conservatives none). Essential to this challenge was the creation of a genuine weekly conservative journal, and Schlamm insisted that Buckley should lead such an enterprise. It took some persuasion, but Buckley eventually accepted. By early 1954 Buckley began the arduous task of raising money, assembling a technical staff, and recruiting a team of senior editors. It took longer than expected. Raising money was especially difficult—some opposed Buckley's internationalism in foreign policy, while others simply did not feel such a magazine could survive in America's current climate. But finally, in November 1955, *National Review* hit newsstands for the first time. The magazine's masthead listed Frank Meyer as one of its "associates and contributors."[2]

In associating himself with *NR*, Meyer was among ideological friends and comrades. Many of the senior editors of the magazine, such as William Schlamm and James Burnham, were former Marxists who believed they had seen totalitarianism from the inside. And the magazine's "credenda," appearing in the first issue, were very much in line with Meyer's thinking, as *NR* linked itself with each of the different factions of American conservatism. Thus, the magazine bowed in the direction of the free market, declaring that in peacetime the federal government's role must be strictly limited. "The growth of government— the dominant social feature of this century—must be fought relentlessly," wrote the editors. "In this great social conflict of the era, we are, without reservations, on the libertarian side." At the same time, *NR* declared itself a defender of truth and of an organic moral order, fighting against "social engineers, who seek to adjust mankind to conform with scientific utopias." And, of course, *National Review* was militantly anticommunist, calling communism "the century's most blatant form of satanic utopianism." "Coexistence" with it, the editors charged, was immoral and impossible besides, concluding that "we find ourselves irrevocably at war with Communism and shall oppose any substitute for victory." No, Meyer could find nothing to disagree with here.[3]

Yet in the first two years his relations with the magazine were distant. Buckley originally hired him to write a monthly column exposing the liberal slant of academic and scholarly journals and to review an occasional book. But he was not a senior editor, and thus not intimately involved with the magazine's editorial line. Nor does it appear that he wanted to be. He was content to be a "contributor," to stay in Woodstock, reading, writing, and telephoning his growing list of conservative friends.

But his column slowly evolved from a rather dry review of academic journals to the more congenial "Principles and Heresies," a discussion of ideas and philosophies behind current events. Appearing in the magazine for the first time in the spring of 1956, Meyer wrote the column at least once a month until his death in 1972; it became one of *NR's* fixtures.

The magazine as a whole also evolved. Problems arose among the senior editors, despite their shared and intense ideological beliefs—minor differences that nevertheless could potentially wreck their cause. There were disagreements concerning the nature of the Soviet Union following Stalin's death; was there a real "anti-Stalin turn" under Nikita Khrushchev, as James Burnham argued, or was it all merely a devious shift in tactics and nothing more, as both Schlamm and Meyer insisted? And deep divisions concerning *National Review's* political position existed. Burnham in 1956 argued that *NR* must either support President Dwight Eisenhower's reelection bid or risk being shunted out of the political mainstream and tagged as "extremists." Schlamm bitterly opposed Eisenhower and implied in *NR* that Burnham's position lacked principle.

Finally, personality played a role. Schlamm had recently suffered a heart attack, which changed his temperament. His writings became shrill and apocalyptic, and he demanded more and more of Buckley, jealous of anyone who seemed to interfere—such as Burnham. It all came to a head in the summer of 1957, when Buckley finally tired of Schlamm's frequent threats to resign, his scheme to form an anti-Burnham faction among other *NR* editors and staff, and his often unusable writing. Buckley had come to depend on Burnham's knowledge, advice, and frequently brilliant editorials. And so, at Buckley's insistence, Schlamm took a "leave of absence" from *National Review*—from which he never returned.[4]

Aside from criticizing some of Burnham's positions, Meyer had not involved himself in *NR's* internal squabbles. But the turmoil did affect him, for after it died down the question remained: What to do with *NR's* book review section? In the first two years of the magazine, first Willmoore Kendall and then Schlamm had run it. But now Schlamm was gone, and Kendall—a brilliant, witty, acerbic, and personally abrasive Yale political science professor—was not right for the post. In the past, his choice of books for review had been too dry, haphazard, and academic.

Buckley decided to give the book section to Meyer. He knew that Meyer read widely and was aware of the latest offerings in all of the major literary and social science fields. Meyer also had experience, having run a book review department for over a year at the *American Mercury.* He could be trusted to run the book section efficiently, to give it more coherence. Buckley wrote Burnham that, in the past, the book section had been "rather promiscuously put together. I think in this respect Frank's administration of it will be an improvement over [Schlamm's]."[5]

Meyer thus began his fifteen-year tenure as *NR*'s book review editor. It was a huge task. Piles of books would be sent to Meyer's home in Woodstock from publishers across the country. He selected the books to be reviewed, decided who should review them, secured their assent, and waited (often impatiently) for the review to arrive. He then edited the writing for style and grammar, and chose the reviews to be sent to New York for publication in *National Review*'s forthcoming issue. Often Meyer's material arrived at the last possible moment, rushed into the waiting hands of managing editor Priscilla Buckley by a hired driver from Woodstock named Homer.[6]

Some within *NR* had doubts about Meyer. James Burnham, although he respected Meyer's anticommunism and did not question his role within the magazine, argued that his selection of books, and his writing style, needed improvement. On one occasion, Meyer ran two long reviews of the latest scholarship on ancient Greek literature and history by *NR*'s two "classics" reviewers, Revilo Oliver and Garry Wills. Burnham wrote Buckley to complain. "I do think that Frank Meyer is going too far," he told him. "Revilo and Garry Wills, both at great length, are just too much to take; and…they are writing in such a way that they can't possibly be communicating to more than a dozen of our readers."[7]

Burnham wanted desperately for *National Review* to expand its readership base and to become a real political force among America's opinion leaders. He wanted the kind of magazine that would be on the desks of politicians, professors, writers, and bureaucrats. But for that to happen, it must be readable and relevant to people's everyday concerns. He was not sure that Meyer's book section achieved that.

But Buckley remained generally happy with the way Meyer handled his department. As time went on, Meyer began to grow into his task and to make *NR*'s book department his own. He managed, for one thing, to be organized. Upon request, he could furnish Buckley with a complete list of all the reviews he had received, all he had assigned, and all of the forthcoming articles and reviews that he and Buckley had discussed. Plus, Meyer's long list of conservative contacts meant that he could find new, young talent for the magazine, something Buckley saw as extremely important. Meyer also took his editing very seriously, gradually working out his own concept of the perfect review. When *NR* publisher William Rusher once asked him about this, Meyer had a ready reply.

> In general, my concept of the ideal book review is one which both gives a feel of the book and sets up a three-cornered dialogue (trilogue?) between the author, the reviewer, and the writer. Reviews can be bad, among other reasons, if they fail to any considerable degree to fulfill both these functions—that is, at one extreme, if they simply give a flat, factual recital of the contents of the book, or, at the other extreme, if they ignore the book almost completely. But since all reviews have weaknesses of one kind or another, to err in one direction or the other does not necessarily make a review unusable. The quality of the writing, specific interest, etc. may make it worthwhile.[8]

It was important that Meyer develop confidence in his handling of the book department, for some book reviews were often necessary for personal, financial, and even political reasons—occasions when Buckley involved himself in the book section. Sometimes, Buckley asked Meyer to review a specific book if it had been pushed by a staunch friend of the magazine—and if the friend was persistent enough. "We must—absolutely must—run a review . . . on [a priest's] book published, I believe, out in the midwest somewhere," Buckley once wrote him. "The priest is a close friend of one of our most loyal investors and friends, and he has written me at least a thousand letters on the subject. Would you look through your files and schedule the review at your earliest convenience?" On another occasion, Buckley requested Meyer to review a book with the odd title of *Mao Tse-tung and I Were Beggars.* "It is a respectable book," Buckley assured him; "[T]he people who printed it have done me a whole series of kindnesses and I should like to reciprocate."[9]

Buckley also made review requests for financial and political reasons. In 1957 a conservative author from Chicago published a volume on "collectivism" in American churches. Buckley wrote Meyer that it should be reviewed as soon as possible. "It is, of course, polemical in nature, but I think we have some obligation to give it a forward thrust—for political reasons," Buckley told him. "We ought to give it a fairly straightforward boost." Sometimes, running a review could improve the financial health of *NR*. At one point, Buckley urged Meyer to run a review by a writer for a New York City religious newspaper. For "in response to our supplications, [he] is doing a big push for the magazine in Sunday's *Our Sunday Visitor,*" Buckley answered. "I don't need to remind you that his last one got us 1,200 trial subscriptions."[10]

MEYER'S MANAGEMENT OF *National Review's* book department, of course, was behind the scenes, invisible to the average *NR* reader. What made him visible was his regular "Principles and Heresies" column. It was here that Meyer laid out his political philosophy, began slowly to build a loyal cadre of readers, and—most importantly—attempted to thrash out his own interpretation of just what "conservatism" meant. It was also an excellent barometer of what many conservatives were thinking in the late 1950s.

Meyer often wrote about what were, to him, familiar themes. He saw his column as a forum for educating his readers on what the prevailing intellectual and philosophical trends were—and why they were wrongheaded and dangerous. Meyer continued to pound away at philosophical relativism and the lack of truth and proper values in modern society. It led men to live like animals in a decadent, corrupt society, he wrote, citing the rise in juvenile delinquency and the vulgarity of modern, mass-market fiction.[11]

Meyer also underscored the importance of tradition. Mostly this emerged in his writings on American constitutional issues. He believed that a correct interpretation of the Constitution rested in the understanding of the original intent of the document's framers, and in grasping the concept of the separation of powers. The public's acceptance of executive supremacy over Congress upset the Constitution's balance of powers, a situation for which Meyer blamed what he called the "Roosevelt Revolution." To rectify this imbalance, he championed Congress's investigatory powers and urged it to exercise this prerogative more frequently. It was no accident that Senator Joseph McCarthy used such powers.[12]

Nor did Meyer agree with several recent decisions of the U.S. Supreme Court, which brought him and other conservatives face to face with a very difficult issue. The Court, under the leadership of its new chief justice, Earl

Warren, moved in a liberal direction in the 1950s. In its most notable decision, that of *Brown vs. Board of Education of Topeka, Kansas,* in 1954, the Court
utilized economic and sociological evidence to declare school segregation
unconstitutional, and later ruled that southern school districts must move
"with all deliberate speed" to desegregate. Meyer, as a conservative, had a
difficult time with such rapid change. The *Brown* decision he denounced as
one "which rode roughshod over precedent and reason and constitutional
obligation." The Court, he argued, was making social policy rather than doing
its job of simply interpreting the Constitution.[13]

Later, events pushed Meyer to go further. In the fall of 1957, violent
mobs in Little Rock, Arkansas, supported by the state's national guard, prevented the integration of nine black students into Central High School. As a
result, President Eisenhower reluctantly sent federal troops to Little Rock to
protect the courageous blacks throughout the school year. Meyer did not see
the event in its racial import, but as purely a constitutional issue. Meyer argued that no one branch of government has the sole authority to interpret the
Constitution. Instead, tradition holds that this power is divided among four
centers of authority: the three branches of the federal government and the
states. Drawing from the constitutional interpretation of John C. Calhoun,
Meyer wrote that the Supreme Court can decide upon constitutional issues
when the differences "are not extreme" and "can be more or less simply
adjudicated." However, when "profound differences" exist, the Constitution
"clearly envisages a suspension of decision," for none of the many different
"constitutional sovereignties" in the American system should be forced to
accept a decision which they view as unconstitutional; this, said Meyer, is a
"settled tradition."

Specifically, Meyer urged Congress to pass legislation limiting executive
power in the area of school integration, and suggested that states utilize the
traditional, Calhounian doctrines of interposition and nullification. Meyer even
advised the southern states to beef up their state militia, should federal troops be
used against them again. Meyer admitted that some might call these proposals
"extreme." But the danger to traditional American liberties was extreme as well,
and he reminded his readers that one of the foremost advocates of states' rights,
as seen in the "Virginia and Kentucky Resolutions" of 1798, had been Thomas Jefferson.[14]

Meyer, along with most conservatives in the 1950s, put tradition, states' rights, and the Constitution ahead of the cries for justice from America's black minority. But Meyer was no racist. At the time of the crisis in Little Rock, he noted that many "thoughtful men" supported school integration because of "compassion for a servile race" and a "devotion to abstract justice." Meyer's point was that the *Brown* decision, and forcible school integration in general, was not the way to achieve justice and liberty.[15]

IN REALITY MEYER AND *National Review* in the 1950s spent comparatively little time on the race issue. They saved their passion for what, to them, posed an immediate threat to the very survival of the United States: international communism and America's stance toward it.

Meyer's writing style, which was often heavy and stiff, gathered verve and crispness when he wrote about communism and American foreign policy. His views fit snugly into the conservative mainstream. He stressed that communism, despite the death of Stalin, had not changed. Its goal had always been, and continued to be, control over the entire world. But what of the Soviet Union's new leaders, such as Nikita Khrushchev and Nikolai Bulganin? What of the growing public split between the USSR and Mao Tse-tung's China? Meyer drew on his experience in the Communist Party to argue that such "thaws" and "splits" were more apparent than real. They were merely shifts in tactics, a common CP practice. Currently the Soviets saw the "balance of world power" shifting in their favor; the "period of socialist encirclement" of the West was about to begin. The only possible obstacle was "a dedicated counterrevolutionary force, clear on the nature of Communism and determined to throw it back." To prevent this, the Soviets wished to humanize their image, to lull the West into complacency. Meyer pointed out that at the Twentieth Communist Party Congress, despite Khrushchev's denunciation of Stalin's "crimes" against his people, the delegates reaffirmed their aim of world revolution. As for Mao, Meyer stressed, he had eliminated at least fifteen million Chinese in the process of consolidating his power; indeed, he was now the "most able" of the international communist leaders. The West should fear him, not romanticize him.[16]

Meyer saw the East-West conflict primarily in moral terms, and said that the West's greatest defect lay in its "lack of courage." Its only hope was to regain that courage, to risk all—"to stand against evil, to vindicate eternal values [and to risk] security, prosperity, life itself." And again and again he pounded away at the idea that American liberals lacked that courage. He even attacked George Kennan, perhaps the principal architect of the "containment" doctrine, as one who had for years been involved in "a grandiose pseudo-metaphysical mining and sapping of the foundations of his civilization."[17]

When the Soviet Union brutally crushed the Hungarian uprising of November 1956, Meyer reacted as most conservatives did—with moral outrage at the Eisenhower administration's failure to take action. Meyer wrote that Dwight Eisenhower's principles "were tested in acid and found counterfeit." America's failure to support the freedom fighters of Eastern Europe showed that Western leaders "did not have the guts to come to their support."[18]

Senior editor James Burnham thought otherwise. Burnham, who had earlier championed "liberating" Eastern Europe, was profoundly affected by the events in Hungary. But he concluded that if the idea of liberation could not even be attempted in this crisis it never would be. Given this reality, Burnham argued, the conservative must adjust his policy prescriptions to fit within "Eisenhower's liberal-humanitarian axioms"; otherwise the American Right would be dismissed as too extreme and never gain a hearing. Burnham thus proposed that both superpowers withdraw all of their troops from Central and Eastern Europe. This would "neutralize" the area and in the long run result in the unification of Germany along the lines of Austria—which, Burnham argued, would be a net gain for the West.[19]

Meyer vigorously disagreed with the "Burnham Proposals" (as Buckley labeled them), and focused on what he saw as their fatal assumptions. He attacked the view that conservatives must operate within the "Eisenhower axioms." When *National Review* began in 1955, Meyer noted, the magazine specifically repudiated Eisenhower's middle-of-the-road philosophy. Had the world changed that much in less than two years? Perhaps it had, he mused; America's foreign policy now seemed to be based on "surrender, surrender, and again surrender." How could conservatives accept Eisenhower's "axioms"? No, they must fight to change the prevailing liberalism, "to educate and to mobilize the forces to change it." Anything else—including Burnham's proposal—would simply reduce the pressure on the USSR, allowing it to solve its "problems" and emerge stronger than ever. Meyer summed up his case: "It is not possible to create a policy that both satisfies the hopes of an Eisenhower dream of renunciation of war, reliance upon the UN, victory without sacrifice, and simultaneously recognizes, as *National Review* has done, the harsh reality of the irrepressible conflict between the aims of armed Communism and the survival of our civilization and our values."[20]

This was a continuation of what would be a long debate between the two men, a debate between the real and the ideal, between pragmatism and principle, between what was possible and what was right. The debate would occur again and again within the magazine, and was one that these two men could never quite resolve.[21]

Not all issues were so divisive. Although Meyer was never involved in the ferocious debates raging among intellectuals concerning Senator Joseph McCarthy in the early 1950s, he did, in general, support McCarthy's anticommunism and his investigatory activities. Upon McCarthy's death in 1957, Meyer summed up his feelings. It was true, he wrote, that McCarthy could be "strident." And one could occasionally fault "the niceness of his discriminations or the tactical acuity of his actions." But Meyer saw McCarthy as a positive force precisely because he was not subtle. McCarthy believed there was "an absolute choice between good and evil" that would not allow compromise. McCarthy's "great commitment" to anticommunism bore witness to the truth. In other words, he was an ally in the great struggle with communism, and on that basis—no matter his imperfections—Meyer would accept him.

The only thing Meyer regretted was the controversy's anti-intellectual turn. Some McCarthy supporters had come to regard all intellectuals with the greatest suspicion. Meyer called this "unfortunate," for society needed thinkers who could articulate a society's basic ideas. But then again, intellectuals had brought society's distrust down upon themselves. Too many had gone "a'whoring after strange gods, whose blandishments both the traditions of their culture and the discipline of their profession should enable them to resist."[22]

Most *National Review* conservatives agreed with Meyer on these points. They also agreed with him when, in 1959, he bitterly denounced Nikita Khrushchev's official visit to the United States. The visit was the culmination of both the Eisenhower administration's willingness to engage the Soviets in "summit diplomacy" and Khrushchev's slow and only partial dismantling of Stalinism. When the visit was announced, Meyer was horrified. It was a sign, he wrote, of the "accelerating decay of the American will to resist Communism"; it was a refusal to see "evil as evil" and to label it as such.[23]

National Review did all it could to publicize its opposition to Khrushchev's visit. The magazine printed bumper stickers with the slogan "Khrushchev Not Welcome Here" and sponsored a rally of anticommunist groups in New York City's Carnegie Hall when the Soviet leader came to the city. Conservatives watched glumly as Khrushchev spoke to the United Nations in New York, stared at the cornfields of Iowa, and glared at Hollywood dancers doing the "cancan." Throughout, Meyer denounced Khrushchev's travels in America in moral terms. President Eisenhower, Meyer wrote, had now "clasped the hand of the Jailer of All the Russians." The visit had become "the greatest defeat in our history," for we had now recognized the Soviet Union as "a legitimate and integral participant in the comity of civilized nations." What especially disheartened Meyer was that the invitation appeared to have come from *fear*—fear of war, fear of nuclear weapons, fear of Soviet strength.[24]

So what *should* U.S. policy be toward the communists? Meyer occasionally tried to address this. In the spring of 1957, he offered two specific alternatives to current policy. First, the U.S. should give no aid or recognition of any kind to any communist leader, whether he be Khrushchev or a supposed "moderate" like Tito. Communists were communists, Meyer believed; any differences between them were nominal. Secondly, to atone for our "betrayal" of Hungary, America should promise to give concrete aid to any insurgent movements rising within Soviet satellite states. Specifically, we should encourage West Germany actively to foment unrest in its East German communist neighbor. Should the Soviet Union so much as "raise a finger" against the West Germans, the U.S. should inform it that "we will regard your act as a *casus belli* and will reply to your aggression with full force."[25]

This again was a radical position, and undoubtedly a dangerous one. As time went on, Meyer seemed to realize this—or was made to realize it, when Buckley refused to run an article coauthored by Meyer and L. Brent Bozell that implied their advocacy of a preemptive nuclear strike against the USSR. Buckley now agreed with Burnham that such proposals were too far out of the mainstream. Perhaps this is what caused Meyer to ruminate on nuclear weapons and their implications for American policy, for in the late winter of 1958 Meyer wrote a remarkable column that he titled "Dilemmas of Foreign Policy."

He now realized, Meyer wrote, that foreign affairs in the modern era carried within it a "dilemma." On the one hand, the conflict with the Soviet Union continued. The USSR's communism was a "materialist faith determined to rule the world and wipe out on the earth the very memory and image of man as a free being. . . ." Therefore "the destruction of this state is a clear duty." But Meyer also realized that nuclear war could lead to "the destruction of the human species." Did anyone have the right to launch such a war?

What were the alternatives? One, Meyer continued, was to endorse an aggressive anticommunist strategy, in which the West would deliver a series of ultimatums to the communists, backed by the threat of force, meant to "drive the Kremlin forces back to their narrowest limits," until communism's power was effectively destroyed. But the dangers of such a policy were obvious. Meyer's alternative was to resurrect the idea of a "Fortress America," a pre–World War II term used by conservatives who opposed America's entry into the European war. Meyer knew that such a term would bring memories of "America First" and "appeasement" of aggressors. But, he argued, we should stop "sneering" at this concept; for if American policymakers were not prepared to be aggressive, then the only moral policy against the Soviet Union was to "retreat to our own borders." Meyer did not mean "isolationism." Our "borders" in this case should include at least Latin America, Western Europe, Japan, and Taiwan, he maintained. "Let us state [to the USSR] that if this line is breached, we will fight with all our power." But that was all. If the U.S. was not prepared to risk war, it should simply focus on defending what it held. "At least," wrote Meyer, "let us draw back from our shameful promises to the oppressed, from our expenditure of money and men in far-flung endeavors that have no aim and only swell the power of bureaucracy. Let us settle in our own sphere, devoting our resources to building a free life."[26]

Predictably, Meyer received mail strongly opposing his "Fortress America" concept. And so a few weeks later, Meyer wrote another column defending himself against charges of isolationism. He emphasized that his policy still aimed at the defeat of the Soviet Union; a "Fortress America" was merely the most feasible way to do so. Ironically, Meyer now seemed to advocate a version of the containment policy that he had always scorned. But it also seemed the only policy that would be taken seriously. Even Frank Meyer could at times be pragmatic.[27]

THESE EARLY YEARS AT *National Review* were important years for Frank Meyer. He began to establish himself at *NR*, both as book editor and as columnist. But he had yet to exercise significant influence within the magazine or within the conservative movement as a whole, and he had yet to make a truly original contribution to conservative thought. By 1960, that would change.

Fighting for the Right

FRANK MEYER HAD PONDERED the need to define a coherent conserva tive philosophy ever since 1955, when he attacked Russell Kirk in the pages of the *Freeman*. He began to contemplate not just what conservatism was *not,* but also what it *was*. He had even talked of writing a book about it, but had not progressed very far. In these early years of Meyer's tenure at *NR,* however, he started to flesh out his conception of conservatism. He did not develop it systematically; instead, it evolved through Meyer's "Principles and Heresies" columns, and through debates in *NR* with other conservatives over various points of policy and doctrine. By 1960, Meyer's particular brand of conservatism began to emerge and to influence many on the American Right.

ONE OF THE FIRST MAJOR doctrinal disputes in *National Review*'s pages appeared early in 1956. Russell Kirk, who wrote a regular column on education called "From the Academy" for *NR,* contributed a full-length article on John Stuart Mill for the magazine called "*On Liberty,* Reconsidered." In it, Kirk argued that conservatives overrated Mill as a philosopher. Mill's utilitarianism was too optimistic about human nature, and its explanation of human beings and the reasons for their actions was too all-encompassing. It also raised serious moral concerns, by basing morality on utility, not on truth.[1]

This gave Meyer a perfect opportunity to define his own brand of conservatism, and he was eager to take it. In his response to Kirk, he began by reminding his readers that while it was important for the Right to have banded together to fight the liberals' domination of American culture, it was unfortunate that this tended to "gloss over differences, the clarification of which can only strengthen our common purpose." Now was the time to clear up these differences. As for Mill, Meyer admitted that the English philosopher's thought contained some "confusion and errors." Utilitarianism did equate morality with what was useful or practical, and such thinking undermined moral standards. But Mill also defended liberty and the freedom of the individual against "state centralism" and its "collective" tendencies. In so doing, he was enunciating the first principle of morality: that no act is truly moral unless it is freely chosen.

Thus, although John Stuart Mill's philosophy was flawed, it still constituted a positive contribution to Western thought and tradition. To Meyer, freedom was integral to that tradition. It was part of man's essence, part of his very nature. Man "fulfills his destiny in the choices he makes." This was man's essence, because only man—not animals, not inanimate objects—can choose. And nothing—no ideology, no government, and no institution—should deny him this right.[2]

Meyer was trying to explain to Kirkian "traditionalists" that freedom, tradition, and belief in an organic moral order all went together. But some were hard to convince. One reader wrote Meyer that the split between "continuity and authority" and "reason and the autonomy of the person" seemed to be irreconcilable. But Meyer disagreed. The problem lay in that traditionalists, by so stressing the maintenance of Western values, had forgotten one of the greatest insights of their tradition—that values "cannot be compelled, that they can only be freely chosen by each individual person."

As for "libertarians," Meyer agreed with their stress on liberty and the need for a limited state. But this too easily led to the pursuit of freedom for its own sake, rather than grounding it in tradition. Libertarians "can lose sight of the philosophical values which are . . . the ends which freedom serves and the very foundation of that respect for the innate dignity of the individual person upon which the defense of freedom rests." Libertarians and traditionalists had much common ground, Meyer insisted. Both believed in immutable values, and surely both knew that these meant nothing if not freely chosen. "Truth withers when freedom dies, however righteous the authority that kills it," Meyer concluded, "and free individualism uninformed by moral value rots at its core and soon surrenders to tyranny." He had begun to develop what many would later call the "fusion" of libertarianism and traditionalism.[3]

In the coming years Meyer continued to attempt to fuse freedom and tradition, and he criticized those who placed too much emphasis upon either or ignored such questions altogether. In 1960 the conservative sociologist Ernest van den Haag wrote a piece for *National Review* defending British economist John Maynard Keynes. Keynes, he wrote, did not espouse a statist ideology. Keynesianism simply allowed economists to understand the causes of inflation and depression, and what government could do to counteract them. True, Keynes prescribed differing levels of taxation, spending, and currency levels. But, van den Haag stressed, this need not lead to statism. Governments have always taxed and spent, and if doing so could avoid or meliorate economic downturns, as Keynes argued, then conservatives should be willing to use them.[4]

Meyer quickly responded, this time emphasizing his libertarianism. He made three main points. First, van den Haag asserted that Keynesian economics must not be repudiated because it "works." But, to some extent, so did third-world dictatorships, or even communism. Should conservatives thus utilize the writings of Marx? A true conservative, Meyer insisted, can never divorce economics from morals and principles. Economics must both serve proper ends *and* be conducted by proper means. Secondly, van den Haag spoke about the needs of the state. But the "locus of value" in the economic sphere was in the individual. History proved that the state, if not limited, would become an agent of coercion. Keynes, moreover, was not "neutral," as van den Haag had said. "No techniques that aggrandize state control of the economy can be neutral to the conservative who is engaged in a desperate struggle—a struggle which has priority over all others—to reduce and limit the power of the state," Meyer wrote. This was the concrete form of "liberal–collectivist ideology": conservatives *must* oppose Keynesianism.[5]

Meyer continued to try to strike a balance. He stressed that "classical liberals" must not allow their thought to be captured by a "secular progressivism." For such progressivists sneered at the idea of an "organic moral order," and would thus inevitably lead the nation toward "collectivistic liberal[ism]" and its "more hideous cousin," communism. Libertarians were correct in assuming that, in the *political* realm, freedom was the primary goal. What they forgot was that, in the moral realm, freedom was only the *means* by which men pursue virtue.

As always, however, Meyer coupled such criticisms with similar reminders to traditionalists. While they understood the "authority of God and truth," and grasped the "moral basis of man's existence," they must avoid the trap of "authoritarianism," for "the *political condition* of moral fulfillment . . . is freedom from coercion."[6] Meyer concluded that conservatives must "draw upon whatever wisdom is available to them, to winnow the true from the false, wherever it appears and irrespective of ideological labels." He might have said that conservatives must *fuse* these two parts of their heritage.[7]

Meyer did not always discuss conservatism in such abstract, philosophical terms. If he had, he would never have built much of a following. But he did attract adherents, and one of the ways he did so was by writing about things that nonintellectual conservatives could understand. Meyer frequently opposed himself to America's intellectual elite, which he referred to as the "liberal establishment." Like most conservatives, Meyer located this elite within the circles of government, academia, and the media. He also identified them by their ideas. Meyer charged that the key figures of the liberal establishment had no base of morality, no bedrock values, believed in no absolutes. They depended not on reason but on the "flow of experience"; they admired not values, but "the taste and choice of each man's natural and untutored desires." To Meyer, this explained the middle-of-the-road Eisenhower presidency; intellectual thought in general was now similarly muddled, a "mishmash." Politicians had few ideas of their own, but allowed public opinion to guide their actions. The age's mediocrity was also reflected in its choice of heroes, such "vulgarians" as Norman Cousins, Albert Schweitzer, and J. Robert Oppenheimer.[8]

"Establishment" criticism of conservatives fanned Meyer's resentment. By 1956, several members of the academic elite, such as sociologist Daniel Bell and historian Richard Hofstadter, had analyzed the popularity of Joseph McCarthy and the growth of a conservative movement in America. They attributed this development not to sincere beliefs and concerns, but to psychological defects, "authoritarian" impulses, and "anti-intellectualism" in American life. The liberal establishment could not accept that there might be any legitimate opposition to their ideas and policies. Therefore, those who did resist liberalism's reign must be crazy.

Meyer labeled this thinking a "delusion," and a dangerous one, for it "creates between the intellectuals and the rest of society a schism which portends ill for civilization." Normally, conservatives are defenders of the established order, not radicals or insurgents. But Meyer saw himself as an insurgent warring against a smug, elitist, and immoral establishment. Almost all at *National Review* agreed. Indeed, this was perhaps the primary reason for Buckley's decision to found the magazine. Far from defending the established order, they fought to destroy it; in an interview with Mike Wallace in 1957, Buckley called himself a "radical conservative." This antiestablishment attitude would become a permanent feature of the American Right.[9]

American politics was another primary concern of Meyer and his fellow conservatives. *National Review* covered it assiduously, keeping a regular correspondent in Washington to report on political developments and chronicling the rise of the Right's favorite political figures, such as Senators William Knowland and Barry Goldwater. It was also one of Meyer's favorite topics; he often spoke of the correct conservative approach to politics. He needed to, for the conservative movement advocated different strategies. Ralph de Toledano was one of America's most respected conservative journalists and a shrewd reporter of the national political scene. But he told conservatives that too often they, "like Trotskyite splinter groups, get their kicks from ideological purity," thus splitting the Republican Party and losing elections. The Right must show more tolerance for liberal Republicans, and seek not purity but victory. Similar thoughts came from another (unidentified) *NR* reader. He wrote Meyer that *NR* was overly negative and was not being "constructive." After all, liberals were not monolithic, were "by no means of one mind on everything. . . . [W]e are not in a civil war situation with the liberals." Why not seek compromise with liberalism on the basis of shared values, and "strive for model ways of translating those values into policy"?

The question of pragmatism and principle, of being "constructive" or holding to what was "right," had appeared again. But Meyer's view remained the same, and he thus tried to articulate his own political vision. Toledano, Meyer said, was too willing to compromise on matters of truth, which (as he often said) a conservative must never do. The Republican Party had done this very thing in 1952, and was stuck with President Eisenhower and his "appeasement" and "statism."

To the correspondent who urged moderation, Meyer admitted that many liberals did share an "inherited moral capital" with conservatives, but liberals were "relativists" who repudiated absolute values and the "spiritual basis" of the individual. They dreamed of being "social engineers" who would "confine the free rhythms of human life and the designs of God." Only by launching a "merciless attack" upon liberalism could conservatives drive "wedges" within liberal ranks. Did this make *National Review* a "radical" opposition? Of course it did, Meyer concluded, but such an opposition was necessary. Power was in the hands of an "Establishment," and although removing it would be difficult, "there is nothing in the political sphere worth doing but to make the attempt." This was modern, American conservatism—a long way from its eighteenth-century forbears.[10]

MEYER HAD BY NO MEANS convinced everyone of the soundness of his political and philosophical approach. Although he always got along very well with editor-in-chief Buckley, in these early years Meyer's relationship with some of *NR*'s other editors and contributors was somewhat strained. These differences were an excellent example of the difficulties faced by *National Review*— and by conservatives in general—in the closing years of the 1950s. The conservative unity that Meyer sought proved difficult to find.

In part, discord within the American Right revolved around broad, philosophical questions such as the concept of "tradition." Ralph de Toledano was not content with conservatism. "The program and the certainty were still lacking," he wrote. "Having accrued a smattering of diverse political postures, [conservatives] tried to live by them, bound more by frustration than by doctrine. . . . [T]hey did not—perhaps they could not—define [their] tradition or their own philosophical roots." Toledano was aware of Meyer's efforts to fuse the ideas of freedom and authority, and his reliance on the American Constitution. But the Constitution was too vulnerable to amendment, or to the machinations of liberal Supreme Court justices. Meanwhile, Toledano argued, "though Meyer had come to grips with the troubling conservative paradox of freedom-in-authority, he had conquered it only to the degree of finality with which a theologian 'solves' the problem of good-in-evil."[11]

Then there was Whittaker Chambers. Ever since the Alger Hiss case, Chambers had lived in relative seclusion on a farm near Westminster, Maryland, although he willingly received visitors and kept in contact with many conservatives and anticommunists. In 1954, after a brief correspondence, Buckley drove out to meet Chambers, whom he had long admired, and the two became fast friends. Buckley then tried to get Chambers to accept a position as senior editor with *National Review*, but Chambers had demurred, largely because he felt his own brand of conservatism did not quite match Buckley's. In 1957, he changed his mind and became an *NR* senior editor for the next two years.

Some at *NR* feared that Chambers would be difficult to get along with; his writings hinted at a dark, brooding presence. But he turned out to be wonderful company—a rather short, chubby man who enjoyed good conversation and funny stories and worked in a perpetual cloud of pipe smoke. But his differences with Buckley and others remained, and Chambers's view of Frank Meyer served as an excellent example.

Chambers contended that the crisis facing the West was not fundamentally about philosophy or free-market economics. Instead, he defined it as a moral and spiritual conflict with the Soviet Union and communism, one which demanded a broad counterrevolutionary struggle by the Right and required compromises and alliances with whomever would join in this struggle. Chambers' views were close to James Burnham's—and "antipathetic" to Meyer's emphasis upon free-market capitalism. "Capitalism, whenever it seeks to become conservative in any quarter," Chambers wrote Buckley, "at once settles into mere reaction—that is, a mere brake on the wheel, a brake that does not hold because the logic of the wheel is to turn. Hence the sense of unreality and pessimism on the Right, running off into all manner of crackpottism." Laissez-faire was no longer relevant to understanding modern society; it no longer appealed to the masses, and its espousal would not help in the fight against communism. Hence, Chambers told Buckley that he had "almost nothing in common with the effort of Meyer or Kirk, whose rationales, no matter how formally logical, seem to me, by contrast with the total reality, chiefly an irrelevant buzz."[12]

Chambers believed that Meyer's views were too abstract, too coldly philosophical. After the Republican Party suffered serious losses in the midterm congressional elections of 1958, Chambers reflected in a letter to Buckley:

> If the [Republican] Party cannot get some grip of the actual world we live in and from it generalize and actively promote a program that means something to masses of people—why, somebody else will. There will be nothing to argue. The voters will simply vote Republicans into singularity. The Republican Party will become like one of those dark little shops which apparently never sell anything. If, for any reason, you go in, you find, at the back, an old man, fingering for his own pleasure, some oddments of cloth. . . . Nobody wants to buy them, which is fine because the old man is not really interested in selling. He just likes to hold and to feel. As your eyes become accustomed to the dim kerosene light, you are only slightly surprised to see that the old man is Frank Meyer.[13]

James Burnham's criticisms of Meyer were similar but on a slightly different subject. Burnham never ceased trying to push *NR* closer to the political mainstream. He wanted the magazine to be a *conservative* influence and was therefore concerned that it not be seen as extreme, a haven only for crackpots and dreamers. Burnham was now in a position to press his agenda. He had become one of Buckley's most trusted counselors and friends, advising him on such things as the kind of articles *National Review* ought to run and the magazine's continuous financial problems.[14]

One way to broaden *NR*'s appeal to the center, Burnham thought, was to enhance its "readability." *NR* conservatives must be willing to "popularize" their views. Meyer was part of the problem. "Many of Frank Meyer's columns do not belong in a weekly magazine," Burnham wrote. "They are not readable; and except by a small coterie, they are not read." Burnham emphasized that he did not consider Meyer's columns bad philosophy, nor his subjects inappropriate. But Meyer's was "a somewhat different genre. I do not find the same confounding of genres in his columns, at least not as a rule. But I think many of them are just too damn difficult to understand, when encountered in a weekly."

In Burnham's eyes all of this was part of a larger problem—the question of whether the magazine could be relevant. "Is *NR* going to rest in a bayou," Burnham wrote Buckley, "or struggle in the main channel (even if at the channel's edge)? Is *NR* trying to talk to those only who are already in basic agreement, or to reach out toward new layers? Is NR only making the record of inevitable doom (a la Trotsky or Whit Chambers), or does it assume that—though the ideal is impossible—some choices are still significant, and results can be if not good then at any rate less bad? Is NR going to express the negation of the defeated part of an older generation, or the still open perspectives of a younger?"[15]

BUT DESPITE ALL of these arguments within *National Review,* Meyer stayed. Buckley liked him and trusted his work. Only a few months after giving Meyer authority over the book department, Buckley listed Meyer in internal memos as one of *NR*'s "critical personnel." And the feeling was mutual. Meyer admired and respected Buckley; the two enjoyed lengthy discussions, not only about the magazine but also about ideas and issues. Both men also had a great sense of humor. On one occasion, Meyer sent Buckley a formal-looking letter, typed on *NR* letterhead and addressed to him using his full title of editor in chief. At the bottom of the page, in Meyer's longhand scrawl, was written: "Bill: I have a young girl doing some stenography for me a few hours a week to take some of the brunt off Elsie—She seems to treat you with a lot more respect than Elsie—who writes you on yellow paper without a title!"[16]

Elsie actually enjoyed Buckley enormously. She found him funny and charming, and she liked his intensity of feeling. She occasionally sent him notes, in her own neat cursive script, concerning something he had written, or perhaps about an article *NR* had run. On one occasion, she praised Buckley for his improved writing style. "A tribute," she began. "I believe you are becoming one of the great English prose stylists! . . . At your best, you manage the incredibly skillful combination of brilliance, polish, elegance, wit, and—robustness. And *then* the moral fervour shines through. . . . I am satisfied that you will be accounted among the company of the great, as you perfect the gift that God has given you."[17]

In time, Burnham's acceptance of Meyer grew as well. He could see that Meyer was there to stay, and his worries about the book section dwindled. Besides, Meyer had his own loyal readership, much as Burnham had. Hence he later told Buckley: "I have a softer attitude than I used to about Frank's column. The prose is frightful, but he thinks pretty deep, and some of his ideas are sweeping. And I believe we have a bloc of readers who like and want his sort of thing. . . . I would myself find it very interesting if he spent frequent columns on trends, controversies, new ideas that he found therein (including sympathetic developments)."[18]

Within *National Review*, Meyer began to establish a kind of legend—mostly because of his use of the telephone, which continued to be extensive. He was very close in these years to fellow editor L. Brent Bozell; the two spent hours discussing and arguing over the phone. Willmoore Kendall joked that an "emergency call" from Meyer to Bozell was "defined as one which interrupts the *regular* call from Frank Meyer to Brent Bozell." Others on *NR*'s staff laughed that Meyer was paid either his salary or his phone bill—whichever was higher.[19]

The legend grew also because of the growing number of his friends and contacts. Meyer became a full-fledged conservative activist, reaching out to traditionalists, libertarians, right-wing politicians, and especially younger people. In 1957 Garry Wills joined *National Review*. Wills was a youthful, conservative Catholic seminarian who had, out of the blue, sent *NR* an article parodying the writing style of *Time* magazine. Buckley loved the piece, and quickly arranged for Wills to visit *NR*'s offices in New York; once there, Wills agreed to do more writing for the magazine, including book reviews, which is how he first met Meyer.

As would happen with so many young conservatives, Meyer soon had Wills visit him in Woodstock to stay the night and discuss conservatism, literature, history, and anything else that came to mind. Wills and Meyer soon became close friends. Wills would typically arrive in the early afternoon; Frank would just be getting up, emerging "bear-like" from upstairs, downing endless cups of coffee, and glaring at Wills from beneath hooded, bleary eyes. He had an "underground" look about him, Wills recalled, with his pasty face, purplish lips, and seemingly perpetual weariness; and the two would then frequently argue loudly about literary authors and political positions. Yet none of this mattered, because in the end it was Meyer's friendship that always came through. Meyer knew that Wills, although he loved books, had few of his own and little money with which to buy more. So, he gave him as many books to review as he could. Later, when Wills married, Meyer helped him apply for and receive a research grant to take him to England so that he could finish work on his dissertation—and have a honeymoon with his new wife. And when Wills ran out of money before finishing his thesis, Meyer secured him a job writing editorials for the *Richmond News-Leader.* This kind of personal attention and caring endeared Meyer to many young conservatives, and helped bring more of them within the *NR* orbit and into the movement in general. It was one of his most significant accomplishments.[20]

Meyer was active in other ways as well. By 1959, once or twice a year he ventured out on lecture tours around the country, speaking mainly to conservative groups and to right-wing student organizations at colleges and universities. The program was something Buckley had helped set up through a speakers' bureau called the Babcock Agency. These were golden opportunities for Meyer to make contacts and win converts.[21]

He especially tried to keep communication open between himself and other crucial figures in the conservative movement. This was not always easy. Relations between Meyer and Russell Kirk were chilly for some time in the wake of Meyer's criticisms. But Meyer did not allow their dispute to become personal. When *NR* received a book for review that was appropriate for Kirk, Meyer sent it to him. When Kirk wrote a column for the magazine which contained praise for "night people," Meyer immediately wrote him: "Whatever our other differences, I am wholeheartedly with you—my own bedtime being between seven and eight. . . . I wonder, incidentally, whether part of the virtue of those hours for work or talk is not that everyone being asleep, emanations of their minds are turned off so that the ether is clear. An unscientific hypothesis, but one I cherish."[22]

Meyer also carefully read each issue of *Modern Age*. This highbrow quarterly journal, begun by Kirk in 1957, focused on broader issues of culture and literature, with a dash of foreign policy thrown in. In 1959, however, Kirk ceased editing the journal due to unspecified differences between him and his financial backers. Meyer quickly fired off a letter to Kirk: "Allow me to say how much I regret your resignation as editor of *Modern Age*. Your journal has been a remarkable achievement—and one which I cannot conceive, under the circumstances, retaining its character without your editorship. I can only hope that you will succeed in establishing your conditions and resume the editorship. However much we differ from time to time in our view of some of the problems of conservatism, I think we share a firm respect for quality and excellence—which I suspect is the area in which *Modern Age* will suffer most acutely from your departure."[23]

Nor did Meyer's bridge-building stop with Russell Kirk. Whenever he scheduled a review of an avowedly conservative book, Meyer let the book's author and financial backers know—"so that they will know we are taking the book seriously," as he once told Buckley. Meyer also occasionally ventured to Washington, D.C., to contact the editors of the conservative newsletter *Human Events,* and kept in touch with the representatives of the William Volker Fund, a California-based foundation that was a prime source of grant money for conservative authors. In 1960, Meyer made his first contribution to *Modern Age,* propounding his "fusionist" thesis concerning freedom and authority. He also had ties to the Intercollegiate Studies Institute, a network and funding source for conservative student groups. It was through his ISI connections that, at a conservative seminar held in southern Indiana, he first met Richard Weaver. Meyer, Weaver, and Milton Friedman were invited to discuss the differences between libertarian and traditionalist conservatives; to Meyer's surprise, he found that he and Weaver were in essential agreement on the possibility of unity between individualism and tradition, with Weaver (in Meyer's view) defending the "dignity" and "worth" of the individual more strongly than Friedman. This was why Meyer befriended young conservatives, lectured across the country, and sought contacts with right-wing groups and organizations. He sought common ground; he sought to build a conservative *movement.* And it was beginning to happen.[24]

IN MEYER'S FIRST FIVE YEARS at *National Review* he was not seriously involved in formulating the magazine's editorial line, partly because of Meyer's decision to spend most of his time in Woodstock. *NR'*s editors did not know Meyer well, nor he them. And what the magazine's staff did know, they were not sure they liked. Priscilla Buckley, who became *NR'*s managing editor in 1958, recalled that Meyer's personality could be hard to get used to: "It was considered a lucky thing that Frank was ensconced at Woodstock, at a safe distance from New York. He was difficult to work with in person. Like the good ex-Communist that he was Frank could go on for hours, pacing up and down, chain-smoking cigarettes, willing to talk into the wee hours to make any point, no matter how minor. The rest of us, with a magazine to get out every week . . . just didn't have the time to listen, or the energy to fight every point, or the inclination to make high drama of any given point. His visits to New York were few."[25]

But as time went on, Meyer began to involve himself more. Buckley occasionally asked all of *NR*'s editors for their opinions on matters great and small, and Meyer would telephone or submit written memoranda. Thus Meyer gradually began to offer Buckley his views. In the spring of 1958, Meyer learned that *NR* was considering its editorial stance concerning the accession of Charles de Gaulle to power in France. Meyer could not reach Buckley by phone, and so sent a brief telegram. "Want to urge strongest editorial support DeGaulle. Despite weaknesses present situation make him I am convinced only alternative to Communism in France."[26]

He was now advising Buckley, and Buckley listened. When *NR*'s young editor in chief began a correspondence with the noted British author Evelyn Waugh, he sent Meyer a copy of the letters the two men had exchanged, and asked for his opinion; was it worth pursuing? Meyer encouraged him to continue. "I think it is definitely worth following up. Partly because he is still laboring under misconceptions, and partly because I would desperately like to get him as a reviewer."[27]

A crucial test for Meyer's involvement in the magazine came through the internal debate concerning the election of 1960. Once again, the *NR* circle of intellectuals considered the relative merits of pragmatism versus principle, and Meyer took a very active role in his attempt to influence editorial policy.

In his column, Meyer had been writing about the forthcoming election for some time. He was convinced that conservatives had been deeply mistaken in their past support of Dwight Eisenhower, a mistake they must not repeat. Eisenhower, Meyer argued, had proven to be too pragmatic and "middle-of-the-road"; the Right's past alliance with him had caused their values to "slip." The result was "creeping socialism," said Meyer, and conservatives supported it "only because it creeps instead of leaping." Those on the Right must no longer allow "their energies to be siphoned off by any right-wing liberal who wheedles them with occasional words of conservative sound."[28]

Therefore, a year before Election Day Meyer wrote that American conservatives should under no circumstances in 1960 support Richard Nixon, the candidate of the Eisenhower administration. Meyer observed shrewdly that Nixon had subordinated everything to his quest for the presidency, that therefore he "drift[ed] with the tide" and supported liberal positions such as the

Khrushchev visit and the growth of welfare programs. "All the arguments urging conservatives to support him," Meyer wrote, "boil down to the argument that there is nothing else for them to do."

If there was no clearly conservative candidate available in 1960, Meyer continued, the Right should organize a "conscious, principled boycott" of the 1960 campaign and focus on electing conservative candidates to the House and Senate and creating a real grassroots organizational base among conservatives in the hinterlands. Then perhaps in 1964 the Right could take the Republican Party back.[29]

Such a boycott appealed to many conservatives, because the candidate they truly wanted was not in the race. Senator Barry Goldwater of Arizona, first elected to the U.S. Senate in 1952, published a book in 1960 titled *The Conscience of a Conservative*. The book was almost completely written by *National Review* senior editor and friend of the senator, L. Brent Bozell, and it not only excited the Right, but became a bestseller. Meyer reviewed the book for *NR*, applauding Goldwater as an "outstanding senator" who had written a book based on "principle." Here was a politician who finally said what many conservatives longed to hear. Goldwater called for sharp cutbacks in New Deal welfare programs, for declaring the USSR an "outlaw" nation, and for severing diplomatic relations with it. "A startling program indeed," Meyer wrote. "By stating [conservative principle] with such clarity and force, Senator Goldwater has placed himself in the first rank of American statesmen." Goldwater had also placed himself in the first rank of presidential contenders.[30]

So, as the fall campaign began and Richard Nixon and John F. Kennedy claimed their respective party's nominations, Meyer was decidedly unenthusiastic. Also worrisome to Meyer, both men seemed to be creations of the television age. They would be chief executives "whose effective opinions are automatically derived by a slide-rule out of the material the poll-takers automatically present, a President whose personal style is externally created by the impersonal prescriptions of the television system."

Meyer noted that some conservatives (perhaps James Burnham again) argued that such developments reflected the new technological age; the creation of such "new men" was inevitable, and the Right must simply adjust to them. But Meyer, who detested admonitions to bow to the "inevitable," thundered that this was an "impossibility." "The conservative may temporarily, on the practical political level, work within its power system, but he cannot accept its assumptions and adjust himself to it as the continuing basis of his thought and action. His aim must be to destroy it, to overturn its assumptions and return society to a proper understanding of the relations of power to principle, of man's true ends."[31]

There was still the question of *National Review's* stance on the 1960 race. The magazine's internal debate over it tells much about the state of mind of conservatives in 1960, as well as about the key questions facing them as a movement. The struggle was an intense one.

It began in May 1960, when Buckley scheduled an editorial conference to discuss *NR's* election stance (the usual length of these meetings led *NR* publisher William Rusher to call them "agonies"). Meyer's strong feelings about the issue led him to rush a lengthy memorandum to Buckley. He wrote with genuine urgency. Conservatism, he told Buckley, was marked by contrasts. On the intellectual level, conservative influence was growing, as shown by the growth of *National Review,* the Volker Fund, and the expanding number of conservative writers. This, combined with "the increasingly apparent bankruptcy of the Liberal position," was creating a climate in which conservatism was "the only live option for the independent and the intelligent of the new generation."

But eight years of "a liberal Republican executive" had weakened conservative political opposition to liberalism, and Nixon's movement "farther and farther to the Left" made it worse. With luck, Meyer continued, America would remain stable for the next fifteen or twenty years, so that "a developing intellectual [reality] can be translated into political reality," thus rescuing the country from the liberal establishment. But Meyer feared that liberalism would lead the country to a "crisis," a crisis in which "the confidence of the American people in the leadership of the establishment will be radically shaken and they will look for new leadership uncompromised by previous association with the establishment." In either case—whether there was stability or crisis—*NR* ("the center of the movement") must be free of "establishment" taint, and instead develop new leaders to whom the country could turn in time of emergency. Hence, "under no circumstances should the conservative movement be compromised by tailing the Nixon kite."

Then what *should* the Right do? Meyer told Buckley to take a "positive position," proposing that *NR* endorse Barry Goldwater as "the only candidate whom conservatives can support" and as the yardstick by which conservatives should judge other candidates. No, Goldwater had no chance at the Republican nomination in 1960. But neither would *NR* appear "silly" in backing him. "We can make it very clear . . . that we have no illusions about the practical possibilities," Meyer wrote, "but that if the Republican Party is to express conservative principles, the nomination of Goldwater is the only way to do so." Meyer also urged that the magazine "to a greater degree than we have ever done before" support specific senatorial and congressional candidates "with the greatest of vigor," thus making clear to its readers "that it is here that for the time [being] we see the only hope of political improvement."[32]

No final decisions were made at the May meeting. The battle lines, however, were clear. Meyer, William Rusher, and new senior editor William Rickenbacker argued for no *NR* endorsement of Nixon, with Brent Bozell helping the cause from Washington, from which he supplied Meyer with arguments in their daily, at times hourly, telephone conversations. James Burnham and Priscilla Buckley urged the magazine (albeit reluctantly) to support the vice-president, saying that conservatives would otherwise be seen as extreme and radical and would fail to oppose the liberal candidate. Buckley for several weeks remained uncommitted. Finally, another "agony" was held in September, at which time the issues were thrashed out once again. Buckley then made his decision. As a sign of the issue's sensitivity, he wrote out the editorial for the magazine himself and circulated it among all the editors for their comments.[33]

In it, Buckley presented the arguments of both sides, stating that both were "rational" stances for conservatives to take. He reminded the Right that "equally well-instructed persons can differ on matters of political tactic, and…it is profoundly wrong for one faction to anathematize the other over such differences." Still, *NR* would endorse no one in 1960. Buckley claimed that this was because its job was not "to make practical politics" but rather to "think, and to write; and occasionally to mediate." But clearly the decision to abstain arose at least partly from Nixon's liberalism ("Who likes Nixon's Republicanism?" Buckley wrote. "We don't."), and from Buckley's unwillingness to alienate a large section of the Right. Meyer and Rusher's arguments had hit home.[34]

The editorial did not stop James Burnham from making a last, impassioned plea for Buckley to change his mind. Just before *NR*'s final preelection issue was put to bed, Burnham wrote Buckley a vigorous memo outlining his arguments once again. But Buckley stood firm. He acknowledged that his colleague's comments were "orthodox and compelling," but they did not deal with the "transcendent" argument, which was that "someone—something—concern itself with maintaining the paradigm." He assured Burnham that he did not intend to isolate *NR* from the mainstream political arena. But, at this crucial time, other concerns took center stage. "I do not feel that ours is a monastic function of bead-saying in isolation from the rest of the world. But I think a very good case can be made—indeed, I think Rusher has made it—for suggesting that we actually increase our leverage on events by failing to join the parade. . . . As the editorial put it, you can't prefer Ike, you must like him. And for us to do so in the teeth of five years' analyses of events to which you more than anyone have contributed the essential masonry, is to run the risk of appearing unintelligible."[35]

And so, this time, Meyer and Rusher had won. They did not receive everything they wanted—*NR* had not given Goldwater any official endorsement, nor backed many senatorial and congressional candidates. But on the question of Nixon, they had emerged triumphant. They won because they believed, and Buckley shared the belief, that America was in crisis. The U.S. was losing the Cold War to the Soviet Union abroad, and the welfare state was eroding freedom at home. In such a crisis, conservatives could not support someone like Nixon, with his diluted—"unprincipled"—views. They would not compromise with ideas they deeply believed to be immoral. This was the most thorough airing of the question of pragmatism that *NR* conservatives had yet experienced, and it was an extremely important question for the future of the movement. For the debate was not over.

For Meyer personally, the whole episode marked a turning point. He had become heavily involved in an issue of *NR* editorial policy for the first time, and instead of being ignored, Buckley had read his memos and understood the argument he was making. He now knew that, despite his distance from the magazine's offices, he could play a significant role in its editorial policy. His role within *National Review* would continue to grow as the years passed.

Thus, despite Kennedy's narrow victory over Nixon, Meyer was upbeat. In his column, he urged conservatives to begin to take over the Republican Party; and he presciently predicted that a truly conservative platform would "sweep into its support Southern conservatives and create a new majority of the South, the Midwest, the Mountain states, the Far West, and some smaller states of the East." The Right must not let liberal Republicans take them for granted again or allow for the approval of a liberal platform in order to reach out to the "center." Should that occur, conservatives should walk out.[36]

On balance, Meyer stressed that conservatism was on the correct path. At *National Review*'s fifth anniversary dinner, a lavish black-tie affair held in New York's Plaza Hotel in December 1960, all the magazine's editors made brief remarks before the large audience. Meyer's focused on hope: "It is not for temporal success that we are promised that the gates of Hell shall not prevail against us. We can only know that we fight for the right. But the possibility of temporal victory is taking shape; the weapons are being forged; the issue rests on our stamina and courage."[37]

In the years following 1960, Meyer's stamina and courage would never be questioned.

$$- 5 -$$

Principles, Politics, Action

THE DAWNING OF A NEW DECADE always seems to augur change; and indeed, as conservatives entered the 1960s, change was in the air. Perhaps its most visible symbol was the new president about to take office in January 1961.

John F. Kennedy seemed to have everything. He was young and handsome, with a famous family name, a Harvard education, a sterling record in World War II, a glamorous, beautiful wife, and a vigorous, energetic approach to life. His administration began auspiciously, with Robert Frost reading poetry during inaugural ceremonies taking place in a crisp, cold, snow-capped nation's capital before a huge throng of celebrants. And in the first days and weeks of Kennedy's presidency there was much talk of the influx of "youth" and "vigor" into Washington, of how the "best and the brightest" were being brought in to solve the nation's problems and launch America into a "New Frontier."

It is often forgotten, however, that when John Kennedy assumed the presidency, many observers were skeptical of him. For he was still largely an unknown quantity. Prior to 1960, his record in Congress had been decidedly undistinguished; his political rise was largely due to the money, connections, ambition, and determined public relations campaign waged by his well-heeled father, Joseph P. Kennedy. Nor did these assets produce an easy triumph in the election of 1960. Kennedy narrowly squeaked into the White House, holding only a 118,000 popular vote majority over his opponent, Richard Nixon, and perhaps benefitting from the questionable tactics of Richard M. Daley's Chicago political machine. Upon entering office, Kennedy was not seen by many as a dominating political figure.

The new president thus opened his administration by focusing on a unifying theme: foreign policy. Kennedy's inaugural address emphasized Cold War issues and contained what, in retrospect, is an amazing anticommunist commitment: "Let every nation know, whether it wishes us well or ill, that we shall pay any price, bear any burden, meet any hardship, support any friend, oppose any foe, to assure the survival and success of liberty."[1]

Kennedy was in fact a committed anticommunist who worried that the Soviet Union and China would support other Marxist movements around the globe. But things did not go well. Shortly after Kennedy assumed office, he learned of a CIA plan for 1,500 anticommunist Cuban exiles to invade their homeland and depose Fidel Castro. Castro had come to power in Cuba in 1959, moved steadily to the Left, and was soon firmly in the Soviet camp; consequently, he became an increasingly painful thorn in America's side. Anti-Castro Cuban exiles had been training in Florida, under thinly disguised American auspices, since 1960; now the Joint Chiefs of Staff told Kennedy that they believed the plan was workable, its goals achievable.

Kennedy gave the operation his approval, but it proved to be a fiasco. Castro was waiting for them, and worse, fearing open American involvement, Kennedy refused to give American air support to the operation. By April 22, 1961, it was all over. Landing at the "Bay of Pigs," hundreds of Cuban exiles were killed, and over 1,200 taken captive.

The pressure did not ease. Only two months later Kennedy met with Soviet Premier Nikita Khrushchev in Vienna, Austria. Khrushchev had been making loud noises about providing Soviet aid for "wars of national liberation." Now, to intimidate the inexperienced Kennedy, he demanded a solution to the question of Berlin, threatening to shut off American access to that increasingly divided city. It appeared that international communism was on the offensive.

Upon returning home, Kennedy responded by calling up the army reserve and National Guard units and asking Congress for $3 billion in additional defense spending. But in early August the Soviets solved the problem in their own way. They began constructing what would be known as the Berlin Wall, a barbed-wire and concrete barrier to any further refugee movement between East and West. Kennedy let the wall stand.[2]

MEYER WAS NOT naïve about the prospects facing conservatives. He knew the new administration would be liberal, the only question being how far to the Left it would drift. In an early 1961 column he noted that Kennedy had appointed mostly "left-wing ideologues" as his aides and advisers (such as Adlai Stevenson and Arthur Schlesinger). But chiefly Meyer worried that the president, in his inaugural address, had not been so much harsh toward the communists as he had been gullible. In his speech, Kennedy urged both sides in the Cold War "to explore what problems unite us instead of belaboring those problems which divide us." Meyer responded that this "betrayed his own, and perpetuated the nation's, deep misapprehension of the very nature of Communism. . . . The hard truth about Communism which our new President, like our old, refuses to face is that we have nothing, nor can we have anything, that will "unite" us with the Communists; that Communism is absolutely alien philosophically— one might almost say theologically—to the very concept of justice, to the very concept of any peace but the peace of the graveyard where Communism would reign supreme over the world."[3]

But in this, Meyer disagreed with many foreign policy experts and Kremlinologists. These authorities argued that the growing split between the Soviet Union and China should be exploited by the West, that communism was no longer "monolithic." Meyer was in sharp disagreement. He acknowledged a disagreement between Nikita Khrushchev and Mao Tse-tung; but he did not believe it was a split in the traditional sense. No, Meyer saw it as "an embittered factional struggle," a "struggle for orthodoxy" within communist ranks similar to past factional fights he had personally observed in both the Soviet and American Communist Parties. It was "an internecine dispute between devotees of the same materialist quasi-religion, not a conflict of interest between great powers." Both Mao and Khrushchev remained "united in their fundamental devotion to the conquest of the world by Communism," Meyer held.[4] Above all, Meyer saw the East-West struggle in moral terms—good and bad, right and wrong—about which American liberals cared little. Over and over again, throughout his career at *National Review,* Meyer made clear that his campaign against communism was based upon principle and honor. "Communism in actual and objective fact," Meyer wrote in a typical column, "does represent an absolute black, and the West as a civilization is *in its essence* as close to an absolute white as is possible in the subdued light which illuminates this imperfect world. Sharp and vivid extremes do exist in reality, no matter how much the liberal and relativist mind strives to cloak the real presence of glorious and desperate alternatives."[5]

All in all, Meyer was not hopeful about the Kennedy administration's prospects. In the wake of the Bay of Pigs disaster, Meyer in his column fumed: "The spectacle of the United States, materially the world's strongest power, allowing the enemy of all civilized humanity to establish an armed base 90 miles off our shores," he wrote, was "politically preposterous" and "incredible." And now, to make matters worse, all the U.S. could do was "to send a few hundred unsupported men to die in atrociously unequal battle." To cap it off, the administration sent Adlai Stevenson to Latin America "to apologize for having even to this degree disturbed the equanimity of the bearded Cuban commissar. . . . One has to pinch oneself to accept what is happening as reality."

Meyer traced this failure to the inner workings of American liberalism. Liberals identified themselves with the risings in the Third World of the formerly oppressed and underprivileged, with which Fidel Castro aligned himself. This "immobilized" the Left. Liberalism's "heritage of anti-Western ideology, projected as the democratic mandate of 'the people,' makes it impossible for them to recognize and act against the danger" of dictators such as Castro. And if they did act, they did so only weakly and by indirection—which explained what happened at the Bay of Pigs.[6]

Roughly a year later, the world's two superpowers were in conflict again—the most serious showdown yet. Interpreting the Bay of Pigs incident, and Kennedy's acceptance of the Berlin Wall, as a failure of strength and will, the Soviet Union secretly installed nuclear missiles in Cuba. But American intelligence discovered the missile sites in mid-October 1962; President Kennedy was quickly informed, and he created a committee to formulate a response. For days, meeting in secret, "hawks" and "doves" argued the merits of a surgical air strike against the Cuban missile sites versus a naval blockade of the island. Fearing that a military response would escalate the conflict to the nuclear level, Kennedy, with the committee's agreement, decided on a naval "quarantine" of Cuba, and demanded that Khrushchev withdraw the missiles. On October 22, the president informed Congress and announced the presence of the missiles and the blockade to the American people.[7]

Meyer devoted a column to the Missile Crisis and the principles he saw underlying it (although owing to *NR*'s publication schedule, it predated the crisis's conclusion). And here Meyer repeated one of his favorite themes—the "Liberal Establishment" was wrong; it was mistaken in its policy toward Cuba, and again proved too weak to stand up to communism. On Cuba, "[t]he American people, with instinctive common sense, realize that in the seventeen years of the Cold War this is the turning point," Meyer wrote. The ordinary American was not "swaddled in the layers of ideology that prevent the Establishment from making contact with reality. He knows . . . that if we do not eradicate a focus of infection so near our vitals it will spread until it destroys us." Therefore, "the Castro regime must be removed by force at the earliest possible moment."[8]

But Meyer was proven wrong. The Kennedy naval quarantine succeeded. After nearly a week of indecision, Soviet ships approaching the American blockade halted—and turned back. Soon came the news that the Soviets would agree to dismantle and remove the missiles from Cuba, and that the USSR would like to continue disarmament negotiations. In the subsequent midterm congressional elections, the American electorate, far from showing outrage over the administration's foreign policy, maintained the Democratic majorities in the House and Senate, while the president's poll rating improved. Meyer had failed to plumb the fright Americans felt in the nuclear age. Not for the first time, he had overestimated the conservatism of the average American.

Perhaps he sensed this gap between his and the American people's views on the use of nuclear weapons. For the next few months Meyer seriously reexamined his own stance toward nuclear arms. Actually, the issue had arisen as early as 1961, when Meyer had a rare clash with an "Establishment" figure—University of Chicago political scientist Hans J. Morgenthau. Morgenthau had recently written an article in *Commentary* that questioned whether nuclear weapons could or should ever be used. Morgenthau thought not, citing the incredible death and destruction entailed. Millions would die, and to allow this merely to gain political or military objectives was morally wrong.

In a subsequent column, Meyer pointed to Morgenthau's article, among others, as an example of the feebleness of a liberal foreign policy; renouncing unilateral use of nuclear weapons led to weakness, nuclear blackmail, and eventually "surrender" to communism. An incensed Morgenthau wrote to *National Review* to complain. "[T]he main point I was trying to make," he contended, "was the qualitative difference between death in the pre-atomic age, such as the death of Christ, or Socrates, or Leonidas, and death in the nuclear age, such as the instantaneous incineration, say, of eight million New Yorkers. I have no quarrel with someone who is incapable of understanding this difference. But it is mere malicious distortion to conclude from this philosophic argument that my position amounts to surrender to Communism. I have always maintained . . . that atomic war is an absurdity . . . but that we nevertheless might be compelled to fight such a war."

In his reply—*NR* editors never failed to reply to criticism from well-known figures—Meyer did not retreat. He argued that under Morgenthau's philosophic framework, the West never would be, or feel itself to be, "compelled to fight." "If we are not willing to risk war by our own volition under any circumstances, there will be no circumstances in which we will be compelled to fight," Meyer declared. "If we are never willing to [risk war], [Khrushchev] will move, as he has done, from success to success without ever 'compelling' us to fight. He will ungraciously accept our piecemeal surrender. . . ."[9]

But then came the Cuban Missile Crisis, after which Kennedy allowed the hated Castro regime to remain in place. Meyer believed the American people would never stand for this. But in fact they rewarded Kennedy and his party at the polls. Was there something about the moral issue of the use of nuclear weapons that Meyer had overlooked? What *should* be the conservative view of nuclear arms? This led Meyer to write a lengthy article for *National Review* in the winter of 1963 called "Just War in the Nuclear Age."

He began by stating what, for many conservatives, had become a dilemma. The Right believed that, both for strategic and moral reasons, the West must seek victory over communism. But the necessary steps meant the risk of war, which in modern times meant the possibility of nuclear war. Was it moral, Meyer wondered, to contemplate "the use of such unimaginably devastating weapons?" Could their utilization ever be justified?

In his answer, Meyer attempted to do what he felt a good conservative *must* do—carefully apply traditional, time-tested truths and values to modern problems. Specifically, he evaluated the morality of the use of nuclear weapons in the light of the traditional Western conception of the "just war," to which many Catholics—and Protestants—have subscribed. The concept of the "just war" historically meant that, to be in accord with morality, military conflicts must meet several criteria. Wars must be conducted for a just cause, and those engaged in war must observe the principle of "proportionality"—that is, the force used must be in proportion to the threat posed by the opponent. According to Meyer's analysis, the use of nuclear weapons did not necessarily conflict with these concepts. Certainly the fight against communism was just. And America had "a moral obligation to resist." True, any resort to the use of nuclear arms must be within strict limits. The West must seek to resolve its conflicts with the East by other methods first; to Meyer, this was an excuse to urge yet again that policymakers seek victory by aiding anticommunist groups behind the Iron Curtain. But if all else failed, and nuclear weapons then had to be used, they must be directed only against an opponent's *military* capability, not upon civilian centers.

Of course, Meyer admitted, this brought further complications. Attacks of this nature would almost have to be first strikes; for if the Soviets had *already* launched their nuclear arsenal, striking only missile delivery systems had little value. But the only alternative—the only apparently effective deterrent to Soviet attack—was to purposely target urban civilian centers, which was clearly out of step with the just war doctrine.

Meyer finally, for himself at least, resolved the dilemma by proposing that only an American first-strike capability against Soviet military and nuclear delivery facilities would both be an effective deterrent and meet just war demands. Only "a first-strike counterforce nuclear blow, minimal in its effects upon the civilian population, meets every moral criterion." Meyer knew that some would argue that nuclear arms were so "devastating" that any use at all was immoral. Meyer's reply was unflinching: "To this I can only answer that, even granted the most horrendous estimates of the effects of their use, the preservation of human life as a biological phenomenon is an end far lower than the defense of freedom and right and truth. These the victory of Communism would destroy. These it is our duty to defend at all costs."[10]

TO FRANK MEYER, the imperatives of the Cold War overrode nearly everything else, even the possible use of nuclear weapons. But as 1963 wore on, it became clear that the Kennedy administration did not agree. It took the first steps in pursuit of what would later be called "détente"—an easing of tensions between the United States and the Soviet Union. There were disarmament negotiations, a direct "hot line" between Washington and Moscow was established, and rumors spread of an impending nuclear test-ban treaty. In June 1963, in a speech at American University, President Kennedy indicated that his own thinking was changing, too. "Let us reexamine our attitude towards the Soviet Union," Kennedy said. "It is discouraging to think that their leaders may actually believe what their propagandists write....[I]t is our hope—and the purpose of allied policies—to convince the Soviet Union that she, too, should let each nation choose its own form, so long as that choice does not interfere with the choices of others." Kennedy insisted that Soviet leaders, and the Soviet people, were not intrinsically evil. Both the United States and the Soviet Union had "a mutual deep interest in a just and genuine peace."[11]

Meyer could hardly believe his ears. This truly was "heresy." John Kennedy simply did not understand. Communism, Meyer explained again, demanded a "unified purpose" that brought together "the politico/military and the agitational-revolutionary elements of its being." The Soviet Union would *never* allow nations within its orbit to make their own "choices." Such thinking was hopelessly naïve. Communism required "a vision of a collectivist, controlled, engineered and utopian world." Communists wanted not peace but *victory*. Couldn't President Kennedy understand this? To Meyer, the Kennedy foreign policy was one of "appeasement and retreat."[12]

MEYER HAD WRITTEN all this publicly, mainly in his "Principles and Heresies" column in *National Review*. But he was also increasingly involved in the behind-the-scenes activities of *NR*, occasionally visiting *NR*'s New York offices, faithfully attending the quarterly reappraisals of the magazine's direction held at Buckley's home, keeping in constant telephone contact with fellow *NR* senior editors and staff, and frequently contributing memoranda concerning what stands *NR* should take editorially, the overall direction of the magazine, and the state of the conservative movement in general.

And in private, Meyer was just as direct and uncompromising as in public. He believed that *National Review*'s editorial stances should be firm and strongly anticommunist, and that the magazine's most sharply defined positions gained it the most notice and the most credit with its readers. "I am of the opinion that we could profitably sharpen somewhat our approach," Meyer once told Buckley. "My experience around the country makes me think that [it] is our more forthright and radical attitudes which are our major attraction and our major service."[13] Meyer urged that *NR* take a very strong stand against Kennedy's foreign policy. He wanted *NR* to make the point that "whatever we do, no one will love us, that if we continue to act as we have no one will respect us either, and that the only way we can win back respect after [the Bay of Pigs] fiasco is to act and act decisively." The administration's failure to carry out effectively its policies toward Cuba raised serious questions in Meyer's mind.

> All the evidence seems to point to the complete paralysis of the Administration—above all, of Kennedy himself [he wrote Buckley]. It may be true, as some rumors have it, that Kennedy is thinking of superseding the major echelon of foreign policy advisors, but even if that is the case ... he himself seems to be the prisoner of their ideological attitude. . . . At any rate, whether he is planning to continue along present lines, or is in a state of nervous collapse, or is about to proceed on a better line, the same kind of pressure from outside is required. In any one of these cases, pressure for a hard line will be effective: to combat him if he continues present policies; to galvanize him if he is directionless; to support him if he should be moving in the right direction...
> . I should therefore propose that we continue a drumfire against the policies which have led to the debacle, insisting steadily that events have proved what we have always said: that liberalism is incapable of fighting communism.[14]

Only such a firm stance could shore up the American position in the Cold War, which Meyer feared was at a crisis point. In several Latin American countries he identified "the tendency of those who have been our friends to look about to make their peace with the Castroist and Communist forces." He further believed that "there are strong signs that what has been in the making since ... last November is some sort of a deal on Berlin. I do not need to spell out the results that would follow from that: neutralization of West Germany and the eventual collapse of European resistance." Frank Meyer, like all *National Review* conservatives, took the Cold War in deadly earnest.[15]

As the international crisis over Berlin raced towards its climax in August

1961, Meyer advocated a continued hard line for *NR*. "[A] protest, of course, unbacked by force is meaningless. But the border closing is a direct violation of the Berlin Occupation Agreement. I would suggest that *NR* propose that the United States give Khrushchev an ultimatum to open the border within a limited period of time or we will inaugurate a sea blockade of the Soviet empire."[16]

To Meyer, it seemed that almost everything was going against the anticommunist cause. In France, President Charles de Gaulle, who Meyer had believed in the late 1950s to be the only alternative to a communist takeover of that country, was now making official state visits to Moscow and Peking, even speaking of granting official recognition to communist China. Meyer was distressed. "My own view is becoming somewhat bitterly cynical," he told Buckley. "De G[aulle] and Kennedy are in a race to see who can first make an agreement with Khrushchev. And the corollary is, why would Kh[rushchev] make an agreement with De G[aulle] if he can con Kennedy?"[17]

National Review editorials did not always reflect Meyer's views. The section was under the general direction of Buckley. When Buckley was away, he delegated the authority to James Burnham, and in any case Burnham often did much of the writing. And while both agreed with the general thrust of Meyer's positions, neither believed his proposals were always appropriate. But the magazine wholeheartedly shared Meyer's overall anticommunism. It referred to certain liberals as "fellow-travelers," discussed the "disarmament delusion," labeled Khrushchev a "Bolshevik," and argued that many American liberals had joined "Camp Appeasement." *National Review* also gave the majority of its editorial space in these years to foreign policy, specifically to the Cold War. In that sense the magazine and Frank Meyer were one. Meyer was clearly a member of the *National Review* circle of intellectuals; his thinking and the magazine's were nearly alike.[18]

NR WAS NOT THE ONLY medium through which Meyer spread his views. Throughout 1959 and 1960 he had been working on a book about communism, for which he had contracted with Harcourt, Brace and World Publishers. The volume was to be part of a series on communism and American life edited by the noted historian Clinton Rossiter. Meyer was chosen because of his qualifications as an ex-communist, as well as his growing reputation as a writer for *National Review.* Besides, Rossiter had known Buckley since the mid-1950s, having debated both with and against him, and the two had formed a "tactical friendship." Rossiter took Buckley and *National Review* seriously, and, in fact, joined a list of people petitioning the publisher to include *NR* in *The Reader's Guide to Periodical Literature.*

Meyer worked long and hard on the book, which as always he dictated to his wife, Elsie. The two worked together for hours every night, Frank pacing about his study enveloped in a cloud of cigarette smoke, searching for the right words and phrases, and Elsie furiously taking down his every word, occasionally completing his sentences for him and polishing his grammar and syntax.

Though loathe to do so, Meyer could work amid distractions. Family legend has it that he wrote this first book "while carrying Gene [his younger son] around on his back." Whatever the interruption to his dictation, he could effortlessly pick it up again and remember exactly where he had left off. Occasionally, while doing another task, an idea or phrase would occur to him that would solve a vexing difficulty. "Dictation!" Meyer would command, and Elsie would quickly appear with pad and pencil.[19]

He decided to call his book *The Moulding of Communists: The Training of the Communist Cadre.* Harkening back to his own days as a communist, Meyer said he had both objective and subjective reasons for writing it. On the one hand, the book was "an attempt to depict as objectively as possible the process whereby the Communist man is created." But it also represented "the conclusions of a large sector of a lifetime spent in acceptance, rejection, and examination of Communism. It reflects fourteen years of active leadership, theoretical and practical, in the Communist movement, followed by fifteen years of reorientation and deep consideration of this modern tyranny over the human mind and spirit."[20]

At first glance the book is a carefully researched, detached, thorough analysis of the making of a communist. Drawing upon histories, personal memoirs, and his own experiences, Meyer stressed that a communist "*is* different. He thinks differently. He is not simply—and this is where many painstaking analyses go wrong—a mirror image of ourselves, with our motivations, ordinary or neurotic, hidden under a net of rationalizations couched in barbarous Hegelianisms or Russianisms." Rather, a genuine communist was *created* through a special training process. Meyer told how the communist's entire personality, subjective desires, and personal history had to be subordinated to an absolute obedience to the Party's will and decisions. Party members devoted all their thoughts and actions to bringing about the proletarian revolution. Also important was Marxist theory. Meyer told how this influenced the average rank-and-file Party member, both in what he did and how he thought.[21] As Meyer explained, "It matters little that the economic developments of the hundred years since Marx contradict his theories at every point. . . . Although the victories of Communism arise from the power of the Red Army, from the corroding infiltration of conspiratorial Communist Parties, and from the weak and divided counsels of the West, every such advance strengthens, in the Communist mind, the certainty of the conquering correctness of this theory."[22]

Thus, although Marxism could be refuted logically and empirically, it still wielded power over men's minds. "Communist theory is powerful not because it is true; most obviously it is not," he explained. "It is powerful because *it is believed*. Each aspect may be intellectually weak enough on its own, but in the total theoretical structure each strengthens the other and a unified view is created. Theories which, standing on their own, would be ludicrous take on the seeming luminosity of truth." Communism was strong because its members preserved a certain quality—Meyer called it "the unity of thought and action"—which Western minds thought belonged only to God. This was a trait, Meyer thought, that was "manifestly absurd in men"; yet through it communists "acquire a strength and confidence which, like the fearful evil they bring into being, can only be described as Luciferian."[23]

Communism's tactics, Meyer continued, displayed a fundamental immorality. For example, fellow CP members constantly criticize one another, trying to expunge each other's "subjective" feelings. "Here for the first time," Meyer noted, "he is likely to experience that curious impersonal approach, amounting almost to brutality, with which the Communist examines an individual very much as a carpenter examines a piece of lumber." The highest loyalty of all Party members was not to their fellow communists, or even to the local or national organization, but to the worldwide CP. The "known realities" of the Soviet Union failed to penetrate the communist mind. "Oppression, slave-labor camps, purge after purge, murder in the millions, brutal and unprovoked aggression, even Khrushchev's exposure of Stalin and the Hungarian Revolution of 1956—[all] slides off the cadre Communist's conscience like water off a duck's back," Meyer wrote. "They make no live impact upon him.

Intellectually he explains them as necessary casualties of the historic process, unfortunate but unavoidable."[24]

Throughout the book Meyer called communism evil and satanic, its tactics brutal. He maintained that its aim was victory and labeled it a threat to world peace. "And by victory," Meyer declared, he meant "domination of the world." This was why communist leaders on the one hand appealed for peace and disarmament, and on the other engaged in an arms buildup and sabre-rattling; this was why they appealed to the working class, yet were capable of smashing popular revolutions in order to hold onto power. "What [the communist] is in his reality no policy, no maneuver, no strategy can disclose," Meyer wrote. "He can only be understood if we understand the end to which he is devoted as the compass is drawn to the magnetic pole: the conquest of the world for Communism—with any weapons, so long as they are effective, by any means if they achieve his end, and at any cost. . . . Only a greater determination can avail. Communist man poses two stark alternatives for us: victory or defeat."[25]

And so Meyer completed what he undoubtedly saw as his most important duty: to educate the West about communism, and to warn it of the incredible danger it posed. The book was widely reviewed and much praised by conservative publications. *Human Events* said that Meyer offered "bold and brilliant insights," and that the book was "an invaluable aid to enlightened democratic citizenship." The conservative political scientist Gerhart Niemeyer in *National Review* wrote that Meyer's analysis "should be ranked among the few that have really illuminated the phenomenon of Communism from within." To several books that had powerfully influenced him in his thinking on communism—works by such authors as Arthur Koestler and Bertram Wolfe—"I should now like to add Frank Meyer's *The Moulding of Communists*," he concluded.[26]

But Meyer's work garnered applause in wider circles, too. The *New York Herald-Tribune* called it "an extraordinarily perceptive book . . . , a systematic and serious analytic study." The *San Francisco Examiner* noted that, with such books as Meyer's available, "it is more than foolish to plead ignorance of the aims, the direction of the Communists." The *Washington Star* wrote that Meyer had made "a notable contribution." The *Indianapolis News* praised him for describing "in detail, and with considerable verbal power, the graduated pressures of Communist indoctrination . . . , a difficult task brilliantly achieved." And the *Wall Street Journal* added that the book "acquaints us with the methods of as sinister a lot of psychological drill sergeants as the world has ever known. We will ignore the lessons of *The Moulding of Communists* at our peril."[27]

The book did draw fire from some liberal and academic quarters. The *American Political Science Review* said it was "marred by the tendency to view Communism as a single, solid system. . . . The idea of a Communist monolith does not help us understand Titoism, the Polish unrest, the strain in Sino-Soviet relations . . . and the identity of Communists with legitimate forces of national-ism in the developing areas." Similarly, the *New York Times Book Review* opined that "the author endows the Communist with a measure of devilish consistency and cleverness which seem, paradoxically, closer to the Soviet-bred image of infallibility than to reality."[28]

Yet overall *The Moulding of Communists*, for Frank Meyer, was a success. It gained him notice and notoriety beyond the circles of *National Review* readers, and the book went through several printings. Meyer was no longer merely a columnist, book reviewer, and editor. He was now a conservative *author,* and an activist for the anticommunist cause.

MEANWHILE, POLITICAL developments were afoot in Meyer's adopted home state of New York, developments that would eventually have an important impact on his life. By 1962, New York had entered the fourth year of the stewardship of its dynamic governor, Nelson Rockefeller. Rockefeller cut an immense swath through both state and national politics. A grandson of the famous millionaire John D. Rockefeller, he had enjoyed a privileged up-bringing, preparing himself for a life among the elite. He eventually went into public service, serving in both the Roosevelt administration during the days of the New Deal (though he was a declared Republican), and in Dwight Eisenhower's State Department as a specialist on Latin American affairs. Even-tually he developed a hunger to be elected to office himself; and so he re-turned to New York in 1958 and ran for the governorship against a sitting incumbent, W. Averell Harriman. And, to the surprise of many, he won.

After the initial satisfaction of seeing the state GOP once again capture the statehouse, New York's conservatives were horrified at many of Rockefeller's policies. In his first term he raised taxes no fewer than five times and spent hundreds of millions of dollars for all kinds of government programs, from pub-lic housing to funding for the arts. To make matters even worse, Rockefeller played a crucial role in the Republican 1960 presidential campaign. For after withdrawing from the race early in the year, he promptly submitted a much-trumpeted nine-point program designed to "rejuvenate" American society, a program full of liberal activist ideas. In so doing, Rockefeller succeeded in pushing the eventual GOP candidate, Richard Nixon, further to the Left. After Nixon met Rockefeller at the governor's Fifth Avenue apartment in New York City, the two announced the so-called "Treaty of Fifth Avenue," in which Nixon agreed to support many of Rockefeller's liberal domestic proposals. Conservatives were incensed. Barry Goldwater called it a "domestic Munich," and many on the Right blamed Nixon's narrow defeat in the fall election on his failure to offer a conservative alternative to John F. Kennedy.

What frustrated conservatives even more was Rockefeller's studied indifference to their outrage. He believed that he had captured the "electoral middle" in New York and assumed he could do so on a nationwide scale. Once in a while Rockefeller would pay lip service to conservatives, but few believed in his sincerity. And since New York had no party primaries, there seemed no way for New York conservatives to challenge his domination of state politics.[29]

Finally, two men, both lawyers and political activists from New York City, decided to do something about it. J. Daniel Mahoney and Kieran O'Doherty were politically active and committed conservatives who knew William F. Buckley Jr. and others at *National Review*. They were furious at Rockefeller. A Republican Party, Mahoney said, fashioned in the governor's image "would simply ape, and in many cases surpass, the most liberal programs of the most liberal Democrats." In addition, early reports suggested that Rockefeller was the front-runner for the 1964 Republican presidential nomination. It seemed Rockefeller Republicanism would dominate New York for years to come.

Hence in 1961 Mahoney and O'Doherty began the process of forming a third party, to be called the Conservative Party. This was not unprecedented in New York state politics. Since it lacked a primary system in its state and local elections, there was great potential for the formation of smaller, independent parties. Indeed, the Liberal Party, based in New York City, had existed for years and had successfully pushed the state's Democratic Party to the Left. New York's Conservative Party would have a similar mission. It did not expect to win elections, but would try to push the state Republican Party rightward.[30]

The first thing to do was to set up an official "organizing committee," for which the two men needed some prominent names known to conservatives and other likely supporters of the party. But whom to ask?

One of the earliest calls made by Mahoney was to Frank Meyer. The two had known each other for several years. Mahoney had admired Meyer's book reviews in the *American Mercury* in the early 1950s, and had then faithfully read his "Principles and Heresies" columns when Meyer joined *NR*. The two met in person for the first time in 1958, and Mahoney was impressed with Meyer's zeal for conservatism and his commitment to seeing conservative ideas become political reality. When Mahoney called him about joining the Conservative Party, Meyer quickly agreed.[31]

The truth was, Meyer was anxious to be more active in politics. While he enjoyed being a writer and thinker, he believed passionately that the conservative movement was meaningless if it did not attempt to advance its beliefs in the political arena, much as he had done when he had joined the Communist Party. His personality, his nature, had not changed; but his political principles had.

And so Meyer busily immersed himself in Conservative Party work. One of his first tasks was to compose a "statement of principles" for the party. Its final form strongly reflected his thinking. The preamble stressed that America "is strong, and everywhere it is in retreat before Soviet Communism. It was founded and grew great on the free energy of free men, and everywhere encroaching bureaucracy overpowers and strangles the free energy of free men"—thus echoing Meyer's two main themes. He devoted a great deal of space (especially for a *state* party) on the dangers of communism, denouncing the "armed might and conspiratorial techniques" of the Soviet Union, which were "step by step enveloping us, preparatory to a final assault or . . . a dictated surrender." Liberalism was incapable of meeting this challenge. At home, Meyer wrote, the Leviathan state reigned supreme—"a crushing burden of taxation for purposes unconnected with defense, never-ceasing inflation, the untrammeled growth of the power of government bureaucrats and union bosses and a constantly decaying educational practice, combine to transform America gradually but unmistakably into a socialist society in which the individual person will count for nothing."

To restore America, the statement called for a strictly limited government, the lowering of taxes, and an increase in defense spending to meet the

Soviet threat. All in all, it was a well-written, concise statement of conservative values and ideas.[32]

In the coming months and years Meyer deepened his commitment to the Conservative Party. He was constantly in telephone communication with party leaders, discussing possible Conservative candidates and thrashing out positions for party platforms. Once in a while he attended meetings of the party's executive committee, often held in New York City; and on election nights, both Frank and Elsie would be there with Mahoney, O'Doherty, and their families, watching the returns.[33]

For some time it was unclear whether the Conservative Party would make it to its first election night. Money was scarce; Mahoney and O'Doherty had little office space and almost no funds with which to pay their tiny staff. And there was doubt whether, in the election that fall, the party could secure the 50,000 votes it needed to win a permanent spot on the ballot. Then, that summer, the state Republican Party organization finally took notice, issuing a formal condemnation of this "splinter group" and urging voters to beware of "political pied pipers." The Conservatives needed not only to respond, but to have a logical, hard-hitting answer that would reassure the party faithful. Meyer was perfect for the job. Soon, in the name of the party's executive committee, he circulated a fierce response to the state GOP's attacks, which was distributed to all New York Republican members of the House of Representatives, as well as to all GOP state functionaries. In his letter, Meyer called Rockefeller and Senator Jacob Javits, another liberal Republican, "little more than carbon copies of the Wagners, Lehmans, and Eleanor Roosevelts who control the New York Democratic Party." The state GOP's call for unity, he wrote, was nothing more than "bluster" and "hypocrisy." "Again and again, they have imposed on the voters of New York a meaningless choice between Tweedledum and Tweedledee." Meyer declared, and yet "we are not out to ruin the Republican Party; we only want to make it possible for the Republican Party to shake loose the tyranny of liberal interlopers." Meyer's circular stirred much comment within the circles of New York political insiders, and although he likely changed the minds of few Republican officials, he accomplished his primary goal: almost all who had committed to the Conservative Party stayed on board.[34]

In October 1962, Meyer attended the party's first big public rally, an evening gathering to be held in New York City's cavernous Madison Square Garden. Unfortunately, it was the same night that President Kennedy made his television speech announcing the presence of Soviet nuclear missiles in Cuba. Only fifteen minutes before the event's scheduled beginning, fewer than one thousand people rattled about in the huge arena. But when, a few minutes later, Mahoney emerged to formally open the night's proceedings, he was greeted by a tremendous roar of approval; in only a few minutes, more than 14,000 people had filled the Garden—nearly everyone had waited for the end of Kennedy's speech. Meyer was one of the featured speakers that night, and he received an enthusiastic reception as he spoofed New York Republicans who had urged conservatives to return to the fold. Meyer was a good speaker. He possessed a loud, projecting voice, and he delivered his talks earnestly and passionately. An attendee of the rally later wrote to *National Review* to praise Meyer's "brilliant" speech that "stirred the audience to that high level of enthusiasm which, as you report, so conspicuously marked the meeting."[35]

The New York Conservative Party not only survived its first year of existence. On election night 1962 it captured over 140,000 votes to win a spot on the state ballot in 1964. In early 1963, Meyer was made the head of the Conservative Party's International Affairs Committee. As a result, he was often in the news. Meyer issued press releases in the name of the party and his committee on important international developments. His statements were often quoted in local New York papers, and occasionally he was interviewed by local television stations.[36]

Meyer offered the party his tactical acumen, too. His experience in the Communist Party had taught him much. For example, in 1963 he wrote a letter on behalf of Conservative Party State Headquarters urging local Conservative leaders to be very cautious in running candidates in local elections that year. "The 1964 elections will be so decisive for the future of the country," Meyer wrote, "and the role of the Conservative Party as a potential veto against any liberal in the Republican national convention is so decisive in this respect, that any participation which would conceivably throw any doubt on our vote-getting potential should be avoided." Meyer held that the party was, in military terms, a "force in being," whose threat to the liberal establishment would increase only when it could show itself to be a "force in action."

Most Conservatives agreed; the party ran few candidates in 1963 but was still a force on the state level in 1964. As a communist, Meyer had learned that an effective political movement must always focus upon broad objectives and not become mired in minor campaigns that could hurt the party's image and clout. He was now teaching those lessons to his new pupils on the other side of the political divide. But there was still the question of what stance *National Review* would take toward the Conservative Party, and here the going was much more difficult.[37]

It was not that Meyer lacked allies among *NR*'s editors. William F. Rickenbacker himself joined the Conservative Party's organizing committee and would remain active in the organization throughout the 1960s, and the magazine's publisher, William Rusher, was very sympathetic. Their goals for the Conservatives vis-à-vis *National Review* were simple: they wanted the magazine to support it as much as possible, to give it editorial endorsement, and to lend it whatever help it could. But the Meyer-Rickenbacker-Rusher faction faced opposition within the editorial board.

James Burnham was dubious about the Conservative Party's prospects. At *NR*'s biweekly editorial conferences and at quarterly meetings, Burnham argued his pragmatic, Machiavellian position: "the nature of politics is to deal with political realities." And the fact remained that New York's Liberal Party existed because it could draw from the "natural forces in the community" that supported it—"the political reality of the close-knit labor groups and some ethnic groups in New York City." But since no such groups supported the Conservative Party, it was "doomed to fail. For it has no relevant function." Given these facts, Burnham thought that *National Review*'s position toward the party "should be—well, friendly, of course," as Rickenbacker summarized Burnham's views, "but—well—aloof." Besides, Burnham believed *NR* was an opinion magazine, not a political vehicle.[38]

Buckley, too, was hesitant. He sometimes complained that *NR*'s readers "expected too much of us." The magazine was still a small entity that struggled yearly to survive, always in the red. Yet its readership "apparently wanted us to act not only as a magazine but as a party, a church, a cheerleader, as well as a *Time*, *Life*, and *Fortune*." Besides, most of *NR*'s senior editors—aside from Rusher and Meyer—had little experience in practical politics.[39]

Even so, a spirited debate developed within the *NR* editorial circle.

Rickenbacker struck back forcefully against Burnham's position, arguing presciently that threads of conservative sentiment *did* exist in New York—among "the upstate farmers, the conservative Republicans, the increasingly disaffected Irish Catholics in New York City." Current political realities could be changed. And did not *National Review* exist to try to change them?[40]

Naturally Meyer participated in this debate as well, both behind the scenes and—most noticeably—in a "Principles and Heresies" column published in *NR* in July 1962. In it, Meyer tried to meet Burnham's arguments and to anticipate the possible objections of other conservatives; for example, that the formation of the Conservative Party was a repudiation of America's traditional two-party system—and thus *un*-conservative. Meyer replied that the Right should indeed respect the American dual party framework. But political parties need not last forever. If they cease to present a viable alternative to the opposing party, they can and should die (as had the Whig Party in the early 1850s). "There is nothing sacred about the Republican Party. . . . [It] deserves conservative loyalty only to the degree that it is conservative." Which was hardly at all.[41]

Eventually, as far as *National Review* was concerned, a firm decision had to be made. Buckley, as always, allowed everyone to have his say. But in the end he sided with Burnham, as he did increasingly during these days. He was impressed with Burnham's entire political worldview, and in this he was reinforced by Buckley's sister Priscilla, a close Burnham friend and ally. Buckley worried about *NR*'s reputation, about what would happen to the magazine if it tied itself too closely to a candidate or party that went in the wrong direction. Indeed, this was already happening; *National Review* had never endorsed the John Birch Society, or any of its leader's many bizarre statements, and yet many people identified *NR* and the JBS as one and the same. Buckley was soon going to have to take care of that problem once and for all. Meanwhile, in respect to the Conservative Party, *NR* finally decided on "no formal support of it, nor hortatory editorials about it; a continuation of our present realistic enthusiasm. . . . [We should] seek to scale down over-ambitious estimates of its growth."[42]

Meyer and his allies were naturally disappointed. But in practice *NR*'s lack of official support for the Conservative Party was a distinction without a difference. Many people associated with the magazine helped the party's cause, and Buckley gladly allowed them to do so. Indeed, Buckley himself was an important ally. When Mahoney and O'Doherty were still in the early stages of forming the party, it was Buckley who, at their request, wrote a letter to several prominent New York state conservatives, urging them to join the party's organizing committee. And, presumably with Buckley's approval, both James McFadden and James O'Bryan—*NR*'s assistant publisher and art director, respectively—helped Mahoney put together the Conservatives' first mass-mailing in 1962; they did so using *National Review*'s mailing list for New York State, a first for the magazine. The members of the *NR* circle were inevitably drawn into active political roles, whether or not the magazine formally endorsed them, as would be the case in coming years as well.[43]

The Conservative Party became an enormously important part of Meyer's life. It gave him yet another outlet for his energies, and his participation was crucial in the party's early days. He helped give it legitimacy among other conservatives and also provided vital tactical advice in foreign policy. Perhaps his most important contribution was to weld together principles and politics, to show that they could be applied—"prudentially" as he often said—in the real world. He was no longer only an intellectual and columnist; he was a political activist, making a difference. The Conservative Party still exists today, and Mahoney always valued Meyer's contribution. "He was in on the ground floor," Mahoney recalled.[44]

THERE ARE MANY WAYS to be an activist for a cause, and in the early 1960s Meyer seemed to try them all. There was so much to *do.* There was a liberal Democrat in the White House, and liberalism dominated the media, the academy, journalism, show business, everything. Hence many people had to be educated, to be convinced, to be enlightened that a conservative position did exist. Meyer tried to do his part.

He regularly traveled on the lecture circuit, speaking at the National War College, the Cleveland Town Hall, the Brooklyn Institute of Arts and Sciences, New Orleans Discussions Unlimited, the Salt Lake City Anti-Communist Forum, the Los Angeles Symposium on Freedom, and the Indiana Conservative Club, to name but a few disparate places. He also appeared on many college campuses, usually invited by a local Conservative Club or a campus chapter of the Young Americans for Freedom. Meyer spoke at Yale, the University of Wisconsin, the University of California, Stanford, and the University of Chicago, among others. He had a number of set topics, including "The Challenge of

Conservatism," "The Reality of Communism," "The Illusion of Coexistence," "The Decay of American Liberalism," and "Freedom, the Forgotten Goal."[45]

It was not always easy to be a conservative on the lecture circuit in the early 1960s, especially on college campuses. Occasionally, unsympathetic university administrators denied conservative groups the best, most convenient campus facilities, or insisted that conservative speakers not simply speak, but debate a liberal faculty member for "balance." And there was always the possibility of loud, rude hecklers to interrupt or stop the speech. Yet as William Rusher—another frequent conservative lecturer—recalls, "we conservative speakers had all the zeal of the early Christian missionaries, and like them we could be sure of a hard core of local supporters, however small."[46]

Meyer enjoyed himself on these tours. He liked meeting and talking with young conservatives, finding out what they thought about current events and controversies. He drew good crowds, and was always surrounded by well-wishers afterwards, anxious to discuss and debate just a bit more. "It was very good meeting you if only for a split second," Meyer told one friend who'd attended one of his talks. "There was such a crush around that I did not know what was going to happen."[47]

Afterwards, he would join conservative friends and acquaintances for food, drink, and long hours of conversation. He especially liked the younger people and would spend the entire night with them, he chain-smoking, with a face now animated as he expounded on this or that point, now darkening as he sensed a younger person's willingness to countenance big government or a less than firm position toward the evils of communism, and occasionally swigging from an old, dented, pewter-colored hip flask full of Scotch that he drew from his back pocket. Sometimes Elsie accompanied him on such trips and would urge him to bed around 3 A.M. so that the students could get some sleep.[48]

Meyer never knew for certain what to expect. This was a time of rapid growth for the nascent conservative movement, but its development was uneven. Some of the groups Meyer spoke to were naïve and unsophisticated. "In Tampa I am speaking at what sounds like a damfool meeting on education," Meyer once told Buckley. "I am supposed to describe John Dewey's philosophy in 20 minutes, to be followed by the leader of the Republican Party in the Florida legislature, who will explain how Deweyism operates in the Florida schools; the man putting it on has a couple of other people to talk about

Clearwater's schools—and wants no questions or discussion. Heaven alone knows what it will be like."[49]

Most often, Meyer could be found on a university campus, trying to spread the conservative gospel within the liberal citadel of higher education. It was not that conservative academics did not exist. Some even contributed to *National Review*, such as the political scientist Gerhart Niemeyer, the poet Hugh Kenner, and the philosopher Richard Weaver. But they were scattered and unconnected, with no network, no way to pool their ideas and forge a more unified movement. How to connect them to each other? Meyer soon came up with an idea.

Meyer wanted to create a kind of newsletter for conservatives in higher education. There, scholars on the Right could advance tentative hypotheses, examine trends in different disciplines, get news of job openings, and generally share ideas. It took Meyer some time to get started. There were articles to be solicited, funding to be sought, and the mechanics of printing and distribution to be worked out. In early 1962, Meyer told Buckley that he was making slow progress with what he simply called the "academic news letter." "The first issue is taking more time than I expected," Meyer wrote, "because I have gotten literally nothing from anyone I have written or spoken to and therefore have had to develop the material myself. I thought it would be much more useful to have something concrete in the first number than simply to say what we are expecting to do, and my idea has gradually paid off. I have now three or four concrete employment offers, with one or two others in the wings, and I shall very shortly be prepared to work up the first number."[50]

By the time the first issue appeared in the fall of 1962 Meyer had decided to call his newsletter the *Exchange*. "Many of us have thought for some time that informal communication among dispersed scholars and writers would be useful and stimulating," Meyer said in his opening essay, titled "By Way of Explanation." This newsletter would "constitute a sort of committee of correspondence for a limited and congenial group who now are too seldom in touch with one another, either on concrete problems of their professions or on tentatives for intellectual exploration." The first issue contained a short piece by Milton Friedman giving a conservative view of the European Common Market, a discussion by an economist from the University of Virginia on whether the concept of "practicality" applied to conservatives, a separate section listing "positions available," and a last page listing "positions desired." Meyer sent this first issue to a

select list of conservative academics around the country, urging them to comment and send submissions and monetary contributions if they could. He
then waited anxiously.[51]

Soon the mail began pouring in, and Meyer was delighted. He had sent
out 175 copies; within two weeks, he received over forty letters or telephone
calls, almost all of them favorable. Reputable conservatives, such as Karl
Wittfogel, Francis Graham Wilson, Henry Hazlitt, Eugene Davidson (the editor of *Modern Age*), Stephen Tonsor, and William Baroody (of the American
Enterprise Institute) gave their praise and thanks freely. Naturally Meyer sent
a copy of the newsletter to Buckley, who gave Meyer what help he could. "I
think *The Exchange* is looking better and that it is going to be wonderfully
useful," Buckley wrote him. "Some day, when you have a chance, I'd like to
go over it with you, sitting down with a copy of it before us." The *Exchange* was
there to stay.[52]

In the coming years, the newsletter was a center of lively conservative
discussion. Nearly every issue contained a "Review of the Journals," which
discussed recent trends in disciplines such as literature, economics, or history
written by a conservative scholar in that particular field, and a "Notes and
Queries" section with reactions to articles or questions about the teaching
profession. Prominent scholars on the Right also occasionally contributed,
including Hugh Kenner, the historian Stephen Tonsor, and Garry Wills. And
sometimes contributors examined new conservative books, such as James
Burnham's 1964 *Suicide of the West*. New trends were identified and analyzed—
the existence of a new and unique generation of young people who were
changing society was noted as early as 1964.[53]

The *Exchange* contained no frills. It was a typewritten collection of single-
spaced articles printed on only one side of the page and copied on thick but
cheap paper. It had no fancy graphics, pictures, or cartoons. Funding was tight,
time was limited, and Meyer patiently explained these facts of life to any who
asked. Why not, asked one friend, print material on *both* sides of the paper? "I
have had so many arguments both ways on printing on both sides of the
paper, that I do not want you to think that I had not considered the matter,"
Meyer wrote back. "For the time I have concluded that it looks sufficiently
better on one side only, that this overbalances space and cost." And cost was
always a worry. But occasionally he had success. "Good news," he told Buckley

in 1963. "The Lilly Endowment has given me a two-year grant . . . at $5,000 a year, for *The Exchange*. So we are in business for 2 and 1/2 years."[54]

And so the newsletter lived on. It would appear three or four times a year until (and beyond) Meyer's death, yet another expression of his determination to be an activist, to weld ideas and action—not simply to talk about the need for things, but to *do* them. In fact, Meyer's influence could be seen nearly everywhere in the growth of conservatism in the early 1960s. When the conservative youth organization called Young Americans for Freedom was born in 1960 at the Buckley home in Sharon, Connecticut, Meyer was there. Emerging from this conference was the "Sharon Statement," a conservative call to action for all young people on the Right which closely mirrored Meyer's position. Among other things, the statement emphasized the existence of "transcendent values"; stressed that the purposes of government were "the preservation of internal order, the provision of national defense, and the administration of justice"; said that "the Constitution of the United States is the best arrangement yet devised for empowering government to fulfill its proper role"; and warned that "the forces of international Communism are, at present, the greatest single threat to these liberties . . . [and] the United States should stress victory over, rather than coexistence with, this menace." All these points Meyer repeatedly stressed over the years.[55]

And Meyer continued to cultivate his contacts in the political arena, too. He knew, and had contacts with the staffs of, prominent Republicans like Senators Barry Goldwater and John Tower, as well as leading conservatives in the House of Representatives, such as Donald Bruce of Indiana. Meyer was especially impressed with Bruce, telling Buckley that he was "a really first-rate person, sharing that balance of conservatism and libertarianism on which we agree, in a literate and intelligent manner." Contact with such political figures testified to *National Review*'s growing importance to the Republican Right. The goal of *NR*'s founders had been to make a difference, to be on the desks of politicians, academics, and opinion leaders all over the country. Bruce now told Meyer that "every Monday morning he reads *NR* from 'kiver to kiver' before he goes about any other business—and his knowledge of what has appeared in our pages confirms it."[56]

Maybe *NR*—and Meyer, too—*were* making an impact. Maybe Meyer's activism, so evident in these years, was paying off. But there was still much more to do. Meyer believed that focusing on political victories without attending to the ideas that lay behind them was not enough. He still had much more to say about these ideas, and as the 1960s wore on, he set to work to put it in writing. Meyer the activist was a formidable figure. He now set out as a philosopher.

In Defense of Freedom

S INCE THE INCEPTION OF THE POSTWAR American conservative movement, several books had attempted to define both the movement and the philosophy behind it. Russell Kirk's 1953 *Conservative Mind* put forward several "canons" of conservatism and discussed whether a conservative heritage in America existed. This was followed in 1954 by Kirk's *Program for Conservatives.* Richard Weaver's *Ideas Have Consequences,* published in 1948, was a fervent condemnation of America's liberal culture, along with relativism and perfectionism, and had inspired many (including Frank Meyer). Friedrich von Hayek's writings stirred many on the Right into opposing the Leviathan state. James Burnham and others urged conservatives to fight against the encroachments of international communism, and thus made anticommunism central to the beliefs of the postwar American Right.

Meyer of course knew of all of these writers, and had borrowed ideas and concepts from most of them. But it was not enough. For one thing, he had reservations about the approach of each of these thinkers. Burnham was too much the pragmatist and historicist; Hayek was too exclusively libertarian, ignoring the need for transcendence and order; Kirk so emphasized community that Meyer had attacked his philosophy as statist and accommodationist; and

Weaver, whom Meyer probably admired the most, was relatively apolitical—and perhaps a bit too close to Kirk.

No, Meyer did not believe that anyone had as yet explicated a positive, conservative political philosophy. No one had integrated what Meyer consistently emphasized were the two main strands of conservatism: the belief in order, transcendence, truth, and the divine, and the idea that freedom was the highest *political* end, it being the only way for the individual legitimately to choose the truth. In fact, many doubted that a synthesis of these two approaches could be achieved. But Meyer had been thinking about the necessity of such a synthesis since the mid-1950s, and in his writings he had slowly constructed a conservative philosophy of his own that he now itched to put into a single volume.

MEYER WAS NOT THE ONLY one concerned about the state of the Right. A number of intellectuals within the *National Review* circle wondered whether conservatives knew what they stood for, whether the American Right truly had a program, a plan, an agenda on which to base itself. Conservatives had succeeded in uniting *against* certain things—such as communism. But what were they *for*? And why?

Whittaker Chambers was one of these troubled souls. By 1961 he was not well; he was tired, and his heart sent him to bed for weeks at a time (he would die of a heart attack later that year). But he continued, in his correspondence with William F. Buckley Jr., to explain that conservatives had to do more than simply oppose; they must think about fundamental underpinnings. As early as 1954, Chambers told Buckley that the Right "can muster great forces. Potentially, it has all the brains, money and other resources it needs. But it can never mobilize them because it lacks one indispensable: it has no program. A distaste for Communism and socialism is not a program." He knew that Meyer was trying to come up with an overall philosophy, but he worried that Meyer was too doctrinaire, too unaware that the events of the twentieth century had changed reality.[1]

James Burnham also feared for the future of American conservatism. He argued that the early 1960s was a crucial period for the Right, but that its organizations and political tendencies lacked an agenda and a coherent guiding philosophy. In which direction was conservatism moving? Which way should it go? For example, Young Americans for Freedom by 1962 had over 25,000 members. Yet it was riven by personal conflicts, factional fights, and battles between liberal and conservative Republicans. As Burnham told Buckley, "fundamental is the question of policy. At this stage, YAF's body has much outstripped its mind. And in truth, YAF does not now have a *program,* or strategy.... Where is YAF going? Nobody knows. It is an established law that a youth tendency must always be politically subordinate to an adult tendency. But where is the adult tendency, and organization embodying it? or which one? YAF is 25,000 young persons in search of a father. Are Barry [Goldwater] and Barryism enough of a man for the job? The Rusher-Meyer-Rickenbacker Conservative Party?"[2]

Meyer reveled in this kind of questioning and introspection. It inspired him to think more deeply, to inquire into the very fundamentals of conservatism. In the early 1960s, Meyer's inquiry became even more intense. In his columns in *National Review,* Meyer occasionally debated (in effect) with Burnham. He believed that Burnham was so consumed with concrete political "programs" that the very idea of exploring the world of *ideas* had to be defended. Meyer wrote in 1961 that it was "ideas and beliefs that decide how men will act. I do not underestimate the hard, steel strength of power. Whether for good or evil, it is power which has the next to last word in the affairs of men—but not the last word. Power is wielded by men, controlled by men, limited by men, as they are guided and inspired by the ideas and beliefs they hold."[3]

Meanwhile, behind the scenes at *National Review* Burnham frequently suggested that the magazine, and conservatives in general, reach out more to liberals and moderates, especially on Cold War issues. Conservatives needed to be more "humane," to avoid "sectarianism" and "clannishness." Again, Meyer thought this kind of thinking was dangerous, and used another of his columns to say so. On specific issues, he wrote, a temporary alliance with liberals would be possible. But liberalism's basic principles rendered it ineffective in fighting communism. Liberals were too relativist, too much beholden to "social engineering," too prone to the belief that communists were simply "black-sheep brothers under the skin." This was why many on the Left favored what Meyer saw as "appeasement." Thus, in another subtle swipe at Burnham's thinking, Meyer said that conservative ideas needed not "watering down, but . . . intensification."[4]

In Meyer's philosophy, ideas had consequences, and Meyer refined his ideas in internal discussions at *National Review. NR* grew rapidly in the early 1960s, becoming for many the focus of the intellectual Right; hence many conservatives, if they had dreams, fears, or misgivings about what was happening within the movement, wrote first to *National Review*—which writings helped shape Meyer's thought regarding the problems of conservatism.

In 1961 Gerhart Niemeyer wrote to *NR,* criticizing the general development of conservatism and the magazine's role in it. The Right was growing too quickly, Niemeyer contended; its ideas were ill-defined. As for *NR,* it placed too much emphasis on politics and not enough on the definition of a coherent conservative philosophy. Buckley sent a copy of Niemeyer's letter to Meyer for comment, and he returned a long memorandum with his overall view of the present condition of conservatism.

Niemeyer was overreacting, Meyer said. Yes, the conservative movement was experiencing "growing pains." But such growth was inevitable, and its leaders must simply "ride the wild mustang and guide it, rather than to attempt to impose upon it the tight check-rein of the carriage horse that characterizes European ideological parties." And of course, the Right must seek electoral success. Electoral victories "*are the bone and marrow of a developing political movement in the United States when those electoral victories reflect, however simply, a truly conservative direction.* They are a visible symbol of things invisibly occurring in the body politic."

This did not mean that conservatives, by focusing on short-range objectives, risked the loss of their long-range, deeper principles. Meyer believed the movement needed a combination of both (as his own life demonstrated). "To forget long-range principle is to be opportunistic," Meyer wrote, "but to renounce the short-range is to be abstract, utopian, aridly ideological."[5]

Divisions within conservatism came from other directions, too. Anticommunist conservatives whom he met on his lecture tours were too often willing to "overlook any degeneration of the conditions and institutions of freedom ... if only they believe it conduces to greater efficiency against the Communist enemy," Meyer wrote. It was wrong to simply ally with "any professed anticommunist, no matter how socialist his views."[6]

On the other hand, many libertarians bothered him as well. Many refused "to recognize the imminently threatening quality of the offensive of armed Communism." Some libertarians were beginning to criticize Cold War foreign policy as merely another form of statism. In answer, Meyer stressed yet again the primacy of the individual person, and that true virtue could not be pursued through state coercion. At the *political* level, freedom must be a primary end. But the conservative was not an anarchist. The state had legitimate functions to perform, one of which was to protect the country from "foreign enemies"—limited, of course, by a "constitutional understanding" that included a division of power and a resistance to intrusion upon the "sacred sphere" of the human person. Libertarians must understand, wrote Meyer, that a true conservative could not "posit freedom as an absolute end nor can he, considering the condition of man, deny the role of the state as an institution necessary to protect the freedoms of individual persons from molestation, whether through domestic or foreign force. He is not, in a word, a utopian."[7]

But just as Meyer threw water on one brush fire, up sprang another. It came in the form of a challenge to Meyer's brand of conservatism by L. Brent Bozell, his fellow senior editor and very close friend. Bozell was quite different from Meyer. Born and raised in Nebraska by Episcopalian parents, he was nevertheless enrolled in a Jesuit high school, which had a slow but inexorable effect on him. He served in the U.S. Merchant Marine and the Navy during World War II, and while on leave in San Francisco he unexpectedly met his father, who had traveled there to announce to his son his intention to convert to Catholicism. Amazingly, Bozell had independently come to the same belief shortly before—he, too, would convert. Bozell became a Catholic as soon as possible, joining the Church in 1946.

Bozell became an increasingly deeply religious man, unlike the ex-communist and generally secular Meyer. After the war he attended Yale University; there he met William F. Buckley Jr., and the two quickly became the best of friends, a friendship cemented when Bozell married Buckley's sister Patricia in 1949. The following year he attended Yale Law School, and after graduation he briefly practiced law in San Francisco. But he developed a keen interest in conservative politics and ideas, and when Senator Joseph McCarthy called him from Washington and asked Bozell to join him, Bozell packed up his growing family and traveled east, remaining in Washington as a speechwriter and political operative (working frequently on a free-lance basis, including ghostwriting Goldwater's *Conscience of a Conservative*). When Buckley founded *National Review*, Bozell was a senior editor, writing a column on the doings in the nation's capital and serving as *NR*'s authority on the Supreme Court.

Yet the intensity of Bozell's religious commitment never wavered, but grew.

Now, in the early 1960s, he was in the midst of an extended stay in the Escorial, Spain, with his family, writing a book on the Supreme Court. In Spain he lived surrounded by Catholicism as a way of life, where he could seek an "ideal, integrated Catholicism."[8]

Hence Bozell's conservatism developed in a different direction from Meyer's; his philosophy was deeply rooted in the authority and tradition of the Catholic Church. At that time he represented an important wing of the American conservative movement; many conservative Catholics found a basis for their political thought in their religious tradition. Bozell therefore argued that Meyer's emphases were seriously misplaced. To prove it, he sent *NR* an enormous manuscript pressing his case. It would begin an important debate into the fundamental tenets of conservatism.

Titled "Freedom or Virtue?" Bozell's piece was over five thousand words long and covered more than seven *NR* pages. But his argument was clear, and he pressed it forward relentlessly, step-by-step. Bozell told the Right that man's first, primary goal was not freedom, but *virtue*. It was man's ultimate "purpose"—"God rewards or punishes depending on how individual man…conducts the quest," Bozell wrote. Moreover, this supreme goal should not be limited to cultivating one's own virtue, but that of all the world—to create a "Christian civilization."

With that assumption, Bozell insisted that the primary purpose of politics must be to *aid* this quest for virtue, this drive for a Christian polity. Since man was corrupted by original sin, and therefore could not find goodness on his own, the state must help him (as well as God). Political and economic freedom were merely ideas and institutions that a "prudent commonwealth," in Bozell's words, would accept "in such measure as they are conducive to the virtue of its citizens." But did this not restrict free will, and thus diminish the very virtue of one's actions? Bozell thought not. Free will, he wrote, was *inherent* in man—especially in his inner impulses and desires, and it was these that truly determined what kind of an act was being performed. A man in chains, forced to commit evil acts, would not be condemned by God, for He would know the man's true inner desires; whereas virtuous acts, commanded by the state, produced order and stability, and promoted a godly civilization. Free will would exist no matter what policies the state adopted; so why should it not pass laws that would prudently regulate man's action, to prevent sin and lawlessness from taking over the world? Did not governments do this already, for example, by prohibiting theft and murder? Was this too an infringement of free will?

To Bozell the drive to raise freedom to the highest political end was in reality an attempt to escape the commands of God. The "urge to freedom for its own sake is . . . a rebellion against nature," he wrote. "[I]t is the urge to be free from God." Bozell charged that libertarians sought to remove God from mainstream American culture; and yet many people longed to believe in something more, something outside themselves. *This* was why some turned to an ideology such as communism. And this was why, Bozell concluded gloomily, "the story of how the free society has come to take priority over the good society is the story of the decline of the West."[9]

Meyer responded immediately, publishing in the very next issue of *NR* a rejoinder called "Why Freedom?" It was not simply a refutation of Bozell's position, but a general critique of the entire traditionalist point of view, to which Bozell had clearly moved. Meyer began by examining this concept of "virtue." He believed that it simply could *not* be coerced; someone forced to be virtuous exhibited "the actions of an automaton." For "being unfree to reject virtue, he is unfree to choose it." Furthermore, allowing the state to promote virtue could only lead to disaster. Power corrupts, and "if the state is endowed with the power to enforce virtue, the men who hold that power will enforce their own concepts as virtuous." Forcing one's own vision of the good upon others deprives individuals of the right to choose what is right and good. Besides, Bozell's conception of virtue was far too limited. The conservative consensus, Meyer wrote, "has conceived virtue not merely in the negative terms of subduing evil inclinations, but also in positive terms—in terms of achievement of potentialities." Performing virtuous acts was "honorable, noble, valorous, glorious, generous." Thus, imposing a state-mandated conception of virtue was not only wrong, but would "destroy [man]'s potentiality for active, creative, positive virtue."

In sum, Meyer put forward what he claimed was not "fusion" at all, but simply the "instinctive consensus" of the conservative movement. He concluded that the "denial of the claims of virtue leads not to conservatism, but to spiritual aridity and social anarchy; the denial of the claims of freedom leads not to conservatism, but to authoritarianism and theocracy." The decline of the West, Meyer wrote, was occurring not because there was too much freedom, but rather "because freedom has declined as virtue has declined. The recovery of the one demands the recovery of the other; the recovery of both is the mission of conservatism today. Virtue in freedom—this is the goal of our endeavor."[10]

This was Meyer's central point—there *was* a conservative "consensus," and his marriage (he didn't like the term "fusion") of freedom and tradition embodied this understanding. And indeed, perhaps such accord was slowly coming.

The Meyer-Bozell debate was metaphysical, philosophical, seemingly divorced from the tug and pull of the political scene. But it inspired considerable response from *NR*'s readers, with a slim majority siding with Meyer. As one reader wrote: "Mr. Bozell, what is the purpose of life if we are marched into heaven at the point of a gun?" Meyer was so stimulated by these exchanges that he wrote Buckley: "I would like to propose . . . somewhat more (not too frequent, but regular) fundamental discussions. . . . I have always thought this was correct, as you know; but I am emboldened to raise it again because of the phenomenal interest in Brent's debate with me." Besides, his relationship with Bozell had not suffered. Unlike what sometimes happened when conservatives debated with each other, the two men loved to argue, but they never quarreled. Their devotion and affection for each other never changed.[11]

BUT IN THE END, MEYER knew that he must do more than argue with individuals. It was time to consolidate his thinking, to pull together the disparate elements of his philosophy and forge them into a coherent whole. In December 1962, through the publishing house of Henry Regnery of Chicago (conservatives' favorite publisher, and one of the few in those days who regularly printed conservative books), Meyer gave to the world perhaps his most important book. He called it, appropriately, *In Defense of Freedom: A Conservative Credo.*

He dedicated the book to his fellow conservatives L. Brent Bozell, William F. Buckley Jr., and Willmoore Kendall: "Companions in battle, whetstones of the mind. . . . None of whom will by any means agree with much of this book; without whom, however, it could not have been written." His intention, Meyer said in his opening chapter, was to "vindicate the freedom of the person as the central and primary end of political society. I am also concerned with demonstrating the integral relationship between freedom as a political end and the basic beliefs of contemporary American conservatism." He disagreed with some who currently called themselves conservatives, specifically the "new conservatives." For while they accepted "the objective existence of values based upon the unchanging constitution of being," they denied what must follow from this—that "acceptance of the moral authority derived from transcendent criteria of truth and good must be voluntary if it is to have meaning; if it is coerced by human force, it is meaningless."[12]

Meyer was determined to show that his vindication of freedom, his defense of the individual person, represented the "crystallization" of the thinking of the wider conservative movement; he would also demonstrate that, contrary to the thinking of critics on the Left, a belief in absolute values *and* in the primacy of the individual was no contradiction. Rather, it was "grounded in the nature of man and in the very constitution of being." Thus his book would deal mainly with the "theoretical soundness" of this position. But first there was the matter of "clearing ground."[13]

The book used arguments mainly hammered out in his *NR* columns, that is, that principles and ideas could not be ignored. Man must engage in fundamental debate over the ideas behind current events. He must not descend into "scientism," examining only whatever *is*, but must imagine what *ought* to be. Meyer, in other words, championed man's free will and urged the use of reason to discover both the true and the good. Man is "a free being," one "who lives between good and evil, beauty and ugliness, truth and error, and fulfills his destiny in the choices he makes."[14]

Having cleared fundamental philosophical ground, Meyer moved on to his second topic: why freedom? Drawing on his earlier debate with Bozell, he defended freedom historically and philosophically, in the process sharpening his differences with the "new conservatives." Meyer argued that, contrary to a widely accepted belief, society was made for *man*, not the other way around. Society is not a real entity; *individuals* make it up. Historically, devotion to an abstract conception of "society" led the state to "improve" it, which in turn led to the oppression of individuals, such as in Nazi Germany or Soviet Russia. Besides, philosophically, ranking the concept of society with that of freedom made no sense. How could man be truly free if he must follow the dictates of "society" or "historical necessity"? To be free means to be able to choose; or, as Meyer put it in the most basic language, a person must be able to say "quite simply—and literally: to Hell with it; it is wrong and it is false."[15]

But Meyer's main purpose was to assail the thinking of the new conservatives. Meyer accused Russell Kirk of wishing to grant individuals freedom
only to choose what Kirk considered "the good." What kind of choice was
that? Then there was Kirk's claim that freedom "subsists in community." Not
so; freedom subsists in the *individual*. "He may find freedom in communal
participation, or he may find it in ignoring community, even in revolt against
community," Meyer wrote. He also rejected the arguments of Kirk's fellow
new conservative, Clinton Rossiter, for a more "inclusive" definition of liberty—the right to "security." Freedom "is *not* all-embracing," Meyer shot back.
"It is a specific aspect of the condition of man; it is neutral to ends—and
presumably, therefore, 'narrow'; and it is as 'negative' as it is 'positive,' since its
exercise demands that it reject all alternatives but the one it chooses." In the
end, freedom "is essential to the being of man." That was what Meyer was
trying to tell the new conservatives; that was "why freedom."[16]

In part three of his book, Meyer asked new questions. For instance, given
that a society must have order, what kind of order should this be? Should it
promote some end? Should it seek to inculcate "virtue" in man? Once again
drawing upon his exchanges with Bozell, Meyer said no. Men must be free to
accept or reject virtue.[17]

As for the state's role in today's society, the "Leviathan" state, Meyer went
on the attack. The state is not synonymous with "the people," as liberals claimed.
Rather, it was made up of those who "possess the monopoly of legal coercive
force." Government should have only three main functions: to protect the rights
of citizens against violence, fraud, and crime; to judge conflicts involving one
citizen's rights versus the rights of another; and to protect the nation against any
aggression from foreign governments. In other words, the state should exercise
the police, military, and judicial functions—what Willmoore Kendall disparag-
ingly called Meyer's "holy trinity.""The image of the state projected in this book
is, of course, an ideal. . . . There is in power an impulsion to more power, which
can only be limited by counter-measures," Meyer wrote. But man must seek to
construct such an ideal, for without it, conservatives could no longer fight the
state's steady accretions of power.[18]

Which led Meyer back to Kirk, Rossiter, and the others. They would "justify any aggression of individual persons so long as it is carried out in the name
of community, of society, or of its agent, the state." "What the New Conserva-

tives are saying," Meyer argued, "is that the state is the proper organ for the enforcement of virtue. . . . Its virtue must be his virtue—which is no more nor less than the central tenet of totalitarianism."[19]

And last, Meyer posed yet another question: where is "the locus of virtue"? Liberals would name the state, new conservatives the community. But Meyer insisted that virtue could only be located in the individual person, and could only truly be found through freedom. Meyer hastened to add: "To assert the freedom and independence of the individual person means no denial of the value of mutuality of association and common action between persons. It only denies the value of coerced association."[20]

In fact, Meyer stressed, most associations *were* voluntary in nature—with two inevitable and necessary exceptions: the state and the family. The state, as long as it was limited to its three vital functions, was crucial in establishing the conditions of freedom. And the family was the only "community," or association, that could legitimately give moral guidance and was intrinsic to a person's existence.[21]

Meyer understood that many moderns would resist the diminution of the state that he and other conservatives proposed. The popularity of the economics of John Maynard Keynes had given the state a practical and philosophical basis, and the comforting, cradle-to-grave security promised by the welfare state was obviously tempting. But Meyer contended that such "security" was illusory and, most importantly, immoral. Meyer defined welfarism as government functions that "belong to individual men," such as "provision for the eventualities of sickness, unemployment, accident, variations in market conditions; the education of children; responsibility for the care of aging members of the family; all the vicissitudes of life." This "is founded upon Keynesian and neo-Keynesian doctrines." But its end "is the security of the anthill or the beehive." "[It] is flatly evil, because it moves towards the destruction of personal freedom."[22]

Meyer also criticized libertarians. "The free capitalist economic order does not and cannot directly inculcate virtue," he wrote. No association, community, or governmental institution could in itself be a source of virtue, Meyer was saying. Instead, it "can only either inhibit the possibility of virtue by suppressing the freedom of men or indirectly conduce to virtue by helping to make men free."[23]

In conclusion, Meyer wondered if perhaps the growth of Leviathan was to be expected. The concept of the sanctity of the individual person was of

Western origin, after all, and relatively new. But "remembrance of the flesh-pots of enveloping security ever tugs insidiously at the souls of free men."[24]

The United States had been caught up in such "fleshpots," and thus its government had created a welfare state to give its people a larger social safety net. But Meyer did not blame ordinary Americans for this. Those at fault, in his view, were the leaders—the possessors of intellectual, political, and moral authority, who had "blinded themselves to the truths of their heritage and rejected the moral responsibility of freedom."[25]

Meyer believed fervently that this could be reversed, that the Leviathan state could be shackled if the natural instincts and energies of the American people were given "intellectual articulation" and "organization"—this was the challenge for modern American conservatism. Meyer declared: "Nothing in history is determined. The decision hangs upon our understanding of the tradition of Western civilization and the American republic; our devotion to freedom and to truth, the strength of our will and of our determination to live as free and virtuous men."[26]

THE NEED TO MARRY freedom to the quest for virtue was Frank Meyer's clarion call to the conservative movement, a stirring summons to battle, a challenge to take those principles and translate them into political reality. It was not a concrete "program," not a blueprint for conservative legislative proposals or a guide to political action, and in that sense, would never meet the approval of critics such as James Burnham. But Meyer believed that a concrete strategy or program *must* have a proper philosophical and metaphysical foundation; if principles were mistaken, all was lost.

Others besides Burnham remained unconvinced. Stanley Parry, who taught political science at the University of Notre Dame and was an occasional contributor to *National Review*, wrote—not unfairly—that Meyer's work was "a revised version of nineteenth-century liberalism, one in which metaphysical realism supplants utilitarianism as the philosophical underpinning for the defense of human freedom." And he correctly identified Meyer's thesis—that "the freedom of the individual is the end both of theory and action in politics." But, Parry argued, Meyer's theory was incomplete. Concerning his view of man, why was there "no consistent indication why the individual establishes interpersonal relations in the first place? . . . Thus we are left uncertain

. . . whether Meyer thinks man is by nature a social animal who *must* enter into a variety of interpersonal relations in order to realize his nature as man, or whether, in contrast, he views man as a 'completed fact,' after the manner of the philosophical individualists like Hobbes." And was it really true that virtue could come only through freedom? Parry held that "actual freedom" could only be acquired by "a virtuous man . . . , one in whom reason rules rather than sits as a spectator of passion-dominated action." Meyer, that is, had not answered "the great question of every political theory: who should rule?"[27]

Then there was Willmoore Kendall, who held that Meyer was too ideological. The American Right, Kendall wrote, "accepts without protest or complaint the fact that American conservatism, though principled, is not . . . doctrinaire, and . . . is not going to become doctrinaire." This ran up against the views of such as Meyer, upon whom, Kendall gibed, "the distinction seems sometimes to be lost." Conservatism must beware of absolutes; it "has sworn no vow of absolute fidelity either to free enterprise a la von Mises, or to a certain list of 'rights' a la John Chamberlain, or to a certain holy trinity of government functions a la (I must mention him again, for he is a great though lovable sinner) Frank Meyer."

Richard Weaver, meanwhile, believed that Meyer had gone too far in criticizing the idea of "community." Meyer's position must lead to "Thoreau's anarchic individualism. . . . [I]f the community got in your way or vexed you, you simply seceded from it." But things were not nearly so simple. "You did not join your community as you might join a musical society or a chess club," Weaver wrote. "You were born into it, and it has been a part of your nurture since long before you started thinking as a political animal."[28]

And Russell Kirk. In some ways, Meyer and Kirk were quite similar. Both were viewed as somewhat eccentric men who defied the conventions of the modern age and lived life in their own ways. Kirk chose to live in the wilds of rural Michigan, eschewing the modern amenity of television (when he found one in his household, he cut all the wires and buried it in the cold ground), taking long canoe rides down Michigan's rivers, eating beaver and smoking "dark, thick" Burmese cigars "looking and tasting . . . like torpedoes." The *National Review* circle referred to him as "the Duke of Mecosta."[29]

But in other ways, Kirk and Meyer were very different. Kirk's experiences with the modern world—he had served in World War II, and later witnessed the ravages of Nazism and communism—taught him to dislike "ideology." Most attempts to devise an integrated "theory," such as Meyer's, would result in rigid, doctrinaire thinking, which must lead to utopianism and revolution, throughout Kirk. Instead, he wanted conservatives to develop a "prudential politics" and a "humane" economics. And Kirk had never forgiven Meyer for his attack upon *The Conservative Mind* in the *Freeman* in 1955. *Freeman* editor Frank Chodorov, apparently with Meyer's assent, had sent copies to many of Kirk's editorial advisers for Kirk's proposed journal *Modern Age,* which Kirk was then working to establish. This was one of the reasons Kirk would not join *National Review* as a senior editor; he would not be a close associate of Frank Meyer. Privately, he wrote in bitter fashion of "ex-Communists.""Very few of the ex-Communists," he told a friend, "manage to cut themselves free of their former tactics."[30]

No surprise, then, that Kirk unleashed a scathing, scornful, sarcastic review of Meyer's book in the *Sewanee Review.* He spared no adjective, saying the book made him "tire," it was "zealous," "abstract," and filled with a desire to "purge." More specifically, Kirk wrote that the book was full of "the weary liberalism of the nineteenth century," that the author was trying to "erect an ideology, with slogans and dogmas . . . to create a disciplined sect of the faithful, to become the law and all the prophets to young persons marching to Zion." Kirk contended that Meyer isolated freedom, removing it from its proper relationship to the other integral parts of the civil social polity, namely justice and order. "Order and justice lacking, man is left with the terrible 'freedom' of the Congo. The eccentric Mr. Meyer himself could not exist for a week under such conditions of absolute liberty as he demands." In sum, Kirk found the book essentially a work of "political pamphleteering." Meyer was "disdainful of doubt," Kirk charged, and this "can appeal to little but the arrogant ego. With this last, he is plentifully equipped."[31]

WHEN FACED WITH such attacks, Meyer sometimes became angry and would let loose volleys of blistering criticism. But he tried not to let the differences become personal. Mostly, harsh criticism of his person and his position frustrated him, for he badly wanted to have an impact on conservatism. And he passionately believed in what he had written in *In Defense of Freedom*; it was his "credo," his belief.[32]

But as time went on, it became apparent that Meyer's position was win-

ning. Not suddenly, nor formally, but seemingly by osmosis, Meyer's philosophical construction was accepted by more and more intellectuals on the Right, and
therefore the debate over conservatism's fundamentals—so intense in 1962 and
1963, when Meyer and Bozell debated the merits of freedom versus virtue—
largely quieted.

Moreover, many who voiced criticisms of his position also paid him great
homage. Richard Weaver called *In Defense of Freedom* "an essay brilliant with
destructive analysis aimed on the one side at Liberal Collectivism and on the
other at a dangerous strain he sees in some of the New Conservatives." Meyer
had "struck hard at those who are interested neither in good nor in freedom."
Murray Rothbard, a staunch libertarian economist, wrote to *Modern Age* to
say that no one within the conservative camp "has as great an understanding
of, or sympathy with, the libertarian, or 'classical liberal' tradition." William F.
Buckley Jr., having seen an early draft of Meyer's work, told Henry Regnery
that "it goes further than anything I have seen to develop a conservative
metaphysic. . . . I think he provides a more satisfactory philosophical answer
to the question why should we have freedom than has anyone else." Even
Whittaker Chambers, not long before he died, recognized (perhaps a bit
regretfully) the effect that Meyer was having upon the American Right. "Frank
Meyer is emerging clearly as the Voice," Chambers told Buckley. "I am not
being sniffy: this, I gather from stray *NR* readers, is what they want to hear.
And, technically, he writes it all well. It isn't my flapjack. But that is of no
interest whatever." He continued to worry about what he saw as Meyer's
inflexibility, his tendency to become too ideological. And he marveled that
NR, with so many different modes of thinking and personalities among its
editorial board, continued to cohere. But it did. "Frank has worked himself
into his shirt until the fit seems nearly perfect to the unpracticed eye," Chambers noted. "But, still, he had (has) to work at it; and there persists, if you have
a sense of these things, a besetting, humanizing pathos. . . . The wonder of Jim
[Burnham] is that, pursuing another quite different and self-contained orbit,
he can make editorial harmony with these so different spheres. So you have
the making of a team or cadre; and I think NR reflects this."[33]

Perhaps in the end Meyer's position triumphed by default. Many on the
Right may have simply tired of the debate. Others knew that conservatives badly
needed to find a consensus and accepted Meyer's fusion as the best compromise

possible. And, after all, much united conservatives—especially anticommunism, in an age when the Cold War dominated the world scene. Meyer himself later told an acquaintance that perhaps the principals in the debate had
"run out of fresh things to say." In any case, by the end of the decade, many of
the central figures in this controversy, such as L. Brent Bozell, agreed that
Meyer had forged a conservative consensus. Even Russell Kirk continued to
write a column for *National Review* on education. And Kirk, Meyer, and almost all of the conservative movement would unite behind the political candidacy of Barry Goldwater. Despite their internal differences, in practice the
Right was unifying. And Frank Meyer had a lot to do with that.[34]

BUT THEN MEYER HAD ALWAYS had a great deal of confidence in himself and his
views. He was convinced that his marriage of freedom, tradition, and virtue was
not only philosophically correct, but inevitable. "The conservative movement is
gradually resolving into a single outlook [consisting of] the two streams of thought
which make it up: emphasis upon the freedom of the individual person, and
emphasis upon the authority of eternal truths," he told Buckley in 1961. Meyer
also emphasized that a conservatism stripped of its libertarian, free-market elements would die. "Apart from my own personal commitment to these doctrines," Meyer emphasized, "I would state as a matter of objective fact that there
can be no American conservative movement of significance which does not
accept them and integrate them with the traditionalist emphasis upon the authority of truth, reasoned and revealed. A conservatism deriving purely from
19th century European conservatism can have no standing in America—nor
should it."[35]

But what of the rest of the country? What of those who did not call
themselves conservatives—who referred to themselves as moderates or liberals?
Was there any hope of Meyer's conservative ideas breaking into and influencing
the wider culture of America? Indeed, what was it like in the early 1960s to be
a conservative in America, especially in relation to the wider intellectual-media
culture of the time? Meyer now had hopes of finding out. "Keep your fingers
crossed for me (if you descend to such superstition)," he told Buckley in the
winter of 1963. "I received a telephone call from *Time* yesterday, saying that they
wanted to send a photographer up tomorrow, because they are going to run a
review of my book. I have no idea of what goes on in the Luce empire or how

certain it is that such a *demarche* will lead to an actual review in print—but I am hoping."[36]

Time did not review Meyer's book, aptly symbolizing the story of conservatives' frustration at, and fascination with, the wider American intellectual culture. The slight was reminiscent of an earlier time when many intellectuals considered *National Review* to be part of the "extreme Right" and beneath discussion. Conservatives such as Frank Meyer were both intensely disappointed at such unfair treatment and were hungry to be noticed, to be taken seriously. Meyer had substantially bridged the gap between traditionalist and libertarian conservatives. But it remained to be seen whether he, or any *NR* conservative, could bridge the gap between themselves and the rest of the world of ideas.

The Establishment

IN THE LATE 1950S AND EARLY 1960S, to call oneself a "conservative" in America was not nearly as common, and certainly not as accepted, as it is today. Of course, within America's rich intellectual and journalistic culture, articles and essays by conservative writers could occasionally be found. But the attitude and the seriousness with which conservative ideas were taken by the "Establishment"—their acceptability—was far different in those years.

In the newspaper world, the important papers were the *New York Times* and the *Washington Post*, and the popular magazines included *Time*, *Life*, *Newsweek*, *Look*, and a few others. The intellectual milieu included journals such as *Partisan Review*, *Dissent*, the *New Republic*, and the *Nation*, various specialized periodicals, and publishing houses big and small. Most conservatives wished desperately to gain notice in outlets such as these, both in the hope that their ideas would gain respectability in nonconservative circles, and in the belief that such attention would allow their beliefs to trickle down to the masses. They were, in fact, being increasingly noticed in circles of power, as well as in the highbrow and popular press—but a true hearing was another matter.

IN ORDER TO DISCUSS conservatism, it was necessary to define it; there had to be some consensus on what conservatism was. *National Review* conservatives had their own definition, and they had presented it in *NR*'s "credenda" in the magazine's first issue; subsequently, Frank Meyer, among others, worked to refine and develop these principles. In general, conservatives agreed on certain common beliefs: the existence of absolute truths, the value of tradition, the primacy of the individual person, a limited central government, and anticommunism. They argued that, although implementing these legitimate beliefs would mean significant changes in America's government and society, such change would return the country to its original, historical practices and traditions.

Interest in American conservatism was also slowly increasing within the academic community. But most of these intellectuals did not think that *NR*'s principles constituted "true" conservatism. They contended instead that no genuine, traditional, historically based conservatism even existed. Louis Hartz, a historian from Columbia University, asserted that the American past was the history of "a liberal way of life." Most thinkers accepted Lockean doctrine—that is, that there is a social contract between rulers and ruled; that if the ruler breaks this contract, the people have a right to rebel; that the masses have certain natural rights; that all men are created equal. But this was liberalism, not conservatism, and American conservatives' acceptance of these principles made them simply modified liberals. What American Right there was, Hartz wrote, "exemplifies the tradition of big propertied liberalism in Europe. . . . It is the tradition which embraces loosely the English Presbyterian and the English Whig, the French Girondin and the French Liberal; a tradition which hates the *ancien régime* up to a certain point, loves capitalism, and fears democracy." To Hartz, conservatism was a desire to protect one's status and economic position, and little else.[1]

Other intellectuals agreed: the principles and programs of current conservatives were not in fact conservatism, and they were contradictory and unworkable anyway. In 1959 the political scientist M. Morton Auerbach wrote categorically: "Conservatism has no way of making the crucial transition from values to reality, from theory to practice, and in the limited periods of history when it *seemed* to make this transition, it was able to do so only for reasons which contradicted its premises."[2] Auerbach defined a conservative as someone who sought "harmony and tranquility, the inner peace which is destroyed by tension." This demanded the "minimizing of individual desires and the maximizing of affection through a 'community,' integrated by traditions and institutions handed down from the past." Auerbach's definition did not for the most part include individual freedom and free-market capitalism. Capitalism, he insisted, upset human tranquility and harmony, and urged man to maximize his desires, to transcend established social limits and tradition, thus upsetting such conservative values as hierarchy and order. Hence the modern Right's attempt to enshrine liberal capitalism as orthodoxy, while claiming this to be "conservative," was inherently contradictory.[3]

And, as had Hartz, Auerbach argued that traditional conservatism did not apply to America in any case. The United States had no social base in which to nurture conservatism—no feudal past, no medieval tradition, no traditional, elitist ranks and hierarchies. It had only business leaders and finance capitalists. The writings of present-day conservatives, such as Richard Weaver and Russell Kirk (Auerbach made no reference to Frank Meyer or *National Review*), were simply irrelevant to the present society, inconsequential to the forces of reaction that in reality constituted the American Right. "The very failure of American Conservatives to analyze clearly the differences among themselves," Auerbach went on, "let alone resolve the dilemmas of each sub-group, makes it clear that they had better do a little 'intramural' debating before they throw down the gauntlet."[4] Some identified the historian Clinton Rossiter as a conservative, but again, his definition of conservatism was much different from that of the *NR* circle. Becoming a true conservative, Rossiter thought, meant being "committed to a discriminating defense of the social order against change and reform." Rossiter described society as "a living organism with roots deep in the past . . . , a grand union of functional groups." He defended property rights, and claimed to be in favor of limited government; but his support of capitalism and private enterprise was only lukewarm. "Few conservatives will assert certainly in their most detached and Burkean moments, that any particular system of production and distribution is, like private property, rooted in the nature of things and men," Rossiter contended. This left little room for the views of Frank Meyer.[5] Other writers claimed that present-day conservatism had little to do with ideas; it arose not out of conviction, but out of a desire to protect status, or from an "authoritarian" personality. Hence, far from believing that conservatives could be legitimate players on the national political scene, these intellectuals feared that conservatives would usher a new authoritarianism, even fascism, into American life. A leading sociologist wrote that conservatives' mentality resembled "in a striking and frightening way the familiar one of the followers of Adolf Hitler." The well-known political scientist James MacGregor Burns concluded that conservatism had no rationality: "[It] can drop bombs but not expand social welfare." Daniel Bell, another oft-quoted sociologist, contended that there was "no coherent conservative force" in America. And the noted historian Richard Hofstadter placed the American Right within the historical context of what he called a "paranoid style" in American politics. It was significant, he argued, that ex-communists were so prominent in the anticommunist cause. They had "moved rapidly, though not without anguish, from the paranoid Left to the paranoid Right, clinging all the while to the fundamentally Manichean psychology that underlies both."[6]

THUS, MANY WRITERS, journalists, and scholars either defined conservatism as being illegitimate and not worthy of the name, or belonging not to the realm of ideas at all. It was instead an irrational, knee-jerk reaction to modernity.

National Review, in what slim coverage it received, fared little better. Almost everyone gave *NR* some kind of label, relegating it to the fringe, to the "extremist" sidelines, far from the mainstream. *NR* was called "radically conservative" or "ultra-conservative"; it spoke for "the far political right" and sometimes engaged in "doctrinaire pedantry."[7]

But mainly the criticism of *National Review* rested on two points. First, *NR* conservatism had no coherent program, no clear vision of what it stood for. A book reviewer for the *Saturday Review* argued that, in the writings of Buckley and those around him, the reader "learns what he should abandon but what is the 'up' is left rather vague." Peter Viereck called the *National Review* circle "rootless, counterrevolutionary doctrinaires."[8]

Daniel Bell, meanwhile, claimed that *National Review* did indeed have a philosophy. But it was an incoherent, jumbled mélange of beliefs and persuasions that made little sense. *NR*, Bell wrote in *Partisan Review,* "proclaims itself conservative" but in actuality is "a strange mix of Thomistic natural law (Buckley), Manchester economic liberalism (Hazlitt and Buckley), Burkean traditionalism (Meyer and Buckley), Platonic *virtu* (Bozell and Buckley), Haushofer geo-politics (Burnham and Buckley), and single-tax, agrarian, libertarian individualism (Choderov [sic] and Buckley). A heady brew indeed."[9]

Other variants on this theme held that, although the country needed a good conservative magazine, *National Review* did not qualify. John Fischer, the editor of *Harper's,* contended that *NR* was "an organ, not of conservatism, but of radicalism." It was too conspiratorial, too convinced that an ill-defined liberalism literally ran the country; its attitude was "dreadfully earnest. The editorial tone is one of humorless indignation, almost indistinguishable from that of the *Daily Worker.*" "No doubt *National Review* will serve a useful purpose in feeding the emotional hungers of a small congregation of the faithful; and it will have a certain interest for students of political splinter movements," Fischer concluded. "But the far greater need for a journal to express the philosophy of modern American conservatism still remains unfilled." Dwight Macdonald, a noted author and critic long associated with the *Partisan Review* circle, made largely the same points in an essay in *Commentary* magazine. He called those affiliated with *NR* "McCarthy nationalists," who expressed the style and the ideas of "the *lumpen-bourgeoisie,* the half-educated, half-successful provincials." "We have long needed a good conservative magazine," Macdonald said, but *NR* was "neither good nor conservative."[10]

Many thought that time had simply passed by *National Review*-style conservatism. It was passé, out of touch with the modern world, and bound soon to die a natural death. Margaret Coit, a writer for the *Saturday Review,* said that while all could agree on the virtues of, say, James Madison, it was "a different matter to conclude that he had the answers for the age of automania and the atom bomb. True, human nature does not change and even human wisdom may not change, but the facts of human life and relationships in a technical age do change, and not solely because of the activities of liberals." James Epstein, in the *New York Review of Books,* bluntly echoed this argument. Many conservatives "rest their case with God. . . . This line of conservative thought . . . may be consoling . . . but as a practical contribution to the question of human freedom as it affects, say, the residents of Harlem, it is not much to the point."[11]

And then there was the charge of "extremism," the other accusation most frequently made against *National Review.* This view was most loudly proclaimed by the liberal *New Republic* in 1962 with a pair of articles by the historian Irving Brant. Brant found that the American Right was essentially made up of "the John Birch Society at the lowest level of intelligence and the *National Review* in the higher altitude of right-wing sophistication." But the two were as "alike as two yolks in one egg. . . . [NR] is the identical twin of the John Birch Society." *NR* and the JBS had the same goal: "driving liberalism forever out of power by deceptive propaganda or by judicial or legislative destruction of the basic rights of citizenship," Brant asserted. "If they could do all they talk of doing, our American society of free men would be trampled to death under a ponderous procession of troglodytes mounted on pachyderms."[12]

Some mainstream journalists and intellectuals predicted the Right's imminent demise. The *New Republic* wrote that conservatism should be relegated to the realm of "discarded ideas," that it was a "relic." True, a "jauntily edited national journal of opinion carries its message to the remaining army of believers," and some conservative politicians remained to carry on the fight in the political arena. "But whatever vitality the movement may ever have possessed has long since petered out. . . . The civilized community has moved on to other things." The *Saturday Review* admitted that William F. Buckley Jr. had become a well-known, popular conservative, with a talent for "showmanship" and the power to "scandalize." But "it remains to be seen whether he will yet make the cause of conservatism respectable in American letters."[13]

Television toed the liberal line, too. Buckley, for example, appeared as a guest on Jack Paar's late-night network television talk show in 1962. His interview proceeded affably enough, but once over, the smears began. Paar told another guest, "What I can't stand is that these people [Buckley and his cohorts] when they talk they have no feeling of humanity—they just don't seem to care about people."[14]

Not all of the attention paid to *National Review* in these years was negative. *NR* conservatives were occasionally complimented on the stylistic quality of their writing, praised for bringing important issues into the open, granted their propositions that liberals had in the past made mistakes in both economic and foreign policy, and admired for their ability to survive. Buckley began writing his own syndicated newspaper column, and was frequently invited to speak and debate throughout the country. *NR's* editor in chief, moreover, despite his "razor-sharp wit" and take-no-prisoners debating style, maintained several friendships with well-known liberals, including Murray Kempton and John Kenneth Galbraith. But mainstream liberal figures could never completely ignore *NR's* political position. Once, the critic Dwight Macdonald visited Buckley's home in Connecticut and went sailing with him. "He's not a bad fellow really," Macdonald later wrote a friend; he "just has bad ideas."[15]

Nothing much changed as the 1960s progressed—despite the fact that conservative Senator Barry Goldwater claimed the nomination for president on the Republican ticket in 1964. The number of *NR* subscribers did increase to nearly 100,000 by 1964. But the reception given *NR* by established journalists and intellectuals did not improve; if anything, it seemed to get worse.

The Goldwater nomination was a shock to many writers and political observers. Richard Crossman, a member of the British Labour Party, an expert on communism, and a writer and thinker with many connections in the American intellectual world, related that up until the last minute, few among his friends thought Barry Goldwater could ever be nominated, viewing him largely as an object of "fun." He now realized how important was the intellectual foundation given to the Goldwater movement by *National Review.* But this foundation was nevertheless radical. *NR* conservatives, such as Buckley and James Burnham, saw liberals as kind of an "enemy within the gates," wrote Crossman, comparing this to the themes found in Adolf Hitler's *Mein Kampf.* Conservatives were "dangerous," capable of rendering "the racial problem insoluble . . . [and] strong enough to prevent the Administration from grasping the opportunities for coexistence with the Soviet Union."[16]

Meanwhile, *Partisan Review* assembled many of its senior editors and contributors for their comments in the wake of Barry Goldwater's nomination. *PR* intellectuals were not at all happy. They saw the Goldwater movement as a threat to American democracy. Conservatives were heavily influenced by "racism" and by other "resentments"; Goldwaterism could eventually "form a fascist totality. . . . [Goldwater] has near him at least one man who can think, William Buckley, an all-or-none theocratic zealot of the most dangerous kind." The ubiquitous Richard Hofstadter added that the Republicans' conservative platform was based on "jingoism, economic ultra-conservatism, and racial animosity." John G. Hollander called Goldwater's rise "an aesthetic prank and a moral disaster," said that his supporters were "the Yahoos of respectability," and compared them to German supporters of Adolf Hitler. Jack Ludwig claimed that Goldwater's conservative support was mostly made up of "tax nuts, Roosevelt-haters, TVA-haters, Kennedy-haters, anti-Communist crusaders, pasters-of-'Red'-labels-on-Polish-hams, fluoridophobes, veterans yearning for the good exciting *win* days, old maids afraid of rape by a Negro, pinchy property owners, county political hacks . . . " And *PR* senior editor Philip Rahv wrote that Goldwater "is a naive idealist of foolish ideas, mostly taken from those extreme groups on the Right (like the little Politbureau on the *National Review,* Buckley, Burnham, Myers [sic], et. al.)." "Once in control of the executive power, they are unlikely to surrender it," Rahv charged. "Devotees of the McCarthyite strategy of smear, intimidation and purge, they might well attempt to disorganize and then outlaw the opposition. . . . [The way would be] opened for large-scale purges of the Hitler and Stalin pattern."[17]

Journalists and political commentators from around America and around the world seemed to agree. The London *Times:* "the thought that [Goldwater] had the faintest chance of reaching the White House would be enough to shake faith in the maturity and stability of American politics." A Stockholm liberal newspaper: Goldwater's run for the presidency was "a victory for the stupidity and massive ignorance of the Republican voters."

Many mainstream American newspaper columnists expressed similar shock. The respected political observer Walter Lippmann found Goldwater's nomination "absurd." The political columnist Emmett John Hughes, a former speechwriter in the Eisenhower White House, wrote that conservatism was "a mood in want of a doctrine. . . . It is, for now, a credo without content, a yell, not a word."[18]

THESE WERE RESPECTED, established people, writing in highly regarded, mainstream books, journals, magazines, and newspapers. Conservatives hoped to be taken seriously by those within the corridors of power. But in Washington, D.C., they met with the same conviction that the Right was "extreme" and their ideas outmoded, and with the same mystified ignorance of why conservatives held such convictions.

In the White House, this view of the Right can be traced back to the Eisenhower administration. Dwight Eisenhower had been elected in 1952 with considerable conservative support; but in the coming years the Right believed that "Ike" had let them down, neither curtailing the New Deal nor challenging the Soviet stranglehold over Eastern Europe.

Eisenhower, for his part, considered many conservatives to be extremists and of little consequence. Besides, he believed Franklin Roosevelt's New Deal was immensely popular with most Americans and essential to a modern state. Once, writing to his brother Edgar, he said he was aware of some "splinter groups" that advocated the dismantling of the federal welfare state; but "their number is negligible and they are stupid." William F. Buckley Jr. told a friend that "Eisenhower goes nuts at the mention of my name."[19]

The atmosphere in Washington, D.C., did not improve for conservatives when the Kennedy administration took over in 1961. John F. Kennedy had nothing personally against Barry Goldwater, or against conservatives in general. But most in the Kennedy White House tended to dismiss conservative ideas out of hand. They believed that they lived in an age of progress, and that it was the federal government's task to further that progress in any way it could. In foreign policy, it was not the *idea* of anticommunism that alienated liberals of the early 1960s, but rather the *tone,* the decibel level, of conservative anticommunist views. Kenneth O'Donnell and David Powers referred to Goldwater's views as "archaic conservatism" and "gung-ho militarism." Theodore Sorensen condemned "the far-right fringe of professional cold warriors and anti-communists" who, he argued, denounced President Kennedy "with poisonous passion."[20]

John Kennedy himself feared that the rhetoric of the American Right led to dangerous levels of extremism and hatred, as embodied in such organizations as the John Birch Society, which in 1961 claimed that the American government was "40 to 60%" under the control of communists. Therefore, in November and December 1961 Kennedy spoke out against the "radical right." At the University of Washington, he maintained of the extreme Right and extreme Left: "Each of these two extreme opposites resembles the other. Each believes that we have only two choices—appeasement or war, suicide or surrender, humiliation or holocaust, to be either Red or Dead." Two days later, in Los Angeles, Kennedy renewed the attack, speaking of "those on the fringes of our society who have sought to escape their own responsibility by finding a simple solution, an appealing slogan or a convenient scapegoat." Kennedy and his associates believed that all conservatives contributed to this climate of hatred and fear; Arthur Schlesinger believed that Kennedy was looking forward to running against Barry Goldwater in 1964 because it would "give him the opportunity to dispose of right-wing extremism once and for all."[21]

The Kennedy administration did not merely give speeches about radicalism on the Right, they also took action. In December 1961, at Attorney General Robert Kennedy's behest, Walter Reuther, the head of the United Auto Workers union, and liberal attorney Joseph Rauh collaborated on a 24-page report to the administration. "The Reuther Memorandum" was titled "The Radical Right in

America Today." In it, Reuther and Rauh defined right-wing radicalism as
stretching from Barry Goldwater on the "left," to the John Birch Society on
the "right." Well funded and well organized, the Right posed a danger to
America and to the administration. It trafficked in "fear" and "slander," and
could hurt Kennedy's legislative programs.

Hence the authors proposed that the Kennedy White House mobilize
Democratic special interest groups and media allies against the radical Right;
place several extreme right-wing groups on its list of "subversive" organizations;
plant FBI informers inside these extremist organizations; revoke the tax-exempt
status of such groups; and have them extensively audited by the Internal Revenue Service.

Kennedy took these recommendations seriously and implemented many
of them. Administration aide Lee White began preparing monthly confidential
reports on the activities of the Right (*National Review* included). J. Edgar Hoover
and the FBI intensified their examination of right-wing groups (the Bureau
focused mainly upon the Ku Klux Klan). And the IRS launched its Ideological
Organizations Project, which was supposed to review and audit the tax-exempt
status of all "extremist" groups, but which in practice focused mainly on conservative organizations.

Some within the administration remained objective. Lee White, for instance, assured his superiors that such rightist groups as *National Review* or the
New York Conservative Party were mainly interested in "the winning of a national election, [and] the re-education of the governing class." And although
dozens of right-wing groups were investigated and audited by the IRS, few
actually lost their tax-exempt status. Still, it was not easy to be a conservative
in the days of Camelot.[22]

When Lyndon Johnson became president, the atmosphere in the White
House changed, but the administration's view of the American Right was essentially the same. Again, it was nothing personal—Johnson, recalled presidential
aide Jack Valenti, harbored no ill will toward Barry Goldwater. But not all in the
Johnson administration were as charitable. The historian Eric Goldman, Johnson's
link to the intellectual world, described conservatives as having "a passion against
the twentieth century." Fellow aide Richard Goodwin watched the 1964 Republican convention with "delight" and "pleasure," seeing it as "a cacophony of
hate and disapproval."[23]

Lyndon Johnson himself was not an ideological liberal. Even so, his conception of the political process was antithetical to that of *NR*-style conservatives, and Johnson knew it. Intellectuals within the *National Review* circle, such as Frank Meyer, believed that politics was ultimately based upon ideas and principles, or at least ought to be, and that endless negotiation and compromise, with no attention given to first principles, led to bad policy. Johnson emphatically disagreed, arguing that such an approach could literally threaten the future of the American Republic. "The biggest danger to stability," Johnson once said, "is the politics of principle, which brings out the masses in irrational fights for unlimited goals." Hence Johnson was convinced that the Right was a long-term threat to democracy; it believed that "some conflicts were irreconcilable and could be resolved only by the total defeat of one or more contending powers."[24]

AND SO *NATIONAL REVIEW* conservatives in the late 1950s and early 1960s felt like an embattled minority under siege from all sides. They were in danger of being defined out of the political debate—of being ignored, consigned to the dustbin of history as a querulous, shrieking, splinter faction. *National Review* conservatives were not surprised. They had long argued that America was dominated by a liberal "establishment." The agenda of the political debate was largely controlled by the editorial pages of the *New York Times* and the *Washington Post*, by the producers, directors, editors, and anchors on network television, and by the publishers and editors in charge of magazines and book publishing—most, to some degree, adherents of the ideology of liberalism. Most conservatives did not believe in any kind of conspiracy. Rather, as *NR* publisher William Rusher noted, if liberal criticisms of conservatism "sounded strangely alike, it was for the same reason that the noises made by a flock of geese sound strangely alike. Conspiracy had nothing to do with it."[25]

Even so, conservatives maintained passionately that a "liberal establishment" did exist. Buckley once told James Burnham that he shared a friend's "pessimism" concerning "the Establishment's power. Did I tell you about a recent journey into the maws of the Establishment?" At *National Review*, assistant publisher James McFadden became so tired of the liberal practice of preceding the word "conservative" with the prefix "ultra" that when he incorporated a commercial arts company as a subsidiary of *NR*, he called it "Ultra

Arts, Inc."—a name it still holds. During the 1964 presidential campaign, Buckley tried to calm the fears of some at *NR* concerning the negative media coverage of Barry Goldwater. Why be surprised? They had been "predicting that as soon as Goldwater announced, they would begin smearing him; so why . . . should we now a) be surprised that this is what has happened; let alone b) permit ourselves to be affected by the smears."[26]

Conservatives were convinced that this "Establishment" possessed great power. *NR* senior editor William F. Rickenbacker recalled that conservatives in the early 1960s who wished to be published "didn't exactly have a hundred conservative publishers bidding against each other for the privilege of running your stuff." Only about a half-dozen publications would handle manuscripts that "might sound a shade to the right of Nelson Rockefeller," and such publishers "were men of courage, leading lonely existences more often than not, and feeding largely upon hope and faith."[27]

Even when conservative books did find a publisher, troubles persisted. They still faced the danger of negative reviews in the mainstream press, and occasionally from some on the Right who thought their fellow conservatives too reluctant to do battle with the Establishment, to defy it. This led to frustration and anger. In 1959 James Burnham published a well-argued and lengthy book called *Congress and the American Tradition,* in which he contended that the role of Congress in the American system had been wrongly displaced by the executive, an innovation that ran counter to America's political and constitutional tradition and was largely the doing of liberals. It was a conservative book, making a conservative argument, and therefore it was no surprise when the *New York Times* ran a negative review. But the book's publisher, Henry Regnery, told friends and acquaintances that "the *New York Times* has killed Jim Burnham's book," and ceased to promote it with vigor. Upon hearing this, Buckley became furious. "Regnery goes about wearing his demoralization conspicuously . . . ," he told Burnham. "Granted the New York Times has power. But it hasn't got that kind of power and it is very bad to go about as though it did."[28]

Occasionally, of course, *National Review* would blast away at its critics, crafting editorials that leveled withering verbal volleys at the opposition. When the *New Republic* published the articles by Irving Brant linking *NR* to the John Birch Society, Buckley struck back hard; a subsequent *NR* editorial labeled the *New Republic*'s writing "super-hysterical . . . paranoid . . . scurrilous . . . darkly conspiratorial . . . stylistically gross. . . . Its logic is obtuse, solecistic, self-contradictory and otherworldly . . . embarrassingly stupid gallimaufry."[29]

Yet, despite their opposition to the established order in America, conservatives knew just where power was being exercised, and they wanted to be heard in those circles, wanted to open ears that had been so long deaf to them. This was why Buckley dared the opposition, and spoke and debated before such a variety of audiences. He wanted to spread *NR*'s message far and wide, in the very heart of liberaldom. "Last night was stimulating," Buckley wrote to Burnham of a visit to Princeton University. "The crowd was small, but the students were bright. I regret to say that I don't think *NR* has made much headway in Princeton, which rather surprises me." When Burnham later wrote another book, *Suicide of the West* (published in 1964), he hoped that it would have an impact beyond conservatives. "By Jim McFadden's account, the *NR* ads have done remarkably well," he told Buckley. "I hope that somehow or other it is going to break through into non-Right circles." Frank Meyer agreed that *NR* should not ignore nonconservatives, especially academics. "Now that we are going ahead with the program of prestige advertisements in the Establishment press, I want to put in a strong plug for the expenditure of what I think will be a comparatively small amount of money for ads in the most important quarterlies," Meyer wrote Buckley. Meyer specifically named *Partisan Review, Dissent,* the *Kenyon Review, Yale Review,* and the *Sewanee Review.* Buckley agreed: "We will take out ads in the quarterlies you mention."[30]

Buckley believed that the 1964 presidential campaign presented special opportunities for the Right. Although conservatives were angry at the way their views were portrayed in the mainstream press, and at the "smears" directed at their candidate, the whole country was watching—it was the perfect time to present the conservative case. That summer, with Goldwater's nomination looming, Buckley proposed that *NR* prepare a special sixteen-page supplement for the magazine to appear at the time of the Republican convention, in which *NR* would proceed as if a Republican victory had already taken place, and thus present some "proposals for a Goldwater Administration." The idea, Buckley wrote to *NR* editors and staff, was to force even liberals to consider the possibility of conservatism becoming reality, and thus

> to recognize that such an eventuality would not only be non-apocalyptic,
> but could be enormously exciting. Since the proposals made to President-
> elect Goldwater would not call for atom bomb rattling or for dismantling
> the social security system, a sense of relief would be felt. Then, on the basis
> of that, proposals would be made whose cogency, and whose freshness,
> should have the effect of heating up tired political blood. Ideally, the person
> who reads through that supplement, and whose mind is not utterly closed
> on the subject, will find himself adjusting to certain realities less painfully
> than he thought would be the case. . . . [H]e sees that Goldwater's election
> to begin with would not apparently mean the end of the world; and then
> that Goldwater's election would signify a certain new view of things which
> he never understood before.

Buckley even suggested that *NR* adopt a special motto for the magazine during the months of the campaign, and the possibilities he listed were revealing. "*National Review*: The Magazine of the New Mainstream" was one; "*NR—The Magazine of the Future*" was another; a third was more fun: "*NR—The Journal That Set the Clock Back.*"[31]

MOST OF THE TIME, *NR* conservatives believed they had failed. It was not that their message had no resonance with the great mass of ordinary Americans. The failure lay in not being able to penetrate the liberal establishment's conscience; in failing to persuade liberals to give their views a fair hearing.

This sometimes manifested itself in bitterness toward the American Left, a professing to be unimpressed with their liberal counterparts. When Daniel Bell published a piece in *Partisan Review* that discussed (in part) *NR* and the American Right, Frank Meyer claimed to be amazed at Bell's lack of knowledge. "My major impression: how shallow Bell is, how little he has learned . . . and how badly he has done his homework," Meyer told Buckley. "Uproarious to me is the footnote you will find in which he characterizes me as a Burkean. Out of charity, I have sent him a copy of my book." On another occasion, Meyer debated Dwight Macdonald at LaSalle University in Philadelphia. Again, Meyer was not impressed. "I was rather amazed at how flabby [Macdonald] has become (no longer the radical or anarchist, but just an eccentric Liberal)," he remarked to Buckley, "and also at how far below his best writing style his speaking style is. My sober judgment, confirmed by Garry [Wills] . . . is that by and large I easily carried away the honors of the evening, and I will admit that beforehand I was more tremulous about him than about anybody I have debated in recent years."[32]

Liberals returned such hostility in kind; indeed, in 1965 a veteran political observer wrote that the hard conservative vote in America "will never emerge from their bemusement with pre-Dickensian sociology, Adam Smith economics and Boies Penrose politics."[33]

It would be hard to blame liberals, or anyone else, for once again believing that conservatism was sick and dying. Voters were finally given the opportunity to elect a conservative candidate for president in 1964, and Barry Goldwater was defeated in a landslide.

Indeed, 1964 was a crucial year for *National Review.* It was an exhilarating time—finally one of their own was running for the highest office in the land, with a real chance to win the nomination of a major party, if not the presidency. But it was also a difficult time. Barry Goldwater's candidacy brought out yet again some of the stresses and strains within the *NR* circle. It again raised the question of how much support the magazine should give to a single candidate, and whether it could fulfill the roles of both objective journalism and advocate. It meant that some of the personal and ideological animosities existing within *NR* would arise once more, when those who wished to advance their own political loyalties through the magazine, and who believed passionately in their cause, encountered opposition within the editorial board. It was a year of tremendous growth and opportunity for *National Review,* and one of tremendous disappointment, one that would test these conservatives' will to carry on their struggle.

It was a time that none of them would ever forget.

1964

B Y 1964, *NATIONAL REVIEW* and the conservative movement were grow-ing at a rapid pace. Barry Goldwater was a serious contender for the Republican presidential nomination. One of his protégés, John Tower, had been elected U.S. senator from the state of Texas in 1961. On campus, Young Americans for Freedom had over 25,000 members, bringing a youthful conserva-tism into the halls of academe. And the Conservative Party was a force to be reckoned with in New York State politics. In general, more people were interested in American conservatism; more writers and journalists were discussing it.[1]

NR too was expanding, faster than its founders had ever dared hope. The magazine during its first years had been frail, its finances awash in red ink. In the late 1950s, *NR* consistently lost over $100,000 per year, and beginning in 1958 editor-in-chief Buckley annually wrote an earnest, passionate letter to all subscrib-ers, pleading for contributions to keep *NR* afloat. Fortunately its readers always responded. It helped that *NR* shifted from its original weekly format to a fort-nightly, while slowly increasing subscription rates. Assistant publisher James McFadden remarked that *NR*'s motto should be "You think you're getting less, but remember: you're paying more."[2]

But now, with the political rise of Barry Goldwater and the increased inter-est in conservatism generally, the number of *National Review* subscribers skyrocketed to over 90,000. *NR* became a very busy place. The positions taken by the magazine—the intellectual fountainhead of Goldwaterism—could become news in and of themselves. Working for *National Review* (on 35th Street in New York City) was now serious business. The magazine, James Burnham observed in 1962, "is now operating on a much bigger scale than before. It is not just a question of how much copy there is to churn out. There is a huge quantity of correspondence (including great numbers of semi-personal letters everyone gets), far more MSS [manuscripts], people telephoning, problems coming up, advertising and promotion questions, more art work, people appearing, translating to do, issues that ought to be followed . . . , occasions where *NR* ought to be represented, more thinking that ought to be done."[3]

Yet the working environment at *National Review* changed little. Buckley wanted the editors' primary mission to be to think and to write, to make *NR* the best journal it could be. Therefore Buckley, and all of *NR*'s senior editors, took the written word very seriously, slashing away at grammatical mistakes, sloppy syntax, and typographical errors. "You asked at Stamford last month whether there were things about *NR* I might have noticed from a semi-aloof posture," Burnham once wrote Buckley. There indeed was one: "That *NR* establish an absolute moratorium for an indefinite period on all expressions of the genus 'heh heh heh'; 'Yup'; 'Gr-r-r'; 'Ugh'; 'glug'; e tutti quanti. Gr-r-r, ugh, glub."[4]

Buckley attempted to go over every issue of the magazine himself, but he could hardly catch all mistakes. He secured more editorial help, but errors inevitably occurred. "It was decided supreme efforts would be made to avoid the howlers that have recently plagued us," reported the minutes of one *NR* editorial conference. Word choices were also extremely important, and could become the subject of extended discussions. "We will avoid even more than at present the use of the word 'egghead,'" Buckley once told *NR*'s staff. "It should be used [only] when the word itself is being lampooned or discussed."[5]

But *National Review* tried to keep the atmosphere from becoming overly grim and solemn; the staff wanted to have some fun at the office, and most had a quick and (often) razor-sharp sense of humor. The editors would bet on the outcome of elections and loved to turn their biting wit against their liberal opponents; James Burnham once referred to a major liberal organization as "the Center for the Destruction of Democratic Institutions." But more often, *NR* editors laughed at themselves. It relieved tensions and reminded that despite occasional differences all within the magazine were striving for the same ends. Once, in the midst of a major internal debate, with feelings running high and testy memoranda flying back and forth, William F. Rickenbacker floated this parody of the passionate writings of *NR* publisher William Rusher:

> The recent encyclical (*in re discutatione redactorialis*) strikes me as a genuinely acceptable effort to regain a modicum of viability vis-a-vis the not uncommon *zeitgeist* of our times. Whether the Republican Party can, or indeed will, stir itself to this new challenge, itself a further degradation that was first touched upon by Bill Rusher in his bull of November 16, 1906, *Quid nunc, vacca fusca?* remains to be digested. I cite in this connection, particularly, Plessy v. Ferguson, Marbury v. Maryland, and the Rule in Shelley's Case (Everyman edition). This should not allow us unseemly confidence in the essential outcome, whether or no the tangential issues arise in the earlier question. Here our guide must be Meyer v. Schlamm (ed. Kendall). That I should be moved to break my long silence in this regard should come as no surprise to those who have followed the long and at times intricate controversy that has surrounded this fretted question.[6]

Frank Meyer's most important contribution to *National Review* remained his editing of its book section. To be sure, his wife Elsie gave him invaluable help, for she was an excellent stylist and wordsmith; she edited copy, improved its flow, and corrected its grammar—something not widely known outside the magazine. Elsie preferred it that way. She "carried her intelligence and knowledge (which were formidable) very lightly . . . [and] she tended to keep in the background of any conversation, interrupting only occasionally," remembered Rusher. "She left the entire 'play,' so to speak, to Frank, who talked loudly and extensively and authoritatively."[7]

Putting together *NR*'s book review section was difficult. For one thing, it contained more than just book reviews. The section's title was officially "Books, Arts, and Manners," and featured reviews of movies, plays, music, television, sports, show business, and social trends. Meyer maintained a wide and varied collection of reviewers; fretted about the proper balance of topics and subjects; soothed bruised egos and fragile temperaments; prodded tardy authors; and often cut and pruned their copy to fit *NR*'s space limitations, thus risking the wrath of touchy reviewers all over again. And if the section did not live up to *NR*'s high expectations, Meyer could count on hearing from his editor in chief. On one occasion, Buckley told Meyer frankly that the previous section

had not been particularly good. Meyer had to agree. "On the last book section: you are right; it was a lousy one," he admitted. "There are always a few
lemons among the reviews I get, and generally I try to hide them in good
sections, but once in a while, through a series of accidents, I end up with a
real wastebasket issue. . . . The answer is to try a) not to get lousy reviews and
b) if once in a while you have one and have to run it for one reason or
another, to conceal it in a good issue."[8]

Some of Meyer's reviewers could be extremely sensitive. A writer once
sent his review accompanied with a note, stating in no uncertain terms that he
wanted it in no way edited or cut. He scolded Meyer to be more careful in
the future of his reviewers' "feelings." With a sigh, Meyer attempted to heal all
wounds, while keeping editorial control over his department. "I am afraid... that
my editorial necessities make it just about impossible for me to accept your
conditions," he replied. "I never can know until I sit down to organizing and
editing a given issue whether it will be necessary to cut a piece . . . [and] as a
matter of fact I do not know until just about the time I am working on any
issue how many pages I will have; but, more importantly, I have to try to get a
proper balance of subjects, etc. into an issue, and, unfortunately, one or more
pieces may have to be cut to achieve that." Privately, Meyer got sick and tired
of these temperamental authors and their fragile psyches. "He is getting insuf-
ferable," Meyer told Buckley concerning the previous reviewer. "Besides,
while I did not say it in the letter, I have always to squeeze the pomposity and
verbosity out of his reviews before using them, or *they* would be insuffer-
able."[9]

He had the most difficulty with authors from the academic world. Their
writing tended to be dry and heavy and therefore required a great deal of
stylistic editing. It was frustrating, especially since such pieces came from friends
of *NR* eager to help the cause of the magazine. It required all of Meyer's
diplomatic skills to remain on good relations with such academic conservatives. "I have received a review," Meyer once told Buckley of copy from a
conservative college professor, "which is simply impossible for an American
audience. After consulting with Brent [Bozell] and Willmoore [Kendall], I
am returning it to him, saying I very much want him to review for us but have
hesitated because he has not been considering his audience, tried to explain
what I mean, and have asked him to re-do the review."[10]

There was also the problem of reviewing books written either by friends of the magazine or by someone close to the editor in chief. Meyer tried to assign these reviews to those likely to admire the books; but if it was critical of the work in question, Meyer never published it without first carefully going over it himself and then consulting with Buckley. Negative reviews could lead to hurt feelings and personal ruptures, and in these years *NR* could not afford to lose any allies. Once, Meyer received an unfavorable analysis of a volume written by Buckley friend and adviser Hugh Kenner. "Can we run it without creating a personal crisis?" Meyer asked. "If you think we can't, I don't know where we will get a reviewer more likely to be sympathetic and knowledgeable . . . but I will try." Fortunately, Buckley was almost always supportive and understanding. "I know just what trouble you are having with him," Buckley wrote Meyer of the professor with the difficult prose style, "and suggest only Brent [Bozell] can get it through [the professor's] thick head that we are not a journal of metaphysics." In the case of Hugh Kenner, Buckley told Meyer to go ahead and run the review; he would "square it with Hugh."[11]

On the whole, Meyer's reviewers did not consider him a difficult or demanding editor; he acted more as a mentor and friend who edited their submissions for style and clarity, but almost never for content. Nor did he try to indoctrinate or "conservatize" them.

Guy Davenport began reviewing for *National Review* in the early 1960s. He was a young writer just out of graduate school, largely apolitical, who considered himself a conservative "only in the broadest sense," and whom Meyer accepted as a reviewer only because of Hugh Kenner's recommendation. Yet the two became fast friends, talking for hours on the telephone about history, literature, and the classics (instead of politics). Meyer consulted him on the reading curriculum he should use in educating his two sons. In return, Davenport received the advice of "an editor who was a wise counselor and teacher. I learned from Frank how to review—I'd never done it before." Davenport mainly reviewed fiction for *NR*, and Meyer's rare cuts were only to remove Davenport's occasional off-color references. "*NR* is a *family* magazine," Meyer would say. Meyer eventually gave him the task of writing "Random Notes"—a department in the book section of news from the entertainment world. Davenport protested that he knew nothing about show business.

"Just the man we're after," both Buckley and Meyer replied; and, armed with subscriptions to *Variety* and *Publisher's Weekly,* Davenport learned by doing.[12]

National Review was now an established fact, a factor in Republican circles. It had a growing cadre of dedicated subscribers, as well as a committed group of senior editors, staff, writers, and reviewers; and it was developing its own culture, its own ambiance. But it was 1964, and important events were taking place that would test *NR.* They would challenge the journal's conception of itself and tax the will and the commitment of many who had dedicated themselves to the *National Review* enterprise.

MAJOR DECISIONS CONCERNING the direction of editorial policy were not taken lightly at *National Review.* There was a process for making such decisions, and, besides Buckley and Meyer, several other important persons were involved. Their backgrounds show how the rise of the American conservative movement—with all its strains and divisions—was encapsulated within *NR.*

William A. Rusher, *NR*'s publisher, tracked all aspects of the magazine's financial situation and had the prerogatives of a senior editor, including full participation in all major editorial conferences. Rusher was an articulate, be-spectacled, charming man who enjoyed good wine and conversation and hated red ink and office disorder. He was born in Chicago in 1923, lived for a time with his parents in Kansas, and then moved with them to New York at the age of seven. He was an officer in the Air Corps during World War II, afterward attending Harvard Law School, from which he graduated in 1948 and settled in New York City as an associate of a respected Wall Street law firm. He was, through the early 1950s, a moderate Republican of the Thomas Dewey variety, an internationalist and cold warrior in foreign policy but resigned to New Deal domestic reforms.

By 1957 Rusher's views had changed, and the evolution of his thinking gives a glimpse of how the rise of the conservative intellectual movement affected the thinking of individual actors. Rusher was powerfully influenced by several conservative books. He read Friedrich von Hayek's *The Road to Serfdom* and was "duly impressed" with its anti-statist arguments. He pored over Whittaker Chambers's *Witness,* which reinforced and increased Rusher's anticommunism, defining fully for him "the philosophical case against Communism." And he examined Russell Kirk's *The Conservative Mind,* which gave him "a new and deeper understanding" of that for which conservatism stood. Soon, armed with an intellectual (not merely instinctive) conservatism, Rusher discovered that he did not like what he saw in the Eisenhower administration. He disagreed with its treatment of Senator Joseph McCarthy and believed generally that Eisenhower was not doing nearly enough to fight communism at home, thus provoking his "emotional break" with the administration. In 1956 and 1957 Rusher served as associate counsel to the staunchly anticommunist Senate Internal Security Subcommittee, where he helped conduct investigations into the activities of the Communist Party in America, focusing on its attempts to clandestinely penetrate mainstream American life.[13]

But in the summer of 1957, Rusher decided to leave the subcommittee; his boss, Chief Counsel Robert Morris, was moving on, and Rusher chose not to serve under Morris's successor, Jay Sourwine. One afternoon he lunched with Buckley. Rusher knew him somewhat; they had mutual political contacts in Washington, D.C., and Rusher had been a charter subscriber to *National Review*. He hoped that the Buckley family business needed another lawyer. But after only a few minutes, Buckley stunned him by asking him to join *NR* as its publisher. It was one of Buckley's intuitive hiring decisions, which more often than not succeeded brilliantly, as it did here.

Rusher would serve the magazine for more than thirty years. He added a badly needed dose of organization and detail, and he gave *NR* his knowledge of the nuts and bolts of practical Republican Party politics. Rusher became an activist; he was involved with the Young Republicans, with the formation of Young Americans for Freedom, and ultimately was one of the earliest organizers of the Draft Goldwater movement. He would be a strong advocate within the magazine of orthodox Goldwaterite policies—that is, a strictly limited federal government and an active anticommunist foreign policy. He believed that *NR* should involve itself more closely with conservative political organizations and not moderate its views simply to win the support of the "Establishment."

Buckley remembered him as a "jaunty," "serene," self-confident man who could in an instant produce charts and graphs marking the magazine's financial progress (or lack of same). He came to *NR*'s editorial conferences "with his notebook and his clippings, to pour vitriol on the ideologically feeble," Buckley recalled with fond amusement. "His scorn is not alone for those in public life whose activities during the week he finds contemptible, but also for those who lag a bit behind in exhibiting similar scorn." Rusher therefore was often much in tune with Frank Meyer on ideas and issues, and was perhaps Meyer's most important ally on *National Review*'s editorial board.[14]

William F. Rickenbacker had only recently joined *NR*'s senior editors; he, too, was a Meyer confederate. Rickenbacker was born in California in 1928, the adopted son of pilot and World War I hero Captain Eddie Rickenbacker. William attended prep school in North Carolina and then went on to Harvard, graduating with honors. Bill Rickenbacker was truly brilliant, with an incredible range of abilities. He was a prize-winning pianist and a superb linguist, fluent in French, German, and Spanish, and an expert in Russian, Italian, Portuguese, Latin, and Greek. In his spare time, he lettered on Harvard's golf and swimming teams, and (naturally) he became an accomplished pilot.

By the late 1950s, Rickenbacker was a stock market and investment analyst. He had also begun to write, focusing especially on his growing antipathy toward big government. He came to the attention of Buckley and *National Review* in 1960, when he sent the magazine a piece announcing, in his soon-to-be customary elegant, pithy, humorous prose, his refusal to fill out one of the forms contained in the U.S. Census. It asked, among other things, how many toilets you had in your home. Rickenbacker's article skewered this governmental intrusion with relish; Buckley loved the piece, contacted Rickenbacker, and hired him as an *NR* senior editor.

It was yet another of Buckley's instinctive decisions, and Rickenbacker stayed with *NR* throughout most of the decade. He was an excellent writer who took his ideas and his politics seriously yet could also be uproariously funny, especially when poking fun at the stuffy and the self-righteous. He developed generally into a libertarian conservative, which explains his ideological kinship with Frank Meyer.[15]

Not all *NR* editors were Meyer allies. James Burnham became *National Review*'s most important senior editor besides Buckley and was the man Buckley entrusted to make final editorial decisions when he was away. Burnham, by 1964, was a tall, thin, balding, gray-haired man whose thick glasses hid eyes that studied the world coolly and analytically, belying his mischievous humor and sense of irony. Burnham was born in 1905; he graduated with honors from

Princeton University in 1927 and later studied literature and philosophy at Oxford. He had come of age in a tumultuous period in American history, an era of economic depression and social dislocation. It convinced him that capitalism was dying, that Marxism was the wave of the future. Burnham throughout much of the 1930s was a Trotskyist, active in the Socialist Workers Party, editor of the Trotskyist newspaper the *Militant,* and a frequent correspondent with Trotsky himself.

But Burnham was never fully at ease within this movement, one reason why he remained a professor of philosophy at New York University. He was uncomfortable with several of Trotsky's positions, especially his insistence that Stalin's Soviet Union, despite all evidence, remained at root a "workers' state." He also became disenchanted with Trotskyist methods of confronting dissent, the doctrinal purity and expulsion of those who disagreed. Hence he left the movement in 1940 and the very next year wrote an extremely influential book called *The Managerial Revolution,* which argued that bureaucratic managers, from both business and government, were becoming the most influential class in society and formed the core of most governments (challenging Trotsky's belief that the proletarian working class was primary).

From there, the end of World War II and the onset of the global Cold War led Burnham to focus on foreign policy, and he became one of America's leading anticommunist authors. His book *The Struggle for the World* was an important theoretical justification for a hard line against the Soviet Union; and his later works, especially *Containment or Liberation?* (1953), gave ammunition to conservatives battling against what they considered to be the failures of the containment policy. Burnham, who throughout the 1930s and 1940s was a fixture on the New York intellectual scene and a frequent contributor to *Partisan Review*—a man of the Left—was increasingly identified as a conservative, and his 1954 book on communist penetration of the American government, called *The Web of Subversion,* reinforced this perception. When Buckley approached him in 1954 about joining *National Review* as a senior editor, Burnham enthusiastically agreed.

As the magazine established itself, his influence with Buckley steadily grew. Burnham possessed an overwhelming breadth of knowledge, and the editorials and columns he wrote were penetrating and readable. Burnham became Buckley's mentor, counselor, and friend. But to others within *National Review,* he was more an obstacle, a threat. For Burnham was a moderate within *NR* circles (he himself once said that he was on *NR's* "left wing") who contended over and over that conservatives must accept certain "realities." Men such as Rusher, Rickenbacker, and especially Meyer sometimes thought that Burnham was too interested in making *NR* "the right wing of the Establishment" (in Meyer's phrase), in gaining power and influence, and not enough with principles and ideas, with what was right and true. Meyer took a special dislike to Burnham— eagerly attempting to engage him in debate, relentlessly and snidely criticizing him in conversations with other *NR* personnel, even half-seriously suggesting that Burnham might be a CIA plant, placed to make sure that the magazine did not stray far from the country's liberal consensus.[16]

But Burnham was not alone on *NR's* editorial board. He was joined by Buckley's sister Priscilla, who had become *NR's* managing editor. Priscilla Buckley, four years older than her brother Bill, graduated from Smith College in 1943 and went on to become an accomplished journalist. She worked for United Press from 1944 to 1948 and then worked for a stretch at a radio station in South Carolina. She was recruited by the CIA in 1951 and stayed there for the next two years. Then, from 1953 to 1956, she took a long-coveted position as a general assignment reporter in Paris, again for the United Press.

In 1956 her brother asked Priscilla to come work for *National Review.* She was his sister, and Buckley knew he could trust her. But more importantly, Priscilla Buckley was an experienced journalist, and her brother realized that *NR* desperately needed people with real journalism skills. He had "lots of professors but no journalists," he told her. She agreed, and remained with the magazine for over thirty years. She was quiet and somewhat shy, but she had also a quick wit and a talent for writing. And she was extremely efficient and well organized. In her outlook, she found herself agreeing more and more with Burnham. The two shared an office, and their laughter echoed down *NR's* hallways. Without ever formalizing it or even discussing it, they became allies.[17]

The wild card in these political and personal dynamics was often William F. Buckley Jr. himself. No one could ever be absolutely certain where he would stand on a given issue. True, he consulted with Burnham more and more frequently, but none of *NR's* senior editors believed his mind was made up in advance, or that he would not *listen*—that he could not be persuaded. In 1960 Buckley resisted Burnham's entreaties and refused to endorse Richard

Nixon for the presidency in the magazine, accepting the arguments of Rusher and Meyer.

And so *National Review*'s editorial board was a microcosm of American conservatism in the early 1960s—with its personality conflicts, divisions between libertarians and anticommunists, and splits between pragmatists and hard-liners. All these elements came to the surface in 1964.

THE PLACE WHERE MAJOR *National Review* editorial stances were argued, debated, and, ultimately, decided was *NR*'s quarterly editorial meetings. These, begun shortly after the founding of the magazine, filled the need occasionally to rethink *NR*'s positions and policies, and came from Buckley's desire that all of the journal's senior editors feel involved in its direction.

By 1964 these gatherings had become legendary within the magazine. For one thing, they were not known as "conferences" or "meetings"; Buckley originally called them "agonized reappraisals," borrowed from Secretary of State John Foster Dulles's statements on foreign policy. William Rusher shortened it to "Agony," and the name stuck. It was also appropriate. They could be interminably long, with each editor vying for his position. "In the beginning," Rusher remembered, "we all tended to take these get-togethers very seriously. . . . [T]hey rather reminded me of meetings of the German General Staff!"[18]

Originally, Buckley wanted only one or two Agonies per year. But by 1960 Meyer, Rusher, and Rickenbacker pressed for more to offset Burnham's influence on Buckley. "The quarterly conference came about because Frank and Bill Rusher and I felt a need to combine our forces to hold the line against JB," Rickenbacker recalled. "With only one meeting a year, we could be picked off one by one during JB's constant talks with WFB. We decided to . . . let Bill see that JB's opposition on the board was organized and not inconsiderable."[19]

The Agonies were held either at the Buckleys' home in Stamford, Connecticut, or at their apartment in New York City. Present would be editor-in-chief Buckley, editors Burnham, Meyer, Rickenbacker, and Rusher, and managing editor Priscilla Buckley. Proceedings always began with a "most agreeable" dinner prepared by Buckley's wife, Pat. Then it was on to business. First, they went over the minutes of the last Agony and discussed the effects of past decisions. Rusher would then report on the finances of *National Review*, followed by Priscilla Buckley, who gave a rundown on *NR*'s current staff. Once or twice a year *NR*'s masthead was discussed; should anyone be invited to join? Be dropped? And the editors almost always analyzed the outward appearance of *National Review*—its cover, typeface, and so on.[20]

Finally, the editors would debate the direction of editorial policy and content. And here the real arguments occurred. Sometimes the controversy arose over what stance *NR* should take on elections, or how much support should be given to a particular candidate, party, or organization; often the most difficult debates were over whether *NR* should criticize, or completely break with, any of its comrades on the Right. Usually it was Meyer who led the charge, directing his ire frequently at Burnham. The two men simply had different approaches to politics, which first surfaced in their disagreements over the proper Western reaction to the Soviet invasion of Hungary in 1956, and which intensified in their separate views concerning *NR*'s position in the election of 1960.

Burnham avoided discussions of philosophy or ideology, preferring to focus on specific events, on identifiable trends in politics and foreign policy and how *NR* might concretely influence them. Meyer, who sought to discuss conservative principles and how the magazine could advance them, suspected that his opponent was refusing to debate fundamentals, which he saw as cynical and dishonest. This was exacerbated by Burnham's stoic, imperturbable demeanor, so alien to the excitable Meyer. "It was at some of these meetings that Frank would occasionally let loose in a frenzy of heated oratory," Priscilla Buckley related, "often directed at Jim Burnham, whose patrician cool could get to him in a second flat." Meyer would sometimes jump out of his chair in frustration. "In the editorial conferences the arguments between Frank and Jim grew so hot that I sometimes thought Frank would leap up and grab Jim by the throat and try to break his neck," remembered an amused Rickenbacker.[21]

Sometimes Burnham, who had a real sense of humor, and some talent for mischief, could not resist adding fuel to the fire. "Jim knew exactly how to get Frank's goat," Rusher recalled, "which was to suggest that the book reviews were too long.... This suggestion that he didn't know what he was doing, and that the reviews were less than the very best, predictably infuriated Frank."[22]

On at least one occasion, the editor in chief intervened with an ultimatum. Priscilla Buckley related that "I do remember Bill once calling Frank to order and demanding that he apologize to Jim B. or, it was implied but not said, resign, since one couldn't say certain things about a colleague, attribute dishonesty to him, and still continue to work with him." But episodes such as these were few, and Agonies rarely produced lasting, permanent damage. Both Buckleys worked very hard to keep the magazine's editorial team together, knowing that what could sink the *NR* enterprise would be a public breakup among its senior editors. Both stressed again and again, privately and during Agonies, that all within *National Review* were on the same side. The editor in chief would talk to Meyer on the day after a fiery meeting and remind him of this; by then, Buckley remembered, he could "be induced to look at [the previous day's] exchanges appropriately."[23]

But the underlying tensions within *NR* could not be banished so easily, and all knew it. Burnham thought that part of the problem lay in personality conflicts, and that perhaps he needed to do more to alleviate them. "I have not done enough to woo Bill [Rickenbacker]," he once told Buckley, "but I am not much of a wooer." He also believed that Meyer added to office difficulties; when a rift developed between Burnham and Rickenbacker in the early 1960s, he wrote Buckley that "Frank joins in a bit, partly for the sheer joy of the intrigue and because he feels he has a spiritual pupil [in Rickenbacker]." But Burnham mainly argued that *NR*'s internal divisions concerned differences over the overall direction and conception of the magazine. What sort of a journal should *National Review* be? What should be its primary goals? What should it *do*? Burnham had definite ideas on this, and he tried periodically to articulate them to Buckley in order to bring him around to his point of view.

> It is of course [Burnham wrote Buckley] a fact that there are differences of opinion on policy and the correlated question of rhetoric. These emerge on this or that topic, but from the point of view of running a magazine it has occurred to me that the main difference may be this. . . . Priscilla and I take a more professional point of view toward *NR*. We want simply to have the best magazine in the world, assuming a (not too sharply defined) conservative and anti-communist point of view. Frank, Bill Rusher and Bill Rickenbacker also want a good magazine, of course, but they first of all want a crusade, a political party and a kind of ersatz church, and they want

NR itself to be all these things or at least organically and intimately a part of all three, rather than a magazine-as-magazine which would have a certain aloofness from crusades, parties and churches even if it altogether agreed with them.[24]

As an ex-communist, Meyer was accustomed to internal battles and faction fights, and occasionally he could not resist engaging in plots, counterplots, and various small conspiracies against the man he sometimes called "the Enemy." "Frank, you must realize, was always a conspirator," recalled Meyer's friend Ralph de Toledano, "perhaps instinctively or because of his long years in the Party where conspiracy and throat-cutting were pandemic."[25]

But as time went on, though Meyer's opinions did not change, his actions did. He adjusted himself to the realities of *National Review*. For example, when Burnham and Rickenbacker had their office rift—Buckley was in Switzerland skiing and writing—tensions grew high, and there seemed to be no one there to defuse them. In stepped Frank Meyer. He took the unusual step of going to *NR*'s headquarters, where he had a series of somber, intense conversations with his protégé Rickenbacker. "I think—at least I hope, with considerable reason—that the WFR side of the problem disturbing you is under control," he wrote Buckley. "I had a very serious talk with him . . . and I am pretty certain that I got across to him what he should do." Meyer could not, of course, simply leave it at that; he went on to complain that "from my own experience, I [know that] JB can be provocative himself." But the main difficulty, Meyer thought, was Rickenbacker's "indirect approach," and so Meyer told him "that it would be much better to raise frankly such questions with Jim on a colleaguely basis."[26]

Meyer would increasingly take on this role, trying to defuse conflicts, to mediate between warring individuals on the Right—which fitted, after all, with his goal of developing a conservative philosophy to which all on the Right could adhere. But it was also true that Meyer—and Rickenbacker, and Rusher—were trying to advance their political commitments to Goldwater and to the Conservative Party, which was bound to clash with the Burnham faction. But what else could someone like Frank Meyer do? His politics were an outgrowth of his ideas and principles, which he passionately held.

ON JANUARY 2, 1964, Barry Goldwater finally made it official, formally announcing his candidacy for the presidency of the United States. *National Review's*
favorite politician was in the race.

To an extent, Goldwater's conservatism stemmed from his upbringing, from
Arizona's open spaces and individualistic traditions, and from his parents, who
preached the virtues of individualism and patriotism. And Goldwater spent much
of his early life as a practicing capitalist, owning a thriving business in Phoenix.

But he was also familiar with the seminal works of the postwar conservative intellectual renaissance—Hayek's *Road to Serfdom* and Kirk's *Conservative
Mind.* And he knew of *NR* from the moment it was founded, writing that the
magazine "burst on us like a spring shower, proclaiming that the liberals were all
wet." By the early 1960s, *NR* was the leading intellectual journal of the Republican Right, and Goldwater its prime political figure. It was William Rusher who
gave Goldwater one of his first significant breaks, asking him in 1955 to speak to
New York state's Young Republican organization, after which he began to receive national attention. L. Brent Bozell for several years was close to Goldwater's
staff, penning for Goldwater his best-selling book, *The Conscience of a Conservative.* And in 1961, Rusher was a founding member of the Draft Goldwater Committee, which worked within the Republican Party to round up delegates to the
1964 GOP convention, hoping to persuade Goldwater to run for the nomination.[27]

It may even have been an attack against the *National Review* Right by an
"Establishment" politician that helped convince Goldwater to run in 1964. By
the summer of 1963, Nelson Rockefeller, a liberal, was gearing up his own
campaign for the GOP nomination. Recognizing the growing power of conservatives, he occasionally attempted to woo them. But, having generally failed,
Rockefeller went on the attack. He made an angry, well-publicized speech that
targeted the GOP's "radical right," claiming that the Republican Party faced
danger from these "extremist elements" who indulged in "threatening letters,
smear and hate literature, strong-arm and goon tactics, bomb threats and bombings, [and the] infiltration and takeover of established political organizations by
Communist and Nazi methods."[28]

Rockefeller's verbal assault could only be interpreted as a direct blast, not
against the "radical right," but against Republican conservatives—against the
National Review Right, the Goldwater Right. The Conservative Party's J. Daniel
Mahoney remembered it as a "flame-throwing attack," an "all-out assault" on

the GOP conservative wing. Goldwater recalled being "shocked and sad-
dened" by Rockefeller's speech. *National Review* struck back especially hard;
in a lengthy editorial, the magazine labeled the governor's comments "preposterous . . . , hysterical accusations." Conservatives were more determined
than ever to fight against Rockefeller for control of the party—and so was
Goldwater.[29]

Now it was 1964, and Goldwater was running for president. Frank Meyer
was delighted. He had admired the senator for some time and recognized
him as the Right's leading presidential candidate. But as the 1964 election
neared, Meyer tried to be cautious. The conservative movement, he told his
NR readers, "looks toward nothing less than a deep-going renewal of American life in the spirit of the Western and American tradition—a renewal at
every level of existence." Such a rejuvenation "cannot be attained by a political victory alone"; it would be "utopian" to believe that. Conservatives should
not expect Goldwater "to stand in splendid purity as champion of the whole
sweep of conscious American conservatism." Goldwater's job was, rather, to
build a "consensus" united by "instinct" and "broad belief."

Some of Meyer's readers must have been scratching their heads. Was not
this the same columnist who had urged conservatives not to support the candidacies of Dwight Eisenhower and Richard Nixon because they were not
"pure" enough? But Meyer anticipated the objection, something he was increasingly more adept at doing (the sign of a good debater). He had not
opposed Eisenhower and Nixon because of a lack of "purity," Meyer contended, but "because nothing in their campaigns showed a determination to
reverse the general trend in American politics. That Barry Goldwater has
shown and continues to show."[30]

Besides, Meyer could never support Lyndon Johnson, who had taken
over as president following the tragic assassination of John F. Kennedy. In his
first days and weeks as president Johnson established task forces to craft federal legislation for conducting a "War on Poverty," and in foreign policy Johnson
continued, wrote Meyer, to "reject victory over the enemy as a national goal,
filling the void with bombastic and empty talk of 'peace' when there is no
peace."[31]

But a number of people in *National Review* had serious doubts about
Barry Goldwater's viability and effectiveness as a presidential candidate. James

Burnham more than a year before the election had worried about the John Birch Society's effect on the incipient Goldwater campaign, and he had questioned whether the Arizona senator had the political sophistication to handle such a problem. "To win an election in this country you do have to make inroads into the moderates and the Center; and the extremist tactical behavior (not necessarily Birchite) does repel the Center," Burnham wrote. "And it is a fact that—more and more, indeed—the extreme Right is active in 'the Goldwater movement.' According to the classical laws of strategy, Goldwater should now take the Right (as a whole) for granted, and go after the Center." Buckley increasingly sympathized with this view. He worried how effective Goldwater would be on the stump, questioned the efficiency and cohesiveness of his political organization, and after the assassination of President Kennedy doubted whether Americans would be willing to see the presidency change hands yet again.[32]

Indeed, Buckley mentioned to Meyer as early as winter 1963 that Goldwater was "perhaps not . . . our man." Meyer did his best to counter the skepticism and misgivings of his fellow editor. "As to your remark about his perhaps 'not being our man,'" Meyer wrote Buckley, "the only *firm* response I can make is: he's the only man we've got. I think it is vital to find a center around which to consolidate political conservatism. I do think, too, that there is a chance of winning . . . with him, and very little chance with anyone else."[33]

As Goldwater officially announced his candidacy and the 1964 political season opened, these misgivings were about to emerge into the open.

NATIONAL REVIEW'S OFFICIAL position toward Goldwater's candidacy—Burnham and Buckley's position—quickly became clear. *NR* would support Goldwater, but would keep a certain distance, thereby retaining its objectivity. A January 1964 editorial said that *NR* "will never be mistaken for a campaign organ which, quite understandably, strains all news involving its candidate through a sort of euphoric dye." The journal's stance would be "as enthusiastic endorsers of Mr. Goldwater's candidacy; as independent evaluators of his statements and his campaign; and as objective analysts of his chances."[34]

Neither Rusher, Rickenbacker, nor Meyer was pleased with the magazine's position. An Agony was coming up, and Rusher and Meyer demanded clarification on *NR*'s stand. Just what did being "objective analysts" mean? "Of course, we should be objective—that is, honest," Meyer told the other editors. "But objectivity (or honesty) taken by itself can hardly define exhaustively the position of *NR*. Rather, I would propose . . . a phrase signifying our commitment—e.g., objective—but committed to the conservative cause, not neutralist."[35]

This led to a stormy Agony, at which Rusher, Rickenbacker, and Meyer urged *National Review* to be more direct in its support of Goldwater, while Burnham and Priscilla Buckley argued for supporting him, yes, but for keeping a certain distance; they "felt rather strongly that *NR* shouldn't commit itself totally to one candidate prematurely or endorse him one-hundred percent for better or for worst. We felt that that would narrow our options unduly," recalled Priscilla Buckley. The editor in chief as always allowed both sides to have their say, but in the end ruled that the magazine's viewpoint would remain. But soon he would leave for Switzerland, and without his strong presence and guiding hand, the internal debate would continue.[36]

Shortly after Buckley left, Burnham became uneasy with the way things at *NR* were proceeding. Buckley, for instance, assigned senior editor William F. Rickenbacker to write a special feature for each edition of *NR* during the 1964 election year. It was called "Focus on November 3," and was to be a column of news, notes, and analysis concerning the ongoing presidential campaign. But Burnham thought Rickenbacker's columns read like Republican "public relation handouts"; and he was troubled by other columns and editorials in the magazine that seemed to tout Goldwater. Burnham argued that most within *NR* knew "that Goldwater is a second-rate person; and he seems to be surrounded by third- and fourth-rate persons. . . . [H]owever unlofty, he is the best of the available bunch. But I can't see why we shouldn't be sharper and more critical of his organization and the conduct of the campaign from both a policy and a technical point of view. And I don't really believe this would in the least injure him practically; it might well help."[37]

The presidential primary in New Hampshire proved to be an especially thorny problem for *National Review*. Goldwater had not performed well on the campaign trail, making off-the-cuff comments that seemed to advocate the use of tactical nuclear weapons on the battlefield. Burnham wanted to map out *NR*'s response to all the different scenarios possible in New Hampshire. If Goldwater won a comfortable victory in the primary, Burnham suggested that *NR* reemphasize its support; if he won only a plurality, *NR* should continue to express cautious optimism, but also propose ways to improve the campaign; if Goldwater should lose, *NR* should stress that, while the senator was certainly not out of the race, important local and congressional elections needed attention and support, and in any case "the function of conservatives and the conservative movement is continuing, and not limited to electing this or that candidate."[38]

Both Meyer and Rickenbacker strongly opposed such a view. To them, Goldwater was their, and *NR*'s, candidate; the Right must continue to support him regardless of the outcome in New Hampshire. "Our reaction to the primary should, I think, combine analytical objectivity with support of our candidate," Meyer told his fellow editors. "We should take cognizance of the distorted analysis in the press barrage which has been directed to reading BG out of the race ever since the assassination." William Rickenbacker went further. "New Hampshire is a battle, but not the war," he told *NR*'s editors in a lengthy memorandum. "I will pin my hopes on Goldwater no matter what happens in New Hampshire. . . . We are willing, I take it, ultimately to sacrifice our lives in the cause of Christian civilization; we should be no less willing to dedicate our magazine to the only major public figure who proclaims our own beliefs. . . . My grandchildren would thank me for doing nothing less."[39]

When the voting in New Hampshire was finally completed, *NR*'s worst fears were realized. Goldwater not only lost the primary, but lost it to a write-in candidate—Henry Cabot Lodge. Goldwater received only 23 percent of the vote. A discouraged Buckley put his crystallizing views on paper in a long memorandum to *NR*'s editors. He was not suggesting (yet) that *NR* withdraw its support from Goldwater. "It is a grave wrong, moral and strategic, to let Goldwater down in any way, now that we have him running for president," Buckley told them. But at the same time it would be "a grave, perhaps graver wrong, strategically and morally, not to leave ourselves the room to say . . . that the community must not despair of the possibility of nominating and electing a conservative in the years to come merely by the experience of Barry Goldwater back in 1964—*who after all, did not really have his heart in the campaign, and was not as well qualified to run or serve as* (fill in the New Hero)."[40]

And so *National Review* editorials continued to reflect Burnham's (and now Buckley's) general outlook. But the Meyer-Rusher-Rickenbacker faction was also heeded. "We are for Barry Goldwater, yesterday, today and tomorrow," the post–New Hampshire editorial declared; "we are for his nomination as the Republican candidate, and for his defeat of the Democratic candidate." Besides, despite his defeat, Goldwater still garnered more votes than did Nelson Rockefeller. The New York governor's quest for the GOP nomination was "crushed."[41]

Even when Goldwater's political fortunes improved, *NR* said that his victories could be "pyrrhic" and "hollow" come November. And it never played any role in the official Goldwater campaign, although a few individuals made a stab in that direction. In the fall of 1963, Buckley and L. Brent Bozell approached several key members of the Goldwater campaign staff and suggested that the two men organize a committee of conservative intellectuals and college professors in support of Goldwater in order to show that Goldwater, too, had intellectual support. The staffers were impassive and noncommittal; but soon, a *New York Times* story detailed how the campaign had repelled a "boarding party" led by Buckley and Bozell. The piece was probably leaked by close Goldwater adviser William Baroody of the American Enterprise Institute, who feared losing power and influence and anyway believed that *National Review*'s reputation as "extremist" would hurt the campaign. Both Buckley and Bozell were offended by the intended slur; and by the time Goldwater understood what had happened, he could do nothing to repair the damage.[42]

In the meantime, Meyer continued to sound the Goldwater trumpet in his *NR* columns, devoting nearly all of them to analyses of the senator's campaign and its meaning. He followed the election closely, compiling stacks of campaign news and election data for use in his writings. In April, he wrote triumphantly that "any detailed state-by-state analysis of delegate strength shows Goldwater not only the leading candidate, but overwhelmingly the leading candidate." Despite the attempt of some liberal Republicans to form a Stop Goldwater movement, such a drive was getting nowhere. "As things stand now," Meyer chortled, "it is the forces of the Liberal cabal, not of Goldwater, that are in disarray."[43]

In May, Meyer the columnist continued as political analyst and prognosticator, asserting that Goldwater was a proven vote-getter—he had gained more total votes in all Republican primaries combined than any other candidate. Furthermore, Goldwater could win in November against Lyndon Johnson. To do so, he must "expose the confusions and the contradictions of the Johnson Administration: the effort to pose both as the symbol of prosperity and as the savior of the country from abject poverty; the double-faced stance of wooing the South and wooing the Negro revolution, with its effective encouragement of both sides to violence." And his allies at *NR* agreed.[44]

At this point, Nelson Rockefeller came back with a vengeance, posting a huge victory over Goldwater in the Oregon primary and enjoying a huge lead in the polls prior to the primary in California. Thus, at an *NR* editorial conference in late May, Buckley suddenly announced that, should Goldwater lose in California, *National Review* should call on him to withdraw immediately from the race in order to avoid a devastating, embarrassing defeat at the Republican convention—a defeat that would harm not only Goldwater, but the entire conservative movement. And in his newspaper columns Buckley, while defending Goldwater's policy positions, bluntly said of the senator's chances in 1964: "This is probably Lyndon Johnson's year . . . and the Archangel Gabriel running on the Republican ticket probably couldn't win."[45]

This set the stage for another crisis, a big one. As the California primary approached, Rusher prepared his resignation from *National Review* should Goldwater lose. And given their like views, Meyer and Rickenbacker might easily have followed suit. *National Review's* future hung in the balance.[46]

Fortunately, Goldwater won the California primary; his nomination was now virtually assured, and everyone at *NR* united behind him. Frank Meyer meanwhile wrote to the editorial board on Goldwater's chances of winning in November. Despite the fact that his candidate trailed Johnson by over forty points in the polls, Meyer truly believed Goldwater could win, and thus indirectly chided Buckley for his negativity (as William Rusher did in another memo). The situation was "dynamic," Meyer told his fellow editors. "As is so often the case in political matters, prediction by an active participant can itself be a factor in the outcome . . . [and] whether Goldwater defeats Johnson or not partly depends on subjective factors . . . [including] the enthusiasm, capability and skill of the Goldwater supporters. *NR* can play an enormous role [here]."[47]

On Wednesday night, July 15, Barry Goldwater was nominated for president on the first ballot by the Republican National Convention, receiving 883 votes. And Frank Meyer, listening back home in Woodstock by radio (he as yet owned no television), must have felt a special gladness—so many had called conservatives like him "extremist" and had laughed at the idea of Goldwater being nominated by a major party. Now it was happening, with the whole nation listening and watching. Yes, conservatism had made it at last. It was part of "the mainstream."[48]

BEFORE FOCUSING ON the fall campaign, Meyer wanted to bask in Goldwater's triumph a bit more—and, not coincidentally, direct some fire yet again upon the "Establishment" that had earlier scorned conservative chances in 1964.

Meyer spoke with disdain of establishment media figures, who had been outraged "that anyone would dare to ignore their acceptable list of truths and appeal directly to the sentiments of the American people." Now they maintained that Goldwater could not defeat President Johnson. But Meyer was confident of the quiet conservative majority abroad in the land, which had finally found a leader. Barry Goldwater's beliefs, Meyer contended, represented "the fundamental American commitment to limited government, individual freedom and individual initiative, prosperity based on productivity and untrammeled by bureaucratic governmental power, and a firm policy against dangers from abroad." As the Goldwater campaign said, the American people would finally have "a choice, not an echo."[49]

Meyer was in fact a bit giddy during the late summer of 1964, positively euphoric about Goldwater's prospects. In August he informed his NR readers of a scenario that could give the Republicans a smashing victory in November. Although Goldwater would lose eastern industrial states such as New York, Pennsylvania, and Massachusetts, Meyer argued that the GOP could claim much of the Midwest, the Rocky Mountain states, the Southwest, and the South. If Goldwater could somehow pull off an upset in either Texas or California, he would win. And "should Goldwater penetrate the East also," an exhilarated Meyer wrote, "he could well win in a landslide."[50]

But soon Meyer came back to earth. Goldwater was a mediocre campaigner. Worse, on the night of his acceptance speech he fell right into the hands of his enemies by uttering the now-famous lines: "I would remind you that extremism in the defense of liberty is no vice! And let me remind you also that moderation in the pursuit of justice is no virtue!" His words allowed the Democrats, and the national media, to portray Goldwater as an extremist, as a candidate outside the national consensus. Goldwater was put on the defensive for the entire campaign, accused of wanting to destroy Social Security and of advocating the casual use of nuclear weapons; Senator Fulbright of Arkansas compared him to Stalin, civil rights leader Martin Luther King and California Governor Edmund G. Brown linked him to Hitler, and labor leader Walter Reuther claimed that "Goldwater is crazy—he needs a psychiatrist." Goldwater appeared certain to go down to defeat.[51]

By October 1964 Meyer was much less optimistic, but he remained defiant. President Johnson's campaign, he noted, was based on one theme: that "conservatism is outside the national consensus," was a form of "extremism." And "this campaign is having its effects." Meyer believed that most American voters were confused. In the past, despite their "deepest beliefs," they had always accepted the "liberal consensus." But the 1964 election had "precipitated a conflict approaching the traumatic, between deeply-held beliefs and a confused sense of shame before the ridicule of the 'sophisticated' organs of opinion." But a "massive undecided vote . . . , the most significant aspect of the campaign" was still out there. It was conservatives' last hope.

In any case, Meyer—here sounding resigned to defeat—emphasized that the American Right had done something important, regardless of the outcome of the election. "Conservative principles have been put forward," Meyer declared, "on the highest political level. . . . The myth of an over-all American Liberal consensus . . . will have been once and for all destroyed by the millions who vote for Barry Goldwater."[52]

The last weeks of the campaign were difficult for *National Review,* and indeed for all conservatives, many of whom had worked so hard for Goldwater, only to watch as he went down to a defeat of landslide proportions. But they vowed to continue the struggle. At an editorial Agony in late September, *NR's* editors resolved "to make [a] special effort in November and December to keep *NR* bright and sassy and relevant." One of Meyer's friends from California, a Goldwater precinct captain during the primary election in June, wrote in early October that "If Our Man loses, I hope he has a good rousing We-Have-Just-Begun-to-Fight speech for the morning of November 4th. Something like 'If Lyndon is in, it's going to take every one of us conservatives to keep this country afloat until 1966 and 1968.' . . . There's an awful lot of Democrats and damn fools out here in California."[53]

On November 3, 1964, Lyndon Johnson was elected president of the United States. He won 61 percent of the votes, compared to Goldwater's 38 percent, and

482 electoral votes to Goldwater's 52. But a few days later *NR* editorial assistant Arlene Croce reported to the editors that "election commentary [is] rolling in by the pound, [and] very many readers [are] expressing appreciation for *NR*'s service to the campaign."[54]

THE TIME HAD COME for conservatives to analyze what had gone wrong, to ponder what the American Right should do next. Frank Meyer, in his column, ruminated on the state of conservatism after such a disaster. What did the election prove? First, it showed that "the mass-communications network, solidly in Liberal hands, is even more formidable an opponent than conservatives had thought." Second, and more important, the election proved "that conservatives have not yet learned how to translate the principles for which they stand into concrete issues that can seize the imagination of decisive sections of the voters." And third, the Right must refute "the Liberal attack on conservatism as a radical tearing down of established institutions," as well as the Left's contention that its foreign policy was "trigger-happy." There was much for conservatives to do.

Meyer decisively rejected the notion that the 1964 election was a "repudiation" of conservatism. After all, Goldwater had still garnered over twenty-six million votes. In addition, Meyer said, the campaign energized thousands of devoted Goldwater volunteers, who would in the future be "a powerful force of committed conservatives as the decisive sector of Republican campaign workers." The election guaranteed that the Republican Party "has become a party which will in practice, outside of a few constituencies, function as a conservative party or will not function at all." Finally, Meyer reminded his readers, "Nothing that occurred demonstrated anything wrong or weak—morally or philosophically or logically—in the conservative position," he declared. This was the first chance the Right had had "to confute thirty years of Liberal indoctrination." There would be more chances; conservatives must stand firm, must not "weaken" their positions, must feed the "energies" released by the 1964 campaign. Indeed, to Frank Meyer and other conservatives, the fight had only just begun.[55]

In December Meyer expanded on his earlier thoughts. He told conservatives that they must create a conservative program "in depth," demonstrating that their proposals were put forward in the context of "a sober and conservatively restrained program of gradual, phased transformation"; for example, they must stress that given the damage that the Social Security issue had done to Goldwater, "conservative opposition to the unlimited state would not mean the cutting off of every social security check on January 21."

It *was* possible, he emphasized, to be "responsible" and to strongly oppose the Left. Meyer thought he saw a new political champion of such a position—the conservative former actor Ronald Reagan. Barely a month after the defeat of Barry Goldwater, Meyer identified Reagan as a rising conservative star. Meyer thought Reagan's now-famous television address on Goldwater's behalf a week before the election was the perfect model of the "responsible conservatism" he was talking about. Reagan "did not soften his indictment of the Liberal way of life," Meyer noted; rather, "if anything, he toughened the conservative position, but he toughened it with a concrete analysis and a living presentation." Meyer thought that, politically, Mr. Reagan was going places.[56]

IN THE COMING WEEKS and months, Frank Meyer tried to practice what he preached. Did American conservatives lack concrete programs? Then they must find and develop them. Had the conservative position been distorted in 1964? Then the Right must find new ways of communicating its message. Conservatives faced a dilemma, Meyer wrote in *National Review* in early 1965. Conservative proposals lacked "the human appeal of the cry to solve immediate and obvious social problems." Yet conservatism must also adhere to its core axioms—the freedom of the individual person, the morality of limited government. The question, then, was "how real human needs can be met without traducing those principles. . . . Conservatives are not social Darwinians. Nor do they share with the collectivists a Utopian arrogance towards human beings, if only an abstract ideological pattern can be imposed." So what was the answer? It lay, Meyer contended, in the combination of "a free polity" and a "free economy," and the notion that these free institutions could be used to solve problems of human welfare—"to the degree they are soluble," he added.

By early 1965 Meyer had begun to discover concrete examples of conservative social policy alternatives. He wrote, for example, about a man named Richard C. Cornuelle, the director of the Foundation for Voluntary Welfare. It promoted projects such as the United Student Aid Fund, a group of private bankers, businessmen, and administrators that loaned money to college students, thus bypassing government aid. Cornuelle's foundation also planned to use Marion County, Indiana, as a pilot project in utilizing "private resources in an attempt to eliminate hard-core unemployment in that county." Such efforts were "of the greatest importance to the struggle to reclaim a free America founded on voluntary effort," Meyer gushed; they were "a complement to conservative political action."[57]

There was also the continuing problem of the Social Security program, a huge thorn in conservatives' side during the 1964 campaign, and Meyer was determined to address it. The 1964 campaign had apparently proved that Social Security was an enormously popular program with most Americans, and that proposals to make it "voluntary" (as Goldwater suggested) equaled political suicide. Yet how could a conservative be for limited government, if one of its largest programs was "immune" from discussion? Meyer argued that such a position would be untenable—there would "remain no *principled basis* for challenging the usurpation by government bureaucrats of any field of private endeavor."

The size of government *could* be reduced, Meyer emphasized, but only through a discussion of fundamentals. Smaller government "will never take place until the principles of the restriction of government are re-established. So long as any area of illegitimate government action is considered beyond discussion, the principles themselves cannot be clarified." Was Meyer advocating more direct conservative attacks against Social Security? No. Social Security, Meyer maintained, had become too ingrained in American government and society to be "precipitately" changed. But "the principle that insurance for retirement and illness is not a proper function of government remains valid."[58]

Indeed, Meyer's primary task at *National Review,* and as a conservative generally, had always been to define and disseminate conservative ideas. Thus in 1964 he found time to edit and see into print a volume titled *What Is Conservatism?,* dedicated to the memory of Richard Weaver (who had died suddenly early that year), in which he called Weaver a "pioneer and protagonist of the American conservative consensus." And that was what this book was about, that despite the different elements of the Right, a "consensus" could be found.[59]

It was another Meyer attempt to promote his "fusionist" marriage of the traditionalist and libertarian strains of conservatism. The opening essay was a reprint of his 1960 *Modern Age* article called "Freedom, Tradition, Conservatism," in which he showed how freedom and order could be combined into a coherent philosophy, and thus that differences among conservatives were mainly ones of emphasis. The Right could still "maintain a common front and a common struggle."[60]

Meyer also solicited, and received, essays from a number of important intellectual conservatives. Willmoore Kendall contributed his unique and penetrating analysis of the U.S. Constitution. M. Stanton Evans, Wilhelm Röpke, and Friedrich von Hayek explained the libertarian philosophy and how it applied to economics and politics. Fr. Stanley Parry, Stephen Tonsor, and Garry Wills gave the "traditionalist" viewpoint on a number of different topics. And frequent opponent Russell Kirk contributed a brief piece explaining his view of conservatism. Meyer then wrote a conclusion.

Unsurprisingly, he found much on which conservatives agreed—no fewer than six points. First, all agreed on the existence of "an objective moral order," and "immutable standards by which human conduct should be judged." Second, most on the Right accepted that "the human person" is the center of all political and social thought, and that this was true whether the stress be on his freedom or on his responsibilities. (In other words, conservatives did not think in collectivities.) Third, while conservatives disagreed on how much the state should be limited, they still shared "a distaste for the use of the power of the state to enforce ideological patterns upon human beings." Fourth, they all rejected state "planning" of any aspect of human life. Humans were not to be "faceless units," led by "the blueprint of the social engineer." Fifth, conservatives all venerated "the spirit of the Constitution," especially the separation of powers, which kept the state in check. And finally, all had "a devotion to Western civilization and an awareness of the necessity of defending it against the messianic world-conquering intentions of Communism."[61]

What Is Conservatism?, as Meyer noted in its introduction, was funded by a conservative organization called the Intercollegiate Society of Individualists, led by its president, E. Victor Milione. This conservative network continued to provide funds to scholars on the Right. Thus, even with Barry Goldwater's devastating defeat, conservative ideas lived on; and, as the appearance of this book showed, the conservative movement did, too.[62]

But what about politics? If conservative ideas were to be disseminated more effectively, would it not require more and better political organizations, groups, and committees? Meyer and others had thought so for some time. As

early as 1962, Meyer had spoken with William Rusher and conservative pub-
licist Marvin Liebman on the need for some kind of umbrella group that
would increase the influence of the mainstream Right. To his fellow editors at
NR Meyer described it as "the organization of an authoritative leading group
which could speak for American conservatism in the way that the ADA speaks
for liberalism." Meyer wanted its membership to consist of academics, activists, politicians, and members of the *NR* circle. Most crucial, however, was that
all should "have a strong connection with the real problems" and be "decisively overweighted with men deeply committed to a responsible conservatism *per se*."[63]

Thus on December 19, 1964, from a meeting of over thirty conservative
activists and politicians at the Mayflower Hotel in Washington, D.C., the American Conservative Union was founded; Republican Congressman Donald
Bruce of Indiana was chairman, fellow House Republican John Ashbrook
vice-chairman, and *National Review*'s William Rusher head of the Political
Action Committee. Meyer quickly joined the ACU's board of directors, and
he served as its treasurer in 1965 and 1966. Now his telephone contacts included ACU leaders and other board members, and he was often on the
phone with them, discussing the organization's overall strategy, what new
position papers or statements it should issue, and he attended several ACU
board meetings per year. His energy, his devotion, and his skill at practical
politics amazed those who thought of Meyer mainly as *NR*'s "house meta-
physician." "The implication was that [Meyer's] concerns were somewhat
rarefied and impractical," recalled M. Stanton Evans, a close colleague of
Meyer's. "Nothing could be further from the truth. Frank was in fact the most
practical of men—quick to execute his organizational duties, a prod to others
who were laggard in performance, a tireless promoter of conservative agit-
prop." By the early 1970s, the ACU had become an important lobbying agent
for the American Right, with over sixty thousand members. And once again,
Frank Meyer was there.[64]

IF THE WEEKS AND MONTHS following Barry Goldwater's defeat had shown anything, it was that American conservatism had been beaten, but not destroyed;
it had lost a battle, but not the war. Frank Meyer had invested as much time

and emotion in the Goldwater cause as anyone; but in the wake of Goldwater's defeat, he continued on, finding new directions for conservatism, establishing new organizations, discovering new issues. Thus *National Review*'s tenth anniversary banquet in New York City in November 1965 was far from a wake; instead, the celebrants were defiant, glorying in their status as liberalism's opposition, and Frank Meyer more so than most. "Conservatism is no more nor less than devotion to the restoration and renewal of the spirit of Western civilization," he shouted to the assembled throng, with his reading glasses perched perilously on the bridge of his nose (a friend told the listening William Rusher that "this is the largest cell meeting Frank has ever addressed!"). "It is a colossal task. Yet from its very grandeur we may take heart when the tides of power swell against us. What we base ourselves upon runs deeper than those tides. The nature of men, firmly rooted in their creation, belies the construction of the Utopians."[65]

But were there deeper reasons for the defeat of Goldwaterism in 1964? Meyer, Buckley, and others in this period more than once referred to "responsible conservatism." What was responsible conservatism, and how did it differ from the irresponsible variety? Who *were* the irresponsible members of the Right? And what could *National Review* do about them? There were further steps to be taken before the American Right could enter into the "mainstream."

Extremists

IN SEPTEMBER 1961 WILLIAM RUSHER decided to send a lengthy letter to his friend and fellow *National Review* senior editor, L. Brent Bozell. Bozell and his family were still in Spain, where Bozell was working on his book, *The Warren Revolution,* while studying and experiencing his Catholic faith.

Rusher told Bozell that *NR's* circulation was steadily increasing, and that crowds at conservative political events seemed to be growing. But expansion brought problems. For one thing, it cried out for leadership, and Rusher feared that *National Review* was not providing it. Bozell had previously asked Rusher why he delayed in pushing *NR* to take a more direct role in organizing the Right. Rusher explained that *NR's* other senior editors had not yet decided how, or even whether, the magazine should be involved in such things. "If those of us here at *National Review* want to lead the American conservative movement, we will have to get over the idea that it can be done solely by means of well-phrased editorials," he answered. "We will either have to form an organization of our own . . . or we will have to decide to lend our support to somebody else's organization." But "the sentiment in the higher reaches of *National Review* seems to be that, when we want the conservatives of America to organize, we will tell them about it; and that meanwhile they can darned well wait. . . . [But] in all likelihood, they *won't* wait." These were people "frustrated" by their country's plight, convinced America faced

a "desperate situation," and "contemptuous" of the established political parties. They could easily "fall into the hands of men and organizations woefully
unsuited to the responsibility—and with just a little further bad luck, into the
hands of the first really slick demagogue that comes along."

If such a scenario occurred, Rusher worried, *National Review* will "righ-
teously denounce it . . . and will wind up where some of its friends . . . have
always wanted it to wind up: i.e. as a 'respected'—which is to say, harmless—
spokesman for a benign brand of conservative Republicanism." The results
for conservatism would be disastrous. "The conservative movement, bereft of its
only chance of really imaginative leadership, may in these circumstances do better for a time than some of its contemnors suspect," he concluded, "but it cannot,
without *National Review,* do what needs to be done—and there will go the ball-
game."[1]

Rusher's fears were neither theoretical nor groundless. For by 1961 the
conservative movement faced a threat greater, perhaps, than any posed by its
liberal opponents.

Robert welch, by the early 1960s, was a pink-cheeked, white-haired, grandfa-
therly looking man who happened to head one of the fastest-growing political
organizations in America: the John Birch Society. Welch was born in 1899, graduated from the University of North Carolina, and spent two years each at the
United States Naval Academy and Harvard Law School. Eventually he went into
the family business—a candy manufacturing enterprise—where he stayed for
over twenty years, a leader in his community.

But by 1957 the fall from political grace and sudden death of Senator
Joseph McCarthy propelled Welch to devote his life to political work. For he
was convinced that McCarthy had been right: the chief danger to America lay in
communists boring their way into American society from within. Indeed, the
peril was even greater than McCarthy had said. So in 1958, Welch founded the
John Birch Society, named after an American army officer killed in China while
fighting against the Chinese communists.

On the surface all this was rather unremarkable. The John Birch Society at
first was simply one of many anticommunist organizations. But the JBS went
further, much further, than most such groups. The society claimed that communism was penetrating every aspect of American life—into schools, into govern-

ment, into all the nation's major institutions. The society's leading publication, called *American Opinion,* argued that the federal government was coming under the "operational control" of the Communist Party. And astonishingly, in a privately circulated book manuscript, Welch argued that a close analysis of President Eisenhower's political life showed he was a "conscious agent of the Communist conspiracy." How else explain the reverses suffered by the West against the communist tide but by conspiracy and treason?[2]

By the early 1960s, more than fifty million Americans had heard of the JBS. It had chapters in at least thirty-five states and raked in annual dues of over $1.3 million. It published *American Opinion,* churned out scores of pamphlets, books, and a weekly "Review of the News," and indulged in various other activities. In Pampa, Texas, for example, the society stretched an enormous banner across the town's main square: "HELP IMPEACH EARL WARREN" (the chief justice of the Supreme Court). "The Birchers . . . ran booths at county and state fairs, rented advertising space, established local chapters, and enrolled members by the scores of thousands," recounts one historian. In California, thousands turned out to hear Robert Welch's speeches, in which he charged that not only was the U.S. government coming under the control of communists, but that thousands of "Comsymps" had burrowed within the American clergy. "Don't worry about the atomic bombs or H-bombs," said another JBS speaker. "It's right here we'll lose the fight."[3]

ROBERT WELCH HAD a number of connections to *National Review.* He had known William F. Buckley Jr. since 1954, and the two men once or twice shared the same platform at anticommunist rallies. Welch donated $1,000 to *NR* in 1955 and again in 1957. He gently admonished Buckley for failing to realize that President Eisenhower was "on the other side"; but Buckley, busy keeping *National Review* afloat and maintaining contact with dozens of anticommunist groups and individuals from around the country, took little notice. When the JBS was founded in 1958, it had among its leadership a number of *NR* contributors, including Spruille Braden, Adolphe Menjou, Clarence Manion, and Revilo Oliver; and among its members was the industrial tycoon Roger Milliken, a key *NR* financial contributor. With these solid conservatives willing to join, how bad could the John Birch Society be?[4]

Buckley's first inkling of trouble came in 1958, when he obtained a copy of Welch's manuscript on Eisenhower, *The Politician*. He shunted it off unread to associate publisher Jim McFadden, who read it carefully and gave Buckley his assessment—Welch was "a nut." Buckley then examined it and was "appalled." To him Welch's writings were paranoid nonsense, displaying an utter inability to discriminate between a conscious traitor and someone who was simply mistaken in his views and policies. To think Dwight Eisenhower could commit treason was, to Buckley, sheer madness.[5]

Other conservatives were also troubled. *NR* senior editor William F. Rickenbacker met a group of John Birch Society members during a lecture tour. Birchers, he said, though "terribly earnest . . . were hopelessly ignorant of history, political theory, philosophy, psychology, intellectual history, and so on. They said . . . if a man acted in congruence and sympathy with the Communist line then he was a card-carrying Communist." Meanwhile, J. Daniel Mahoney fought to keep the Birchers from infiltrating his New York Conservative Party. JBS members would regularly attend Conservative Party meetings and attempt to pass out society literature. Mahoney further became aware that an important party official—a county chairman—was also a member, and in the higher councils, of the John Birch Society. Was the JBS attempting to subvert other conservative organizations?[6]

So by 1960, many at *National Review* felt uneasy about the Birchers and "extremists" on the Right generally. They worried about what JBS views could do to the Right should their liberal opponents link them to all conservatives. But for now, Buckley and others believed that nothing could be done. They were more concerned about opposing American liberalism and about unifying their ranks, not criticizing their ostensible allies. Barry Goldwater, for example, hoped to solve the problem by simply ignoring them. When asked about JBS approval of his programs and policies, he always replied that they supported him, not he them.[7]

But by 1961, this became more and more untenable. Robert Welch seemed to be everywhere, making speeches and appearances and giving interviews. And slowly Welch's extreme views began to be aired by the mainstream media. *American Opinion* made matters worse by asserting that the federal government was between 40 and 60 percent under the "operational control" of the Communist Party. Suddenly, a wave of news media attention landed on the John Birch Society, and, as a result, many liberals began voicing alarm about the society's impact on the country. Senator Jacob Javits called for a congressional investigation. The Union of American Hebrew Congregations stated that they were "fearful . . . that national discussion is being corrupted by the hatred and fear fomented by ultra right-wing groups." And some members of the Kennedy administration began voicing dark concerns about "right-wing extremism."[8]

By the spring of 1961, Buckley believed that *National Review* could not wait any longer. Robert Welch was making the Right look bad, and *NR* must sever its connections with the Birchers in order to stop the bleeding. Buckley did a similar thing in 1959, prohibiting all who served on *NR*'s masthead from having anything to do with the *American Mercury.* The *Mercury* had been purchased by a bigoted businessman named Russell Maguire, who made the magazine overtly anti-Semitic. Too many on the pre-World War II Right had espoused such prejudice, and it had given conservatism an odor of know-nothingism which it had yet to completely shed. So no more of it. *NR* would divorce itself as firmly as possible from the likes of Maguire. "Now we are cut loose from that dragging filth; it is a liberation," rejoiced Whittaker Chambers. "How good, and how strong it is, to take a principled position." Now it was time to do so again. Buckley wanted to attack the John Birch Society and its thinking—and soon.[9]

But some within *National Review* opposed a direct, public confrontation, and urged Buckley to proceed cautiously. Conservatism could not afford fratricidal strife. William Rusher, for one, contended that surely not all JBS members agreed with Welch's bizarre opinions. The society contained many good, solid conservatives. If *NR* assailed the society, and its members began deserting it, where would they go? There must be an alternative organization which ex-Birchers could join. Yet one did not yet exist. Buckley's criticisms of Welch, Rusher told him, seemed "based rather more upon your impatience with an organization of conservatives that is not obediently following *our* lead, rather than upon a conviction that all of these people are somehow irretrievably tainted." In sum, as Rusher recalled in later years, "an outright denunciation would simply hurt the feelings of a lot of basically sincere and simple people . . . [and give] the leftist media, who certainly didn't need it, another excuse for a feeding frenzy at the expense of the conservative movement as a whole."[10]

Frank Meyer also urged discretion. He had known of the society and its growth for some time, of course. And he had little use for the John Birch Society's overt ideology, "their absolute refusal to recognize a) the qualitative differences between Communism and liberalism and b) the degree to which our society remains in its essence far even from fully liberal," he wrote to Buckley in 1961.[11]

But he was uneasy with the size, and the apparent ferocity, of the attack Buckley wished to wage on the society. "Welch's own extravagances are of such a nature that the conservative movement, and in particular *NR*, must in some way or another dissociate itself from them," Meyer acknowledged. But "some of the solidest conservatives in the country are members of the John Birch Society, and we should act in such a way as to alienate them no more than is strictly necessary from a moral, political, or tactical point of view." *NR*, moreover, should explain carefully the reasons for taking such an action. "Whatever we do should be done in such a way as to carry [our readers] most effectively along with us."

Meyer also thought that the magazine should not ignore its main target: liberalism. *NR* must remind any angry readers that its real enemy remained American liberals. Any *National Review* editorial on the JBS should say clearly, Meyer wrote, that "we repudiate Welch's analysis of recent history" but also "strongly reject the word 'fascist' which is being thrown around in California as in any way applicable." The magazine must "point out the motives and long-range purposes of the Liberal attack which is now being made and place ourselves firmly in defense of [the JBS] against any action by the state."

Of course, any course *National Review* took was fraught with danger. A severe assault against the John Birch Society could anger many on the Right, costing *NR* subscribers, money, and possibly its existence. But failure to act would tie *NR* forever to the extremist, paranoid views of Robert Welch, which could destroy it in the public eye. It was an important and difficult decision. Frank Meyer knew it. "I should add that I do recognize the extreme difficulties that *any* action on our part will create with Welch and his supporters, and [with] some of our readers and contributors," Meyer advised Buckley. "But there seems to me to be involved here a responsibility both morally and politically to which we have to face up, in the role we have acquired . . . of the conscience of American conservatism. The other side of the matter, however, must not be lost sight of—that we have to continue to exist and exert influence."[12]

Buckley did think things over; and, at least partly at Meyer and Rusher's urgings, he wrote a brilliant editorial for the April 22, 1961, issue. He placed it in a question-and-answer format, and he directed most of the editorial not against JBS members, but against the troublesome views of Robert Welch.

Buckley titled the piece "The Uproar" (referring to the tremendous media coverage the JBS was receiving) and began with soothing words. He assured readers that he agreed with the basic goals of the society. "Its principal aims are to arrest the Communist conspiracy, and resist the growth of government," Buckley wrote. *National Review*'s problem was mainly with its founder. Robert Welch was a "courageous" man and passionately devoted to the anticommunist cause. But *NR* "rejected totally" Welch's assertion that Dwight Eisenhower was a conscious communist agent, as well as that the U.S. government was under the effective control of the worldwide communist conspiracy.

Here Buckley paused to explain in more detail, carefully and with precision. Why did *NR* "reject totally" Welch's theses? Because they were nonsensical. "If our government is in the effective control of Communists," Buckley said, "then the active educational effort conducted by conservatives . . . is a sheer waste of time. . . . The point has come, if Mr. Welch is right, to leave the typewriter, the lectern, and the radio microphone, and look instead to one's rifles." But, he made clear, "I myself have never met a single member who declared himself in agreement with certain of Mr. Welch's conclusions." What, then, should be the future of the John Birch Society? Buckley was optimistic. "I hope it thrives," he concluded, "provided, of course, it resists such false assumptions as that a man's subjective motives can automatically be deduced from the objective consequences of his acts."[13]

In the short term, the editorial proved to be an unqualified success. Even some members of the Birch Society were impressed. JBS executive council member T. Coleman Andrews lauded its "very objective manner," and Welch himself told him that "despite the differences of opinion between us, which remain and are stressed, I think the article is both objectively fair and subjectively honorable." William Rusher was partly pacified. He later admitted to Bozell that all of the attention given to the society had indeed caused problems—"the tremendous publicity they have received this year has made them a haven for every crackpot in America." Buckley's piece thus was "a masterpiece, winning the approval of everybody from *Life* magazine to Welch himself." One staunchly conservative *NR* reader told Meyer that "The Uproar" "was perfect." Meyer replied that now "my attitude towards [the] JB[S], by the way, is essentially that of Bill's editorial."[14]

Immediately after it appeared, Meyer went on one of his lecture tours. He wrote Buckley: "I should report that traveling through New Orleans, Dallas, and Phoenix, where three-quarters of the best people I met were John Birch members, I found no dissatisfaction with the editorial nor with my own public answers to questions, which followed the line of the editorial. I believe that if we maintain that tone, we will be successful in our aims." Meyer still, however, had hope that the organization could be saved. "Despite all we agree upon about the John Birch Society, a very large number of its members are outstanding and sane conservatives."[15]

Other members of the *NR* circle were not so sanguine. Rusher believed that the JBS's extremism was likely to grow. And if the John Birch Society were to wither away, where would its members go? What had *National Review* done to establish an alternative home for them? "My own hunch is that we are in the early stages of a conservative trend which is going to grow and harden and quite possibly get out of hand," Rusher warned Buckley, "as the scope and pace of the free world's collapse becomes apparent to the American people and the desire for a scapegoat takes hold. That is why I have been so pathologically anxious for us to encourage some reputable substitute for the John Birch Society. I herewith say again, for the umpteenth time, that we cannot prevent, or control, or even materially delay the organization of the American Right solely by means of well-phrased editorials in *National Review*."[16]

But *NR* was still too small, with too few resources, to enter the political game itself. *NR* was a journal of thought and opinion, not a political party. As far as the John Birch Society was concerned, most within *National Review* believed that it had gone as far as it should for now. Meyer, although in the end supporting the anti-Welch move, dealt with the JBS very gently in his *NR* column. In May 1961, he argued that liberalism "weakens the fiber of society, but . . . liberals are not, as are Communists, conscious enemies conspiratorially organized for the conquest of world power." However, to satisfy his more rabid readers, Meyer assured them that liberals must indeed be "fought"—but by using the methods of education and political action.[17]

As Meyer said often during this period, the conservative movement was undergoing "growing pains." Mistaken and extreme ideas must be rebutted; but it must be done carefully, with "prudence." *National Review*, Meyer told Buckley, would have to "patiently move with the movement. . . . Not to accept, of course, the phoniness of a Nixon or the paranoia of a Welch; but to support wholeheartedly those who represent the movement and . . . even if somewhat simply—move in the right direction."[18]

Perhaps *NR*, for now, had gone far enough.

BY THE TIME 1962 dawned, it became clear to Buckley and others that the JBS remained a problem. For one thing, *National Review*'s criticisms of Robert Welch had apparently not affected his position within the John Birch Society at all. Nor had his positions changed. The election to the presidency of John F. Kennedy had changed nothing. If anything, Welch's views were becoming even more preposterous. Now he charged, in an interview with the *Boston Herald,* that the failed operation at the Bay of Pigs had been the result of a communist plot. And *American Opinion* said that the federal government was now 50 to 70 percent under the operational control of the communists. Then Major General Edwin Walker was removed from his army post for circulating JBS material to his troops and loudly castigating his commander-in-chief. Walker initially won much conservative sympathy; but when it became clear that he subscribed to Welchite views, he lost favor within the *NR* circle.[19]

It was not only the paranoia of the society's leaders and followers. There was also the organization's effect on the Right as a whole—its influence was spreading; its members were infiltrating other groups. A board member of Young Americans for Freedom, a Bircher, consistently voted with a small, liberal Rockefeller faction within YAF in order to try to drive from power the *National Review* bloc; he was only halted by the heroic efforts of William Rusher and Marvin Liebman. There were also continuing efforts by the society to infiltrate the New York Conservative Party. And even though JBS penetration was consistently rebuffed, any association with it dragged all conservatives down. In early 1962 New York state Republicans began whispering to the press that the Conservative Party was becoming a front for the John Birch Society, a rumor soon duly reported by the *New York Times*. Supporters of the party were furious.[20]

And so by the winter of 1962 Buckley was convinced that *NR* must again take a stand, this time taking a tougher line. He was supported in this view by both Priscilla Buckley and James Burnham. Both had argued for some time that *NR* must distance itself from the "radical" and "kooky" Right, and they thought that Robert Welch "had a screw loose when it came to Communism." Hence "we felt we must dissociate ourselves from such ideas if we were to continue to be taken seriously," Buckley's sister recalled. "It was touchy and also painful."[21]

Buckley was as firm, as resolute, as he had ever been. When he visited his friend Bozell and his sister Trish in Spain, the three of them went for a long walk one afternoon, "and Bill advised Brent that he was thinking of severing relations with the Birchites in the magazine, no matter the cost," Mrs. Bozell remembered. "Brent was in full and enthusiastic agreement." Others, such as Rusher and Rickenbacker, were not so sure. Rusher, worrying that *NR* would lose subscribers, argued that *NR* should instead concentrate its fire on communists and liberals. Rickenbacker agreed. Burnham seemed to want to "annihilate Welch," Rickenbacker charged, and that was going too far.[22]

Frank Meyer was torn; his unusual indecision reflects what a wrenching episode this was for everyone on the Right. In January 1962 Meyer tried to analyze the dilemma in a long memo to Buckley. In his view, the society was the symbol of a much larger problem. *NR*'s overall objective was to establish "responsible leadership over the conservative movement" and to achieve "the magnification of the influence of that movement," Meyer wrote. But this was made difficult by "the disorientation of Welch to reality."

Meyer believed that groups such as the John Birch Society had deep, historical roots in the history of modern-day conservatism, that they had formed from an "uncompromising, instinctive opposition to the kit and kaboodle of the Roosevelt revolution, which had supplied a large proportion of the troops in every right-wing movement from the days of the Liberty League and America First through the Taft campaigns, the McCarthy days, and today." Many members of such groups were sensible, knowledgeable conservatives, but with "undoubtedly a strong element of know-nothingism in it." Extremists existed within any movement. What should *National Review* do about it? Meyer believed that "necessary criticism of either opportunist politicians or of demagogic mass leaders should be conducted in such a way that their followers will still listen to us."[23]

Meyer wanted desperately to stand for sound principles. But he did not want to alienate and divide conservatives, either. And so mostly he urged caution. But this time, although Buckley as always heard everyone's views, he stood firm. Hence "The Question of Robert Welch" appeared in the February 13, 1962, edition of *National Review.*

Once again Buckley chose his words carefully, taking pains to distinguish between ordinary, sensible JBS members and their leader. But in his lengthy (six pages) yet eloquent editorial statement, he made no bones about the depth of *NR's* differences with Robert Welch. Buckley began by reviewing the long list of Welch's statements and positions, emphasizing their extreme, unreal nature. Indeed, *NR* now believed "that Robert Welch is damaging the cause of anti-communism. Why? Because he persists in distorting reality and in refusing to make the crucial moral and political distinction. And unless that distinction is reckoned with, the mind freezes, and we become consumed in empty rages. The distinction is between 1) an active pro-Communist, and 2) an ineffectually anti-Communist liberal."

Buckley acknowledged that the JBS held "some of the most morally energetic, self-sacrificing, and dedicated anti-communists in America." But many of them had told him that Welch's opinions made no difference to them. Such rationalizations were not acceptable. How could they, he asked, be part of a group whose head is so completely wrong on central issues? What of the moral question? Buckley challenged the members: "Can one endorse the efforts of a man who, in one's judgment, goes about bearing false witness?"

He concluded by emphasizing conservatism's main goals and how Welch's actions were damaging the Right's ability to achieve them:

> If we are to win the war against Communism, we have no less a task before us than to change national policy. Nothing is clearer than that Mr. Welch is not succeeding in doing anything of the sort, precisely because, by the extravagance of his remarks, he repels rather than attracts a great following. . . Mr. Welch, for all his good intentions, threatens to divert militant conservative action to irrelevance and ineffectuality. There are, as we say, great things that need doing, the winning of a national election, the re-education of the governing class. John Birch chapters can do much to forward these aims, but only as they dissipate the fog of confusion that issues from Mr. Welch's smoking typewriter. Mr. Welch has revived in many men the spirit of patriotism, and that same spirit calls now for rejecting, out of a love for truth and country, his false counsels.[24]

Buckley wrote Burnham shortly afterward that he believed his gambit might work. "I am cautiously optimistic," he told him, "though I know we shall not hear the end of it for many months." Burnham in turn attempted to encourage the editor in chief. While Buckley was away in Switzerland, a huge conservative political rally was held in Madison Square Garden that March, sponsored by Young Americans for Freedom. A full house was expected, with almost every major conservative political figure scheduled to attend (Barry Goldwater would give the evening's keynote address). Burnham watched the event closely to see if *NR*'s intervention against Welch would "neutralize" the extremism issue. Afterwards, he happily reported to Buckley that neither Welch nor General Walker was there. "The Rally wholly reconfirmed the necessity of the anti-Welch move," Burnham assured him. "Walker would have completely loused up the affair. . . . Indeed, his absence, and the general turn against Welch and Birchism led to a most happy and widely publicized result *outside* of the Garden: the simultaneous picketing against the Rally by Rockwell's Nazis, some sort of ad-hoc Birch-Walker outfit . . . , pacifists, and the ADA [Americans for Democratic Action] and Young Democrats." The national press corps was (briefly) favorable to *NR*. The *Washington Post* admired the magazine's action, and *Time* magazine wrote that "many a liberal organ must have envied the *Review*'s devastating analysis of the thinking of the John Birch Society's founder."[25]

But *NR*'s public attacks against the John Birch Society were painful as well. *National Review* received over 350 hostile letters, along with seventy subscription cancellations and twenty disavowals of further financial support. (All told, there were more than 1,300 letters written in response to the magazine's stand.) Some of the correspondence spewed forth the most vile and hateful venom that many had ever seen. Others were less emotional but still sharply critical. One of conservatism's problems, said a typical *NR* reader, was the conservatives' "habit of destroying themselves and giving aid and comfort to the left wing by devoting so much of their energy to fighting other conservatives. . . . [Y]our obligation, if you expect to continue as a leader and molder of conservative opinion, is to stop fighting other conservatives and devote your wit, satire and biting pen to the greater task of exposing the folly and greater danger of the Left." The crisis with the John Birch Society, moreover, was at times intensely personal. Some on the Right warned darkly against the attack—"the JBS could destroy *NR*, we were told," recalled Priscilla Buckley. And some contributors to the magazine had ties to the society; many now felt they must choose one or the other—or even came to believe that *NR* was on "the other side." "Susan Huck, a brilliant Hunter College geographer, had written some excellent pieces for us on the Middle East," remembered *NR*'s managing editor, "but she too was beguiled into contributions to *American Opinion*. . . . I remember trying to persuade her that if she was interested in a career as a writer a continued association with the JBS would be the kiss of death, but to no avail. . . . It ended only in destroying our friendship." The episode was marked with pain and emotional scars. "[S]o many of the people involved were our friends; so many were genuine patriots and fighters, ready to stand up and be counted. But to their minds we had struck out at an ally, and were guilty of treachery, the unforgivable sin."[26]

Perhaps owing to the pain the move had caused, and the financial losses *NR* had to absorb, many at the magazine wanted it to go no further. The question came up because, at a January 1962 editorial Agony, Burnham raised the possibility of "going forward" with *National Review*'s break with the John Birch Society, of widening its "breach" with Robert Welch. Absolutely not, responded both Rusher and Meyer. Meyer said he had understood that the most recent anti-Welch stance was "the most advanced position we want to take, and that now we are prepared to allow the forces in the Birch Society time either to succeed in toppling Welch or . . . to learn that they cannot and draw the necessary conclusions." Far from staging further attacks, Meyer contended that *NR* should "cover our rear" by "stepping up our attacks upon the Liberals. . . . [We must] make what we did not a tablet-keeping gesture but a step towards consolidating a responsible leadership of American conservatism. Therefore we have to make it uncontestably clear that our attack on Welch was an attack based upon a solid conservative foundation, an attack carried out . . . because Welch is morally and intellectually not a conservative."[27]

Meyer had come to see the reasons behind the second anti-Welch editorial. Thus, he soon wrote a column in support of the magazine's general editorial line—though again he was gentle, never mentioning the JBS by name, referring only to an obsession in general with "conspiracies" and stoking his writing with enough anticommunist fire to satisfy the most conservative reader. Needless to say, an international communist conspiracy still existed, he began. But today many on the Right "exaggerated [this] out of all proportion." And others created "still deeper, more devilish conspiracies, hatched in the murky regions of the intellectual underworld—conspiracies encompassing Communists, international bankers, Freemasons, Jews, Catholics, and Heaven knows whom else, all directed by some mysterious 'They,' some arcane 'Invisible Government.'" Certainly communists in the U.S. "should be exposed, harried, persecuted… as if [they] were an armed contingent in the rear of a fighting army." This done, the important task would then only have begun: reversing the course of the global conflict with the Soviet Union, and countering the effects of liberal ideas in the United States.[28]

Another lecture tour, this time through the Midwest, confirmed Meyer's positive impression of the editorial. Meyer wrote Buckley that most of the "sober" conservatives he met, including the publisher Henry Regnery and Congressman Donald Bruce, were "happy the issue has been so sharply raised." But he did not think the overall problem—establishing a "responsible conservatism"—had been solved. "I have run into good intelligent sober people who are upset (I ignore here the wild ones), and I think a serious problem still exists … of finding ways of retaining and intensifying our leadership over them," he concluded.[29]

For the time being, *National Review* did not pursue further its break with the John Birch Society and Robert Welch. Rusher and Meyer had won a small victory. And *NR* had other issues to address. There was the rise of Barry Goldwater, the 1964 election, and the ever-present Cold War foreign policy situation to deal with; and besides, most assumed it would take time for the internal situation within the JBS to resolve itself. Many at *NR* were undoubtedly so exhausted from the 1962 confrontation with the Society that they welcomed the respite. For more than two years, *NR* mentioned the John Birch Society editorially not at all.

But, incredibly to some at *National Review,* Welch remained in charge of the JBS—despite all their hopes that the "sensible" members of the society would depose him. And the media continued to mention the Birchers synonymously with a dangerous extremism. Burnham worried about this, especially with regard to its effect upon the Right's political fortunes. "The extreme Right does seem to me a very difficult problem (there are so many difficult problems, alas)," Burnham wrote Buckley in the summer of 1963. "When you come down to it, our anti-Welch strategy has not proved to be so hot; about all it accomplished was, to a certain extent, to keep our skirts moderately clean. … Is it possible that the JB Society is the embryo, or an embryo, of the genuine American form of fascism (whatever it will be called) that might deepen and spread when 'objective conditions' are ripe?" The society, in short, was a lead weight that the Right could not seem to shed.[30]

Buckley agreed. "It looks to me as if there is no stopping these bastards," Buckley told Burnham. "We did not break the back of the movement. We came very close to doing so, but let's face it, we didn't, and it is growing in strength.... [T]he gravamen of its criticisms has not altered; our country is dominated by the Communists."[31] But throughout 1963 and 1964, nothing happened; the emphasis was on Goldwater, and to have any chance at winning in 1964, conservatives had to be unified. *NR* decided to wait.

IT WAITED UNTIL the summer of 1965, when finally Buckley decided *NR* could delay no longer. The John Birch Society had launched a new membership and fundraising drive and now claimed that the U.S. government was somewhere between 60 to 80 percent dominated by communists. To Buckley, the JBS had reached new levels of "virulence" and "panic."[32]

Worse, Welch and his followers, despite claiming that communism was their primary target, came out against the deepening American involvement in the war in Vietnam. Their opposition was based on a typical Birchite progression: since the U.S. government was controlled by communists, the costly, protracted conflict in Vietnam must be a Red plot, designed to weaken America. "Get US Out!" blared headlines in Birch publications. This was paranoid fantasy, no longer harmless or irrelevant. *NR* had to break with the John Birch Society, once and for all.[33]

Or so, at least, Buckley and Burnham believed. Once again, however, they faced opposition from within *NR's* editorial board from Rusher and Rickenbacker. They feared that a new attack upon the JBS would lead to worse losses than before. Further, they argued again that "right-wing cannibalism" played into the hands of the Left. Rusher, again and again, asked: Where could these people go? What new organization could they join?

Thus, at the magazine's quarterly editorial Agony in the heat of late August 1965 in Stamford, the editors sweated through a long, sometimes anguished discussion about a new assault upon the John Birch Society. The decision to go ahead with it was inevitable, of course. Buckley was determined. But as a result of Rusher's prodding, the Agony decided that "WAR [Rusher] will attempt to organize a division of the ACU to receive JBS members and others who desire JBS-type relationship. Details, strategy, etc. are his to devise." And *NR's* general tone in this newest anti-JBS move would "be tactful, will make the point that the disillusion of the members is understandable, that they are not to blame."[34]

National Review's most decisive break with the Birch Society would run in a special section of the magazine, set to appear in October. With the decision made, excitement steadily mounted among many of *NR's* staffers and editorial assistants, who were united in their desire to see the magazine go after the Birchers once again. Some talked apocalyptically of beginning a "Thirty Years' War" against the JBS, that this would be a "knock-down drag-out fight." But Rusher remained deeply concerned and continued to raise objections to the new anti-Welch stand. He argued that there had not been enough consultation on the overall tone, length, thrust, and emphasis of the upcoming *NR* special issue. The magazine should not "compel the Bircher to admit, by necessary implication, that he was a fool to join the Society at all. . . . [W]e should leave these people an avenue of retreat; if we insist upon surrounding and destroying them utterly, they have nothing to lose by fighting us to the very end." He also deplored some of the tough talk he heard from various *NR* staffers. "Knock down, si; drag out, no," Rusher snapped. "I have better things to do with my next thirty years."[35]

Nerves at the magazine grew even tauter as the deadline for the attack neared. Rusher continued to agitate and demanded an editorial conference be called to further discuss matters. But Buckley, busy with other concerns (he was running for mayor of New York on the Conservative Party ticket at this time), and disliking conferences anyway, resisted. Increasingly testy memos passed between *NR's* offices, and finally an exasperated Buckley called a halt: "I do not believe that thoughtful resolutions are only arrived at after collective (!) conferences."[36]

Finally *NR's* special edition on the John Birch Society appeared in the October 19, 1965, *National Review.* This time the headline, "The John Birch Society and the Conservative Movement" was splashed across *NR's* front, with fourteen pages devoted to it, along with signed columns by *NR's* most important senior editors. First, a background section gave the reasons for the magazine speaking out again. Then its heavy hitters took their swings. Buckley's reprinted newspaper columns emphasized the extremity of the JBS's most recent stands, such as that current U.S. attorney general Nicholas Katzenbach was taking his orders directly from the Communist Party and that Supreme Court Chief Justice Earl Warren was covering up evidence of communist participation in the assassination of President Kennedy. Such JBS rantings were "paranoid and unpatriotic drivel," Buckley said. This was joined by a lengthy analysis of the JBS's foreign policy views by James Burnham, who stressed that its opposition to the Vietnam War put it on the side of the Left. The Birchers had strayed into waters where "no conservative can prudently venture."[37]

One of the strongest attacks on the John Birch Society, however, came from an unlikely source: Frank Meyer. Meyer had grown more and more disgusted with the ideology espoused by the Birchers. It was heresy; and early in 1965 he signaled his support for an ultimate break with the JBS, telling Buckley that *NR*'s editors should soon discuss "the ideological problem of the rise of other conspiratorial theories besides Welch's in the conservative ambient, and the need of *NR* to come to grips with them." His support was crucial in giving Buckley the momentum to move; and now Meyer wrote a hard-hitting column for inclusion in the issue, called "The Birch Malady."[38]

In the past, Meyer wrote, the John Birch Society's extremism had seemed "harmless." But now the society reflected increasingly "the underlying paranoid theories of Robert Welch"; and more importantly, it urged an American pullout from Vietnam, "placing the Birch Society alongside of SNCC, Staughton Lynd, the sit-iners and the draft-card burners"—and all this came when, finally, America's political leaders had moved in Vietnam to "counter the Communist danger." On this issue Meyer stood shoulder to shoulder with James Burnham.

But Meyer devoted most of his column to explaining just where the society had gone wrong, to analyzing their "malady"—carefully, patiently trying, one last time, to convince them of the error of their ways. Frank Meyer always believed in the power of ideas; it was never too late. What then were the heresies in the Birchers' thinking? First of all, they showed no awareness of the existence of *liberalism*. "There is no room here for misplaced idealism, intellectual error, the lures of power, the weakness and vanities of men," he wrote. Liberals were wrong, misguided; their ideas must be fought against. But they were not part of some kind of communist plot. "It is not a simple arming of the good for a casting out of satanic enemies," Meyer insisted.

Furthermore, members of the John Birch Society participated in a historical and philosophical error. They believed "that there are two kinds of men, good and evil, and that evil only arises in society as the result of the conscious effort of evil men, banded together to produce it." Birchers saw everything as part of "a vast conspiracy of evil." This ignored life's complexity; it left out the complicated nature of human beings. In conclusion, Meyer returned to the JBS's view of Vietnam. This was the last straw. The membership of the society was being mobilized "in ways directly anti-conservative and dangerous to the interests of the United States," he charged. Serious, conservative adherents of the Birch Society, if there were any left, must understand that "it is rapidly losing whatever it had in common with patriotism or conservatism—and [must] do so before their own minds become warped by adherence to its unrolling psychosis of conspiracy."[39]

MEYER'S COLUMN WAS a virtuoso performance—firm, argued with care and precision, its central point unmistakable. So was the entire issue of *National Review.* *NR* received over 1,500 angry letters of protest and a number of subscription cancellations. But the magazine survived and, in the coming years, prospered. Most importantly, the whole episode between *NR* and the John Birch Society eventually accomplished exactly what Buckley had desired.

Almost every editor at *National Review* had been discussing for some time the need to establish a "responsible" conservatism. This was why *NR* had been founded in the first place; and this was why its positions on the Soviet invasion of Hungary, the Mao–Khrushchev split, the 1960 election, and the Goldwater candidacy had been debated with such passion and intensity. The Goldwater movement, the New York Conservative Party, and the American Conservative Union were attempts to convert this "responsible" Right into political reality.

But try as it might, *NR* had been unable to leave the "extremist" tag behind. For always, lurking in the background, was the dead weight of the John Birch Society. But after the October 1965 attack upon the JBS, it was much harder to make such an argument. It allowed the magazine to move on to other issues; Buckley and the other senior editors could now participate in more public forums and debates. Many people still bitterly opposed *NR*'s conservatism, but they slowly came to admit that it was in fact a "responsible" viewpoint. Could this have happened had *NR* not divorced itself from the JBS? William

Rusher, looking back over his thirty years as *NR*'s publisher, wrote, "I freely acknowledge that [the break with the JBS] was an important, and indeed an essential, step not only for *National Review* but the conservative movement as a whole."[40]

Frank Meyer had perhaps been slow to realize the extent of the threat of the John Birch Society to the American Right. But he had no illusions about the alien, anticonservative principles it espoused. Once he saw the society was unsalvageable, Meyer, as usual, committed himself totally to the break. His support for the October 1965 special edition of the magazine was important; his column, definitive. Frank Meyer had again played a crucial role in a critical episode for American conservatives.

AFTER 1965, THE John Birch Society faded from the nation's news. For if even *National Review* thought it beyond the pale, what more authoritative opinion could there be? JBS members were briskly swept out of mainstream conservative organizations. J. Daniel Mahoney, for one, soon cleansed the New York Conservative Party of any residual Birch influences. And the county chairman in the party who also belonged to the JBS? Mahoney eventually confronted him, telling him that he simply must choose: would it be the party, or the John Birch Society?

The chairman chose the Conservative Party. But then, as Mahoney told all who would listen, the Conservative Party was merely following "a *National Review* view of the world."[41]

The Long Road Back

NATIONAL REVIEW'S BREAK with the John Birch Society was an important episode, both in the life of the magazine and in the development of the conservative movement. But it was emotionally exhausting for all involved. And it remained unclear just what difference this would make in broadening *National Review* conservatism's appeal to the wider public.

In the mid-1960s, the obstacles to a conservative resurgence in America appeared more insurmountable than ever. Whatever *NR* did or said concerning the Birchers, just one year earlier *National Review*'s presidential candidate had suffered a huge electoral defeat. Pronouncements of the death of conservatism were everywhere. On the day following the 1964 vote, the *New York Times*'s James Reston wrote that Goldwater "not only lost the presidential election yesterday but the conservative cause as well." *Time* magazine added that "the conservative cause, whose championship Goldwater assumed, suffered a crippling setback. . . . The humiliation of their defeat was so complete that they will not have another shot at party domination for some time to come."[1]

The image of *NR*-style conservatism, at least as interpreted by many cultural leaders, did not immediately improve. The historian Allen Guttmann dismissed *NR*, writing that its "rhetoric is ordinarily that of nineteenth century Liberalism, but it is hard to imagine Thomas Jefferson, John Stuart Mill, or even

William Graham Sumner assessing the political situation in quite the same way as *National Review*." At Harvard University, a course on conservatism was called "Fascism and the Far Right in the Twentieth Century." It lumped anti-Semitism and American Nazism with the Goldwater movement, and implied that since 1960 a crucial concept in understanding the Right was "authoritarianism as a psychological problem." Within the Republican Party, meanwhile, liberal Republican intellectuals tried to move the GOP away from Goldwater conservatism. One way was to attack *NR*. George Gilder and Bruce Chapman, in their 1966 manifesto arguing the case for liberal Republicanism, contended that many conservatives' view of the average voter was "narrow-minded, selfish, xenophobic, and racially-prejudiced. This view is often enunciated, somewhat evasively, in olympian polysyllables by *National Review*."[2]

Then there were the politicians and other activists in the political arena. The head of the Women's International League for Peace and Freedom said that Americans "must rid [themselves] of the obsession of anti-Communism. Obsession is a mental disease, you know." Liberal Republican U.S. Senator Thomas Kuchel of California described the Republican Right as "a fanatical, neo-fascist, political cult, overcome by a strange mixture of corrosive hatred and sickening fear, recklessly determined to control our Party or to destroy it." President Lyndon Johnson, proclaiming his electoral victory in 1964 a "mandate," proceeded merrily along creating the "Great Society," paying no heed to conservative calls to respect the "permanent things." Indeed, Johnsonian rhetoric seemed like a direct slap in the face to conservatives. "Is our world gone?" Johnson asked in his 1965 inaugural address. "We say farewell. Is a new world coming? We welcome it, and we shall bend it to the hopes of man."[3]

This led to some resentment and frustration among conservatives. Sometimes it was vented in simple, direct ways, as when on the night of Goldwater's 1964 defeat, Donald Lukens, a future Republican congressman and a tireless Goldwater activist during the campaign, kicked in his television set and bought a one-way plane ticket to Australia. A right-wing newspaper editor wrote that politics in the mid-1960s was an arena where all assumed that "major societal questions have long since been determined, and everyone is agreed on the proper goals of political action."[4] William F. Buckley Jr. strove, even during the darkest days of the 1964 presidential campaign, to keep *National Review*'s tone optimistic. But in the post-1964 letdown, even *NR* occasionally sank into pessimism. When the 1965 off-year elections did not go well for the Republicans, *NR* pled for the relevance of the party's conservative wing, tempered with political realism. "[W]ithout the conservative wing of the Republican Party, the GOP is dead," the editors wrote. "Nominate a [liberal Republican New York City mayor John] Lindsay for President, and Mr. Goldwater's showing would appear like the Golden Age of Republicanism. On the other hand, the GOP cannot nominate a hard conservative and win—not as things are presently constituted...." Buckley believed that the Republican Party and conservatism had been so shattered by the 1964 loss that it might not win a national election for at least another decade. "The GOP will lose the next Presidential election," he wrote in 1966, "and perhaps the one after; but there will, hopefully, be one after that, towards which a party of opposition . . . should look with confidence." Perhaps some of Buckley's pessimism was provoked by the declining fortunes of *NR*. Subscriptions were down. William Rusher reported that the 1964 defeat, a libel suit filed against the magazine by liberal scientist Linus Pauling, and the magazine's attack on the John Birch Society had had "a powerful and long-lasting depressant effect." 1966 would likely turn out to be "the worst year in the financial history of the publication." The road back for conservatives would be a hard road indeed.[5]

BUT THE POST-1964 depression did not last long—partly due to the rush of events in the 1960s, but also because of the efforts of many dedicated individual conservatives, who were convinced not only that the cause was not lost, but that the fight had only begun. The mood at *NR* quickly improved. Most thinking conservatives knew that Goldwater would lose in 1964; among other things, the American people would not accept three different presidents in a twelve-month period. Thus, although upset at the size of Goldwater's defeat, recalled Priscilla Buckley, "*NR* considered the whole Goldwater operation a major victory for the conservative movement. . . . What happened at the Cow Palace was a revolt of the masses against the Eastern Republican establishment and that set the scene for the eventual takeover not only of the party but of the Presidency." As Rusher presciently told *National Review's* editors on the day after the 1964 vote, "historical turn-abouts seldom occur all at once. Goldwater's nomination was the first—not the last—battle of resurgent conservatism; there will be others."[6]

Besides, the conservative political counterestablishment of groups and organizations continued to function. Frank Meyer had an active and important role in this. The American Conservative Union weathered some difficult times in its first years of operation. It nearly died in the first months and years after the defeat of Barry Goldwater. But soon Rusher reported to *NR*'s editors that the organization had made a smooth transition to the "able chairmanship" of *National Review* ally and member of Congress John Ashbrook. It was now in good shape, and ACU treasurer Frank Meyer "remains our major contact with the world of serious research, and is limited only by the amount we have to spend along this line." Many of the active personnel in the American Conservative Union were alumni of Young Americans for Freedom, who "form a valuable *NR*-oriented reservoir of talent for the ACU." The organization had definitely "turned the corner."[7]

Meyer performed many tasks for the ACU. In 1965, he organized a conference of conservative leaders to deal (for example) with the split between responsible and extremist conservatives, to be called "The Crisis in the Conservative Movement." "And American conservatism is, indeed, in crisis," he warned. "We have no doubt that the breach will affect all organized conservative action— both through organizations such as the ACU and within the Republican Party itself." Meyer was also in charge of assigning authors to do studies on important topics, which the ACU then published in order to influence the national debate. In a typical year he found well-known conservative scholars to do analyses on labor policy, military strategy, and voter attitudes.[8]

Meyer also remained an important member of the executive committee of the New York State Conservative Party. It was Meyer who helped convince William F. Buckley Jr. to run for mayor of New York City on the Conservative Party ticket. Buckley's colorful, active campaign confounded liberals and skeptics and garnered over 340,000 votes. On a more mundane level, Meyer continued to advise party leader J. Daniel Mahoney on candidates, platforms, and issues. And he watched with pride as the party slowly grew. In the 1966 race for governor, the Conservatives not only nominated a candidate, but had a full party convention, complete with a platform arrived at through open hearings before a platform committee—over which Frank Meyer presided, Mahoney recalled later, "with extraordinary skill and meticulous impartiality." The party's gubernatorial candidate, an unknown college administrator named Paul Adams, gained over 520,000 votes. Furthermore, the party finished ahead of the Liberals, thereby gaining the coveted third rung (row C) on the state ballot. Perhaps, indeed, things were looking up.[9]

Meyer was also a key adviser to another conservative organization that sprang up in these years, called the Philadelphia Society. Founded in 1965, the society was designed to bring like-minded conservative thinkers and scholars out of isolation and into contact with each other, as well as to focus on deeper societal issues and the principles that should underlie public policies dealing with them. It met once or twice a year, with Meyer helping in setting up its initial meetings. As Meyer wrote Buckley, "[T]he greatest need of the conservative movement today is for the deepening of its theoretical understanding." Meyer hoped to see topics discussed such as "the decay in the American intellectual outlook," "the insurrection in our cities," or "the disorder in our foreign policy." He remained active in the society until his death.[10]

He stayed on the lecture circuit, too, going out once or twice a year and increasing the amount of speaking he did on college campuses. This was where new recruits could be found, and where liberalism and radicalism had to be challenged. In one instance, Meyer spoke at Indiana University, where a brash, iconoclastic recent convert to conservatism named R. Emmett Tyrrell had founded a magazine, the *Alternative,* through which he launched elegant but deadly verbal salvos at the dominant IU student Left. Meyer appeared on campus during a weeklong barrage of conservative speakers brought in by Tyrrell, afterward journeying to his ramshackle forty-acre farm, sitting up into the wee hours of the morning in an old barn around a keg of beer with the *Alternative*'s staff, discussing issues great and small. Tyrrell became yet another of Meyer's telephone contacts, and his publication eventually became the *American Spectator,* until the century's end an important voice on the conservative political scene.[11]

Meyer's sphere of influence also included Young Americans for Freedom, which left behind a greater legacy than could have been imagined at the time. The movement against the Vietnam War and the youthful "counterculture" in the 1960s has been well documented. Not so the sizable segment of youth who wound up on the Right. "For me," recalled conservative activist Lee Edwards, "as for most conservatives, the '60s were the decade not of John F. Kennedy but Barry M. Goldwater, not Students for a Democratic Society but Young Americans for Freedom, not the *New Republic* but *National Review,* not Herbert Marcuse but Russell Kirk, not Norman Mailer but Ayn Rand, not Lyndon Johnson's Great Society but Ronald Reagan's Creative Society, not a 'meaningless' civil war in Vietnam but an important battle in the protracted conflict against Communism."[12]

Meyer knew these young people existed. In 1965, he was one of the featured speakers at a YAF-sponsored "Conservative Unity Rally" held in Teaneck, New Jersey. Later, he delivered the keynote address at YAF's New England Regional Conference in Bridgeport, Connecticut. And in 1966, the group sponsored a kind of summer leadership seminar, bringing to Lancaster, Pennsylvania, 175 conservative student leaders representing 192 YAF chapters. Frank Meyer was the featured speaker one morning on "the role of the contemporary conservative in America." "Out of the Catskills came Frank Meyer, everybody's favorite intellectual leprechaun," reported a participant. "As always, he spoke as if he were still lambasting the Trotskyites at a Communist cell meeting. As always, his audience loved it." After his talk, Meyer could be seen outside, elaborating on his lecture. A cameraman captured the image of a short, intense-looking man, clad (for once) in jacket and tie, with a silver mop of hair topping his baggy, sunken features. This "intellectual leprechaun," an unlikely goodwill ambassador for conservatism to America's youth, was surrounded by a bevy of eager and equally intense young people.[13]

So CONFIDENCE IN conservative principles remained high. But now, owing to his defeat, Barry Goldwater was the leader of conservatism in name only. The Right needed a new star.

Thanks to the rise of Ronald Reagan, who this would be was never much in doubt. And this important conservative political figure had plenty of ties to *National Review.* He was a former Hollywood movie actor and political activist, past president of the Screen Actors Guild, and a certified liberal Democrat who had voted for Franklin D. Roosevelt for president four times. But since the 1950s Reagan had been moving to the Right, endorsing first Eisenhower and later Nixon for the presidency, becoming a spokesman for General Electric, and traveling about the country giving speeches endorsing individualism and free enterprise, while denouncing taxes and big government. He first subscribed to *National Review* in 1956, read the magazine closely, and had been a personal friend of William F. Buckley Jr. since 1960. His television speech during the latter stages of the Goldwater campaign brought him to serious national attention as a possible conservative candidate for office. "The Reagan phoenix rose very early and very fast from the ashes of Goldwater's defeat," remembered William Rusher.[14]

Nor did it hurt Reagan among *NR* conservatives when, in 1965, he clearly echoed the magazine's position on the John Birch Society. By the fall of that year, Reagan's candidacy for governor of California was gaining steam. Then came the accusations that he had ties to the JBS. Reagan was never a Bircher; now, he put out a carefully worded press release that echoed the *NR* position— it attacked the extreme views of Robert Welch, but avoided slighting the honest conservatives still in the society. "In my opinion those persons who are members the John Birch Society have a decision to make concerning the reckless and prudent statements of their leader, Mr. Welch," read Reagan's statement. "I wish at this time to reaffirm my criticism of Mr. Welch and restate that I am in great disagreement with much of what he says." Sure enough, the issue was not a serious threat to the Reagan campaign.[15]

Buckley and *NR* cheered Ronald Reagan's candidacy on to victory throughout 1966. As early as January, Buckley lauded Reagan for having "the mind of a true conservative, who recognizes limits of political action, recognizes that every problem does not beget its own solution." Reagan won the GOP primary convincingly and went on to a smashing victory against the Democratic incumbent Edmund G. (Pat) Brown. In fact, 1966 proved to be a banner GOP year. Republicans captured twenty-five of thirty-four governorships nationwide. In the House of Representatives, Goldwater stalwarts such as John Ashbrook, John Rhodes, and Edward Derwinski all won their races; and in the U.S. Senate, John Tower was reelected, Carl Curtis (a Goldwater floor manager at the 1964 GOP convention) won election for the first time, and Strom Thurmond—running in his initial race as a Republican—achieved an overwhelming mandate. Republicans, and conservatives, were on the road back.[16]

As Reagan took over the governorship of the nation's largest state, some disagreement arose among *NR* conservatives over how far he could go in national politics. Buckley himself showed a bit of skepticism about the affable, rising conservative hero. Referring to Reagan's early confrontations with the California legislature, Buckley wrote, "[T]here is a great deal of potential support available to a right-bent public figure, but he must know how to discharge the correct vibrations to shake it out, and Governor Reagan didn't know how to do that in January 1967, and does not know—and here is his most baffling dereliction of the moment—how to do so even now." As for Reagan's presidential ambitions, Buckley worried out loud that Reagan would be unelectable, laden with the tag of "actor."[17]

Frank Meyer had a different view. Meyer had noted Reagan's speech on Goldwater's behalf in 1964, and had been quick to tout him as a potential conservative figure following the election. And now he believed Reagan's 1966 victory in California was supremely important, not only for the political future of the Right, but for the salvation of the Republican Party.

Meyer wrote in his "Principles and Heresies" column shortly after the 1966 elections that now "the Republican prospects for 1968 look a good deal brighter." But the question remained: What kind of Republican Party would it be? Meyer feared that a heresy was creeping into Republican thinking; namely a willingness to "settle for any candidate who could win for the Republican Party, no matter how little he would achieve for conservative principle." Probing deeper, Meyer saw this as a sign of the continuing tendency among some conservatives to "regard the Republican Party as somehow a good in itself," no matter its candidates or their principles and policies. This was no idle worry. Liberal Republicans such as Nelson Rockefeller, Michigan governor George Romney, Illinois senator Charles Percy, and New York mayor John Lindsay were prominent in the party, busy calling for "a 'positive' program of *Republican* big government," which would mean "that Republicans instead of Democrats will be expanding the coercive welfare state" and also making "insidious passes" at the anti-Vietnam War vote.

If any such liberal became the party standard-bearer in 1968, it would mean a "Liberal" and "opportunist" GOP that would most likely lose its conservative base; hence, it would wither and die. The stakes were high. If a "Republican mystique" was placed over and above conservative principle, much of the conservative electorate could fall into the hands of George Wallace, whose "right-wing demagogy," Meyer wrote, "masks socialist welfare practice."

Conservatives could still emerge triumphant in 1968, Meyer insisted. But they needed a candidate "who can stir conservative enthusiasm"—in short, Ronald Reagan. "By the principled positions he has taken, and by his proven ability as a campaigner . . . Ronald Reagan, should he prove the governor he promises to be, qualifies for this role." Meyer had not forgotten the experience of 1964. He was more pragmatic now. He would not identify himself totally with one candidate. Thus, he went on to note that "if it became necessary [in 1968] to accept a man of the center"—he specifically mentioned Richard Nixon—"he would be strongly influenced [by the support for Reagan] in the conservative direction."[18]

But for now, it was Reagan who stirred conservative hopes and energized their dreams. And someone like Frank Meyer, in whom the fires of conservative zeal always burned brightly, needed little to fuel him.

MEYER CONTINUED TO DO more than simply espouse conservatism. He lived it. It was a part of everything he did and every role he assumed—husband, father, intellectual, conservative activist. Frank Meyer at home was no different from Frank Meyer anywhere else.

Meyer was an active intellectual who read constantly and widely. He subscribed to numerous magazines—*America*, the *New Republic*, the *Reporter*, the *New Leader*—and he daily scrutinized the *New York Times*. He also looked the part. In his youth, Meyer spent time in the smoky, bohemian, intellectual coffeehouses of New Jersey and New York; he still sported that slightly seedy look. During a time when tight pants and button-down shirts were the norm, Meyer wore loose-fitting trousers and baggy, worn shirts. Brent Bozell once asked Frank's wife why he dressed as he did; and "Elsie, with that twinkle, said in slight embarrassment that Frank and she had decided that since he looked Mediterranean he might as well dress that way."[19]

Elsie Meyer remained an important part of Frank's life. In addition to running the household and minding their two sons, she did the bulk of her husband's typing and dictation and helped him edit *National Review*'s book section. It was a heavy workload, but Elsie kept her sense of humor. At the bottom of one Meyer memo to Buckley was the following brief typewritten note: "Dear Bill: forgive the typing anomalies. I dropped (!) the typewriter on the floor New Year's Eve. I was cold sober; just annoyed that everyone was so busy talking that I could get no help in moving the typewriter, so I exerted more strength than I knew I had. Anyway, since then the poor thing has never been put back in working order."[20]

Elsie was an active intellectual herself, following politics closely along with her husband. But she was a different kind of thinker than he, much more focused on literature (and exuding less passion and heat). She had a deep knowledge of English literature. "I cannot think just where in the tradition of English letters you fit," she once wrote Buckley. "Curiously, the *spirit* of your writing reminds me of Chaucer. . . . It is interesting, though, that he was a public figure, as well as a poet, and did bring some French lightness into the powerful Anglo-Saxon armory—which could also be ponderous as well as powerful. . . . I shall keep in mind comparisons with the great prose stylists and let you know what I come up with." Her learning was deep and considerable, but it was channeled in somewhat different directions than Frank's. As she wrote on another occasion, she was "averse to flamboyant political broadsides, from Tom Paine on. Being what my husband unkindly calls an 'incurable 19th century rationalist,' I have a penchant for what *I* choose to consider dispassionate analysis."[21]

One thing both could agree on was the education of their two sons. It would be done at home, never at government-run public schools. And it would be a traditional education, emphasizing classic works and the understanding of basic principles. When John and Eugene were very young, Elsie did the bulk of the teaching. Frank did not have the patience to sit and teach young children their ABCs. But as the children got older, teaching duties became equally divided between husband and wife. Frank taught mathematics, science, and history; Elsie tutored the boys in English (her major at Radcliffe), geography, and spelling. The boys were given specific assignments and were closely monitored on their progress via oral quizzes from either Frank or Elsie. The Meyers' homeschooling was very effective. There was no way for either of the two boys to get away with not having done their homework. They *knew* each day that they would be called on, and hence knew that they must get their work done.

The Meyers emphasized not so much memorization as the learning and understanding of basic concepts and principles. They stressed the classics: in philosophy, Plato and Aristotle; in history, Herodotus; in literature, Homer and Shakespeare. The boys studied Latin along with formal logic. Most important, perhaps, was the whole atmosphere of the household. Both parents were writers and thinkers who read widely. Thanks to Frank's job as book review editor for *National Review,* books were literally everywhere, strewn throughout the house.[22]

Given their parents' habits, the boys also worked much of the night and slept much of the day. Thus, as the Meyers had intentionally not sought approval from the educational authorities for their homeschooling practices, Meyer once told a friend that going out publicly with the boys during the day was dangerous. Someone might ask why the boys weren't in school. At one point, a state truant officer visited the Meyer house and told Elsie that she would need the state's permission to educate the boys at home. Frank, awakened early, called angrily from the next room, "You need *my* permission to do anything with my children, I don't need *yours*!"[23]

The teaching at the Meyer house came in many different ways. Frank had diverse interests, which he passed on to his sons. For example, he was a connoisseur of good wine who was familiar with the different vineyards of France and other nations (he was convinced that "there is just no wine made to go with ham"). He was also a baseball fan, taking his boys once a year to New York to see a game and faithfully listening to the World Series each autumn on the radio (always rooting *against* the New York Yankees). And he was a student of chess. He found the game intellectual and challenging; both of his sons excelled at it. Four or five times a year the three of them would travel to chess tournaments held in the New York area, in which the two boys would compete. Elsie encouraged this, for chess gave Meyer time with his sons.[24]

Much of Meyer's time was also spent in keeping up his voluminous contacts with conservatives far and wide, mostly by phone. "We spoke so often, in fact, that our long phone conversations were cutting into my reading time," recalled Conservative Book Club founder Neil McCaffrey, "and I had to ask him, clumsily, if perhaps we could ration our conversations. The truth is that, living in his mountain eyrie, he craved stimulation and got it over the phone. I think he lived vicariously by way of those who led more active lives."

The telephone relationship between Meyer and McCaffrey was typical. They talked about everything. "We gossiped about what was going on among conservatives, argued about politics and religion, and in general exchanged ideas about anything and everything," McCaffrey remembered. In these conversations, Meyer showed a quick mind, a faster tongue, and a sometimes ruthless judgment of human character, whether of friend or foe. McCaffrey recalled later that Meyer's thinking was "much sharper than his heavy-handed literary style would suggest. He had . . . a keen knowledge of psychology and how it could be turned against people when he analyzed them. Yes, Frank had an instinct for the jugular. In fact, I think he over-indulged it. Rarely did he describe anybody, even his very closest friends, without adding a few notes of denigration. This of course made him superior to the person he was denigrating. It was not one of his nicer qualities." But, as with most of Meyer's acquaintances, McCaffrey believed he could always count on Frank as a supporter and confidante. "I counted him a close friend," he wrote years later. "Yet part of his genius for friendship was in making literally scores of people think that each was among his special friends."[25]

There were also the visits. Many conservatives, one or two per month, maybe more, visited the Meyers at their Woodstock home for dinner, drinks, and all-night conversation. Meyer especially seemed to enjoy the younger, up-and-coming conservatives, wanting to encourage them. A number of those who would play an important role on the American Right in the 1970s and 1980s paid a visit to Frank Meyer in Woodstock sometime during the 1960s. They never forgot it. Edwin Feulner, the future president of the Heritage Foundation, one of the Right's most important think tanks, was one such young conservative. "A small man with a gray crewcut and piercing, deep-set eyes, often wearing a turtleneck, Frank Meyer was constantly in motion," Feulner wrote years later, "pacing as he thought and talked, reciting English poetry by the yard and spouting Shakespeare—whole soliloquies at a time." Feulner found him a "likable" man, charming, "pleasantly argumentative." The two discussed "everything from gardening and baseball to chess and the classics, frequently touching on such favorite topics as Abraham Lincoln's un-American characteristics or the dangers of federally-mandated zip codes." All this followed a good but "simple" meal and occurred amidst "a jumble of books—stacks, racks, pieces of books . . . [that] careened in perilous stacks up and down the stairs at the Meyers' charming farm house." The talking lasted until 5:30 A.M., which left Feulner a bit unsettled but glad for the experience. "I was woozy for the next week," he recalled, "but that weekend stands out in my memory as one of the intellectual high points of my early education in the conservative movement."[26]

MEANWHILE, MEYER remained a well-established figure in *National Review*, where he had by now carved out his own niche. He was not the most popular *NR* personality, nor the most well known, nor the most colorful. But Meyer had his own band of followers, his own readership, and (he believed) his own job to do at *NR*.

The most popular, well-known, and colorful person at *NR* was of course William F. Buckley Jr. Meyer did not see him as often these days, for by the mid-1960s Buckley's fame had blossomed. His newspaper column, his books, his television show "Firing Line," and especially his run for mayor of New York had made Buckley a national figure, a kind of celebrity. He was constantly in demand and thus frequently on the road lecturing and debating. His time became valuable and in short supply. As his sister Carol recalled:

> Fame brings with it a great loss of privacy as one becomes hostage to the public fantasy. Bill would sacrifice a great deal for celebrity. It began slowly, being recognized here, approached there. Personal time slips away in small increments, and soon there is almost none left. For you do not belong to yourself but to the people on the street who ask for autographs, the drunks on the plane who accost you, reporters, journalists. I seldom saw him now without a crowd of admirers (or detractors). His life was appointed to the minute, and so it was mostly on his sailboat, away from the limelight and surrounded by close friends, that Bill was allowed simply to be himself.[27]

But Meyer and Buckley remained fairly close, staying in touch frequently by phone and remaining generally in harmony concerning *NR* politics and policy. *NR* was Buckley's first love, and he kept himself fully informed on its every aspect. Since he trusted Meyer to run the book section well, the two men were free to deal with routine matters rather quickly and thus to spend time developing their friendship. Buckley would occasionally send Meyer new equipment and other gadgets to help him in his many works, such as a new copy machine. It "has arrived and is a godsend," replied a grateful Meyer. Buckley also occasionally sent him manuscripts that had arrived at *National Review* and asked Meyer to recommend their suitability for publication. In return, Meyer sent Buckley articles and news clippings that could be used as fodder for a newspaper column.[28]

Indeed, as with any ideological enterprise, personal relationships were key to the success of *NR* and the conservative movement as a whole. For it was only too easy for disagreements about ideas to become personal, which could lead to costly splits within the movement. A legend grew that Meyer was doctrinaire and unable to get along with those who disagreed with him. This was not true. Although he and Russell Kirk at one point exchanged fierce verbal salvos and continued to disagree on certain issues, by the mid-1960s whatever "feud" had existed had largely quieted. Kirk later noted that "while Frank Meyer was *NR*'s book review editor, [I] often was asked to contribute to the magazine's literary pages, and all [my] own books were reviewed therein; it would be otherwise with *NR*'s later book-review editors."

Sometimes, of course, personal breaks were unavoidable, and even necessary. Meyer disagreed, at times sharply, with both L. Brent Bozell and Willmoore Kendall. But he remained good friends with Bozell, and broke only with the prickly, incredibly difficult Kendall (who insulted nearly every friend he ever had at one time or another). "WK rides again," an exasperated Meyer wrote Buckley in 1965. "He has finally, for the final time, irrevocably broken with Brent, and rather hurt Brent. I broke down the other night for the first time and told Willmoore off in no uncertain terms, precisely on this account. So I suppose, except for the fact that he still has to be associated with me on the book [*What Is Conservatism?*], that I am in the same boat." "Is this yet another final break with Brent, i.e., to be distinguished from the final break with Brent of two weeks ago?" an amused and frustrated Buckley asked in reply. "I'm losing count."[29]

Among *NR*'s readers, Meyer was not the magazine's most popular writer, but his column was generally approved by most subscribers and *NR*'s coterie of disciples. A *National Review* reader poll conducted in 1965 found that the most popular column in the magazine was Buckley's "On the Right," with 80 percent of the readers sampled "strongly approving"; the second most popular was James Burnham's "The Third World War," with 63 percent strongly approving; and third was Meyer's "Principles and Heresies," with 54 percent strongly approving and 22 percent mildly approving. On the other hand, only 33.6 percent of *NR* readers strongly supported Meyer's book section, with 28 percent mildly approving; and only about 1 percent named his column their favorite feature. But then *NR*'s subscribers were sometimes guilty of anti-intellectualism (over 40 percent consistently opposed a poetry page) and hence may not have appreciated what Meyer was doing. Meyer moreover did not have the charisma of a Buckley or the sharp immediacy of topic such as Burnham's. Yet 52 percent of those polled believed that *NR* was "improving, becoming more effective." And all at the magazine would have agreed that Meyer had much to do with that.[30]

Behind the scenes at *NR* Meyer remained a stickler for principle. He could become fixated on what seemed, on the surface, to be mundane issues. But keeping *NR* and his colleagues "principled" had become his role. At one point a conservative friend of Buckley's wrote, saying he believed the magazine's tone was too shrill, that it did not make *NR* appear "responsible" enough. Meyer disagreed. Meyer labeled *NR*'s tone "ironic" and "indignant," and launched into a lengthy discussion of "tone":

> I am afraid [he wrote to Buckley] that we *are* still an opposition and that we are likely to remain to a considerable degree in social and philosophic opposition even if our political power increases. For our situation the ironic tone is ideal. Even, indeed, if we represented a great deal more political power than is likely in the short range . . . in a world where material developments have been what they are, that ironic tone is the only possible one for a Christian approach to the social world as it is and is likely to be for a very long time to come. To be "grave" would be either hypocritical or idolatrous.[31]

Sometimes even word usage and letter capitalization could inspire a debate over fundamentals—and demonstrate Meyer's influence. In 1966, for instance, new *NR* senior editor Arlene Croce committed what to Meyer was a *faux pas* of principle. Croce, a Meyer discovery, had been writing for an obscure, leftist Catholic magazine when he came across one of her essays. Meyer liked her writing style and immediately telephoned to inquire if she would like to write for *NR*. She did want to; she had been powerfully influenced by Whittaker Chambers's book *Witness* and had been steadily moving rightward. So Meyer introduced her to Priscilla Buckley, who put her on the magazine's editorial staff. She was rapidly promoted and soon became a senior editor.

Now, Croce had submitted a memo arguing that it was time for *NR* to cease capitalizing the "L" in the word "Liberal.""I am unable to see the point in our habit of spelling 'liberal' with a capital 'L' when all we mean is an Arthur Schlesinger type," she wrote."I submit the term 'liberal' in its modern, degraded sense is sufficiently understood without our having to punch it home every time with this troublesome capital letter." Meyer disagreed and fired off his own memo. This was not merely a question of style, but concerned the magazine's entire understanding of the difference between nineteenth-century Manchesterian free-market liberalism and twentieth-century statism. Capitalizing the word

"Liberal" "is absolutely essential if we are not going to yield the concept of true liberalism to the statists," Meyer asserted. "From the beginning of *NR*, it was this usage that made possible the association under the name conservative of many who like myself have a large liberal component in their position." This issue was not "a matter of style at all, but—petty as it may seem on the surface—is a highly significant political and principled question." Eventually the issue was thrashed out at an editorial Agony, where Buckley helped devise a compromise.[32]

DURING THE MID-1960S, Meyer's purpose remained what it had always been. In the introduction to a book he published in 1969, which brought together a collection of his columns and other writings, his goals remained twofold: to "express and formulate the consensus of the contemporary American conservative movement"; and "to champion one emphasis within that consensus, the libertarian as opposed to the more traditionalist." Or, put another way, Meyer was trying "to show in concrete circumstances the living meaning of the conservative outlook."[33]

Meyer spent a great deal of time in these years reading the ancient texts of both Greek and Jewish philosophy, seeking to understand fully the history and philosophical foundations of the West. Eventually his ruminations resulted in a piece for *Modern Age* titled "Western Civilization: The Problem of Political Freedom." It examined the historical roots of human freedom. Meyer, displaying a deep knowledge of the ancient Hellenic and Judaic texts, argued that freedom arose from the influence of both ancient Greece and Israel. Both traditions adumbrated more than any other the conflict between, on the one hand, the individual and his rights, and, on the other hand, the goal of "transcendence" and the building of a perfect social order. While both societies developed the idea of the need to protect the individual, both also faced the temptation to achieve transcendent perfection here on earth, to *force* people to do the true and the good. Thus began the West's fateful, on-again-off-again romance with utopianism and overweening government. Meyer was adding to his "fusion" thesis, arguing that such a marriage was not merely a twentieth-century creation, but had firm historical roots. Human freedom rested on solid historical ground.[34]

History was an important mode of inquiry for most conservatives. For most believed that the tradition, values, and principles handed down through the ages were worth conserving, or at least deserved careful consideration. But exactly what ought to be conserved, and what not? Sometimes members of the Right could not agree on an answer.

In the summer of 1965, Meyer published in *National Review* an innocuous-looking brief review of a book called *Freedom Under Lincoln,* by Dean Sprague. Given the reverence accorded Abraham Lincoln in America, few dared challenge the Lincoln myth. But Meyer would. "Mr. Sprague is a courageous man," he wrote. "He has dared to pierce the myth of Abraham Lincoln's benevolence and examine the realities of an authoritarianism that was, in terms of civil liberties, the most ruthless in American history. His detailed recital of the naked use of federal power against individual citizens, as well as against the press, throughout the North might be entitled 'Repression Under Lincoln.'"[35]

Thus began an interesting debate, one which exposed yet another side of conservatism—the bifurcation between the traditionalist, agrarian Right rooted in the American South, with its belief in states' rights, and the conservatism more oriented to America's capitalist, nationalist, urban tradition. A few weeks after the appearance of Meyer's "brief," William F. Buckley Jr. took the unusual step of penning a letter for *NR*'s letters-to-the-editor section. It was fine to criticize Lincoln, Buckley said, but to imply, as Meyer did, that Lincoln was somehow "anti-humanitarian" was "worse than mere tendentious ideological revisionism. It comes close to blasphemy to say such a thing about a President whose recorded words preaching love and reconciliation, because of their sublime quality, could not have come except from a pure heart, words which do more even now to inspire lively sentiments of faith, hope and charity than the millions of words and deeds of the little Florence Nightingales in and out of the world of ideology."[36] A debate was on, and Meyer loved a debate. He responded in *National Review*'s "Open Question" feature.

Meyer opposed Lincoln first because Lincoln had destroyed the traditional check upon centralized power, states' rights. The right of secession was a state's "last sanction," needed if the federal government was not "to grow so strong as to destroy the tension that guaranteed liberty." Lincoln had attacked this state "autonomy." His reason for doing so was to preserve the Union. It did not matter "that he would have preferred to achieve his ends without war; so would every ideologue." Lincoln "waged [a war] to win at any cost." His government became a "repressive dictatorship" upon the northern states; and in prosecuting the war, he allowed Ulysses S. Grant's "brutal meat-grinder tactics" and the "brigand campaigns waged against civilians" of William T. Sherman. Lincoln's war aims made "no effort at reconciliation, only the complete triumph of central government."

In sum, and drawing out the relevance of the debate to his contemporaries, Meyer argued that without Lincoln "it would have been infinitely more difficult for Franklin Roosevelt to carry through his revolution, for the coercive welfare state to come into being." The sixteenth president "undermined the constitutional safeguards of freedom" and "opened the way to centralized government." Such actions would always draw Frank Meyer's hostility.[37]

But what if someone accepted Meyer's fundamentals yet arrived at a very different answer? This challenge came from conservative political scientist Harry Jaffa. Jaffa had been a speechwriter for Barry Goldwater. His rightwing credentials were not in doubt. Yet he drew very different lessons than did Meyer from Abraham Lincoln.

Jaffa professed to be shocked that an individualist such as Meyer never mentioned the issue of slavery. Furthermore, he maintained that America's founding fathers did not believe that the states and the federal government were in some kind of co-equal "tension," as Meyer implied. The founders established the Constitution in order to create a *stronger* national government. Jaffa also denied that there was widespread acceptance of the right to secede. Even Robert E. Lee did not think that secession was right or legal. Moreover, Jaffa argued, Lincoln was not an "ideologue" but a "genius" who asked how one man could "enslave another, without conceding that the other might, if he can, enslave him."

In sum, Jaffa believed that Lincoln was a conservative, not a statist. Lincoln showed his opposition to the relativism of the modern age; he challenged the idea that an idea—such as slavery—was acceptable so long as a majority desired it, as in the Confederacy. It was Lincoln, more than anyone else, who said "that just government must be controlled by moral purpose, and that no counting of heads can turn wrong into right."[38]

This debate goes on still among conservatives. Both sides presented powerful arguments, but it did not become at all personal. Buckley was almost never angered but was instead amused by some of the contrarian stands taken by his book review editor, and the tenacity with which he held them.

"FSM [Meyer] will submit a letter for publication together with editorial commentary," Buckley playfully wrote at the end of a summary of an editorial Agony, "in order to dis-entangle the confusion between himself and the bad Frank Meyer."[39]

Then there was the secretary of defense in the Johnson administration, Robert S. McNamara. In May 1966 the secretary gave a speech in Montreal to the American Society of Newspaper Editors, at which he called, as Meyer quoted him, "for universal service in non-military activities for all young people not in the armed forces." McNamara asked for "every young person in the United States to give two years of service to his country—whether in one of the military services, in the Peace Corps, or in some other volunteer develop-mental work at home or abroad."

Meyer was outraged. McNamara was calling for compulsory national service—"from dentistry in Da Nang or baby-sitting in Burma to garbage collecting in Gawanus or social work in Waukegan," Meyer wrote. He was shocked at its "unconstitutional and totalitarian implications." What American liberals were saying was that "we can eliminate the Communist threat not by fighting the Communists, but by 'building bridges' to them and social work-ing the rest of the world." In other words, liberals "are in a splendid position to eat their ideological cake and have it too." They could use the continuing threat of communism "to expand their coercive welfarist programs and steadily increase the scope of government action."

Naturally Meyer saw this as the result "of decades of governmental in-fringement upon the rights of the individual person." Meyer had hold of some raw meat, and he went after it with relish. McNamara's speech was "disturbing," "outrageous," his proposal "characteristic of such regimes as fas-cism and communism." This was the Frank Meyer to whom conservatives always responded. At about this time, Buckley too wrote a column on McNamara's proposals, sounding the same themes as Meyer and reflecting his influence. "The implications are enough to take one's breath away," Buckley wrote.[40]

But these were changing times. By the mid-1960s, opposition to the war in Vietnam and hostility toward the military were growing. And some of this feeling was leaking into the libertarian Right. In his column Meyer had not denied that the state had the power to have a military draft *per se,* but that

McNamara's proposal was an unjust, coercive use of that power. Many libertarians spotted this interpretation and wrote in, urging Meyer to oppose the draft in all cases, that it was "coercion."

So once again Meyer must show conservatives how "fusion" worked, how his brand of conservatism in concrete circumstances was a living doctrine. He argued that libertarians forgot an important principle: that in a society citizens not only have rights but "obligations"—such as to fight for one's country if its national security were threatened. If a person's conscience told him that his government's policies violated the "moral law," then "he has the ultimate right to secede from his obligation—*but only if he simultaneously renounces the benefits and protections of his citizenship.*" It was "invincible moral insensitivity," he thundered, for some libertarians "to prate in the name of freedom about the civil rights of disruptive practitioners of civil disobedience or the free-trade beauties of commerce with the enemy or the iniquity of the citizen's military obligation, when the very structure of our freedom depends from moment to moment on the vigilant maintenance of an armed watch that only the American state can provide."

But Meyer went on to say that while he did not question the legitimacy of a draft, he wondered whether at present it was needed. "A free state has the right to enforce it only when such enforcement is the sole way to defend the structure of freedom itself—that is, only in circumstances of paramount necessity," Meyer continued. And "this has not been the case during the long stretches of the cold war or during the limited wars in Korea and Vietnam." Advocates of the draft seemed to believe that universal conscription was good for citizens, or they argued that shifting to a volunteer military would cost too much money. Neither position convinced Meyer. "A free society can of necessity morally demand universal military services of its citizens," he summarized, "but when overriding necessity is not present, conscription is immoral—be the excuse ideology, convenience, or expense."[41]

So Frank Meyer appeared to be against the draft—but for reasons quite different than the anti-war student Left's. Meyer would always go where his principles took him. Holding to one's principles—that was the important thing, and Meyer increasingly understood his role within conservatism as seeing that those on the Right held onto theirs.

But Meyer remained influential with younger conservatives. At the 1966

Young Americans for Freedom summer leadership school, a poll was taken concerning the philosophical camp to which students belonged. Eight percent identified themselves as "radical traditionalists," allying with L. Brent Bozell; 11 percent saw themselves as libertarians, following Ludwig Von Mises; 15 percent were Objectivists, and were led by Ayn Rand; 32 percent were Russell Kirk traditionalists; and leading the poll by a small plurality (34 percent) were "fusionists," who named as their primary influence Frank Meyer. Later, when the YAF journal *New Guard* saw its pages become the focus of heated dispute between Ayn Rand Objectivists and more traditional conservatives, it quieted the controversy by reprinting Meyer's classic 1962 article "The Twisted Tree of Liberty," in which he had perhaps most effectively propounded his fusionist thesis.[42]

IT WAS NOT ENOUGH, however, for Meyer to explicate conservatism's principles more effectively, or to help consolidate both his own and *National Review*'s leadership and influence within the conservative movement (which Meyer surely did). It was also necessary to address the changing world of the 1960s, to make both his own and *NR*'s worldview relevant. It was an era that saw a domestic increase in crime, violence, and social unrest in the nation's cities; a steady increase in the use, and the social acceptability, of hard drug usage; and an explosion in the popularity, and social influence, of television.

Meyer believed it important to examine social trends so that conservatives could deepen their "understanding" of them. By 1966, the rising crime rate in America's urban areas greatly concerned Meyer. America was approaching the point, he thought, "where the civil society cannot protect us. . . . Daily we see crimes of violence mount. Every year mob actions, whether inspired by ideology or by the senseless savagery of amoral teenagers, become more common."

To all of this, as usual, Meyer believed the liberals had no answers. All they could do was call for gun control or attribute crime to the fact that many were "underprivileged." But Meyer was also critical of the "usual conservative response" to crime—reference to "the breakdown of moral standards" which called for a "revitalization of the Western ethos . . . is no solution to the immediate problem." Other conservatives "would attempt to restore order by increasing the number and power of the police." Meyer thought "that alone would not be enough."

Meyer's answer? "Self-defense," he argued, "has become not a right but a duty." Not vigilantism. Meyer meant the "hiring of private policemen or the volunteering of individual citizens. . . . Rather than talk of government control of firearms, private citizens should be encouraged to arm themselves," as guaranteed in the Bill of Rights in the right to bear arms. The "inherent right to self-defense" must become a conservative watchword.[43]

Meyer's column struck a chord with *NR's* readers. "Enclosed is my check for $5.00," wrote in one *NR* subscriber. "Please send Frank Meyer's marvelous article on the right of self-defense to those nine candidates for self-destruction on the Supreme Court. And ask them if they ever got mugged on a dark night." Months later, Meyer's piece was still drawing favorable reader mail.[44]

Drug use was a somewhat different matter. Hallucinogenic drugs, particularly LSD, became a big story in 1966. Cover stories appeared on the phenomenon in *Newsweek*, *Life*, *Time*, and the *Saturday Evening Post*. Alarmed, Congress banned it, and the Food and Drug Administration sent letters to over two thousand colleges and universities warning of its dangers.[45]

Meyer was concerned that some conservatives might be drawn to a social fad and that libertarians might justify drug usage on purely individualist grounds. LSD was being trumpeted, he wrote in his column, as something that could "raise your consciousness" and would somehow be "educational." Meyer did not believe it. He argued that LSD and other drugs destroyed intellect, that they ruined the "ordering of experience" that had taken generations to create.

Times were changing, and Meyer was having a difficult time comprehending what it all meant. One thing he was sure of: these changes were signs of the "corrosion" of the West, signs of the inroads made by relativism and existentialism. Timothy Leary said that young people should "turn on, tune in, drop out." What it really meant, Meyer charged, was to "turn on the attack on civilizational restraints, tune in on the animal and the instinctual, drop out of civilized society. It epitomizes the rejection of structure, differentiation, order." And he had little use for "the jellyfish sloppiness of mind and body which characterizes the *avante-garde* youth."

But, more profoundly, Meyer believed that people were no longer as concerned with the content, with the meaning, of what they were reading and seeing, but with how it was presented to them, how it entered their consciousness. For this he blamed Marshal McLuhan, who in the mid-1960s, writing on the importance of television, had popularized the phrase "the medium is the message." McLuhan's enemy, Meyer wrote, was "the word—in all its connotations. It is the word, the essence of language and the bearer of thought, upon which civilization is built, which carries from generation to generation knowledge and tradition. McLuhan would deny meaning to all this. The content is nothing. Everything dissolves into the momentary mode of presentation: yesterday, the printing press; today, television." The world was seeing the destruction of "distinction, form and structure," and this was McLuhan's goal. Achieving it, Meyer ruminated sadly, "would constitute a surer assault upon civilization than the Hun or the Goth before the gates of Rome."[46]

The provocative Meyer once again landed himself in controversy. He was deluged with letters and phone calls, most of which said the equivalent of "isn't McLuhan describing what is actually taking place, and shouldn't we all catch up with it and learn to live with it?" But Meyer believed that such an attitude was precisely the problem. This "absolves" the intellectual, the statesman, and all elites from their societal "responsibility." It was the symptom of a society "simultaneously suffering from a deep spiritual malady and from the disruptions of breathless technological change."

Meyer would not back down an inch. McLuhan, he maintained, was "a crank and, like all cranks, has a single explanation for everything." He was an exemplary proponent of the current philosophy of "technological determinism." Meyer well remembered his communist days and the Marxist analysis of history, heavily driven by the question of who owned the means of production. That was determinism at its worst, and it led to totalitarianism. McLuhan's determinism could be just as dangerous; it declared that "nothing substantial results from the conscious will of men"; there was no room for the "fruits of reason," for "the intuitive sweep of the human imagination." The "discrimination and differentiation" so essential to society must, we were now being told, be "submerged in an interpersonal, electronically-linked collective of 'cool' togetherness."

Meyer then quoted McLuhan as saying that a new society was coming, indeed had arrived, and that it must have a new "faith"—"a faith that concerns the ultimate harmony of all being." Meyer would have no part of this global "collective" either, would not buy into this celebration of the television age. "The medium is the medium—no more," he declared. "Whatever its protean technological changes, the human spirit will use it for good or evil. The fate of men is in their own hands—in their understanding of the wisdom of tradition

and their mastery of the gifts of reason." For Frank Meyer, free will and human freedom must always be the message, and nothing else.[47]

SOME MUST HAVE believed that Meyer was out of touch with modern society,
petulantly rejecting all change. But it would not be fair to say that Meyer did not
try to understand what was happening to America, or that he himself never
changed. .

By the spring of 1966, he could see that politics, society, and the conservative movement were becoming fundamentally altered, and he urged *National
Review* to address this. In a memo to *NR's* editors, he argued that "a partial
reassessment of *NR's* role and therefore of its content" was needed. On politics,
this Goldwater conservative, who along with Rusher and Rickenbacker had
pushed the magazine to involve itself in the political arena, now took a very
different view:

> The 1964 election was the last chance to unite under responsible leadership
> the right-wing populist and know-nothing elements with the new conser-
> vative movement of the past dozen years. Since then they have split wider
> and wider apart. The net result as far as politics is concerned is that the
> Republican Party now consists of four separate groups—Liberals, Birchite
> know-nothings, sober conservatives, and opportunist politicians. In the reac-
> tion against the extreme right, the best that can be expected is the leader-
> ship of this last group. Such a principled conservative movement as the
> Goldwater movement is in the immediate future just about ruled out.

Thus, although *National Review* could not ignore politics, it would be "un-
faithful to its function if it continued to give the same commitment to party
politics that it did during the Goldwater years. Politics in this sense, I think,
should be de-emphasized."

Meyer argued that the country was increasingly affected, and divided, by
such things as the Vietnam War, the civil rights movement, and the generation
gap. It was important for *NR* to recognize these changes and deal with them. He
continued:

> On the other hand, profound changes are occurring in American society,
> many of them just beneath the surface, as well as in those intellectual areas
> that will determine the issues two or three years from now. The Establish-
> ment is splitting, and not merely on foreign policy. All sorts of real issues exist

which conservatives have not seriously recognized, and to which certainly they have not given creative thought. Simultaneously, the readership of *NR* is gradually changing. We have a great many less of the Neanderthals, and we are being taken seriously by intelligent and troubled people of varied formal persuasions.

In sum, Meyer hoped *National Review* would "shift our emphasis and devote a good deal more attention to developing conservative analyses of our national life."[48]

Hard it must have been for Meyer, the ardent political activist, to advocate a step back from politics. But as even Meyer's frequent opponent James Burnham said, Meyer thought deeply and was always in touch with current developments. He obviously realized that sometimes change is necessary, especially for an enterprise on the road back from a devastating electoral defeat. And the 1960s gave Meyer and *National Review* plenty of opportunities to develop "conservative analyses of our national life."

Civil Rights

NATIONAL REVIEW AT FIRST had little sympathy with the civil rights movement. These conservatives believed in the primacy of tradition—in slow, gradual, organic change—and constitutional processes over high-pressure social movements. Most of those at *NR* had spent little time in the South and understood little about the reality of what segregation meant, save for Buckley and his family, who had ties to South Carolina, which perhaps led Buckley (for a time) to absorb some of the white southern view toward segregation. But the seeds of change in their thinking existed. The views of the *NR* circle, and those of Frank Meyer, evolved over time, and eventually a first step was taken toward moving responsible conservatism away from any association with racism. To understand fully Meyer's views on race, they must be put in the context of what other *NR* conservatives believed during these turbulent years.

IN THE 1950S, *National Review* had raised all kinds of objections to the movement for civil rights, especially the Supreme Court's insistence that southern school districts desegregate "with all deliberate speed." Editorially, which usually meant the copy of Buckley or James Burnham, *NR* argued that the primary issue was that the Court's rulings were based on unsound constitutional reasoning. The Court, wrote the editors in June 1957, "is sitting no longer as a judicial bench, but as the nation's supreme legislature, unmaking and making the nation's laws." It now reached "into our schools, our recreation, our smallest business enterprise, our entertainment, our hospitals, our churches." The liberal establishment on the Court wished to establish "absolute social equality" between whites and blacks "independently of their own wishes, and of the will of local communities."

Soon thereafter Buckley published a piece on the integration controversy by the noted southern traditionalist conservative Richard Weaver. Weaver argued provocatively that the current changes in race relations were the leading edge of what he called "racial collectivism," which eventually could lead to communism. Civil rights laws had weakened the concept of private property, since one now could not discriminate in selling property and businesses were prevented from discriminating by race in their hiring. Was this not the kind of state control found in a communist state? Furthermore, Weaver charged that forced integration "would ignore the truth that equals are not born identical. . . . In a free society associations for educational, cultural, social and business purposes have a right to protect their integrity against political fanaticism. The alternative to this is the destruction of a free society and replacement of its functions of government, which is the Marxist dream." NR editorially stressed that there was an alternative to such social engineering: "The contrary conception—organic, historical, traditional it can be called—proceeds from a conviction of the limitations of man and his works, a humility about his ability to achieve or even define perfection, a belief that the perfect society is not of this world. . . . If we believe that these institutions should—and can—be changed for the better, then let the change not come by arbitrary and catastrophic decree from without but principally by a slower, more organic growth from within."[1]

As fall 1957 approached, and the possibility of conflict between Arkansas and the federal government over school integration grew more likely, Buckley wanted NR to take a bolder stand, to make the case against federal interference in a daring and provocative way. An editorial appeared in late August 1957 titled "Why the South Must Prevail." The central question in the current debate, wrote NR, was "whether the white community in the South is entitled to take such measures as are necessary to prevail, politically and culturally, in areas in which it does not predominate numerically. The sobering answer is *Yes*—the white community is so entitled, because, for the time being, it is the advanced race." It continued: "If the majority wills what is socially atavistic, then to thwart the majority may be, though undemocratic, enlightened."

Many would consider this thinly disguised racism. But *NR* took pains to disassociate itself from the southern racism of the Ku Klux Klan variety. The editorial concluded: "The South confronts one grave moral challenge. It must not exploit the fact of Negro backwardness to preserve the Negro as a servile class. It is tempting and convenient to block the progress of a minority whose services as menials are economically useful. Let the South never permit itself to do this. So long as it is merely asserting the right to impose superior mores for whatever period it takes to effect a genuine cultural equality between the races, and so long as it does so by humane and charitable means, the South is in step with civilization, as is the Congress that permits it to function."[2]

This was not enough for then-senior editor L. Brent Bozell. Bozell was the magazine's resident constitutional expert and political reporter. He argued that *NR*'s editorial was "dead wrong" and would harm the conservative cause. *National Review* was in effect sanctioning southern lawbreaking to preserve its culture, he maintained. For since the South was ignoring the Fifteenth Amendment, *NR* was indirectly giving its assent to the intimidation of black voters and other racist practices. It called into question "how seriously *National Review* takes the law and the Constitution." Bozell understood conservatives in general "to be telling Supreme Courts and Presidents and legislatures and their Liberal advisers out over the land that, except for transcendent reasons of conscience, the American system does not permit private judgment as to whether the Constitution and valid laws should be obeyed...." But if *NR* now supported opposition to constitutional law, its position collapsed. It was unacceptable "when we begin to pick and choose between constitutional provisions and laws we like and those we don't, when instead of urging repeal of those we don't like, we condone violation of them."[3]

If *NR*'s position on civil rights was nuanced, it still had far to go. When the crisis in Little Rock broke, and Governor Faubus used state militia to keep black students from attending an all-white school amidst shouting, racist mobs, *NR* argued that the entire crisis could be traced back to the Supreme Court's

interference in the nation's race relations. The racial situation had been improving until the Court interposed itself. Now conservatives found themselves in a difficult position. "Unless we are prepared to abandon the whole
scheme of a limited, mixed, and divided sovereignty, we must defend Governor Faubus, and his right and duty to preserve and defend the domestic peace
of his state according to his oath of office," *National Review* wrote. But "we
cannot advocate the defiance of due and lawful process, however distasteful it
may be, without risking the breakdown of law in general, and of constitutional government. . . . Therefore the situation in Little Rock has no just
solution, and can be settled only by violence and the threat of force." Bozell
again disagreed, contending that Governor Faubus was not truly defending
traditional constitutional positions, such as interposition. He simply sought
racist votes: "Governor Faubus may have struck just the right balance for his
private political purposes, but in the process he would seem to have weakened the South's position, and cheapened it."[4]

THE CIVIL RIGHTS struggle slowly escalated. There was more discussion of the
issue in Congress, and southern "freedom riders" were brutally beaten by a
white mob in Alabama. But *National Review*'s position changed slowly. In response to the freedom riders, the magazine pleaded that outsiders must try to
"understand" the South.

> [Jim Crow] does not strike the average white Southerner as wrong, nor does
> experience argue that the average white Southerner should be reasonable in
> making this one concession. . . . The South views the attack on Jim Crow as
> merely one proposition in a soritical series whose necessary end is the aban-
> donment, to a strange and cosmopolitan government lodged in the remote
> eastern capital of Washington, of the right to determine the shape, and the
> quality, of Southern life. Never mind that we (whose Jim Crowism is more
> sophisticated) disagree with, or disapprove of that regime, or that part of it
> that requires the social separation of the races. That is what *they* feel, and *they*
> feel that *their* life is for *them* to structure; that the Negro has grown up under
> generally benevolent circumstances, considering where he started and how
> far he had to go; that he is making progress; that the coexistence of that
> progress and the Southern way of life demand, for the time being, separation.
> A conspicuous, theatrical, cinemascopic bus ride into the heart of things to
> challenge with language of unconditional surrender this deeply felt belief
> was met, inevitably, by a spastic response. By violence . . . Let us at least
> attempt to understand.[5]

The tug-of-war within *NR*'s thinking continued until 1962, when James Meredith attempted to enter Ole Miss. This time there was a notable toughening of the journal's position toward southern racists, including Mississippi Governor Ross Barnett. To be sure, it was also skeptical of the civil rights movement. William Rusher wrote to a friend that "I suggest to you that it takes a special kind of blindness for Americans to concentrate so furiously and so emotionally on the delicate social problem which is gradually working itself out in the southern United States, while tolerating amiably the infinitely more brutal despotism that is the daily bread of people behind the Iron Curtain." Meanwhile, *NR* editorialized that the crisis at Ole Miss showed Meredith "wants that campus and Mr. Khrushchev wants the Western Hemisphere, and the Kennedy Administration is slowly running out of time to figure out which area most needs a show of force." Buckley, writing for himself, argued that those "who continue to honor the federal system" should "despise the Barnetts of this world," but should also "feel considerable sympathy for the right of a community up against the rights of a Supreme Court which . . . has recently converted itself into a 'third legislative chamber.'"[6]

But when President Kennedy used force to quell the worst rioting on the Ole Miss campus, and when angry crowds of hate-filled whites continued to harass Meredith, *National Review* lashed out against southern racism. "If Mr. Meredith is looking for changes in the attitude and actions of his fellow students," it stated in early 1963, "whose matchless rudeness toward a minority of one ill suits a society that cherishes its tradition of polite manners, personal honor, and bravery, he has a point. The gentlemen of the South are not alone in regarding states' rights as a matter for principle. And *National Review* is not alone in remarking that the cause of principle is never served by jeering mobs." Even such mild rebukes as this gained the magazine some vicious hate mail. "To hell with you, Buckley!" wrote one outraged Mississippian.[7]

NR for a time would hold to this position, hewing to its constitutional and legal point of view while speaking out against racism in all its forms. When Martin Luther King and his Southern Christian Leadership Conference began an antisegregation campaign in Birmingham, Alabama, in the spring of 1963, *NR* criticized "that crew of professionals who spend their time rioting from city to city like a traveling crap game, leaving behind them the emotional and material ruins that usually follow upon speculations against the laws of probability.

And that is true irrespective of the intrinsic merits of the Negroes' case." But then Buckley, on viewing Bull Connor's attempts to repress black demonstrators, bluntly told Alabamans that they must allow black Americans to assemble peaceably, that blacks too were included in the Bill of Rights. "Continued failure to do so," he wrote in *NR*, "will as a matter of hard political fact have the effect of easing over into the hands of a strong Federal Government, whose symbol is the paratrooper with bayonet, a greater and greater role in the evolution of Southern affairs."[8]

When in 1963 President Kennedy proposed a sweeping new civil rights bill, *NR* was opposed. While someday black Americans would be free, this would not happen "tomorrow": "no, not tomorrow—they can never be free tomorrow, so long as they are thought of, are pandered to, and act, as a monolithic minority; any more than they became truly 'free' upon Mr. Lincoln's proclamation to that effect." When blacks did gain their freedom, the magazine hoped they would find a society "free of domination from those external forces which have suppressed minority and majority rights wherever they have seized control, and free of that domestic menace—overweening government—which discriminates against freedom without reference to race, color, or creed."

A short time later *NR* published a lengthy article by the *Richmond News-Leader's* James Jackson Kilpatrick that strenuously quarreled with the bill's constitutionality. Kilpatrick wrote passionately that legislation cannot eradicate racial prejudice, that while he did not favor discrimination he did defend an individual's right to discriminate should he so desire. This was what the Constitution was all about, Kilpatrick contended, not about the "right to be right." When over 200,000 people marched in Washington, D.C., for civil rights in August 1963, *NR* editorialized that "nothing is clearer than that the way to induce a philosophical discussion on [the civil rights bill] is not to encourage a stampede of several hundred thousand people into Washington who lust after a piece of legislation, and damn the arguments against it."[9]

On the other hand, *National Review* also published a surprisingly positive review, by Garry Wills, of James Baldwin's *The Fire Next Time*. Baldwin, a young, militant black author, had written such things as that "the only thing white people have that black people need or want, is power—and no one holds power forever." Wills in response wrote that the United States, and the West in general, had in fact a racist past, had been hurtful to the black race, but that even so

Western civilization should not be torn down in response, as Baldwin seemed to suggest.

But then African-American leaders began to demand economic as well as civil rights, and some urged more radical actions than King's nonviolent demonstrations. In response, early in 1964 James Burnham wrote lengthy analyses of the civil rights movement, studying it as a sociological phenomenon. For one thing, Burnham asserted that it was not a civil rights movement, but a "social revolution," as could be seen in its methods. It relied no longer on the legal system, the ballot box, or on mass demonstrations, but took to "huge extra-legal, often bluntly illegal, mass operations—mass sit-downs, blocking of the public highways, interference in private and governmental business, deliberate provocation of mass arrests . . ." Most importantly—here was where it "plunged into darkness"—it had no realizable goal. "How could a series of mass demonstrations, sit-ins and sit-downs bring knowledge, wealth, skills, culture, happiness? These are prizes that individuals only can win. . . . [T]here is no short cut in East Africa *or* the United States. . . . [W]hat the movement is now trying to rebel against is not the peculiar fate of Negroes but the human condition itself, against Man's Fate."[10]

The violence in early 1965 against civil rights marchers in Selma, Alabama, however, symbolized most conspicuously by the antics of Selma police chief Jim Clark, led *National Review* to take its strongest stand yet in admiration of what the civil rights movement had accomplished. Thus, Buckley in his column was as usual both philosophical and provocative, arguing that *both* whites and blacks in some parts of the country lacked the education for an informed vote, and perhaps the vote should be taken from them both. Buckley also stated that "on the single issue of whether a Negro in Alabama should be deprived of the vote, simply because of the color of his skin, it seems to me that there cannot be any argument: none moral, and certainly none constitutional." *NR* editorialized that there was no justification "for the undoubted and indefensible violation of Negro rights by the State of Alabama and its officials." The magazine further congratulated King on his successful strategy.

> [T]here is no doubt at all the Reverend Martin Luther King has out-maneuvered and out-fought the State of Alabama. Dr. King has again shown his very considerable mastery over the methods and arts of modern psychopolitical warfare. He has used Selma as a lever to move public opinion and

the national government in his chosen direction. There was nothing in the Selma situation that guaranteed him so favorable an outcome as . . . he is gaining, if his opponents had shown more intelligence and flexibility in their counter-measures. Blind prejudice, big-bellied bullhorn sheriffs, and club-swinging cops are not enough equipment for government in our time.[11]

BUT 1965 PROVED TO BE a turning point, both for the American civil rights movement and for *National Review*'s position on it. The magazine had slowly grown in its sympathy for the movement. When Congress at President Johnson's urging passed the Voting Rights Act, *NR* stated that it was touched to see, among blacks voting for the first time in the South, "in the photographs, the seriousness and hope and quiet pride in their faces and to read their deeply felt statements, so often religious in root, of the meaning to them, as they struggle to express it, of this act of entering the electorate of their country, the earth's greatest nation."[12]

Yet the wheel of history continued to turn. Only five days after President Johnson signed the act, a huge race riot erupted in Watts, a suburb of Los Angeles. In six days of violence, 34 people were killed, over 800 injured, more than 4,000 arrested. Damage was estimated at over $45 million. It was only the beginning. In the 1966–67 period, there were riots in over two hundred American cities. The civil rights movement subsequently splintered, some elements holding to Martin Luther King's nonviolence, others becoming radicalized, speaking of "black power" and advocating violence against whites. In 1967, H. Rap Brown, head of the Student Non-violent Coordinating Committee, was quoted as saying in Maryland that his followers should "burn this town down. . . . When you tear down the white man, brother, you are hitting him in the money. . . . Don't love him to death, shoot him to death."[13]

NR conservatives were horrified at these calls for mindless destruction and joined the "backlash" against the civil rights movement and its leaders. After the riot in Watts, an *NR* editorial argued that the best way to guarantee that it would occur again was "to moon over the affair and yap about injustices by whites to Negroes, about the notorious guilt of the white slave trader, and the rest of it. The other way is to recognize that the Hitler in ourselves surfaced; that it must not be permitted to surface; that those in whom it surfaced must be prosecuted and punished and above all denied the solace of sophistical defenses."[14]

Soon Buckley wrote that the nation needed a "hiatus" from new civil rights legislation. "The realization has dawned that all those legislative enactments calculated to produce equality before the law were not enough to reify the heavenly kingdom," said *National Review.* And should King overzealously attempt to change national policy through disruptive sit-ins and demonstrations, "Word should be gently got through to the non-violent avenger Dr. King, that in the unlikely event that he succeeds in mobilizing his legions, they will be most efficiently, indeed most zestfully repressed."[15]

Nor did it help when, in a major speech in New York City in 1967, King came out strongly against the Vietnam War. *National Review* opined that in the speech King's "demagogy" was "soaring," that from it "he would have won an anti-American shouting contest against the principal hog-caller for the Red Guards." *NR* conservatives were becoming tired of the civil rights movement, tired of the violence that seemed to accompany it in the inner cities, and tired of its opposition to the Vietnam War. Buckley called Stokely Carmichael, the origi-nator of the "black power" phrase, "the exact opposite number of the Ku Kluxer, and if he were white he would no doubt be in the front rank of the bitter-drunk zealots calling for 'the lynching of the niggers.'" Buckley said the rioters in Newark, New Jersey, had "a raging disease of the spirit"; they possessed "the anarchic passion to smash." And when Martin Luther King was assassinated in April 1968, Buckley could write that "his virtues were considerable . . . [but] a year ago he accused the United States of committing crimes equal in horror to those committed by the Nazis in Germany. One could only gasp at the profana-tion." It was "terrifying," he concluded, that "the cretin who leveled his rifle at the head of Martin Luther King may have absorbed the talk, so freely available, about the supremacy of the individual conscience, such talk as Mar-tin Luther King, God rest his troubled and compassionate soul, had so widely and indiscriminately made." Yes, things had changed.[16]

FRANK MEYER'S interpretation of the civil rights movement did not differ sub-stantially from the line taken by Buckley, Burnham, and *National Review.* Like the magazine, Meyer in 1957 opposed Eisenhower's handling of the crisis in Little Rock, stressing even more than *NR* his constitutional and states' rights objec-tions to the Supreme Court and the federal government's position on integra-tion, while hoping that eventually blacks would receive equal treatment through natural evolution.

But by 1963, as the movement gained national attention, Meyer began

to speak out. He dealt with the issue somewhat differently than did the magazine, examining the ideas behind the movement and its titular head, Martin
Luther King, and assessing their relationship to conservative principle. In June
of that year, Meyer for the first time wrote on King and his campaign. The
debate, Meyer said, was "loaded with ideology and sentimentality," weighted
with "established egalitarian cliches." He hoped to get beyond those. Meyer
was careful to emphasize that he believed there had been "undoubted wrongs
suffered by American Negroes," and that he believed in the "justice of some
of their aspirations. . . . I know that the Negro people have suffered profound
wrongs—not least in their original enslavement by Northern merchants and
Southern plantation owners." Meyer further stressed that he assumed "the
innate value of every created human being and the right of every American
citizen, enshrined in the Constitution, to equal protection before the law."
But however much he agreed with their goals, he opposed the civil rights
movement's "unmeasured" and "unlimited" demands. A "typical modern revolution" was in the making, with the passion of blacks being stirred to "fever-
ish heights." The result could be the "destruction of the constitutional order."
This was Meyer's key point: any change in the legal position of American
blacks must come through "prescriptive legal modes." Relations between
human beings were "multifarious," "delicate," and could "never be regulated
by governmental power without disaster to a free society." Laws enforcing
segregation in the South were a "monstrosity," Meyer averred; but so too
would be laws that would excessively "regulate the behavior" of private citizens.

The lawmakers of the nation, Meyer wrote, must not be pressured by "rioting mobs, intemperate demagogues and rampant ideology." The situation was
"becoming starkly revolutionary and devastatingly dangerous. It is time for sober men of both races to take counsel and establish a consensus that will satisfy
the claims of justice *in consonance with the constitutional guarantees of freedom and
order.*"[17]

Meyer continued to hammer away at the theme of constitutionalism:
change must come through the ordered workings of the American governmental system. In 1965, after the violence used against civil rights marchers in
Selma and the intense reaction it provoked across the country, Meyer decided
to analyze King's theory of nonviolence. Not surprisingly, Meyer found it

wanting. As he understood it, King's theory involved four steps. First, nonviolent demonstrators must go out into the streets and exercise their constitutional right to protest. Next, opponents of civil rights would respond with violence against the demonstrators. Then the American public, its conscience pricked by the scenes of repression, would demand the federal government's involvement through corrective legislation, and eventually the legislation would be passed.

Meyer contended that King's theory contained a hidden subtext. It depended, in order to succeed, on provoking the defenders of the status quo to violence. Meyer denounced this as "hypocrisy." "It is violent in its very essence," he charged, "relying as it does upon the terror inspired by mobs to destroy the processes of constitutional government." Why use the word "mob"? Because King's forces were "an assemblage of persons, themselves a militant minority of a minority, devoted to over-awing constitutional processes . . . by the threat of creating terror and civil chaos." Meyer called this "the violence of nonviolence."

He did not deny that there were times when civil disobedience was justified—in combating Nazi or communist totalitarianism, for example. But "against a constitutional order with inbuilt modes for the redress of grievances, there is no such justification." True, in the American system of governance, righting wrongs was often a slow process. Drawing upon his Burkean side, Meyer wrote that representatives were not meant to be "mere messenger boys required to register the opinion of a majority of their constituents on any issue that arises." King and his followers did not seem to realize this. Thus, his movement could "destroy the very possibility of representative government. For deliberation, adjustment, and justice he would substitute the assemblage of a militant mob, the provocation of violence, the stirring up of mass emotion, culminating in the *forcing* of his ideological prescriptions upon the constituted representatives of the republic. It is a program for government by force and the threat of terror."[18]

By 1966 Meyer toughened his criticisms. A persistent question lurking in the background of his writings on civil rights was libertarianism. How could he, a *libertarian* conservative, assail King's use of the freedom of speech and assembly? Was this not guaranteed in the Bill of Rights? Was this not the essence of freedom, of which Meyer spoke so often? After some serious reading of "the analyses, the pronouncements, polemics of the protagonists, black and white, of the Negro movement," he concluded that it was entering a "new phase." The key to understanding it was not to examine the differences between moderates and radicals, or between the advocates of "black power" and Reverend King. Instead, the civil rights movement had "passed over from a program of 'civil rights' to a program of confiscatory socialism, revolutionary in its essence." There were "threatenings of unfocused violence," a call for a $100 billion "freedom budget," as well as "the threat of blackmail by violence" behind nearly every minority demand. A libertarian must oppose the current civil rights movement, because it no longer advocated basic civil rights for African-Americans but aimed at a socialistic program of governmental redistribution of wealth, which conservatives, wedded to the freedom of the individual person, must always oppose.

Meyer reminded his readers of what was still conservatism's first and foremost enemy: liberalism. In his eyes, American liberals greatly exacerbated the civil rights crisis in America. Men such as Lyndon Johnson, Hubert Humphrey, and Robert F. Kennedy had been "condoning violence and blaming the worst outbreaks in the history of this country not on the immorality and barbarism of the participants, but on 'poverty' and 'conditions.'" Liberalism "encouraged an alliance of agitators with criminal elements to create a climate of terror."

Meyer seemed especially irked that certain (to him) important questions were not even being asked. What of individual differences, of differences between races? "If individual A fails while individual B succeeds, it is always the fault of external circumstances," Meyer grumbled, "and not of his quality or his effort or his moral fiber." And if one racial group lagged behind others in its achievements, "it is forbidden to inquire of the qualities of the group in its average." Black leaders must encourage "hard work and free enterprise, the rallying of the community against its own criminal and disruptive elements." Blacks must devote themselves to "the task of self-improvement which is the only answer to its condition."[19]

Reliance on government was not the answer. Nor could Meyer let go of the idea that certain "forbidden questions" were disallowed by liberalism. Meyer in private made the blunt argument that the "civilizing process [of blacks] has not been completed." Much of it resulted from slavery, and from their subsequent difficulties. But how to raise the issue and not be accused of racism? In a later column, Meyer tried to do so obliquely. Liberals, he wrote, held that any distinctions between the races were due solely to "environmental" factors such as poverty, racism, or lack of education. But Meyer believed that "heredity" should also be considered—a taboo subject that many considered racist. Typically he did not back down an inch. "While it has seemed to the common sense of the ages that human beings and groups of human beings exhibit in their character and their performance the mutual interplay of heredity and environment," he concluded, "it is an all but universal liberal dogma that environment is decisive." A "dilemma" for the American Left emerged: "social dogma or freedom of inquiry?"[20]

By early 1968, as Martin Luther King announced an upcoming "Poor People's Campaign" in the nation's capital, and after two consecutive summers of rioting in America's cities, Meyer's attacks against the civil rights movement and its allies intensified. Meyer believed that America was coming apart, that nothing less than the defense of its civilization was at stake. He spoke of such fundamentals more and more often now; he wrote less of a clash between liberalism and conservatism and more of the need to protect "civilization" itself. He followed the development of King's Poor People's Campaign carefully. A gathering of multiracial demonstrators in Washington, D.C., it hoped to bring the federal government to a standstill until it addressed the problem of black poverty. King promised "massive dislocation" in the nation's capital; his methods would include trespassing on the White House and Capitol Hill, sit-down strikes on Washington's thoroughfares, and various kinds of boycotts and demonstrations.

First riots, and now talk of disrupting the day-to-day actions of the U.S. government itself. Meyer had grudgingly admired King's continuing adherence to nonviolence. But it had become clear, he wrote, that this had only been a "fig leaf" that was now "rakishly askew." Meyer angrily contended that King's new program removed "any doubts as to his insurrectionary intentions against constitutional government." It meant that "it is obvious on the face of it that such actions will have to be met with force unless the government is to surrender to Dr. King." The situation seemed to be moving toward a "coordinated rebellion," to "a crisis that, if it is not met by the firm methods available to constitutional government to maintain itself, can only end in bloody race war, with a resulting movement of government towards that dictatorship which always follows anarchy." To Meyer, there could be no freedom without order. This distinguished him as a libertarian conservative, as opposed to a radical libertarian.

Having said that, Meyer strove to show his sympathy for black Americans. His "extensive reading" on the state of American blacks, as best he could tell, showed they had two main goals: "respect and employment." Neither could be gained through "government action," nor through "revolutionary methods." As soon as African-Americans realized this, they could move down "the only road to advancement. It is the road that other ethnic groups have successfully taken, and while the difficulties for the Negro are greater, the prejudices deeper, the principle is the same." The most important asset of black Americans, Meyer asserted, was "the great fund of American good will toward any group striving to improve itself. That good will still continues despite the excesses of the past few years. But if civil order is not restored quickly in our cities, it will soon vanish."[21]

Meyer was appalled by the riots of summer 1967. As spring 1968 approached, Meyer believed America to be in a state of "endemic disorder," with established authority threatened by "mob violence." He compared the rioters to the Jacobins of the French Revolution, and thought that his country was on the verge of "incipient revolution."

In the midst of all this the Report of the National Advisory Commission on Civil Disorders, led by former Illinois Governor Otto Kerner (often referred to as the Kerner Commission), was released. The commission essentially warned of the development of two Americas, one white, and one black, and in short that government should take a stronger role in trying to alleviate America's racial problems. Meyer, predictably, blasted the report as "one of the most preposterous ebullitions of the liberal spirit ever seriously submitted to the public." It "has put the blame everywhere but where it belongs, everywhere, that is, except upon the rioters and upon the liberals who, with their abstract ideology, prepared the way for the riots by their contempt for social order and their utopian egalitarian enticements and incitements." Once again liberalism was the enemy. The liberal solutions that the commission proposed embodied "a utopian theory that if sums massive enough to bankrupt the nation and heavily penalize the productive, tax-paying section of the population were spent, and if simultaneously deep-ingrained prejudices were eliminated, then at some point in the future . . . everything would be solved."

Meyer contended that the only way for American blacks to advance was by developing "economic and social skills and disciplines," which millions were in fact doing. What the government should be doing was to examine "how our free economic system could be motivated to assist in this decisive endeavor." By 1968 things had become very simple for men such as Frank Meyer: it was either order or anarchy, civilization or barbarism. As he wrote in response to a libertarian critic: "I am a libertarian conservative, not an anarchist. I will always support whatever expenditure of force is necessary to defend the order of a free society against sabotage or sedition, as I will against a foreign enemy."[22]

WHAT FRANK MEYER and *National Review* conservatives said publicly concerning the civil rights movement differed little from what was discussed internally at the magazine. But civil rights never assumed the importance at *NR* that it did for many other Americans, and that, perhaps, it should have.

Many within the magazine watched in sympathy as the movement unfolded. William Rusher recalled the "education" that Martin Luther King and his crusade provided conservatives. Lee Edwards, an occasional *NR* contributor and enthusiastic Goldwater activist in 1964, was there when Reverend King gave his "I have a dream" speech, and found his rhetoric and his sentiments "soaring."[23]

But to many conservatives King began to rely too heavily on "radical leftists" to advise him on foreign policy, which led him to oppose the war in Vietnam and to be critical of both the American military and of capitalism in general. "I could not understand his odyssey," Edwards recalled, "in just a few short years, from Christian pastor and disciple of Gandhi to strident prophet and anti-war activist." This bothered men such as Frank Meyer and James Burnham, too. Meyer, as Buckley remembered, "was always fearful of a consolidation of statist authority," while Burnham leaned "very heavily on his sociological feeling that equality was a sociological achievement, not one effected by the state."[24]

Also, through William Rusher *National Review* possessed a conduit for inside information on some of the nation's important political players; this came through Rusher's FBI contacts, which he had made while working with the Senate Internal Security Subcommittee in the 1950s. Thus the editors were privy to the FBI's worries about supposed procommunists on King's staff. Rusher also heard rumors, apparently credible, that through FBI wiretaps there existed recorded episodes of Martin Luther King's womanizing, which supposedly were being played for the amusement of those attending government and FBI stag parties. "I duly advised the editors," Rusher recalled, "and clearly recall that they were distinctly unamused."[25]

Overall, within *NR* there were occasional calls for a fuller discussion of the issue—"I have several times attempted to get a full-dress discussion of the Negro question at one of our formal conferences," Meyer wrote to Buckley in 1966; "I continue to think it is vital that we have such a discussion"—but other issues always seemed to interfere. Foreign policy remained most important to the magazine's editors, and with the war in Vietnam escalating and disrupting the nation, *NR* spent much time on it. And then there was politics to worry about; the 1968 race was coming up, and it spurred questions concerning whom (if anyone) *NR* would support, what position it would take on the various candidates, what it should say about George Wallace, and so on. On race, *NR* would only go so far. As Buckley later reflected, "I rather wish we had taken a more transcendent position [on civil rights], which might have been done by advocating civil rights legislation with appropriate safeguards."[26]

In the end, the civil rights movement of the 1960s was a lost opportunity for Frank Meyer and *National Review*. Surely it could have advocated freedom and equal rights for American blacks without violating its libertarian, antigovernment credo, and without disturbing America's social "order." On the other hand, *NR* did perform one important service for conservatism in these years, and that was to speak out against southern racism and violence. This was not always easy; the magazine took some fire from southerners who saw such criticism as a betrayal. Nor did many people in mainstream, establishment circles necessarily notice the stand the magazine had taken. Perhaps it would take a national election, in which the race issue played an important part, to allow *National Review* to take a stronger, more noticeable stand against racism. That opportunity would come in 1968. But for now, another issue arose for *NR* and Frank Meyer to address, one that was to tear the country apart even more than civil rights: the war in Vietnam.

Vietnam

WHEN, IN THE EARLY 1960S, Marxist guerrillas, strongly supported by communist North Vietnam, began to pose a serious threat to the pro-American Diem regime in South Vietnam, the Kennedy White House greatly escalated the number of American military personnel in South Vietnam. Over 16,000 Americans were in Vietnam by 1963, and U.S. aid reached into the hundreds of millions of dollars per year.

The situation in Vietnam became a crisis during the presidency of Lyndon Johnson. The communist insurgents (soon known as the Viet Cong, or VC) were sweeping into the South. An American pullout, leaving all of Southeast Asia exposed to the communists, would be a significant American defeat in the Cold War and a blow to U.S. prestige and credibility. The Johnson administration thus continued to increase the American military presence in South Vietnam until July 1965, when, in order to advance the war effort by carrying the fight to the VC, Johnson ordered 150,000 U.S. troops to South Vietnam. The U.S. had gone to war.[1]

NATIONAL REVIEW CONSERVATIVES followed the events closely. But what particularly galvanized NR on the Vietnam issue was not only America's involvement in yet another Cold War struggle, but the organized anti-war movement within the country.

The "movement," as some called it, was a mix of elements reaching back to the 1950s "Beat" poets and other cultural nonconformists. By the early 1960s, it included many "baby-boom" students opposed to nuclear weapons, racial injustice, and a society dominated by machines and computers. By 1965, the movement took on the war in Vietnam.[2]

But these protesters were not only against the war; some seemed actually to want a communist victory in Vietnam. Others—with their long hair, their beads, blue jeans, drugs, and "counterculture"—appeared to want to destroy America's traditional values. Those on the Right hardly knew what to make of it all. At the first significant protest against the war in Vietnam, held in Washington, D.C., in April 1965, Students for a Democratic Society leader Paul Potter said bluntly, "I would rather see Vietnam Communist than see it under continuous subjugation or the ruin that American domination has brought." Soon, anti-war leaders Tom Hayden and Staughton Lynd, in a book on North Vietnam titled *The Other Side,* praised North Vietnam's "socialism of the heart," which they saw in "the freedom to weep practiced by everyone—from guerrillas to generals." Radical leader Jerry Rubin, just before marching on the Pentagon in 1967, was quoted as saying that he and his movement were "now in the business of wholesale disruption and widespread resistance and dislocation of the American society." His occasional comrade Abbie Hoffman proclaimed, "I think kids should kill their parents."[3]

Those against the war paid little attention to, and had a very low opinion of, movement conservatives and anyone associated with *National Review.* Anyone not actively opposing the war was part of the "establishment." Conservative Republicans, wrote a radical academic, were representative of "the most reactionary forces in American life." Others on the anti-war Left saw conservatives as simply "slack-jawed, Social Darwinian, and predictably hopeless." "We really did not know who William F. Buckley Jr. was, or what he stood for," recalled then-radical author David Horowitz.[4]

BUT THEN, FRANK MEYER and the rest of *National Review* did not think much of the anti-war movement, either. *NR* had noticed the development of significant anti-war protest early on and had taken it deadly seriously, with rhetoric to match. As early as March 1965 *NR* saw the "serried ranks of the coexisters, appeasers, defeatists, pacifists, beatniks, socio-masochists, leftists, fellow-travelers, Communists, and mischievous Hate America Firsters make their Pavlovian response" to President Johnson's bombing campaign against North Vietnam; it was "all as familiar as baseball in springtime." Buckley soon began calling those opposing the war "kooks," and those intellectuals supporting them "pro-Communists." *National Review* editorialized that anti-war activists were the "frothing guerrillas of the campuses, streets, and gutters." James Burnham, in addition to occasionally referring to the Vietnam War's opponents as "Vietniks," "nihilists," and "revolutionists," argued that many protesters, given their actions, proved that they, not conservatives, were "fascists." "To shout down the speaker when you disagree," Burnham wrote, "to walk out of an assembly instead of discussing, to summon to lawbreaking and violence, to solidarize with an enemy-in-arms, to vilify the lawful magistrates with obscenities and monstrous lies: these are the tactics . . . by which brown and red hooligans have in our century proved their ability to bring democratic government down in ruins."[5]

Frank Meyer, if anything, believed *NR* did not go far enough. The "New Left" had to be seen in the context of the Communist Party. Meyer wrote in a 1968 column that many radicals tended toward "a violence of rhetoric and of action which leads towards no coherent or realizable goal." If the New Left "disrupts the civil order" of America, or served "to corrode national determination" on Vietnam, then it objectively acted to "weaken the forces resisting Communism and therefore to tip the balance in favor of the forces of Communism." If so, the Right must call a spade a spade.

Besides, Meyer maintained that "nature abhors a vacuum." The major opposition to Western civilization in the twentieth century was communism, and given its historical track record, Meyer wondered "whether a violently-oriented movement of opposition, which has no steadying ideological direction, can in the circumstances of the world today, preserve its ideological emptiness from infiltration and domination by Communism." Meyer seized upon a recent article which showed that Communist Party membership had increased since 1960 and that Party members were active in anti-war activities. Meyer trumpeted that the Party was "rapidly gaining strength—and gaining it in symbiosis with the radical movement." In sum, "whenever there has been a vacuum in radical movements in the twentieth century, Marxism has filled that vacuum ideologically and the Communist Party has filled it organizationally."[6]

Behind the scenes, Meyer and his fellow editors were even more alienated from the anti-war crowd than they let on publicly. Meyer, for example,
urged *NR* to take a tough line on the rights of anti-war demonstrators, arguing that the magazine should call for "social repudiation." Specifically, "If we
were at war officially, most of this type of problem would not arise. Treason in
time of war is palpable." Therefore the magazine should consider "coming
out bluntly for a Congressional declaration of war."[7]

William Rusher was even more direct. At an early 1966 Agony, Rusher
said that he did not "favor approaching the question with undue reverence or
in any spirit of assuming that these peyote-inflamed *barbudos* have scored
some sort of cosmic breakthrough on the insight front." He wondered if some
believed *NR* needed to figure out "what we think of [the New Left]." Why?
"Isn't it obvious that they are precisely the end-products (though—to be
sure—and very humanly—the *rebellious* end-products) of the great liberal critique of the Western dispensation? . . . The New Student Left—the Beatniks—the Vietniks—the alienated—the drop-outs: they are here. . . . Let us
get busy saying *why* they are here—and let us stop supposing there is any very
instructive mystery about it." No, *NR* had no sympathy with the anti-war Left.[8]

NATIONAL REVIEW FOR A TIME sympathized with what the Johnson administration was trying to do in Vietnam. *NR* of course vigorously opposed Johnson's
"Great Society" domestic program, but the magazine was always anticommunist first. *National Review* had learned some hard lessons about what was ideal
and what was possible, about what would get one tagged as "extreme," thus
denying one a hearing, and what was politically practical.

Thus, when Johnson said that the United States would never be "forced"
from Vietnam, *NR* proclaimed he had "spoken like a true commander-in-
chief." South Vietnam would survive, wrote James Burnham, "if Lyndon
Johnson's resolution endures." By now, *National Review* believed in the containment doctrine; or at least saw it as the only realistic alternative, as the only
"hard" anticommunist policy available in the atomic age. Burnham held that
"what is fundamentally at stake in the Vietnam conflict, whether recognized
or not, is the question whether the Communist enterprise will be blocked
from further expansion into Southeast Asia, the Indian subcontinent, the South
Seas and the Pacific and Indian oceans."[9]

If *NR* supported the war, it also criticized the Johnson administration for the way it fought it. The U.S. limited its means and methods far too much. America must fight to *win*, *NR* argued. "Is it not ridiculous, really, to send a squadron of million-dollar jets to destroy a couple of trucks on a road when a thousand truckloads of military supplies are simultaneously being unloaded in Haiphong harbor?" *NR* queried on one occasion. "Is it not tactically suicidal to forbid our Marines from seeking out the enemy in his sanctuaries just above the DMZ when he is free to fight where and when it is to his maximum advantage? . . . We have entangled our operations in a set of political, diplomatic, humanitarian and ideological restrictions that make no military sense; indeed, no sense of any kind."[10]

Internally, *NR* was not riven with the kinds of divisions over the Vietnam War that by the 1960s cleaved much of the rest of America. But on a few occasions—a very few—some wondered whether the fighting in Vietnam was worth it, given the restraints on waging the war. "In the many discussions on the war and how both *NR* and the nation should proceed," recalled Priscilla Buckley, "I heard Bill just once say that perhaps we should get out, as the protesters insisted, *if we didn't have the guts to go all-out and fight the war to win*." But many in the magazine knew that liberals would use any diminution in *NR*'s support for the war to buttress the anti-war position. "The slightest hint of a pull-out from us," Rusher told the editors in 1967, "without major and well-emphasized qualifiers, will simply be used by the left to undermine the present military position." No, *NR* would not change its views. "It would have been too disheartening for the *NR* troops and if pressed, I doubt the editors would have gone along," writes Priscilla Buckley. And indeed, the issue was never seriously pressed.[11]

Instead, *National Review* searched for ways to further bolster the effort in South Vietnam. Many in the *NR* circle worried about public apathy concerning the struggle. There was discussion in *NR* editorial meetings of forming a "Committee to Win the War in Vietnam." Though little came of this, the magazine consistently published and promoted the names and addresses of anticommunist groups acting to support the war, and it hoped to do whatever it could to aid the fighting men in the field. "Lady who passes her [*NR*] mags and bulletins to a serviceman in Vietnam encloses a letter from him," reported a pleased *NR* staffer scrutinizing the monthly mail, ". . . he says they get handed all around the unit, and are appreciated."[12]

THIS IS THE CONTEXT in which Frank Meyer addressed the Vietnam issue. As with most other policy matters, his views did not differ significantly from those of *National Review.* "It is the Communist drive for world power that defines every world political problem in these decades," he wrote in his 1969 book *The Conservative Mainstream.* He still saw the world in crisis, a crisis brought on by continued communist aggression and the lack of will to contest it. In the first half of the 1960s, Meyer thought the crux of the Cold War would continue to be in Europe, as he occasionally told Buckley:

> France under De Gaulle is a maverick; France after De Gaulle is almost certain to be neutralist at the best. Italy is very possibly only a year or two from a Popular Front government. The pressure of our appeasement policy and the decay of Europe upon Germany is tremendous, and it may not be very long before a neutralist Social Democracy rules Germany and attempts to make a deal with Khrushchev. . . . [M]ay we not be approaching a situation where the only viable policy will be a policy based solely on American interests and expending energy only upon our own defense and interests and those of the very few peoples who by their own straightforward decision are prepared to fight with us?[13]

But by 1965–66 Meyer maintained that perhaps America was *not* following a policy of "appeasement" in Vietnam; the U.S. was making an anticommunist stand there and had found people who were "prepared to fight with us." His role concerning the Vietnam issue, as with other issues, was to hold all those involved, both Democrat and Republican, to first principles; to expose any contradictions in their positions on the war; and to help distinguish true principles from the heresy of mere partisanship and opportunism. He would also show that he too—he who (along with others at *NR*) once advocated the forcible liberation by the U.S. of Soviet-controlled Eastern Europe—now accepted the limits beyond which a realistic, pragmatic policy on Vietnam could not go.

In early 1966 Meyer spoke out in his column on the Vietnam War for the first time and showed that he, along with many other Americans, felt some qualms about the conflict. Meyer was in a bit of a "quandary," he told his readers. "Just the fact that we are fighting the Communists somewhere is a tremendous step forward after years of retreat under the slogan of 'coexistence,'" he wrote. But there were many problems in *how* America was prosecuting the war in Vietnam. Our policy was "obscure," our conduct of the fighting "ambiguous," the goals for which America fought "uncertain." There was "the contradiction between the assumption of peaceful intentions on the part of the Soviet Union and common interests between us and the Soviet Union on the one hand, and the maintenance of NATO as a war alliance or the prosecution of actual war in Vietnam on the other hand." How could the United States do both? How could it both fight the communists, yet at the same time profess to be making peace with them? No wonder the American people were confused! The only solution, Meyer went on, was again to return to first principles. U.S. policymakers must recognize the involvement in Vietnam for what it was, "one battle in the continuing war with Communism. . . . So long as we fail to understand that the Vietnam struggle is but a battle in a long war it will not be possible to have any clear objectives, any clear definition of what we could regard as victory."

American objectives in Southeast Asia, as Meyer saw it, were three, "in ascending order of necessary commitment and expenditure of men and *materiel.*" First, "the destruction of the Vietcong and the sealing off of South Vietnam, to permit the establishment of a firm anti-communist regime in South Vietnam." Second, "the overthrow of the Hanoi government and the establishment of an anti-communist government in all Vietnam." And, since Meyer could not help but be provocative, third, "in case vigorous prosecution of warfare directed towards (1) or (2) should bring about the threat of Chinese intervention, the welcoming of war against China as an opportunity to destroy its nuclear potential and set back its development as a serious military power for years."

But here, as in his discussion of the use of nuclear weapons in the early 1960s, Meyer the realist appeared. In discussing which option he would prefer, Meyer wrote that "since the Asian continent is hardly the ideal strategic arena for American arms, it may well be that the first of these objectives is to be preferred." Meyer, then, advocated essentially a containment strategy in Vietnam—to protect South Vietnam from communist attack and foster an anti-communist government there. But, he added, America must not fail; Johnson must escalate rather than fail to achieve this objective. And again he stressed that *no* policy would be effective unless U.S. policymakers stated clearly "that we see it as part of the broader war with Communism and that we are pre-pared to take all steps necessary to achieve it." Containing communism by defending noncommunist South Vietnam—that was Meyer's position.[14]

Meyer was also frequently, and at times scathingly, critical of the Republican Party's performance on the Vietnam issue. There was plenty to criticize, for as the war escalated the GOP had a difficult time coming up with a consistent position. Some in the party sounded much like *National Review*. But others preferred to exult in the divisions over the war within the Democratic Party. The House Republican Policy Committee in 1966 stated that "the deep division within the Democratic Party over American policy in Vietnam is prolonging the war, undermining the morale of our fighting men and encouraging the Communist aggressor." Then there were the liberal Republicans, the anti-war "doves," who flatly opposed the U.S. commitment. As early as 1965, prominent Republicans such as Michigan governor George Romney and Oregon senator Mark Hatfield refused to sign a party statement supporting Johnson's commitment of 150,000 men to Southeast Asia. The young, handsome senator from Illinois, Charles Percy, who many touted as a Republican presidential candidate in 1968, damned Johnson for "sucking us deeper and deeper into Southeast Asia. . . . We have battles to fight in our own country, battles against poverty and hunger and ignorance, battles for justice and equality."[15]

Frank Meyer followed Republican Party affairs as closely as anyone, and when he saw opportunism and dovish thought developing among Republican politicians he resolved to speak out forcefully against it. Vietnam, Meyer stated again in his column in the spring of 1966, was a "serious confrontation with Communism," and worthy of support. It required of the opposition political party "the most responsible exercise of its indispensable function as the balance wheel in a free representative polity." Republican support for President Johnson's Vietnam policy would in no way tie them to Johnson's "coattails." They could still offer "scorching" critiques of how effectively the president's policies were being carried out.

Republicans, however, were failing in their duty to be a "loyal opposition." GOP leaders, Meyer charged, had "indulged in a display of petty partisanship, apparently devoid of principle . . . , which is just about limited to gloating over the dissensions on Vietnam in the Democratic Party." Republicans appeared to be motivated only by the desire "to achieve political advantage on a non-principled level."

What had happened to the Republican Party? What had caused this? Meyer argued that the roots of it went back Goldwater's massive defeat in 1964, which "traumatized" many within the party. Some believed that this was "final proof that the Republican Party could never win under conservative leadership." For its part, the liberal wing of the GOP "had so thoroughly disgraced itself by its sabotage of the campaign" that it too was "effectively disqualified" from a leading role. Hence, in Meyer's analysis, leadership of the party had passed to "the center"; and many conservatives accepted this as "the best that could be expected for the next few years." But, Meyer stressed, the Republican performance on Vietnam demonstrated that "the concept has foundered on the hard fact that leaders must have some idea of what they stand for and where they are going." Unsurprisingly, Meyer said that "the time has come for conservatives to reassert their leadership of the Republican Party." The "bulk" of the GOP would respond and the party's message would become clear and principled again if it was given "clear, responsible leadership. But this the center has shown it cannot give. It is up to the conservatives."[16]

It was significant, however, that Meyer, the newborn realist, did not insist on a movement conservative candidate for president in 1968. As we shall see, he was willing to accept a nominee from the "center," as long as that nominee was primarily influenced by the conservative wing of the party. For that to happen, the liberals and opportunists within the GOP must be routed, their leverage and sway reduced. By late 1967, high-ranking GOP elected officials such as Senators Mark Hatfield and Charles Percy and Governor George Romney were not only making anti-war statements and urging a U.S. pullout from Vietnam, but (Meyer suspected) doing so at least partly in an attempt to gain votes from the anti-war Left. So a furious Meyer again banged out a column critical of the Republican performance. As always, he began by placing what he was going to say in a broader context. Political parties need not be "paradigms of ideological purity," he wrote; but on important national issues they must take a "broadly principled position." Currently, a new "opportunism" threatened party "integrity." "This is the despicable proposal to truckle to the Left-liberal and radical ideologues who are kicking up a storm against the Vietnam war," he raged, "and join with them in confusing the

American people on the deadly issues of national interest and civilizational survival our prosecution of that war represents." GOP liberals such as Hatfield, Percy, or Romney advocated "a dishonorable peace policy," and sought "to win an election cold-bloodedly at the cost of national disaster." Thank goodness some conservatives in the party continued to speak up; Meyer even lauded Richard Nixon for taking "a firm line in general" on the war and opposing the "destructive cynicism" of the liberals. Meyer contended that the war in Southeast Asia exemplified the kind of "sporadic hot wars" we could expect, for communists employed "wars of national liberation" as a "primary offensive resource" in their drive for domination. Americans were likely to see more of these "dramatic, painful, drawn-out confrontations"—"the price we have to pay for national and civilizational survival."[17]

WERE THERE NO DIVISIONS among NR conservatives concerning the Vietnam War? There was one, and it erupted between those two old antagonists, Meyer and his bête noire, James Burnham, in 1967. It concerned the military draft.

Meyer the previous year had written a column that, though it defended the principle of a government imposing a draft in time of emergency, opposed the current draft system in America; since it was not needed, it was an unnecessary infringement on individual freedom. Now, a year later, there was a growing movement on the Right against the draft. Barry Goldwater, Russell Kirk, and Milton Friedman came out against it. David Franke, the leader of Young Americans for Freedom, devoted nearly an entire issue of YAF's magazine, the New Guard, to the promotion of arguments against conscription. An organization called the Council for a Volunteer Military was formed, with a number of prominent conservatives (including Frank Meyer) listed as sponsors.[18]

James Burnham, however, refused to join the stampede, and soon he devoted one of his "Third World War" columns in National Review to the antidraft phenomenon. Burnham noted that the Council for a Volunteer Military had been formed initially by Milton Friedman and Sanford Gottlieb, and that Gottlieb was the political director of SANE, a left-wing, pacifistic anti–nuclear weapons organization. Moreover, the council's sponsors, in addition to a number of conservatives, included many prominent liberals and leftists. To Burnham, an ex-Trotskyist who knew something about creating ideological alliances and their pitfalls, this showed that many on the Right had fallen into the trap of entering into "an unprincipled united front," even though Left and Right had joined for very different reasons. Conservatives were only an "adornment," a "cover" for the Left. Burnham charged that "the antidraft movement, as a fact of the present, is an element—a major and effective element—of the *existing* anti-war movement, which is the movement to get the United States to pull out of the Vietnam war . . . , a defeatist campaign to induce the U.S. to accept a Communist victory in Vietnam. This is the bitter logic of antidraftism, 1967 version." Some, he speculated, may have fallen for such a ploy through "naïveté." Others, he concluded, were simply "seduced by ideology—always an untrustworthy guide to practical conduct."[19]

Ironically, Meyer and Burnham had been getting along rather well lately. Meyer agreed wholeheartedly with Burnham's analysis of the Johnson administration's failings on Vietnam. But to have Burnham attack those associated with the council as in any way helping the American Left, to have him denigrate the importance of "principle," as well as to attack the sponsors as naïve and "seduced by ideology," when everyone knew that Meyer was one of the sponsors of the council—this was too much to take. Less than a month later, Meyer struck back hard in his "Principles and Heresies" column. He began by pointing out where supporters of the draft stood: the idea of conscription was "typical of the authoritarian liberal approach to all political problems," symbolized by Robert McNamara, a "prototype of the coercive social engineer" who made outrageous proposals for national service in a nonmilitary "labor corps."

But mainly he directed his fire against Burnham. Why was it "impossible," Meyer demanded, "to support the struggle against Communism and simultaneously believe that it can be better prosecuted by an army of properly paid volunteers? . . ." And he went to great lengths to show that he was *not* against the Vietnam War. "I stand for a volunteer army so long as it is militarily feasible," Meyer asserted. "And I stand not only for the intensification of the Vietnam war but for a firm policy against Communism conducted as aggressively as it is advantageous to our interest. But so long as military needs remain anywhere near the present levels of less than 10 per cent of the male population of military age, there is no moral excuse for conscription." And "if conservatives succeed in gaining the support of those to their left [to further their conservative principles], then so much the better. Mr. Burnham mocks at principle, putting the word in quotation marks and equating it with ideology; but if conservatives do not stand on principle, their entire reason for being vanishes." Support for the council was "vitally important," and to refuse to join it because of possible dangers "would be timidity, not prudence." Living without the threat of conscription was "both the right," Meyer wrote, "and the privilege of citizens of a free society."[20]

It was a heated exchange. But Meyer and Burnham had argued in print before; it shocked no one, and it allowed them to get their disagreement out of their system. Buckley, as always, wished for the editors to concentrate on what they had in common, rather than on what divided them. And on this issue, as usual, Burnham's thinking influenced Buckley, though he remained a bit on the fence. "I tend to feel that most of the people on the New Left who oppose the draft, oppose the draft simply as a useful way of opposing the Vietnam War," he told an interviewer. "And that under the circumstances I find myself, and some of my colleagues disagree with me, declining to join some of those abolish-the-draft committees, even though I do believe in abolishing the draft."[21]

There is little evidence that the Republican Party was significantly influenced by either *National Review*'s analysis of the war or by Frank Meyer's calls to return to first principles. By 1968 many in the party embraced, more or less, Richard Nixon's vague call for an "honorable" peace. But *NR*'s performance on Vietnam was very important for the continuing evolution of the enterprise. *NR*'s position, and Meyer's, was of course hawkish. But they also had more or less accepted the containment doctrine and argued within its parameters. *National Review*'s position was not that different from what many other "hawks" were saying at the time, and it thus fell within the mainstream debate. Furthermore, the distinctions *NR* made, the differences it (especially Meyer) drew with some in the Republican Party, kept it from being too closely identified with any GOP faction or with any specific politician. Burnham had wanted *NR* to have an independent voice, without ties to any specific candidate or faction, for some time. Meyer (perhaps without knowing it) advocated the same thing back in 1966 when he urged that the magazine pull back from politics and concentrate on conservative societal analyses. *NR* was now doing this, and doing it effectively.

And actually, although *National Review* could not have known it at the time, it—or, more precisely, "the Right" in general—*did* influence the Johnson administration and its Vietnam policies. Much of this influence was based on fear and had two components. First, Johnson and many of his advisers worried that if they did not act firmly in Vietnam it would "create a war hysteria that might in turn give rise to a new Joe McCarthy or create pressure for a more confrontational Cold War policy. He feared an anti-Red frenzy that would create openings for crazies on the right and might lead the country into a wider, perhaps even nuclear, war." Johnson himself once said that he "believed that the loss of China had played a large role in the rise of Joe McCarthy. And I knew that all these problems, taken together, were chickenshit compared with what might happen if we lost Vietnam."[22]

Second, one of the reasons Johnson took such strong action was his desire to forestall any criticism of his policy on Vietnam from Goldwater conservatives. Johnson aide Kenneth O'Donnell recalled discussing the 1964 Tonkin Gulf crisis with Johnson at the time, and the two believed that "the attack on Lyndon Johnson was going to come from the right and the hawks and he must not allow them to accuse him of being vacillating or being an indecisive leader." And when Johnson began his sustained bombing campaign against North Vietnam early in 1965, he did so at least partly to blunt expected conservative criticism of his support for the upcoming civil rights and Great Society legislation. Johnson once told an aide that he was "far more afraid of the right wing than I am of the left wing." He occasionally referred to American conservatives as the "great beast." The Johnson administration most likely knew little of the work of *National Review*, but it certainly was aware of the larger cause, the larger movement, on behalf of which *NR* conservatives strove so mightily.[23]

BOTH FRANK MEYER and *NR* were evolving and adjusting to the changing times of a turbulent decade. Both of their voices had changed somewhat over the years, but they were still conservative voices; and they had an influence that they perhaps could not have imagined years earlier. *NR* had come a long way since 1955, had come a long way, indeed, since 1964. And now there was another election year approaching, one that would again test that voice, would test *NR*'s positions on race and Vietnam, and would test whether, and how, the magazine would influence political events. Elections were always important events for the magazine, full of excitement and danger. The year 1968 would be no exception.

1968

RACIAL CHANGE, RIOTS in the streets, the war in Vietnam—the American people had already experienced a great deal by 1967. But 1968 proved to be the stormiest year yet, one that made many question the very foundation of American society and wonder whether it would long survive.

The devastating events of that year began in January, when the North Vietnamese and their Vietcong allies launched the so-called "Tet Offensive," attacking provincial capitals and even supposedly impregnable targets in South Vietnam, such as the American Embassy. Thousands of American soldiers died. But communist forces failed to hold their initial gains, and the Johnson administration claimed a military victory. Still, many Americans were shocked at the fierce communist attack, given the administration's recent cheerful reports on the war. In the New Hampshire presidential primary, anti-administration candidate Eugene McCarthy surprised experts by gaining over 40 percent of the vote. At the end of March, the president stunned almost everyone when, in a nationwide speech on television, he announced that he was freezing U.S. troop levels in Vietnam, temporarily halting the bombing of the North, and would seek new peace negotiations. And he shocked them further by solemnly stating that he would not be a candidate for reelection. Vietnam had claimed its latest, and most significant, victim.

That was only the beginning. A few days after Johnson's withdrawal, Martin Luther King Jr. was assassinated in Memphis, Tennessee. A new round of rioting in hundreds of major cities erupted, with millions of dollars of damage done. Meanwhile an increasing number of student protests paralyzed college campuses. At Columbia University that spring, students occupied several campus buildings for days, including the president's office. And that summer, the orgy of violence and disruption reached a crescendo with the assassination of Democratic senator and presidential candidate Robert F. Kennedy in June, followed by the chaos and confusion at the Democratic National Convention in Chicago, where police and anti-war protesters scuffled and brawled in the streets. What indeed was happening to American society?

THE EVENTS OF THE 1960s had a significant effect upon Frank Meyer and all those clustered around *National Review*. *NR* conservatives had already loudly denounced rioters, the disruption of social order, and the anti-war protesters. But 1968 would have an even more powerful impact upon *NR*, greatly affecting the positions the magazine took on the year's major issues.

The Tet Offensive caused soul-searching in the offices of *National Review*. Buckley, who visited South Vietnam in 1967, was shocked at the intensity of the communist assaults on Saigon and its environs. He saw a picture of a little South Vietnamese girl who had been killed in the fighting. "We haven't the strength to secure every little hamlet in South Vietnam from the enemy," he wrote, "but how can we fail military compounds within the suburbs of Saigon in which little girls live?" All the "chaos" exhibited eloquently "the failure of Lyndon Johnson's foreign policy."[1]

NR's global strategist, James Burnham, whose support of the general commitment in Vietnam had never wavered, doubted more strongly than ever the administration strategy. "Politically and strategically there seems to have been no fundamental improvement since the 1965 clinch," he contended. American forces wallowed in "defensive swamps," battling the enemy effectively in direct combat but always "on the receiving end of the enemy's initiative." The war was a "strategic stalemate"; the Johnson policy of gradual escalation was a failure.

As Burnham saw it, administration policymakers faced a choice, especially given the increasing evidence of North Vietnamese leadership of the communist forces: to institute a complete *cordon sanitaire* around North Vietnam to prevent it from aiding and abetting the revolt in the South, which could take over a million more men; or "the only other way"—hurt "North Vietnam badly enough to compel its government to stop intervening in the South." If the U.S. government believed that either of these two alternatives was impossible, or was unwilling to take the necessary steps, then, he concluded starkly, "isn't it time to get out?"[2]

Burnham was of course not *advocating* a pullout; still, in the past, even broaching the possibility had been unthinkable at *National Review*. But events occurred with lightning speed these days, and old assumptions tumbled quickly. The pace of events was incredible, and it was hard for those at *National Review* to know just what to think. Frank Meyer, for one, believed that these were historic times. "The ten days from the night President Johnson ran up the white flag of surrender in Vietnam to the afternoon Martin Luther King was assassinated," he wrote breathlessly in his next column, "will, I believe, one day impress the historian as the most fateful point in American history since Fort Sumter was fired upon 107 years ago." April 1968, he held, "ushered in a massive crisis."

Meyer had been in Washington, D.C., for a political meeting shortly after King was killed, and he saw first-hand the pall of smoke hanging over the city and the destruction of property from the riots that followed, as well as the fear these created. He warned that continuing disorder could lead to fascism. America's predicament was a result of a "breakdown of moral authority," he contended. The causes of the riots were "not social and economic, but moral. . . . We are reaping the harvest of two generations of contempt for the constitutional tradition of law and ordered freedom," Meyer maintained. But if the state could not protect its own, then ordinary citizens had the right to protect themselves, "and the outcome can only be Hobbes' anarchic 'war of all against all.'" Even dictatorship was a possibility. The crisis involved preserving civilization itself. America needed a "renewal" of "moral authority." Perhaps, Meyer speculated, this "crucible of crisis" would produce such results "with startling rapidity."[3]

Later that April, *National Review*'s usual quarterly editorial Agony was held, at which the editors had a long discussion about the occurrences of that winter and spring. Concerning the riots, Buckley recorded, the editors concluded that *NR* "should raise the point, what has happened to the governing elite? We should ask whether the consequences are some form of fascism, avoiding the use of that word. Might 'authoritarianism' serve?" Concerning Vietnam, the consensus was, "let us be prepared to admit that we have lost the war in Vietnam but remind ourselves what the consequences are of that loss; we should spell them out."The blame must be placed squarely on the liberal establishment. *NR* "should identify the nexus between the demoralization of the governing elite in connection with the first crisis and with the second." Burnham in a later column put it more plainly: "if American power decays, what remains? Internationally as externally, the anti-Americans are vindicated and thereby strengthened; the rioters, law-breakers, vandals, revolutionaries, and nihilists are emboldened to redouble their onslaught against the Power Structure which has displayed its vulnerability."[4]

Student unrest on college campuses flared up anew in 1968, and it had a personal impact on *NR*. The massive, well-publicized confrontations between radical students and the administration at Columbia University occurred in the magazine's backyard. The editors read how militant students took over the office of university president Grayson Kirk, drank his brandy, smoked his cigars, and leafed through his books. Then too, Meyer's son John was a graduate student in political science at Columbia and belonged to the conservative "Students for a Free Campus," which waged fierce battles with Students for a Democratic Society over allowing recruiters for the U.S. Marines and the CIA on campus. After the radicals took over a campus building, John wrote: "I was one of the few to watch the bedraggled mass flow out of Hamilton Hall, break into Low Library, and disappear therein, all without a single sign of administration awareness, let alone opposition."[5]

Occasionally Frank Meyer saw what was happening for himself. His new friend at Indiana University, R. Emmett Tyrrell, kept him informed on happenings there. In 1967 a member of the SDS was elected student body president. He proceeded to: plaster his office with posters commemorating the fiftieth anniversary of the Bolshevik Revolution; set up an official office for "draft counseling"; go to his army physical examination with anti-war slogans painted on his body; interrupt a speech on campus by Secretary of State Dean Rusk with shouts of "murderer" and "fascist"; and then "serenely defend . . . his actions on statewide television." In order to counter all this, Tyrrell asked Meyer and other conservatives to speak at IU during a week-long celebration of conservative thought that he and his student magazine sponsored. Meyer found that the 1960s' madness affected conservative students, too. Self-styled Russell Kirk traditionalists marched about brandishing walking sticks, peering through monocles, wearing long, flowing capes, and occasionally taking a pinch of snuff. Followers of Ayn Rand sported huge dollar-sign medallions around their necks. One young, earnest conservative ate nothing but carrots, which slowly turned his hands orange. "There I was," Tyrrell marveled, "with a man who at one instant had been holding forth thoughtfully on *The Federalist Papers,* and who later over drinks demonstrated quite convincingly that he was a genuine nutcase, with the table manners of Bugs Bunny."[6]

Meyer could tolerate individualism and eccentricity, even a little bohemianism; he was himself at times still a bit of a bohemian, and certainly an eccentric. But the onslaught of the Left at America's universities he could not abide, and later in 1968 he devoted an entire column to it. To Meyer, the problems in higher education were many, including "the mobs of SDSers and black militants who race across the campuses in their arrogance, obscenity and Neanderthal brutality," and the demand that courses have "relevance" to students' daily lives. Fundamentally this was all part of a "deep systemic disturbance," a "failing sense of authority." Just as with riots in the cities, riots in the universities should be blamed squarely on higher education's leaders, on professors and administrators. They had "repudiated the truths of Western civilization and even, in the orgiastic relativism of the contemporary academy, the very concept of truth itself." This was crucial: in order to teach students effectively, there must be a sense that there is a truth to convey. "This does not require," Meyer hastened to add, "a rigid dogmatism; truth may be held guardedly, circumspectly, humbly, with full knowledge of one's human imperfections and limitations; but some broad belief in truth, rooted in civilizational tradition, there must be." Otherwise, on what basis could university leaders criticize radical students and their actions?

This was Meyer the traditionalist, the stickler for "ordered freedom," talking. Student rights? "A student *qua* student has no rights except the right to be well-taught," he went on. "Nothing compels him to enter a university and partake of the munificence of private benefactors or the public purse. . . . [O]nce he decides he wants to be taught, all decisions about the condition of his studenthood are the prerogative of those who provide him the opportunity of studying." As for "relevance," Meyer maintained, this meant "students telling teachers what to teach, on the basis of their tropisms to the surface of contemporary life; it means a wild drive to universal coeducation, introducing sex where all history has shown that it is specifically incompatible with the conditions of study; it means substituting, for liberal education in the free civilization of the West, courses in hotel management or the barbarian history of African tribes." If this "nihilist" attitude triumphed in American higher education, it portended "the anarchy of impulse in place of the discipline of ordered learning, the chaos of fleeting opinion in place of the search for truth, barbarism in the place of civilization."[7]

Suddenly, questions of party and candidate did not seem quite so important. Instead, for many *National Review* conservatives such as Meyer, it came down literally to protecting civilization from barbarism and anarchy. And it seemed as if the forces of chaos and disorder were closing in. In June, demonstrators—part of the "Poor People's Campaign"—camped out in the center of Washington, D.C., leaving litter and promises to disrupt governmental operations in their wake. An *NR* reader described the scene: "The capital of the strongest nation in the world cowers in the presence of 'the Poor'—it has been turned into a vast playground for malcontents and misled honest folk.... [There has been] an increase in car thefts, with the abandoned autos being found at the campsite. . . . And the statue of Lincoln stares down at the filth and litter left by those he emancipated. I wonder where we are going?"[8]

Then came the appalling news that an assassin named Sirhan Sirhan had gunned down Senator Robert F. Kennedy just after his victory in the California primary. Once again the nation went into shock and mourning, and commentators across the country raged in unison that this latest catastrophe proved that America was irretrievably violent and diseased, a "sick" society. *National Review's* editors were sick of being told that America was sick. Something obviously *was* wrong. But the magazine's diagnosis of the country's ills differed from most others:

> In a civilized nation it is not expected that public figures should be considered proper targets for casual gunmen. But in civilized nations of the past it has not been customary for parents to allow their children to do what they feel like; for students to seize their schools and smash their equipment; for police to be ordered to stand by while looters empty stores and arsonists burn down buildings; for poor people, or rich, to pitch camp in the center of government and undertake mass intimidation of the magistrates; for parks

and streets to become unsafe for decent citizens; for the courts, dealing with such a state of affairs, to make rulings year after year that protect the law-defier, the violent and the criminal over the victim; for the priests, ministers, and ideologists to justify the breakers of the law and condemn those who seek to uphold it. . . . We Americans had better get one thing straight. If we are going to begin settling our affairs by violence and shooting, before long the professionals at that sort of thing are going to take charge. We may discover some day that the military junta as a political form is not confined to South America.[9]

Many at *NR* well remembered the heyday of the Nazis and Stalinists. They knew that in the Germany of the 1930s, when social permissiveness and political crises had lasted too long, the people turned to a strongman to fix things. Some worried it could happen here, too. Meyer feared that, in its current agitated state, the liberal establishment would take action that would only increase the likelihood of authoritarianism, not reduce it. He had in mind specifically gun control. Meyer summarized the liberal view of the need for gun control: "Violence is bad? Of course: then let us do away with it. Problem; solution; instant Utopia. Guns kill people? Put government control on guns: domestic peace in our time." In the practical sphere, Meyer argued, there was little evidence that the availability of weapons created violence. "Violence, for good or ill, arises from the souls of men," he wrote. "Gun control would have no more effect ultimately upon the quantum of domestic violence than disarmament agreements have had upon the prevalence of warfare." And worse, "it would be the criminals, the rioters, the insurrectionists, who would find illegal means of procuring weapons"—not law-abiding citizens. There was also the Second Amendment to the Constitution to consider. To Meyer, far from making America "sick," the presence of guns was keeping the U.S. from descending further into sickness—or into fascism. "An unarmed citizenry," he concluded, "is potentially the victim, first of anarchy; then of tyranny and totalitarianism."[10]

Was anarchy that far away? The scene shifted in August to the Democratic National Convention held in Chicago, where radical protesters fought in the streets with enraged policemen, viewed by a shocked nation on television. *NR* let loose. "No loyal citizen of this country, no matter how eager he may be to see the Democratic rascals thrown out by the November election, can be undismayed at the spectacle in Chicago," the editors stated. "Where indeed are we rushing if a city must be turned into a concentration camp in order that the nominating convention of a great political party, founded in our nation's early years and incorporating in its membership more than half the nation's voters, may assemble? If in the streets of that city, while the proceedings carry fitfully on, thousands of citizens, police and troops battle to the sound of screaming obscenities and treasonous cries?"[11]

The trouble in Chicago had a direct impact upon *National Review*. Meyer's friend Garry Wills wanted to cover the Chicago convention for *NR*, and Buckley was willing. But Meyer and others detected a growing leftward drift in Wills's politics, especially in his sympathy for the tactics and goals of the civil rights movement; some at *NR* feared he was succumbing, "on a reverse road to Damascus," to the siren song of the Left. Buckley, however, "was very anxious to stem this tide and to use Garry as much as possible in *NR* in the hopes of salvaging him politically," Priscilla Buckley recalled. "He was a huge talent and we didn't want to surrender him to the Left without a battle for his political soul." Thus, despite Meyer's doubts, Buckley allowed Wills to keep the assignment.[12]

Sure enough, Wills turned in a controversial article on the happenings in Chicago. Again and again he slammed the authorities, writing of "Mayor Daley's untenable first-line toughness," and condemning Daley for "forswearing diplomacy for propaganda." And he appeared to exonerate the demonstrators; Daley's toughness meant that "the kids see in the whole process a vivid symbol of the fact that the System has no place for them." Wills contended that the few professional agitators were "panting along behind the kids, trying to catch their coat tails, catch a ride. . . . Whatever triggering mechanism launched the kids simultaneously from a hundred cities is one that no one controls in Moscow or Havana or Hanoi." Yes, Wills marveled, the young protesters, with relatively few numbers and no money or planning, disrupted the city and tied up thousands of policemen. "The kids have obviously struck an Achilles heel of some sort in our society," he concluded. "We seem to have no defense against them."[13]

When Wills submitted the piece, there was a "great silence" concerning it at *NR*'s offices, and a junior staffer told him bluntly that it had "struck out" with most. Buckley ran it despite the opposition; but he allowed the other senior editors to blast away at the article's thesis in their own corners of the magazine. James Burnham led the charge. Without mentioning Wills's piece, Burnham held that "riots like this year's at Columbia, Cleveland, Chicago,

Berkeley, etc. are and are intended to be paramilitary operations in revolutionary warfare aiming at the destruction of 'the power structure'—i.e., the existing order of government and society." Were these young people angered by a "System" that had no role for them, as Wills argued? "The great majority," Burnham answered, "are merely raw material manipulated by the militants of SDS, the Youth International Party, the Trotskyite, Maoist, Castrovian, and Muscovite Communists, Black Panthers and other extremist Black Powerites."[14]

Here Burnham marched arm in arm with Frank Meyer. In the very next issue, Meyer rushed into print with a column that also did not mention Wills by name. But Meyer, far from criticizing Daley, praised him to the hilt. "He refused to appease the forces of nihilism," he raved. Daley "insisted on fulfilling his constitutional obligation to maintain conditions of order," and proved "that the constituted authorities can act." Meyer then heaped scorn on liberal cries that this was "police brutality." "As if violence could be subdued by anything but violence," he growled; "as if violence were not the essence of mob attack upon constituted order." Meyer admitted that individual Chicago policemen committed isolated acts of "brutality." But he also cited press reports of demonstrators arming their boots with razor blades, tossing beer cans full of urine at the police lines. The very existence of such a "mob" was a "provocation," Meyer wrote angrily, and was not a "peaceable assembly." Naturally it was always a "historical misfortune" when force must be used against "militant minorities." But otherwise such fringe groups would grow in "strength and arrogance," spurred on by the "feebleness" of authority. And if so, Meyer again raised the specter of fascism—a "terrible simplifier" who "destroys at one blow all freedom, all criticism, all civilization."

Once again Meyer presented conservatives with a choice—very simple and very stark. "Either the forces of revolution and nihilism will bring the republic down in a welter of disorder," he maintained, "or . . . the people will rise in their wrath and bring into power those who can *restore* order, at whatever cost to constitutionality and freedom." As time went on, many ordinary Americans seemed to agree with Meyer and *NR*. National polls soon showed that a majority approved of Daley's actions; bumper stickers appeared reading WE SUPPORT MAYOR DALEY AND THE CHICAGO POLICE. Perhaps the majority was finally moving in *NR*'s direction.[15]

ONLY THE 1968 ELECTIONS would tell that for sure. For *NR*, this would be a very different experience than was 1964, when one of their own ran for the presidency in a campaign with the feel of a crusade. But now no candidate with a legitimate chance at winning was a *National Review* conservative. Instead, the front-runner for the Republican nomination was a man with whom the Right had always had its differences: Richard M. Nixon.

Nixon lost narrowly in 1960 to John F. Kennedy in the race for the presidency. In 1962 he ran for governor of his home state, California, and was decisively defeated by the incumbent, Edmund G. (Pat) Brown. Having suffered in both 1960 and 1962 from loss of support on his Right, Nixon began to try to mend fences with conservatives. In 1964 he campaigned hard for Barry Goldwater and sharply criticized party liberals for their listless effort. And in 1966 he traveled the country speaking on behalf of Republican congressional candidates, including many conservatives.

But was Nixon a conservative himself? This question vexed many on the Right, then and now. The evidence is contradictory. Much of it points to Nixon being a "centrist"—though perhaps a right-leaning centrist. Nixon himself wrote later that Goldwaterism "was further to the right of my centrist position than Rockefeller was to the left of it." Again, in the late 1960s, he referred to "the extremists on the Right of the Goldwater type."[16]

Perhaps it was simply that Richard Nixon was a politician, one who wanted the 1968 Republican nomination and knew that he could not win without conservative support. "Nixon must have promised himself [after 1962]," speculated aide John Ehrlichman, "that he would never again alienate the politically active conservatives who can make such a difference in a close election." But he also believed that he could be the GOP nominee only by playing along with the liberals as well.[17]

Whatever Nixon's past might have indicated, 1968 would be a very different campaign in respect to the American Right than Nixon had waged previously. This time around he wooed many conservative leaders, and with some success. Shortly after 1964, he won praise and promises of support from Barry Goldwater, who appreciated Nixon's help in the darkest days of his race against Lyndon Johnson. The following year Nixon hired Patrick J. Buchanan as an aide and speechwriter. Buchanan, an outspoken conservative who was familiar with the writings and importance of *National Review,* served as Nixon's liaison with the *NR* right.[18]

Even so, Nixon got off to a rocky start with conservatives. In 1965, political reporters Rowland Evans and Robert Novak quoted him as saying that "the Buckleyites are a greater menace to the Republican Party than the Birchers." William Rusher was outraged, and he complained when he thought *NR's* editorial line in response was not tough enough. "I do not intend to enthuse about Mr. Nixon until he changes his mind about us," he told the editors, "and even then, I will stop short of licking his hand." But thanks to an admittedly "tortured" letter by Buchanan to *National Review* claiming that Nixon had been misquoted, any rift was soon smoothed over. Nixon's personal efforts then began to take effect. In 1967 he held private meetings with leading conservatives, seeking out their views and explaining in broad terms his own conception of what America's foreign and domestic policies should be. He met with Russell Kirk and discussed Vietnam. He had both Rusher and Buckley over to his apartment, taking them on a *tour de force* of his foreign policy views. He let on to at least one reporter that he read *National Review* regularly. In short, he was clearly courting the support of *NR* conservatives.[19]

"THEY DON'T LIKE ME," Nixon once said of American conservatives, "but they tolerate me." In a nutshell, in 1968 Nixon hoped to convince the Right at least to "tolerate" him. In respect to Frank Meyer, Nixon had a difficult job. In the past, Meyer had had little use for him, opposing any *National Review* endorsement of him in 1960 and damning his "phoniness" in the years immediately thereafter. Nixon was engaged in "an effort to make the Republican Party totally dependent on middle-of-the-roadism," Meyer told Buckley in 1961. "His statement [in a March 1961 speech] that large industrial states and junior labor leaders are decisive to Republican victory, if accepted, builds me-tooism into the Republican Party."[20]

Meyer saw Nixon as another unprincipled politician who could not hold a candle to the conservative hero, Barry Goldwater. But times had changed. Americans now lived in an age of crime, riots, anti-war movements, and drugs. America had to return to sanity. Perhaps there was no longer the luxury to insist on an explicitly conservative candidate, or to sit the election out. At least this is what Meyer seemed to be saying by the summer of 1967.

Meyer and his conservative colleagues had been much "perplexed" about the 1968 race, he confessed in his column, because of the uncertainty of conservative influence on the nomination. Therefore, Meyer urged the Right to keep several guidelines in mind. First, this was not 1964. There would be no "emotionally satisfying" primary campaign waged by a conservative candidate. The nomination would be decided through "hard bargaining" and a "complex of pressures." The issue was not necessarily who would win the nomination, but who would control the convention. Would conservative dominance of the Republican Party be "consolidated," or would liberal Republicans regain power?

Second, Meyer stressed that, even though 1964 had been an electoral defeat, it could still be "a potential massive victory for conservatism." Conservatives must continue what they started in 1964, to work "within the Republican Party from the bottom up." And they must continue to loosen the "liberal grip" on the GOP. "It may not bring about the nomination of an ideal conservative candidate, but it can make certain that no liberal . . . will be nominated. Furthermore, it will insure that the candidate nominated . . . will owe his victory to conservatives and will hold to broadly conservative principles."

About specific 1968 candidates, Meyer opined that conservatives could "rule out" Illinois senator Charles Percy, owing to his "miserable" position on Vietnam, and Michigan governor George Romney, "who has no discernible principles at all." Meyer's favorite candidate was California governor Ronald Reagan. Reagan, Meyer averred, "obviously has the most consistent principled conservative stand" on the issues. But, he added, Richard Nixon "has an honorable anti-communist record and, if he has been somewhat ambiguous on domestic questions at times, he would seem to be, on balance, acceptable to conservatives." This would be true as long as he didn't assume that the Right was "in his pocket," and therefore be tempted to "court the liberals." "If Nixon is nominated," Meyer concluded, "he will owe it to conservative support"—which would in other words "guarantee that conservative control of the Republican Party will be consolidated."[21]

Nixon was being tolerated. His strategy was working. But Meyer kept his distance from all the candidates. There was danger, he warned in a column, in taking "the spirit of political realism" too far, by arguing that *any* victory by *any* Republican equaled a victory for conservatism. When conservatives flirted with the idea of supporting the nomination of Charles Percy, or when they considered a Rockefeller-Reagan ticket, "that ultimate monstrosity in cynicism," they were "making Republicanism per se, instead of conservatism, their end."

What was needed, Meyer believed, was to restate "broad views which are in general consonant with the conservative consensus," so that conservatives would have something by which to judge the candidates. Therefore he reproduced his summary of the conservative philosophical, political, and theoretical consensus which he had written in his conclusion to his 1964 book *What Is Conservatism?* Once again he stressed that all conservatives believed in an objective moral order, that the primary reference of their political and philosophical thought must be the individual person, that conservatives are anti–utopian, anti–big government, and anticommunist. Although Meyer did not say so here, the totality of his writings in this period suggests strongly that Reagan was the man he believed came closest to these ideals, but Nixon was acceptable. Nixon made the cut.[22]

BUT WHAT POSITION would *National Review* as a whole take on the 1968 campaign? It was one thing to find Nixon acceptable, but should the magazine endorse him? Once again *NR* found itself awash in questions of pragmatism vs. principle, personalities, and the differing political positions staked out by its editors. As in 1960, some at *NR* wanted nothing to do with Nixon. But unlike 1960, the majority wanted to have influence with him, and indeed would finally endorse him.

A key to forecasting *National Review*'s position lay in the thinking of William F. Buckley Jr. Buckley received special Nixon attention. By 1967 Nixon was regularly sending him complimentary notes on his newspaper columns that dealt with Vietnam. On more than one occasion, Patrick Buchanan had lunch with both Buckley and Rusher. Nixon spent an entire Sunday afternoon with the editor in chief and publisher, expounding on a wide range of issues; Buckley was especially impressed with Nixon's intellect. Later that year, Nixon appeared on Buckley's *Firing Line*.

Buckley believed that Reagan would not run for the presidency, and in any case he was not sure that he was qualified for the office. He saw Nixon as the most conservative candidate available and liked the way he thought. Barry Goldwater's early support for Nixon played a role, too; as early as 1965, during a visit to Goldwater in Arizona, Buckley was impressed by the fervor with which Goldwater defended Nixon. Hence by early 1968, though he did not formally come out and say so, it was clear that he supported Nixon for president. There were, he wrote later that year, "those attracted to Nixon as a reasonable conservative with a granitic determination to contain the Communists abroad."[23]

William Rusher had a different view. Rusher had remained active in conservative Republican Party political circles after 1964, and he was not, as the year began, for Nixon. "Unlike many of my colleagues in the conservative movement, I never for a moment regarded Nixon as in any serious sense a conservative," he wrote later. "We had to be sure some of the same enemies (notably the liberal media), but Nixon was at heart a Machiavellian."[24]

Instead, in a series of memos to his *NR* colleagues in 1967 and 1968, Rusher carefully laid out the Republican political scene and made a case for the conservative candidate he had already chosen to support. In early 1967, the media's anointed Republican front-runner was George Romney, but there "are already signs that he is not going to last the distance," he wrote in January. Rusher respected Nixon as a serious player in the upcoming race, but he believed that GOP professionals wanted an alternative candidate. They saw Nixon as "too old and familiar, and his general image too timid, to give the GOP a really good chance against Johnson." Rusher feared the liberals would use this Nixon weakness to begin a stampede towards a young, fresh, vigorous (and liberal) face, such as Senator Charles Percy.

To counter this, conservatives needed a candidate. "And it seems perfectly obvious," Rusher maintained, "that there can be only one possible choice: Governor Reagan. . . . The only other choices are: to go down to probable defeat in November with Nixon, or to settle for the vice-presidential spot and supinely help the Liberals avenge themselves on Johnson by nominating Percy, as a Republican Liberal, for the presidency." For conservatives, now a majority within the Republican Party, "to settle for less than the top spot seems unnecessary and indeed irresponsible."[25]

As the months rolled by, Reagan did not officially declare himself a candidate—but neither did he take himself out of the running. And so *NR* continued to be uncertain about what exactly its position in 1968 should be. Quarterly editorial conferences in late 1967 brought "inconclusive" discussions of the 1968 Republican candidates. Eventually, therefore, because conservatives in the country (as well as within *NR*) were divided about whom to support, and in order to keep lines of communication open to all, the editors decided to have *National Review* adopt an "evenhanded" approach—to be analytical and reportorial toward all GOP candidates, to give them all a relatively positive press, and to see who emerged the winner. Buckley and others, Rusher remembered, "didn't want an uncomfortable amount of daylight to appear between [*NR*'s] position and that of Reagan and his growing band of supporters."[26]

This did not please everyone. Rusher continued to plead that Reagan had a legitimate claim "to be the voice of responsible conservatism in this campaign." There was also too much "blare and certitude" in the magazine's editorial discussions, he complained, too much talk that Nixon had it "all locked up." It was primarily Burnham who "annoyed" Rusher by frequently repeating this. Such thinking could become a self-fulfilling prophecy.[27]

Frank Meyer, Rusher's usual confederate in such matters, was somewhat and uncustomarily undecided on just what *National Review* should do. Reagan unmistakably was the candidate to whom he felt closest, and during the Republican primary season Meyer publicly supported him. He fleshed out his thinking and helped explain why members of the Right would remain loyal to Reagan in coming years in an article published in the liberal *New Republic,* which had asked leading thinkers from across the political spectrum to explain whom they were supporting and why. Meyer was Reagan's advocate. He argued that politics was changing. The old Roosevelt coalition was breaking up, with the New Left attacking mainstream liberals. Moreover, the old voting coalition of the South, labor unions, the urban poor, Democratic political machines, and farmers no longer had interests in common.

Instead, a new coalition was rising, one that cut across regional differences and united rural and urban citizens. "This body includes office worker, service worker, and industrial worker," Meyer argued, "farmer and small owner, technician and salaried executive, in a mode of life varying widely in detail but giving birth to broadly similar attitudes and aspirations." Meyer did not rejoice in this homogenization—"as a conservative I much prefer variety of every kind"—but it was a fact. This was a new "producing majority," and to it Ronald Reagan gave expression. Meyer especially emphasized that Reagan was a responsible conservative. "In a world buffeted by the storms of ideology, he is sane, decent, moderate," he held. "The central themes of his position are moral order in society, personal freedom and national dignity." This was true concerning the issue of race relations, too, though Reagan had taken some heat on that score. Reagan "has been meeting all over the state of California with groups of Negro leaders to attempt to find solutions. His conclusion, like the conclusion of all those who have looked into the problem without ideological blinkers, is that the key to Negro advancement is employment."

Reagan desired less government regulation and a lighter tax burden, but would move slowly and deliberately to achieve those goals. "He has shown as Governor of California his awareness that 35 years of governmental aggrandizement cannot be reversed overnight," Meyer emphasized, "particularly by a conservative who understands that too rapid a reorganization of social arrangements—even in a conservative direction—would be as dangerous as any revolutionary dislocation of society." But Reagan had begun to slow the growth of government in California. His principles remained intact. Meyer thus concluded that Reagan could unite the "producing majority" against the threat of "demagogy" from both the Right and the Left. Reagan could end the threat of fascism.[28]

But privately, within *National Review*, Meyer agonized. He was deeply concerned about Nelson Rockefeller. Rockefeller, like Reagan, was not an official candidate. But as George Romney's star plummeted, Rockefeller's ascended, and he continued to be active on the national scene, sounding at times for all the world like a candidate for the presidency. Meyer believed him to be a legitimate threat to gain the nomination. On the contrary, the Republican Party had become even more conservative than Meyer thought; the main threat to Nixon would come from Reagan. But Meyer detested Rockefeller as he detested few politicians, and he was not alone in fearing Rockefeller's liberalism. Senator Strom Thurmond told F. Clifton White that Nixon had to be supported in order to thwart Rockefeller.[29]

Still, Meyer's thinking had changed: he now saw himself as more pragmatic and realistic, and he wrote a long letter to Buckley outlining his shifting views. He urged Buckley not to breathe a word of it to Rusher, whom Meyer had not yet told and whom he feared offending.

He had been entertaining some "second thoughts" about the 1968 election, Meyer confessed. Now that George Romney was out of the race, Rockefeller's chances of gaining the GOP nomination must become the "first concern" of conservatives. "Apart from my fundamental objection to him as a liberal and one who will probably have a much worse position on Vietnam than Johnson," Meyer wrote, "[Rockefeller's] nomination would shatter the conservative movement." For some on the Right would never vote for Rockefeller. Some would .defect to George Wallace, the southern racist, and others to the incumbent administration, which "would create a bitterness that would be very hard to overcome." Furthermore, Meyer detected that some Reagan supporters thought that Rockefeller could eliminate Nixon, and that Reagan could then defeat Rockefeller. But Meyer was "not at all sure that in such a case Rockefeller might not be the final victor."

Besides, Meyer had been impressed with Nixon lately. Nixon had "been stiffening up his position in a conservative direction the past few weeks," he wrote. "He was extraordinarily courageous and sharp on the report of the Kerner Commission. His position on Vietnam seems to be firm. He has come out for ending the draft and instituting a voluntary system as soon as the Vietnam war is over." And Meyer was a little "disappointed" with Reagan recently, especially when the California governor announced that he would support Rockefeller, should he become the Republican nominee. "Generally I still would prefer Reagan," Meyer conceded. "But the issue is not drawn that way. . . . The issue seems to me to be now the urgent necessity of stopping Rockefeller and I would think that we should direct all our energies that way." He did not think that *NR* should yet endorse Nixon. "But I do think that we should consider it and above all that we should open our main attack on Rockefeller." Meyer added that he had "talked some of these things over with Jim [Burnham], and we seem to be thinking on rather parallel lines."[30]

Back in 1964, Meyer and Burnham had held diametrically opposed conceptions of *National Review*'s role in that year's presidential campaign. But much had changed since, and as Meyer said, the issues were "drawn" differently. The situation would soon shift again, however. Shortly after Meyer wrote Buckley, Rockefeller announced that he would not be a candidate for the presidency, which forced Meyer to revise his thinking a bit. "This means, of course, that Nixon almost certainly has it," he wrote Buckley a few days later. But "with the wide vacuum on his left, Nixon may be tempted to move in that direction," he reminded Buckley. "Therefore I suspect that we had best put pressure on him from the right, i.e., keep Reagan alive at least as a rhetorical pressure point." Thanks largely to Rusher's continued advocacy, and the fact that Reagan did not issue any Shermanesque statements about not serving if elected (in fact, he eventually did enter the race, though very late), this is basically what the magazine did.[31]

The primary campaign still caused some stress within *NR*. Nixon remained in the lead and was the clear favorite, but Reagan was at least a distant possibility. And at the end of April, after Johnson's withdrawal and Martin Luther King's assassination, Rockefeller suddenly reversed himself and announced that he *was* a candidate. Liberal Republicans were still a threat. It caused a bit of a disruption within *National Review*'s editorial ranks when, at the end of May, Burnham began to argue that, given the realities of the situation, for "journalistic reasons" the magazine should concentrate its support on one single candidate, and that, further, Reagan should be "ruled out as a serious possibility (except as a vice-presidential tail to Rockefeller's kite) and Nixon should be supported." Meyer would not sit still for this; any alliance of his with Burnham was at an end. In a memo to the editors, he reminded all that the decision had been made earlier in the year to "implacably oppose Rockefeller and to treat Nixon and Reagan with complete even-handedness." By doing so, *NR* represented "the spectrum of conservative opinion" in the country. An endorsement of Nixon now would undoubtedly alienate a good portion of that conservative opinion. Besides, "I insist that Reagan is a serious candidate," Meyer went on. "If it were journalistically advisable to support a single candidate, it would unquestionably be our duty to make Reagan our choice, with Nixon as our second choice."

Meyer believed that *NR* had to hold to its principles, and, whatever the realities of the current political situation, its principles dictated that it must support Reagan. And it must at all costs oppose Rockefeller. "I think we should intensify the sharpness of our attacks on Rockefeller," Meyer said again, "who in my opinion is a greater evil than [Hubert] Humphrey." Moreover, "Should any softening on Rockefeller, tolerance toward the Rockefeller-Reagan idea, or any preference of Nixon to Reagan be decided upon or appear in the magazine," he declared, "I reserve the right to an 'Open Question' dissent, which would take the form of a full endorsement of Reagan."[32]

Rusher felt strongly about this too, as did Rickenbacker; and, on second thought, there was no pressing need to change *NR*'s editorial position. Thus Buckley and Burnham left it as it was, a decision Meyer could live with. Nixon was, after all, sounding quite conservative by the summer of 1968. *National Review* quoted approvingly a number of Nixon statements on the current scene. On students, Nixon said that universities should crack down on radical protesters, "and a good place to start would be the anarchic students at Columbia." On government spending, Nixon stated that "more welfare from Washington will not buy human dignity." On the Poor People's Campaign going on in Washington, D.C., he argued that "the Government must not be coerced into acting because the machinery of Government has been distracted and paralyzed by protesters." Meyer could have written some of these lines himself.[33]

Still, at the end of July, with the convention only days away, Meyer in his column made one last pitch for Reagan. He argued that Reagan was not "extreme," but rather "represents the essentially moderate and anti-ideological outlook of the great majority of American citizens." Meyer went on to introduce his readers fully to his "producing majority" idea, which he had already expounded in the *New Republic,* and he contended that "no Republican candidate who does not give expression to this broad consensus of the overwhelming producing majority of American citizens, white and black, can hope to win." And he blasted the left wing's darling, Senator Eugene McCarthy, who had recently proposed declaring a "national emergency" in response to hunger and poverty in this country. Meyer scorned the idea "that power-hungry men should be allowed to achieve power, using the poor and the alienated of city and university as their battering ram."

What Republicans must do was "express the underlying conservative consensus of the American majority." And he was careful, again, to include Richard Nixon among Republicans who could accomplish this—perhaps a bit warily, because Nixon, he wrote, "has continued to display an ambiguity . . . that it is to be hoped he will drop if he attains the nomination." There was hope that Nixon would be firm. "It is because of that hope that conservatives can envisage supporting him if he is nominated," Meyer continued, "but it is because Reagan's position is clear while [Nixon's] is not, that many conservatives still hope that it is Reagan who will be the nominee."[34]

Eventually, at the GOP convention held in the heat of August in Miami

Beach, Richard Nixon did in fact capture the Republican nomination, despite a late official entrance by Ronald Reagan. Reagan came closer to gathering enough delegates to deny Nixon a first-ballot victory than many people realized. Rusher attended the convention and worked in Reagan's headquarters, telephoning wavering delegates and trying to shake their allegiance to Nixon. He returned to New York frustrated at Reagan's defeat, yet almost exhilarated at the show of conservative influence at the convention. In a prescient memo to *NR*'s editors, he said: "This was a convention wholly dominated by conservatives. . . . [T]he conservatives were able . . . to indulge in the luxury of having *two* candidates." He referred to Reagan, of course, but to Nixon too. "Make no mistake; Nixon was the candidate of a strictly and highly conservative bloc, put together in the first instance by Goldwater, financed by Milbank, blessed by Buckley. . . . He had almost no liberal support whatever. Nixon's nomination may have been (as I believe) an error; but if so it was at least the error of a group of indisputable conservatives." Therefore, "We have every right, logical as well as moral, to assume that on the big issues that really matter Nixon will be (within the limits of his inherently ambiguous personality) essentially conservative," Rusher maintained, "indeed, that he is to an almost frightening degree the creation and prisoner of one bloc of conservatives." Yes, Nixon "received this nomination from a party that, thanks to intervening events of seismic force, bears gratifyingly little resemblance to the one that picked him in 1960."[35]

Meyer, fortified with Rusher's on-the-scene analysis, was clearly pleased. He wrote in his column that the convention was "a miracle of sanity in a madly ideological world," a "conservative convention" which featured three basic conservative points. First, Republicans made "the simple call for order in our society." They reflected the realization "that order is the first condition of civilizational existence, the only foundation of freedom and well-being for anyone and everyone." A second crucial point was "the assertion of the greatness and the stature of this country, the denial of the masochistic whining that we are 'sick,' the vindication of the goodness and power of our institutions, public and private." And third, Meyer approved of the "programmatic assertion that peace in Vietnam, or in the world as a whole, can only be won by national strength and the re-establishment of national dignity."

Yes, these were all "fundamentally conservative positions," and the choice of Spiro Agnew as Nixon's vice presidential running mate gave them an important boost. Meyer noted with glee that the choice of Agnew had been made "against every pressure of the *New York Times*, the television networks, [and] the dolorous warnings of the Northeastern liberals." Agnew's speech at the convention "showed that he is no ideological liberal." Meyer also approved of Nixon's acceptance speech, in which Nixon sounded a theme that was very much like Meyer's "producing majority" thesis; Nixon spoke of "the non-shouters, the non-demonstrators" who went to work every day and paid their taxes. Nixon's words were "firm in content and a fitting challenge to liberalism in tone," Meyer wrote. "This was a very different Nixon from the always cautious, often trimming, Nixon of 1960. If the rest of the campaign is conducted on this level, conservatives can support the Republican ticket with confidence."

But then, there really was no alternative, and the near-revolutionary nature of the times had much to do with it. Meyer hinted at just how much recent occurrences affected his thinking. In 1964, he continued, Republicans pointed to a coming crisis in America—but only on the distant horizon. "Today, the crisis is upon us," Meyer stated. "It has become a stark matter of the survival of the conditions of civilization. Is a great, law-abiding, producing people to be held ransom by small minorities of *lumpen* slum-dwellers and *lumpen* students, aided, abetted and directed by liberal ideologues turned nihilist?" To this, Meyer said with a sigh of relief, Nixon and the Republicans had answered "with a clear and decisive No." If Richard Nixon and his party maintained this stance, his presidential administration could "turn the tide of the anarchy that threatens to engulf us."[36]

FRANK MEYER AND *National Review* in the end supported Richard Nixon in 1968. As with any election, the formulation of *NR*'s stance had been complex, filled with potholes and minefields. But for responsible conservatives, the biggest complexity in 1968 lay, as Rusher said, "out in the darkness." It was George Wallace, who mounted a serious third-party candidacy for the presidency of the United States and presented real problems for the conservative movement.

Wallace was from Clio, Alabama, and from his earliest days he had cultivated a career in politics, along with a "populist" image. He served in the army during World War II and deliberately avoided being tracked into the officer corps, for fear of being seen as elitist. On his return home, he quickly was elected to the state legislature, and he prepared to run for governor.

Wallace was not known, at first, as a racist. But in his 1958 gubernatorial race Wallace was narrowly defeated by a candidate who had an explicit prosegregation platform and significant backing from the Ku Klux Klan. An angry Wallace allegedly vowed never to be defeated on that issue again. Thus, in 1962, when he ran again for the governorship, it was as an avowed segregationist. And he won, promising in his inaugural address "segregation forever." When in 1963 the Kennedy administration put pressure on him to admit the first black students to the University of Alabama, Wallace literally stood in the schoolhouse door in symbolic opposition to integration; and although he could not stop the black students from enrolling, as the decade went on he never stopped arguing the case for "states' rights." But what endeared him to some conservatives was the antigovernment rhetoric that became a corollary to Wallace's segregationism. He damned "pointy-headed" bureaucrats, ridiculed them as people who "couldn't park their bicycles straight," and condemned busybody "theoreticians" and "pseudo-intellectuals" who wished to interfere in the lives of others. These words were music to conservative ears. In 1964, Wallace entered several Democratic primaries and did surprisingly well. Now he was running again, and serious political analysts predicted that he could throw the election into the House of Representatives.[37]

Most at *National Review,* led by Buckley, were deeply concerned. They knew that Wallace was garnering some conservative support, and they feared its implications. By early 1968, the mainstream media were reporting that some Wallace supporters were from the "kooky" Right—from the anti-Semitic *American Mercury,* the Liberty Lobby, the John Birch Society, and the White Citizens' Councils. This support could smear all conservatives with the brush of "extremism," something those at the magazine had worked hard to eliminate.[38]

But it was more than that. Wallace was attempting to cloak racial segregation in the language of constitutionalism; and besides, his arguments were made in the most vulgar terms, seeming to those at the magazine to appeal to the basest of human emotions, to Americans' lowest common denominator. "He was a racist," remembered Priscilla Buckley, "and we had fought hard to clear the conservative movement of racists; he was a vulgarian and a demagogue and a populist." He presented a "danger" to conservatism, threatening to splinter the movement into different and opposing factions, thereby reducing its influence. Thus, as early as the spring of 1967, the quarterly editorial Agonies of the magazine began to be taken up with "lengthy and inconclusive" discussions of Wallace. The questions centered on when and how vigorously to oppose him. By November 1967 *National Review's* position was clear. Wallace was beginning his "assault" on the White House, it editorialized, which was "in the authentic tradition of twentieth-century demagogy: a continuous offensive, with no retreats, answers, or explanations. . . . His skills are coarsely made, but they carry a heavy charge."[39]

This all had to do with principles, of course. That is, what were the principles of George Wallace, and did they truly make him a conservative? Such questions were right in Frank Meyer's bailiwick, and his position on Wallace was important in determining the magazine's overall stance and *NR's* emphasis on Wallace's "demagogy." Wallace, Meyer wrote in a May 1967 column, was a "demagogue" and a "populist," which was the "radical opposite" of conservatism. Yet many conservatives, Meyer knew, were "attracted" to Wallace and highly critical of *NR's* hostility to him. The Right must ask why Wallace attracted such support "if his candidacy is not to tear apart the American conservative movement and poison the moral source of its strength."

Meyer analyzed the problem of Wallace as he had the other radical right-wing groups he had written about over the years. The attraction to Wallace came from the "diverse" nature of the American conservative movement. Some were mainly anticommunists, opposed to the expansionism of the Soviet Union. Others were implacable opponents of domestic communists, fearful of the spread of spies and traitors. Still others wished to end liberalism's "encroachment on the liberties of individual citizens," and called themselves libertarians. And, finally, there were those who worried about the "decay" of law and order. All these "strains" occasionally rose to the surface.

When they did, Meyer continued, "those of us who attack certain positions as alien to the spirit of conservatism are inevitably criticized on the grounds that those whom we are attacking are also enemies of liberalism." But consider the possibility that some who attacked liberalism might pose "other dangers to conservatism and to the civilization conservatives are defending." Meyer thought George Wallace posed such dangers. For Wallace was a "populist," and populism, Meyer lectured, arose, as did conservatism, out of opposition to liberalism—"the

arrogant and naked elitism of the liberals, isolated from the ethics and tradition of the people." But this "polar opposite of a political perversion" was not
conservatism. Liberals wished to impose a "utopian design" upon society;
populism "would substitute the tyranny of the majority over the individual...untrammeled by considerations of freedom and virtue." This was "alien"
to the traditional conservative desire for limited, constitutionalist, republican
government.

Such populism, Meyer went on, was "the air that Wallace breathes. Every
speech he makes, every interview he gives, is redolent of it." Yes, Wallace
agreed with conservatives on Vietnam, on crime, on the need to reduce the
federal bureaucracy. But, Meyer also pointed out, Wallace's record as governor of Alabama showed that he was willing, very willing, to buy votes with
government spending. "When it is a question of socialist welfare measures or
when he builds a welfare state in Alabama, he is as far from conservatism as
any liberal," Meyer declared. "His combination of nationalist and socialist
appeals couched in the rhetoric of incitement of the masses and contempt for
the intellect in all its manifestations, is radically alien to conservatives."[40]

Frank Meyer and *National Review* had decided to read Wallace out of the
conservative movement, if they could. The decision was backed with action, led
by Buckley. He took a real dislike to Wallace, partly because of his populist
demagogy, but also because of what Buckley perceived as his obvious racism and
his crude railings against intellectuals. Thus he tried to mobilize his conservative
and Republican contacts against Wallace. He told one correspondent, "What I
resent most is his abuse of the rhetoric and analysis of conservatism." And Buckley
wrote Barry Goldwater: "It seems to me that we ought to have a real chance at
winning this year and that the important effort has got to be to discourage
conservatives from voting for George Wallace." He had Wallace as a guest on
Firing Line, where Buckley attacked him for his racist views, for blacks in Alabama being "inadequately protected," for the violation in Selma of the basic
rights of blacks. In the fall, Buckley wrote several articles and columns highly
critical of the Wallace movement. Conservatives "despise what they know to be
[Wallace's] venture in political profiteering on grave mutual concerns," Buckley
wrote. Wallace would give the country little but "the disintegrating penetration of Big Daddy government, accelerated by the thumping dissent of the
backwoods heckler." He also prevailed on two leading conservatives to attack

Wallace in the pages of *National Review.* Congressman John Ashbrook, the head of the American Conservative Union, wrote that the "only thing Wallace has against Washington is its racial policy. In all of his other attitudes he is one of the biggest centralizers of them all." Barry Goldwater put it simply: a vote for Wallace, he told *NR* readers, would go nowhere "but right down a rat-hole."[41]

NR and Meyer took some severe criticism for their anti-Wallace stand. After Meyer's 1967 column attacking Wallace appeared, hostile letters poured in from readers, most of them accusing *NR* of being elitist. "All right, all right, you Eastern intellectuals, let's simmer down," said one reader from Iowa. "You'll soon be screaming at George Wallace as hysterically as the beatniks who harass him at every meeting." Now even Meyer had "joined the chorus." A man from New York City wrote that "the implication, however veiled, that Wallace is another share-the-wealth demagogue is a deliberate distortion worthy of the *New York Times*. I have a feeling that Wallace's greatest sin, in your eyes, is that he doesn't amuse himself by attending opera and reading T. S. Eliot."[42]

BUT *NATIONAL REVIEW* held firm, and, although at one point Wallace's standing was at over 20 percent in the national polls, toward election day his numbers began to fall down to the roughly 13 percent of the vote he eventually got. Perhaps *NR* played a small role in that. Meanwhile, in its last issue before election day, the magazine finally officially endorsed Richard Nixon for the presidency, arguing that he was "capable of giving the country the impulse it needs on the way back to sobriety."[43]

Nixon's narrow victory meant that, for the first time in nearly a decade, a Republican would be in the White House. Conservatives would be in the unusual position of having someone they supported in a position of power, an unfamiliar role. Meyer wrote that this time he had voted for Nixon (as had Rusher). He was "the choice of a preponderantly conservative convention," and was one who could "restore order" at home as well as "American honor and prestige" abroad.

Although Nixon represented "an overwhelming American conservative consensus" his main "danger," to Meyer, lay in reaching too far for harmony, in attempting to split the difference between Wallace on the Right and the black powerite/student "nihilists" on the Left. Meyer stressed his now-familiar thesis that any conservative candidate's "center of gravity" could be found in "the essentially undifferentiated continuum of the great producing majority of Americans." What specific issues united these producers? Meyer contended that the election demonstrated four areas of agreement. First, all wished for "civil peace." Second, they wanted "an honorable and powerful American presence in a world beset by Communist aggressions." Third, producers desired an end to "massive social experiments financed by taxes on their hard-won earnings." And finally, they wanted a "defense against the nihilism that would destroy the very structure of their lives." This, then, Meyer declared, was the "mandate of 1968." A failure to follow it "could plunge America into massive social chaos."[44]

THE YEAR 1968 WAS another important one for *National Review*. Though like the rest of the country the magazine had been powerfully influenced by the tumultuous events of that year, they had not driven *NR* conservatives to radical extremes. Instead, *NR* (and Meyer) had acted almost as a mediator between the Reagan and Nixon camps during the spring primary season, both hinting at the loyalty the American Right would show to Reagan in the coming years and cementing its links to the Nixon campaign by endorsing him when the time came. It further lived up to its responsibility in relation to the Wallace campaign. *NR*, in the past critical of the civil rights movement, had taken a formal stand against racism. To have been neutral toward Wallace would have been hypocritical at best. Neither *NR* nor Meyer engaged in such hypocrisy. Their opposition was clear; their hands were clean.

More importantly, there were unmistakable signs by 1968 that *National Review* was now, in the eyes of people with influence, a responsible, influential, conservative voice on the national scene. Many in the elite cultural and media circles vigorously disagreed with *NR*, but they had to take what the magazine said seriously. This respect had been long in coming. Around the time that *National Review* began, the dominant view of conservatism could be summed up in the words Mary McCarthy wrote to her friend Hannah Arendt: "the great effort of this new Right is to get itself accepted as *normal,* and its publications as a *normal* part of publishing . . . and this, it seems to me, must be scotched, if it is not already too late. What do you think? I know you agree about the fact, the question is how it is to be done."[45]

It was certainly too late by 1968. *National Review* was now a player on the

national scene. When it held its tenth anniversary dinner in 1965, House Minority Leader Gerald Ford attended; cultivating contacts at *NR* was important
to a career in the GOP. When people around the country searched for an
example of responsible conservatism, they looked to *National Review*. And
when the Washington State Republican Party wished to denounce the John
Birch Society in 1966, it put out a pamphlet that reproduced much of what
NR's special issue had to say about the JBS. Even the liberal Republicans at
the Ripon Society had to give *NR* conservatism its due. "Ripon's ideological
premises may not be those of a libertarian-conservative like Milton Friedman, let alone a traditionalist-conservative like William Buckley (and it's time
we learned to distinguish the two varieties)," said one Ripon writer, "but we
can at least grant that some intellectuals on the right are thinking." Another
Ripon member gave grudging praise for the work done by *National Review*
and right-wing enterprises like it: "Such organizations work constantly to
propagate a conservative ideology," he declared, "a body of belief which will
set right a world gone out of kilter, a dogma for which mothers will work
long hours and fathers will sign large checks. Their adherents are given the
sense of a movement, a cause, a crusade. As a result all of these groups have
important influence in Republican politics." Respected *New York Post* political journalist Nick Thimmesch wrote that *NR* was "the nation's best Tory
magazine."

And *NR* had really arrived when it gained recognition from the noted
political reporter David Broder of the *Washington Post*, who with his colleague Stephen Hess published a book in 1967 on the state of the Republican Party. Broder and Hess conceded that the magazine was "never dull," that
now "Americans can get a steady stream of conservative comment coated
with style and wit." They noted that within the Republican Party there was
now a "*National Review* crowd," which acted "as guardians and advisers to
many of the groups that seek to influence the Republican Party, notably the
Young Americans for Freedom, the Young Republicans, the American Conservative Union, and the Intercollegiate Studies Institute." Furthermore, *NR*
had influenced the party; it had been "scrupulously careful to disassociate
itself from extremists like the Birchers. . . . [I]n fact, Buckley was in advance of
many national Republican leaders in his condemnation of Robert Welch's
organization." Now all responsible Republicans had adopted this position;

one of the most "divisive" intraparty issues was no longer subject to debate. "Gradually," Broder and Hess wrote, "Republicans are learning to stop shouting and to start reasoning with each other."[46]

All this was reflected in the fortunes of *National Review.* By 1966 the magazine could report that its readership was up 5 percent, comparing favorably with the *New Republic,* down 31 percent, the *Atlantic,* down 8 percent, and the *New Yorker,* down 10 percent. In 1968, the Magazine Publisher's Association cited *NR* for excellence, for "brightening the solemn business of political discourse by mixing humor with its strong opinions." By the summer of 1968, Buckley proudly informed *NR's* readers that the magazine had finally crossed the magic 100,000 subscriber mark; and, in what he considered its highest honor, he reported that *Pravda* had attacked *NR* as "the theoretician of the ultras."[47]

It showed in concrete political and electoral terms, too. The political organization most influenced by *NR* was the New York Conservative Party. Its fortunes improved in these years as well. Its low point was 1964, when it got only 3 percent of the total state vote. But then came Buckley's run for mayor of New York, which generated much-needed publicity (and 13 percent of the vote). In 1966, its relatively unknown gubernatorial candidate, Paul Adams, got over 500,000 votes statewide. And in 1968, Buckley's brother James, running for the U.S. Senate on the Conservative ticket, astonished nearly everyone by getting over 1.1 million votes in the state, 17.3 percent of the total, which more than doubled any previous party vote total. Something was happening; indeed, Richard Nixon that fall had felt the need to seek out the Conservative Party's support. "I welcome the support of the Conservative Party, which I regard as a responsible political organization," read a Nixon statement. And in the really big test in November 1968, the presidential candidates identified as being on the Right, Nixon and Wallace, together garnered over 56 percent of the votes cast nationally.[48]

National Review conservatism seemed to have arrived. William F. Buckley Jr. deserves much credit, and he received much recognition for his efforts. But Frank Meyer played an important role as well. He held responsible positions in nearly every major conservative organization, and he was an important force on the positions taken by *National Review.* It had been difficult at times; both Meyer and *NR* were often frustrated, and at times they frustrated others.

But the enterprise was achieving its goals, and Meyer had much to do with that. Of course, what life would be like under a Nixon administration remained to be seen.[49]

Nixon Conservatives

A S THE YEAR 1969 DAWNED, conservatives, though encouraged by the electoral successes of 1968, were sobered by the problems America faced. The United States had over 500,000 soldiers in Vietnam engaging in a war that seemed no closer than ever to being won. At home, millions of American citizens, disenchanted with the war, spilled over into large, divisive anti-war protests. And many young Americans, with long hair, grungy clothes, and drugged eyes, lived in "communes" and formed a "counterculture" seemingly opposed to everything *National Review* conservatives stood for. The country was as polarized, as divided, as ever.

NR conservatives, however, comforted themselves that a new presidential administration was about to take the reins of power in Washington. Richard Nixon may not have been "one of their own," but he clearly sympathized with much of what conservatives had to say—and the *NR* circle would have a line of communication open to him. Had he not personally courted the support of William F. Buckley Jr.? Had he not said that he read *National Review*?

And yet this also posed a challenge for conservatives like Buckley—and for men like Frank Meyer, who had also supported Nixon. How much allegiance did they owe Nixon? Must they defend everything Nixon did? How easy would it be to oppose him, should Nixon stray from what conservatives expected? What conservatives, and Meyer, discovered in the Nixon years was that their ties to the new "establishment" presented them with more dilemmas, with more challenges, than ever. Indeed, it could be argued that the election to the presidency of Richard Nixon was one of the most troubling periods ever for American conservatives.

AND YET, AT FIRST, it seemed to be the best of times for *National Review*. For one thing, William F. Buckley Jr.'s stature among conservatives was such that Richard Nixon believed he must pay attention to him and even consult with him. And so in 1969, as the Nixon administration got under way, some of Buckley's friends became Nixon appointees, such as former CBS executive Frank Shakespeare. Nixon later appointed Buckley to the Advisory Commission on Information of the United States Information Agency. Buckley began occasionally to receive invitations to administration state dinners, along with frequent notes from the president on Oval Office stationery congratulating him on his columns. He was also periodically invited to the White House itself, often with only one or two others present, for face-to-face meetings with the president.[1]

Moreover, Buckley had been friends with Nixon's new National Security adviser, Henry Kissinger, for years. They kept in close telephone contact throughout the Nixon years, and on over twenty occasions Kissinger had Buckley come to Washington for private, personal briefings on administration foreign policy. Former YAF chairman Tom Huston was also part of the Nixon White House, and he became known in Beltway circles as one of the administration's house conservatives, armed with positions smacking of his long association with *National Review*.[2]

It must have been exhilarating for *NR*'s resident political activist, publisher William Rusher, occasionally to receive telephone calls from Huston that were, as Rusher once wrote to Buckley, a "blunt appeal for pressure from you [Buckley] and [James Jackson] Kilpatrick on Nixon, to stem the tide of what Huston (and inferentially the other conservatives in the White House) regard as the disastrous series of liberal appointments that have been made recently. . . . The only conservatives [Nixon] respects, according to Huston, are you and Kilpatrick (among the writers)." Patrick Buchanan was important in this regard as well. Buchanan, one of the few ideological conservatives on Nixon's staff, had served as Nixon's liaison with the Right through the 1968 campaign, and now in the White

House occupied, as Rusher once put it, its "conservative desk." Buchanan served as a channel through which *NR* conservatives could reach the Nixon administration, as he sought out *NR*'s views on appointments and issues.[3]

There were plenty of questions, of course, both at the time and later, as to just how much good all of this did. Some worried that all the attention Buckley and *NR* received simply meant that they were being used. Buckley realized that it was important for *NR* to not be seen as an administration house organ. Reminded at one point by Rusher that he had agreed to speak at an American Conservative Union function, Buckley dutifully agreed to come. "Much though I despise these things," he told Rusher, "we should probably put a brave corporate front on and keep the administration honest."[4]

Yet it was a fine line to walk, especially when storm clouds loomed. Such a "dance along the precipice," as Buckley occasionally called it, required strong moral and philosophical tethers. And it was here that *National Review*'s guardian and arbiter of conservative principles and heresies, Frank Meyer, tried to teach conservatives one of his final lessons. Meyer was a somewhat reluctant Nixon supporter in 1968; he had always had his doubts about him. Thus, if and when the Nixon administration departed from conservative principles, Meyer, with no real ties to the Nixon White House, would be ready to keep the Right on the correct path. But all of that was yet to come.

FIRST, IT WAS TIME for a little fun. And it was a sign of the shifting political winds, and *NR*'s growing prominence, that those clustered around the magazine could have both fun and influence. In this case, the issue was John Lindsay. Lindsay had been mayor of New York City since 1965, having weathered the wild, rollicking campaign that William F. Buckley Jr. put him through—a campaign which, although Lindsay won, cemented Buckley's place as a national conservative political figure. Since then, Lindsay's administration had had its ups and downs. But by 1969, as the mayor's campaign for reelection neared, many worried about his growing strength, fretting that liberal, Rockefeller-style Republicanism might yet emerge triumphant within the GOP. It was thus taken as a given at *NR* that the mayor must be knocked down a peg or two. The question, as Rusher told Buckley in 1969, was "how best to dramatize Lindsay's shocking apostasy from Republicanism for the purpose of permanently destroying his national ambitions."[5]

Thus *NR*, editorially, fired many a verbal salvo at John Lindsay that summer, with Meyer tooting away on his anti-Lindsay horn. The mayor's mode of governance was, Meyer wrote, "tax, tax, tax the productive citizenry, black and white; spend, spend, spend on the non-productive." He rooted openly for Lindsay's "toppling" within the Republican primary later that summer, and he hoped that Lindsay's opponent, John Marchi, endorsed by the Conservative Party, could pull an upset. If that happened, Meyer wrote, it would "dim the mystique of liberal Republicanism's leading glamour boy and save the country from the calamity of a Lindsay drive for the Presidency."[6]

It was in fact becoming more and more difficult for a liberal Republican to survive in the GOP. The Republican Party had changed. Ever since Barry Goldwater captured the party's nomination in 1964, it had become clear that a transformation was taking place. Richard Nixon's nomination in 1968, owed mainly to conservative support, provided more evidence that the Republican Party was becoming a conservative party. And Lindsay's loss of the primary election to John Marchi, by a fairly healthy margin, confirmed this yet again. "Lindsay has in effect," *NR* editorialized, "been drummed out of the Republican Party by the rank and file." The mayor himself could only splutter at a post-election news conference that his opponents were "extremists," "reactionaries," and members of the "ultra-Right." Thus, as Meyer wrote, Lindsay's dreams of being elected to higher office within the Republican Party had been extinguished. Meyer had it right: "the Republican Party in New York will never be the same."[7]

THE QUESTION OF Richard Nixon and his administration was another matter entirely. How *National Review* as a magazine handled the first two years of the Nixon presidency illustrates the difficulties facing all conservatives, and especially activists such as Frank Meyer.

Some in the *NR* circle had never trusted Nixon. Back in 1960 William Rusher had written that there was a "central problem that confronts a Nixon supporter. *If* Nixon could be demonstrated to be a conservative in his own thinking and instincts, a little guile would be a small price to pay . . . , but [many] do not demonstrate Nixon's conservatism—they merely assume it. I, alas, do not; and without that assumption, Nixon becomes—not a sort of underground Hero of the Resistance—but just one more collaborator." On the other hand, many were thrilled to see the Republicans in control of the White House again and therefore tended to give Nixon the benefit of the doubt. *NR* occasionally applauded, in its editorials, the conservative "tendency" it saw in Nixon—his appointments of conservative judges, his relaxations of federal guidelines. Buckley told an interviewer that in his view Nixon "needs to be protected from that part of the right whose emphasis is unbalanced in the direction of the paradigm."[8]

Unfortunately, in the first years of Nixon's presidency, many of the initiatives that *NR* conservatives hoped for—a major military offensive in Vietnam, significant cuts in domestic spending at home, a radical assault on the size of the federal government—did not happen. Yet, again reflecting James Burnham's thinking, *National Review* sought to be analytical, objective, and reportorial as it analyzed what the Nixon administration was doing and why it was doing it. After Nixon had been in office for approximately a month, it was clear that the new administration was not going to take the United States in a direction radically different from its liberal Democratic predecessors. *NR* tried to examine calmly what was happening: "Mr. Nixon combines a mildly conservative, or square, temperament with some of the evangelical populism that is so common in the American tradition. But he is not an ideologue and not solidly committed to either Right or Left. . . . The Nixonologists are looking for something that isn't there. You cannot define or predict Mr. Nixon's basic policy line because he doesn't have one. The policy line is going to be defined by the nature of the first sharp challenges or crises that arise and by his response thereto. . . . Then we shall see what stuff President Nixon is made of; then and not before."[9]

Besides, Nixon had many of the same *enemies* as did conservatives, and in the politically charged times of the late 1960s, that mattered, too. In 1969, the war in Vietnam remained a major issue in American politics. Although the president kept his cards very close to his vest, it was evident that he would not immediately withdraw from Vietnam. *NR* took Nixon's side against anti-war protests, denouncing the "sentimental claptrap" the news media spread about the demonstrations and damning the protesters as "fools, opportunists, and America-lasters; bamboozled housewives, hare-brained clergymen . . . and a hard nucleus of just plain anti-Americans." What Nixon needed to do in order to retrieve the situation, both at home and in Vietnam, was to lead.

"Only if he now asserts his leadership," the magazine editorialized, "will the weak in heart, and the weak in mind, be frustrated in their impetuous efforts to bring about American defeat and international calamity."[10]

There were also times, in Nixon's first two years as president, when *NR* opposed him. The magazine eventually decided not to support Nixon's proposed Family Assistance Plan, which would have provided cash grants—a "negative income tax"—for poor families who fell below a certain income level in exchange for a work requirement. The *NR* editorial board decided that the plan would cost too much and create too much dependency among the poor. The magazine "regretfully" opposed the bill, the editors wrote, "on the grounds that its passage will be a victory that neither the President nor the nation can afford."[11]

And in foreign policy James Burnham became a frequent Nixon critic. He was unimpressed by Nixon's plans for a gradual American military pullout from Vietnam, along with continued U.S. aid and support for South Vietnam—a "Vietnamization.""Signs have multiplied," he wrote in his column in April 1969, that the president would "pull out ('disengage from') South Vietnam. To pull out on the best available terms but to pull out in any event. (It is hard to see how terms can be expected to be much good when you have decided in advance to settle anyway.)" "[L]et us at least hope," Burnham went on, "that Mr. Nixon is not going to try to fool us about what a pullout signifies, which means he will first have to make sure not to fool himself. A defeat is a defeat is a defeat."[12]

What *NR* mainly sought to do during Nixon's first two years was to exhort the president to more conservative alternatives; to urge him to do what many at the magazine seemed to suspect he wanted to do, but the political consequences of which actions Nixon feared. On Vietnam, *NR* repeatedly stressed the conflict's importance to the anticommunist cause, and that the U.S.'s minimum objective must be to maintain a noncommunist South Vietnam. Nixon, the magazine said over and over, must explain to the American people why such a goal was important. "The voice of their President is still a powerful and moving force in the minds and hearts of his countrymen," it said at one point. "If he fails to win them to the task he knows to be essential to the nation's future security and interest, it will be a blameless and honorable failure." Furthermore, *National Review* frequently urged Nixon to use such counterinsurgency methods as were necessary to achieve victory in Vietnam, and not merely to hold the line. "Let

[President Nixon] demand of the Joint Chiefs prompt transmission of a plan not for quitting by stages but for winning," the editors wrote. "He will get it if he asks."[13]

And so it went—never completely unqualified praise for Nixon, and never sharp, bitter, untempered criticism. When he pursued policies conservatives supported, *NR* tended to remind its readers that he may have done so, not because of his belief in conservatism, but because of its ultimate political benefits. So too for actions taken by the president which conservatives did not favor. Midway through Nixon's first year in office, for example, journalist James Jackson Kilpatrick, in offering an early assessment of Nixon's presidency for *NR*'s readers, opined that there indeed had been some disappointments, such as not demanding North Vietnamese withdrawal from South Vietnam; nor had he made as many conservative appointments to government as he had promised. But Nixon was "trying," he was "studying everything," and perhaps more could be done after the 1970 elections. "At the end of his first semester, the record is mixed: Not bad; not bad at all," Kilpatrick continued. "But not Dean's List, either. From the conservative point of view, it is about what we should realistically have expected; and if some of us have reacted with disappointment, the fault may not lie with Mr. Nixon's performance, but with our own giddy hopes. We hoped for too much."[14]

It was a fine line *NR* had to walk. Which of Nixon's policies were necessary compromises with liberals and Democrats, and which were unnecessary sellouts? Some conservatives were unhappy no matter what *National Review* said. At one point American Conservative Union member Robert Bauman complained, in a long letter to Buckley, that *NR* should not accept Social Security as a given, and in general should press harder for reductions in the size of government. Bauman claimed that otherwise "there is really little point in either the continued existence of *NR*, the ACU or any other anti–collectivist efforts. . . . Conservatives look to *NR* for leadership, and this kind of offhand treatment of major issues, even though minor in extent, is somewhat unnerving." On the other hand, when *NR* ran the Kilpatrick piece assessing Nixon's presidency, many readers thought it somehow disloyal. "One says how *dare* we give Nixon a report card?" wrote an editorial assistant summarizing a fortnight's mail. "Since when do we rate the President of the United States?"[15]

In response, Buckley wrote to Bauman and suggested that "if you know of any election results or specific opinion polls that suggest that the American people have turned away from the notion that it is the job of government for instance to subsidize education or medical care, you have got quite a news-beat. . . . I continue to believe what I expounded several years ago, back in Goldwater days, that the conservative has two functions, the paradigmatic, and the expediential." In attempting to fulfill these functions, *NR* tried to remain evenhanded in its overall editorial policy and in its treatment of Richard Nixon. Although no one knew it yet, as Rusher later remarked, many would come to consider the 1969–70 period "as near as Nixon and conservatives would ever get to a honeymoon."[16]

THE MAIN REASON it was a honeymoon was not so much because of what Nixon did as because pragmatism had made many inroads among conservatives. Of course, Richard Nixon and *NR* conservatives also had a common enemy: the anti-war movement in the United States, which after 1969 seemed to become louder, more radical, and more threatening to the survival of the nation itself.

The anti-war movement was everywhere, especially within American higher education. At Harvard University, militant students took over a number of campus building and evicted several deans from their offices. At Cornell, armed radicals first took over the campus administration building, and then were allowed to leave without penalty. On one occasion, William F. Buckley Jr., attempting to give a commencement address, was repeatedly shouted at, interrupted, and heckled by black power militants and representatives of the Students for a Democratic Society. At other commencements, a radical student, upon receiving one of her institution's highest academic achievement awards, turned her back upon the local archbishop conferring it and raised a clenched fist in defiance; forty students stood with their backs turned during an entire commencement speech given by Nelson Rockefeller; at Harvard, members of the SDS went to its president, Nathan Pusey, and demanded that one of them be allowed to speak at the graduation exercises, or else they would disrupt the proceedings—and Pusey agreed; at Brown, three-quarters of the graduating class turned their backs on their commencement speaker, Henry Kissinger. "What does one do about . . . the girl who violates sacerdo-tal proprieties, the band of students who turn their backs on someone who is called on the scene to be honored?" Buckley asked. "Where reason does not obtain, power will, and this is the ugly truth the growing consciousness of which is haunting more and more people. You cannot have ceremony without a certain decorum, and you cannot have a workable society without ceremony. The choice society is being handed is to abandon ceremony, or to repress demonstrators."[17]

The situation did not immediately improve, either. Early in 1970, a conservative student at the University of Michigan wrote *NR* that, in the previous week, there had been "two major police-student confrontations, two nights of 'trashing' by roving bands of radicals . . . , two episodes involving the 'unshelving' of several thousand books in the University undergraduate library by black students—rendering the library useless to all others during midterm exams—a parade on the drag complete with balloons and kazoos, and a bullet found lodged in President Fleming's house." Later that same month, at the University of Washington, an ROTC building burned to the ground. When asked to comment on it, the university's chancellor said: "While I disapprove of violence, you've got to understand the way the kids feel about that bloody war in Vietnam." After President Nixon ordered the incursion into Cambodia in the spring of 1970, events seemed to spin out of control. Over 450 colleges and universities across the nation were paralyzed by student strikes. In California, Governor Ronald Reagan shut down the entire state university system, citing the threat of violence. Dozens of state governors called out the army and the National Guard. At many institutions of higher education, anti-war rallies turned into riots. At Kent State University, such a riot led nervous National Guardsmen to fire upon and kill four student protesters, which only inflamed the situation. Many universities simply canceled the rest of the school year. "I have seen a once great university," wrote one conservative student to *National Review*, "become a third-rate political tool for a mob of Vietcong flag-waving animals, who trample the rights of anyone who dares to disagree with them." Buckley, attempting to give a commencement address in California, was heckled and hooted; finally, after fighting to speak over the noise and through the fumes of a smoke bomb, he was presented with a live pig by an anti-war student leader. "Can American Education Survive One More Year Like the One We Have Just Been Through?" blared the headline of one *NR* article late in 1970.[18]

Nor was it only in academia. In the San Francisco Bay area the Black

Panther Party, led by Black Power militants such as Huey Newton and Bobby Seale, talked of violence and revolution. Children at Black Panther functions were given comic books that portrayed heroic African-American guerrillas fighting against pigs in policemen's uniforms. And then there were the bombs. In late November 1969, in a span of forty-eight hours in New York City, explosives were found in the RCA building, in the Criminal Courts building, and in the headquarters of General Motors and Chase Manhattan bank. Later a police station and Navy recruiting office were firebombed, and four Molotov cocktails were lobbed at the home of a judge presiding over a trial involving several Black Panthers. In 1970 in San Francisco, an explosive device detonated at a police station, killing one policeman and injuring nine others. In Santa Barbara, amidst anti-war rioting, a Bank of America building burned to the ground. Two Weathermen, part of a radical and violence-prone anti-war organization, were killed by their own homemade explosives. And in April 1971, the last big anti-war rally took place in Washington, D.C.; over 300,000 attended, but there was so much violence, open drug use, and petty disruption that even liberal, anti-war columnist Mary McGrory called it "the worst planned, worst executed, most slovenly, strident and obnoxious peace action ever committed."[19]

What some of these militants said was hardly believable. Angela Davis was quoted as saying that "the first condition of freedom is violent resistance." Black Panther leader David Hilliard said, "We will kill Richard Nixon. We will kill any [expletive deleted] that stands in the way of our freedom. . . . We advocate the very direct overthrow of the government by way of force and violence." A leader of Students for a Democratic Society stated flatly that "we're moving towards armed struggle in this country." Militant anti-war leader Abbie Hoffman, speaking at Columbia, outlined its future: "BOOM! BOOM! BOOM!" Jerry Rubin, in his book *Do It!,* wrote that, in the years to come, "Every high school and college in the country will close with riots and sabotage and cops will circle the campuses, standing shoulder to shoulder. The schools belong to the pigs. Millions of young people will surge into the streets of every city, dancing, singing, smoking pot, f——— in the streets, tripping, burning draft cards, stopping traffic." "The time for words is over," shouted radical lawyer William Kunstler. "You must resist, and resistance means everything short of revolution. And if resistance doesn't work, revolt." "We're against all that's good and decent in honkey America," seethed John Jacobs of the Weathermen. "We will burn and loot and destroy. We are the incubation of your mother's nightmare."[20]

What did this kind of polarization mean? *National Review* conservatives struggled with this question increasingly during these years while remaining rather fascinated by the phenomenon. Anti-war disruption, the magazine said at one point, was often "carried through the mass media as typhoid germs used to be carried through the water supply." And after detailing some suspicious-looking bombings, *NR* solemnly intoned: "Two unmistakable hallmarks of decadence are the inability to recognize blatant evil and a reluctance to call it by its name."[21]

FRANK MEYER WAS as profoundly affected by the rise of radicalism and the counterculture as anyone, especially as it was manifested in American higher education and in the anti-war movement. One son (John) had already graduated from college; another (Gene) was soon to enter. Meyer had many contacts within academia who kept him up to date on the latest campus outrages. He contended, quite simply, that civilization was being threatened by barbarism—strong language indeed. But Meyer believed that New Left abominations justified such a view. In the spring of 1969, at Cornell University, it had just come to light that three black students, angered at statements made by their economics professor (he had, for example, defended the superiority of Western civilization), seized the main offices of the economics department and held its chairman prisoner. Eventually the little siege ended peacefully. But most significant to Meyer, Cornell's administration pressed no charges against the students. Indeed, one administrator expressed admiration for their protest, since the professor's defense of the West was "a specially obvious case of the racism which black people find throughout the white community. . . . [A]cademics cannot use the cloak of 'academic freedom' to cover up statements which might anger black students."[22]

Meyer was outraged. To him, the students' actions, and Cornell's response, was a perfect example of "the terror, ideological, professional, and sometimes even physical, that is being directed against champions of Western civilization and its values." Many students were striking out at "the very foundations of Western civilization"—not merely the Vietnam War, or racism, or militarism (as

they claimed). It was going further, much further, than that. And liberal relativism had prepared the way. Liberals preached that all values, all beliefs, must
be left to the individual. From this it was only a short step to the approval of
"the black student who curses at his teachers because he is taught Bach
rather than 'soul.'" But, in the midst of the chaos, Meyer saw hope. He noted
the increasing visibility of former left-wing faculty members such as Sidney
Hook, who by 1969 had become an outspoken critic of the anti-war counterculture, as well as the appearance of some antiradical articles in *The New Republic*. Perhaps, Meyer wrote, "enough of our intellectuals may yet be shocked
into sanity by the anarchy for which they have prepared the way." Indeed, so
many did move away from liberalism and the Left that they were labeled
"neoconservatives." They had not escaped the notice of the ever-vigilant
Meyer.[23]

But the denizens of the counterculture were what most interested Meyer.
In late summer 1969, he leveled yet another broadside at them, calling them
"pseudo-revolutionaries," "cheap pot mystics," "morally uncouth" and "intellectually lazy." They assumed they knew all, that they should dictate the curriculum
and demand an undefined "relevance" in all of their courses. "I want, I want, I
want," Meyer mimicked, "and if I don't get it, I'll burn the place down." The
typical extremist student, he went on, was like "an outraged baby who has not
gotten what he wants—but, sadly for our society, a baby who has achieved the
physical stature to demonstrate, occupy, and throw Molotov cocktails."[24]

Later, Meyer, analyzing the "counterculture" more carefully, argued that it
was misnamed. It should be called the "anti-culture," because it opposed what
was essential to any civilized culture: civility, reasoned discourse, standards. Instead, the counterculture was an "amalgam of dope, rock, scruff, amorality and
superstition." The "scruff" found in late 1960s hairstyles broke down self-disci-
pline, Meyer contended; the "incessant and insisting" drumbeat of rock portended the "sensual destruction of an ordered universe." And marijuana was
being "celebrated as a mode of escape from conceptual thinking." Thrown all
together, along with some other fads of the late 1960s—Eastern mysticism,
Satanism—these elements spawned revolutionary thinking.[25]

Meyer had also learned through the years that it wasn't enough merely to
attack and condemn. What should conservatives *do?* Meyer heard from two different camps. Some on the Right gleefully relished the thought of "the sowers of

the wind reaping the whirlwind." Liberalism, which gave birth to the radicals, would be "swept away" and conservatives could fill the power vacuum. But others believed the radical threat to be so great that, as Meyer summarized their view, "common cause must be made with all liberal forces who are willing to resist the radical onslaught."

Meyer held that both sides were correct. It made sense in certain situations to work with liberal allies "where outrageous demands must be resisted, violent demonstrations suppressed, the norms of social existence defended." On the other hand, he reminded his readers, the civilization that liberals were helping to defend had become "corroded," and it was the liberals' fault. The revolutionaries were liberalism's progeny. "On sex, on drugs, on responsibility, in its refusal to read and study, the hippie movement is no more than the extreme extension of liberalism's relativist attack upon the standards of civilization," Meyer asserted. But neither could one "watch supinely as the radicals overwhelm our social order." Responsible conservatives must strike a balance. Frank Meyer, the "fusionist" seeking compromise, was still at work.[26]

Meyer had strong views about the anti-war movement as well. In the fall of 1969, in the wake of the massive protests created by the Moratorium movement, Meyer argued in his column that, far from being the orderly expression of democratic protest, as claimed by many in the news media, this was an attempt "to subvert the orderly processes of representative constitutional decision" by "a small minority"—one million people, out of two hundred million total American citizens. It involved "ambitious leaders mobilizing a mob-like minority to destroy the true processes of a constitutional polity." The current anti-war opposition presented a new challenge, combining "Marxist and Deweyite intellectuals" with the development of television, which was staffed mainly "by the intellectual flunkies of the academic intellectuals." This combination, Meyer believed, created a "pseudo-reality . . . , an *illusion of public opinion* to overawe constituted government." Indeed, Meyer was most concerned about the need to defend constitutional, representative processes, what Meyer called "the greatest feat of intellectual force combined with common sense in the history of mankind." This was Meyer the Burkean traditionalist talking.[27]

Meyer stayed on the attack. In 1971, when anti-war activists again invaded Washington, D.C., an increasingly angry Meyer drew a parallel be-

tween these raucous opponents of the war and the Nazi and communist street
fighters in Germany's Weimar Republic during the 1920s. Their mutual goal,
Meyer argued, was to "terrorize" the government, to "bind it to the will of an
impassioned and violent minority." Indeed, Meyer's contempt for the
counterculturists had greatly deepened. They were "more despicable" than
ever. They were "spoiled," and Meyer thought it was time to take action against
such "children." He wondered aloud in his column whether it wasn't time to
pass legislation keeping demonstrators a certain distance away from the seats
of government. It was time to return to a primary responsibility of legitimate
government: the just exercise of authority.[28]

It is important to realize that *National Review,* by now, represented the
mainstream of conservative thinking in America, and that, on the anti-war
movement and the counterculture, Meyer fit squarely within that mainstream.
Burnham bluntly wrote that many counterculturists were devoted to violence as a good. "Civilization, men being what they are, is never far from the
brink of savagery," said Burnham, ominously, in his column. "It does not take
so very many savages within to push it over."[29]

In May 1970, after the four student protesters were killed at Kent State
University, *National Review* in essence assumed Frank Meyer's position on demonstrations in general. Referring specifically to the students shot at Kent State,
the editors wrote: "Mob rule is by definition revolutionary in its relationship to
representative democracy, and it is by nature lawless and violent. Inevitably it
leads to bloodshed. Those who have encouraged the mob, often very respectable
and 'moral' individuals, might just as well have pulled the trigger."[30]

Nor were views such as this unique to *National Review.* California governor Ronald Reagan wrote that it must have seemed "incomprehensible that a
portion of our population—including some students, some faculty members,
and outsiders—are attempting to overthrow our democratic way of life. It is
equally incomprehensible in a democratic society . . . to find so many of its
citizens standing mute and helpless while their basic values and fundamental
processes are assaulted." Many conservatives who read *National Review* believed
that it should take an even stronger stand against the revolutionaries. "Lots and
lots of calls and letters," reported an editorial assistant to *NR's* editors in November 1969, "urging us to do something against the Moratorium."[31]

One of those most powerfully affected by the violence and the divisions in society was William F. Buckley Jr. He wrote an entire speech on the issue, called "Reflections on Current Disorders," which he circulated to his colleagues at *National Review.* "Reason cannot apprehend the revolutionary vapors on which the revolutionaries are stoned," he told his audiences. "What is required, I think, is a premonitory Sign; a sign of firmness; such a sign as Hamilton foresaw might have to be shown. Repression of the lawbreakers . . . is the defense of the rule of law." Twice in 1970 the taping of Buckley's television show, *Firing Line,* was interrupted by bomb threats. "One can hardly deny," Buckley wrote in his column after the second incident, "that the atmosphere is violent, remorseless, uncontrolled and uncontrollable, and *very* nearly unfathomable."[32]

Even more unfathomable to the editors of *NR* was the fact that the changes of the late 1960s sometimes proved irresistible even to conservatives, especially young ones. They too were wearing their hair longer, listening to rock music, experimenting with hard drugs. It was very difficult for older men of the Right, such as Meyer or Rusher or Burnham, to understand. Yet they strove mightily to do so. A conservative on campus "may be seriously torn between a perfectly human desire to accommodate himself to the prevailing behavioral patterns on his campus," Rusher wrote Buckley privately, "and a perfectly sincere loyalty to the higher principles and more profound commitments of Young Americans for Freedom. Shall he wear his hair long and smoke pot, or wear a vest and read *National Review,* or both?"[33]

The best example of how the many social movements of the late 1960s affected even the rock-ribbed conservatives of the *NR* circle came in the spring of 1970, when a letter from a young conservative named Tom McSloy reached William F. Buckley Jr.'s mailbox at *National Review.* McSloy was in many ways a perfect example of a young man of the Right. He had just returned to the U.S. from a stint in the army, was involved with the Conservative Club at Northwestern, and had volunteered in the 1964 Goldwater campaign. But he was also a member of his generation, one who liked Bob Dylan, enjoyed the Rolling Stones, and through it all remained "an inveterate *NR* fan."

But McSloy believed there were many things wrong with *NR*; and it was this that caught Buckley's attention. *National Review* had not, in recent years, given "equal time" to college students and their complaints, McSloy argued; it had not fairly represented "legitimate" student demands. A 1969 *NR* editorial paragraph had labeled his favorite rock group the "Rolling Scum." *NR* was not being fair, McSloy went on, condemning everyone, especially Frank Meyer. "There are a lot of *NR* subscribers under thirty and we're not freaks, either, or radicals or hippies," he told Buckley. "But I am damned tired of those little innuendoes about the things young people like, and of the fact that every pomposity uttered by some SDS moron is duly punctured, while you let all sorts of foolishness pass if it happens to be directed at young people, or by some totem conservative. (Frank Meyer springs to mind. You really need to give him the horselaugh frequently, you really do.)"

McSloy wanted more space devoted to issues relevant to the young. He hoped *NR* would be critical of the Right as well as the Left. "You certainly haven't thumped on the Nixon administration with the gusto of old," he wrote. "The bureaucracy is still enormous and parasitic, the debt mounting, taxes oppressive, inflation spiraling. Have you sold out to the Establishment? . . . I really do like *NR*, but you can be terribly stuffy at times really."[34]

The letter struck a chord with Buckley; maybe the magazine *had* lost some of its zest, perhaps it had gotten too "stuffy." Buckley sent McSloy's letter to both his sister Priscilla and to Meyer, calling it "superb" and urging that it be run in *NR*—"the sooner the better, as far as I'm concerned." And soon it was, in Buckley's "Notes and Asides" column.[35]

More importantly, Buckley allowed all of *NR*'s senior editors to respond to the letter in the same space. Surprisingly, given that he was singled out by McSloy for attack, one of the more thoughtful replies came from Frank Meyer. He rejected McSloy's thesis that *NR* should give a great deal more space to "youth" issues. But in doing so, he demonstrated that he had given much more thought to the whole question of the "generation gap" than many might have suspected. Student protests, Meyer wrote in his response, were "a revolt against the standards of Western civilization," and therefore, *NR* must be "committed to the sharpest opposition to the 'student revolt,' which is the nasty spawn of liberalism. Being conservatives, we must base our position on principle, not on the dictates of the latest fads and fancies."

But Meyer did not end there. McSloy had jokingly written that *National Review*'s position on youth and the anti-war movement put it in the "Pig Camp." Meyer thought this an important point. "If it is to be defined as Mr. McSloy defines it," he answered, "as the camp of defense of the standards of Western civilization, then all I can say—and with enthusiasm—is 'oink.'"

McSloy's "complaint," Meyer went on, was mainly that *NR* should say more about pot, rock music, and the sexual revolution. These, however, were mainly "symbols"; long hair was in a way a "uniform," and uniforms were nothing new. Meyer was not totally unsympathetic; but he tried to place these issues in a historical context, and to explain how a true conservative must seek to think and therefore to act. Marijuana, for example, was in his analysis "a drug characteristic of Eastern civilizations, over which the West towers as civilization towers over barbarism. The West has its own drug, alcohol, integral element in song and story, love and battle, material substance of its highest mystery. How encompassing a rejection of tradition would conservatives be condoning, to bless the turning from this to the leavings of dying civilizations?" As for the sexual revolution, Meyer held that "one need not be unmoved by the tragedy of a Tristan and an Isolde, a Lancelot and a Guinevere, a Paolo and a Francesca, to recognize the height of spiritual achievement in the Western concept of sacramental monogamy."

No, Meyer said, conservatives could not, should not, change for change's sake. Younger conservatives like McSloy must know that conservatism, properly understood, did not mean adopting new ideas simply because they were new, and it certainly did not mean rejecting tradition and the historical achievements of the West simply because they were old. Far from it. No, "to ask conservatives to withhold their support from those in authority over the young," Meyer concluded, "who attempt to maintain the tradition of the civilization, is to ask them to cease to be conservatives."[36]

It was a serious, thoughtful response, as were all of the comments by *NR*'s senior editors. The magazine received a "fantastic inundation," as Rusher later put it, of letters from readers in response to the whole controversy; and, significantly, when McSloy was given space in *NR* to respond to the senior editors, he had two specific points to make. First, he showed how some younger conservatives differed from *NR* in their views on the Vietnam War and changing sexual mores. "I am not sure," McSloy wrote in his reply, "that the threat which marshaled the conscript army that crushed Nazi Germany is equally present in Indochina. And I do not believe that society should restrict the sexual behavior of its members, as long as it is done in private, and by consenting adults." And secondly, he had something to say to Frank Meyer, something that illustrated his and other young peoples' differences with Meyer, but which once again showed

Meyer's tremendous influence. "'My intention in writing . . . is to vindicate the freedom of the person as the central and primary end of political society,'" McSloy quoted. He then added, "I almost wrote that without attribution, so familiar is it to me. Those ringing words are Frank Meyer's, whose nose I elsewhere tweak, but whose thought has guided me at least part of the way to the positions I here defend. Though we may not always agree, we fight on the same side."[37]

National Review did eventually make some accommodation to the changing times, instituting a column on rock music and other youth issues. Significantly, it was assigned to another of *NR's* stable of young writers, C.H. Simonds, a close Meyer friend who frequently stayed overnight with the Meyers and worked closely with him on the book section. *NR's* overall position, however, did not change; it remained closely informed by the overall philosophical framework that Frank Meyer provided. Buckley, in fact, would occasionally refer to "ground control" in Woodstock, guiding *NR* towards the correct path. He meant it.[38]

NATIONAL REVIEW WOULD not try to become "hip" and "cool." And it would not join with the antiestablishment spokesmen who bashed Richard Nixon concerning the Vietnam War, either. If anything, the counterculture's hostility to Nixon made Frank Meyer and *NR* feel closer to him. But the war was not the only issue placing Nixon and the *NR* circle on the same side. There was also the rise of Spiro Agnew.

When Agnew first arrived on the national scene, few envisioned that he would become a conservative hero. He was first elected governor of Maryland in 1966 as a champion of racial integration, and in the 1968 presidential race, Agnew at first supported Nelson Rockefeller. Nixon chose him as his vice presidential candidate mainly to appeal to the moderates in the party, not the conservatives. That fall, Agnew's campaign was plagued with so many gaffes, and so much media hostility, that most thought Nixon won in spite of him.

But, although almost no one realized it, by 1969 the new vice president's thinking had become conservative. The evolution of Agnew's thought was partly inspired by the times in which he lived. As governor of Maryland, he had watched helplessly as severe rioting and social disruption roiled the streets of Baltimore in the wake of the assassination of Martin Luther King Jr. And he apparently became angry at black leaders who, in his opinion, did not do enough to denounce the rioters. Furthermore, during Agnew's fall campaign as Nixon's vice presidential nominee in 1968, William F. Buckley Jr. was one of the few columnists to write in support of him, praising Agnew's "toughness, sincerity, decent-mindedness, decisiveness."[39]

So, when William Rusher, always on the lookout for possible conservative allies within the Nixon administration, and always hoping to discover "presidential timber," called on Agnew early in 1969 at his Washington office, he received a warm welcome. Rusher later heard from others that Agnew read *NR* closely, discussed its articles with people, and handed out copies of the magazine to friends. Before long, the two men were meeting occasionally to discuss politics in general, the Republican Party, and how to advance the conservative cause. Occasionally Buckley or conservative strategist F. Clifton White were with him. Had *NR* conservatives found a new ally?[40]

It soon became evident that they had. Agnew's growing conservatism—plus the influence of hard-liners such as Patrick Buchanan and William Safire, who both occasionally wrote speeches for him—made him eager to denounce the administration's enemies, especially those in the anti-war movement and the news media. Nixon let him. Agnew could be the administration's point man on such issues; at the very least, it would secure Nixon's conservative flank. Agnew took to the job with gusto. He attacked anti-war opponents by claiming that a "spirit of national masochism prevails, encouraged by an effete corps of impudent snobs who characterize themselves as intellectuals." As for violent anti-war protesters, it was time "to stop dignifying the immature actions of arrogant, reckless, inexperienced elements within our society." And he fiercely denounced what he saw as the liberal bias of many members of the news media, the "nattering nabobs of negativism."[41]

Conservatives had long yearned to hear this kind of direct, even contemptuous language. It expressed what they felt. Agnew and his staff, meanwhile, made sure that conservatives knew in what direction he was heading. Patrick Buchanan occasionally sent advance copies of the vice president's speeches to *NR*. And the magazine, while keeping in mind the obvious—that the administration was using Agnew to appeal to conservatives and to attack their anti-war opponents—could not contain its enthusiasm. "The public has now been told dramatically that another position does exist," it remarked; "as a result of

[Agnew], the Administration's position on Vietnam has been rescued from the realm of the subliminal."[42]

Surprisingly, one member of the Right remained somewhat aloof. William F. Buckley Jr, with the air of the aristocrat about him, believed that politics should maintain a certain class, dignity, and elegance, and not descend into down-and-dirty, unthinking, demagogic, populist appeals. When Agnew made his speech containing the "impudent snobs" reference, Buckley in his column severely criticized him. "I wish that Spiro Agnew hadn't said it," he wrote. "It was careless, silly, and analytically indefensible." Buckley contended that, in fact, it would be highly unusual for a snob to be "impudent," and besides, attacking intellectuals echoed the style of George Wallace. Later, when contemplating *National Review*'s fifteenth anniversary celebration, Buckley was very cool to the idea of inviting Agnew as a speaker. "*NR* is after all a project of some literary and philosophical subtlety," Buckley told the senior editors privately, "and however much we applaud the Vice President's performance, it is rather objurgated in character, and I think it would hurt us if he chose our dinner as an opportunity to say something raucous."[43]

But his senior editors would change his thinking. Naturally, Frank Meyer was involved. Meyer was delighted with Agnew. He for quite some time had been complaining about the liberal bias of the news media. The attacks on Agnew, Meyer wrote in his column, came because he had confronted the "old liberalism, New Left, and the communications media." Agnew had "clearly and simply called things what they are." Meyer took pains to state (perhaps hoping to influence Buckley) that he did not believe Agnew's rhetoric to be excessively populist or demagogic. Words such as "snob," "impudent," or "effete" were "arguable and subject to confirmation," very different from George Wallace's unanswerable "pointy-head" rhetoric. Agnew's speeches "drive straight to the actual reality of the situation," Meyer went on. "There are dozens of issues today on which this kind of straight talk is necessary if we are not to be immobilized in a semantic paralysis while the forces of disorder run unchecked." Agnew, to Meyer's relief, challenged "the consensus of the ideologues. Those who yearn for clean intellectual air are in his debt."[44]

Once again, Meyer found an unlikely ally in James Burnham. Burnham shared Meyer's distrust of the American news media, and he also believed that Agnew's speeches were substantive and important. As he told Buckley early in 1970: "I have got hold of the full text of quite a number of [Agnew's] . . . speeches, and I must say I thought them pretty good. . . . In fact, I think that Agnew's speeches are intellectually superior to those delivered by any other U.S. political big shot for many years, intellectually more serious; to begin with, they really do say something about serious subjects. Now there is also, no doubt, something else in them and in him that is harder to evaluate because it is down deeper. . . . Maybe it's very bad, but just possibly it's what the doctor ordered."[45]

If even the sober, rather cynical Burnham was foursquare behind Agnew, then support for the vice president within *NR* was strong, indeed. Buckley came around, partly owing to the influence of Meyer and Burnham and partly due to Agnew himself. Almost immediately after his column critical of Agnew, Buckley wrote another to correct the assumption held by many readers— including Agnew—that Buckley "disapproved" of the "substance" of the vice president's thinking. Wrong, said *NR*'s editor in chief; he had subsequently read another Agnew speech, and its condemnation of the "reckless" and "arrogant" actions of the anti-war movement was a "bullseye!" On the whole, Buckley went on, "the occasional rhetorical misfires aside, Mr. Agnew is doing okay, and the impudent yelping of some of his snobbish critics is music to the ear." Later, in December 1970, Buckley, Rusher, and *National Review* arranged for Agnew to attend a special *NR*-sponsored lunch in Buckley's apartment in New York City, where he could meet with business leaders, significant financial contributors to *NR* and the conservative movement, and some of the *NR* staff. It was quite an occasion for the *NR* circle—"we have never before had a lunch for the vice-president," Buckley wrote later—and was yet another example of how far the magazine had come. At the gathering, Agnew gave a brief talk, and Buckley, who had not quite lost his skepticism toward him, lauded Agnew's "quite extraordinary analytical and syntactical resourcefulness, his sense of decorum and balance. A very nice guest." Rusher later told Agnew that he had won a "convert" in *NR*'s editor in chief.[46]

Agnew thus became a sudden, but welcome, conservative icon. Nor did it hurt when he put John R. Coyne, a former *NR* editorial assistant and contributor, on his staff as a speechwriter. The vice president was yet another reason why many conservatives, swallowing their doubts, were willing to continue to support the Nixon administration. Richard Nixon knew very well how much Agnew appealed to conservatives. He believed Agnew had now "become a really hot property, and we should keep building and using him," wrote his chief of staff. Soon, the question would be: Were conservatives too being "used"?[47]

But few were asking this question yet. On a number of fronts, conservatives still needed the Nixon administration, and they received some help from it. On no issue was this more apparent than the candidacy of James L. Buckley for the U.S. Senate in the state of New York in 1970.

Jim Buckley, a lawyer who helped run the family business, was the brother of William F. Buckley Jr. and had mainly operated in the shadow of his more famous sibling. He was very much a conservative and did his bit to help the cause. In 1965, he managed his brother's campaign for mayor of New York City, thinking it would be his only foray into politics. But it was not. James Buckley was articulate and affable; people liked him. And so Conservative Party leaders urged him to run on their ticket for the U.S. Senate from New York in 1968 against the liberal Republican Jacob Javits. Buckley finally agreed and surprised almost everybody by garnering some 17 percent of the vote, over 1.1 million votes. Once again, many thought—Buckley included—that this would be the end of his political career. Then came 1970 and the election for New York's other senate seat. From 1964 through 1968 this seat had been held by Robert F. Kennedy. After his assassination Governor Nelson Rockefeller appointed Congressman Charles Goodell, a relatively conservative Republican (at that time), to replace him. But then Goodell suddenly became an outspoken liberal, demanding an immediate American pullout from Vietnam.[48]

At this point, James Buckley decided to make a move. He was distressed at the path that Goodell had taken and that there was no one to carry the conservative banner in the race. But he did not want to run a symbolic, minor-party campaign again, as in 1968. He told close friends and associates that, although he was interested in running, he had one question: Did he have a chance of winning? William Rusher leapt into action. He had his friend F. Clifton White commission a quick poll, and Rusher himself sounded out the views of key newspaper editors and other opinion-makers around the state. The news was good. Buckley's poll numbers were respectable; he had fairly high name recognition among New Yorkers. Rusher meanwhile found that many influential media members were receptive to the idea of a Buckley candidacy, with the thought "that Jim should stress that his candidacy is a serious one, and that this is not in any sense a 'spoiler' race." Which it wasn't. Buckley then made his decision: he was in the race, and in it to win.[49]

It quickly became a significant campaign in the larger scheme of things. This was the first time since 1964 that any kind of serious candidate for national office had campaigned on a platform that was explicitly congruent with most of *National Review*'s positions. Thus the old questions surfaced again. Was *NR* conservatism part of the mainstream now? Or would such a conservative candidate still be seen as an extremist and go down to ignominious defeat? Frank Meyer had been a part of New York's Conservative Party since its founding; and his friendship with the Buckleys meant that he knew Jim Buckley quite well. He was yet another of those with whom Meyer would talk over the telephone, discussing the issues and dispensing advice to Buckley about his campaign. Meyer knew him well enough that, at the Conservative Party's seventh anniversary dinner in October 1969, he introduced Buckley and presented him with an award. And later, Buckley, in talking with a reporter, identified Meyer as an adviser on important issues.[50]

The imprint of Meyer and the rest of *National Review* could be found all over the Buckley campaign—unlike 1964, when Goldwater's staff had kept the magazine at a distance. It was *NR*'s publisher, Rusher, who did much to encourage Jim Buckley to run and who remained with the campaign as a close adviser. Many of the campaign's foot soldiers came from *NR*'s allies in Young Americans for Freedom, whose 1970 chairman, Randall Teague, upon hearing of Buckley's decision to run told him that "we are elated at your announcement for the U.S. Senate seat and, as always, we stand ready to serve." Campaign manager Arnold Steinberg sought, from all *NR* staff and personnel, ideas regarding policy issues, press relations, and ways to utilize *NR*'s research department. The campaign used the magazine's photocopying and research facilities so extensively that Rusher felt forced to bill it for their use. Jim Buckley later told reporters that his "brain trust" was the staff of *National Review*.[51]

The message expounded by the Buckley campaign reflected the position that Meyer and the rest of his colleagues at *NR* had been espousing for years. In the three-way race between Buckley, Goodell, and Democrat Richard Ottinger,

Buckley was the only conservative candidate and thus could appeal both to conservative Democrats and to what Nixon called the "silent majority" (and what Meyer referred to as the "producing majority"). A confidential staff memo early in the Buckley campaign opined that Buckley would be "the only candidate remotely representative" of this voting group. There was "a division between those who basically support and believe in this country and its institutions and those who are attacking or apologizing for them. In an essential sense, Buckley will be entering the campaign as the only pro-America candidate. . . . [Liberals] have staked their political lives on the support of the vociferous minority, leaving the silent majority to Buckley. Our task is to reap the harvest."[52]

But could he win? In the early summer things began to go Jim Buckley's way. Some conservative New York state Republican leaders began openly discussing the possibility of endorsing him instead of Goodell. In July, former Goldwater strategist F. Clifton White became Buckley's campaign manager. The New York State Uniformed Firefighter's Association shocked the political establishment by endorsing Buckley, and soon so did the Patrolmen's Benevolent Association. The *New York Times* anointed him as a "serious contender" in the race. In early September, a statewide poll found the Democrat Ottinger leading Buckley by only 4 percentage points. Goodell lagged far behind, with only 14 percent of the vote.[53]

Very important for Buckley's success—and thus important in keeping Meyer and other *NR* conservatives from too stridently criticizing the administration—was the quiet support he received from Nixon and the Republican Party. Senator John Tower, heavily involved in the national Republican campaign committee in 1970, wrote to William F. Buckley Jr. to tell him that while there wasn't anything official he could do for his brother, he would be glad to do anything "extra-official" for him. Buckley replied that "it does occur to me that what Jim needs most is money. Now that is relative; i.e., he needs, say, to spend fifty per cent of what Goodell spends; from which it follows . . . that the less money Goodell gets, the less Jim needs. Enough said?" In July, Rusher had a secret meeting with Patrick Buchanan, during which they thoroughly discussed the campaign and what strategies Buckley could employ. Nixon himself, during the 1970 campaign, seized on the radicalism of the Left and told chief of staff H. R. Haldeman that he "really wants to play the conservative trend and hang opponents as left-wing radical liberals."That fit in with what the Buckley campaign was trying to do quite nicely.[54]

This explains why Spiro Agnew was sent to New York to campaign that fall; and while he could not officially endorse Buckley (who was a member of the Conservative Party, while Goodell nominally remained a Republican), he fiercely denounced Goodell as a left-wing member of the anti-war movement who was out of step with his party, a member of "the radical–liberal clique." And on election night, Nixon telephoned William F. Buckley Jr. to say that "if a quiet Quaker prayer will help, you've got it. Tell Jim to go to the bar with the warm beer and relax a couple of hours after the polls close."[55]

Meanwhile, Frank Meyer had not written a single word about the Buckley campaign. He held an official position with the Conservative Party, and everyone knew that he was advising the campaign behind the scenes. Thus any column written by him on the subject would be seen not as an honest analysis of politics or principle, but rather as self-interested, partisan politicking. In any case, James Buckley pursued themes approved by Meyer in his speeches. Buckley supported the incursion into Cambodia, Nixon's Vietnamization policy, and a stronger national defense. He denounced the anti-war movement: "The primary responsibility for peace on our campuses rests with campus officials," he said. He condemned the tendency of "weak and indecisive officials to romanticize the radicals." He voiced his concern about drug abuse, crime in the streets, and the environment. And he urged mandatory prison sentences for anyone possessing a gun while committing a crime. He didn't need Meyer's help.[56]

And in the end, he won. It was close. Buckley emerged the victor with only 38 percent of the total vote. But it was a victory, and, as in 1964, many in the national news media were shocked and dismayed at conservatism's rise. On CBS-TV on election night, commentator Eric Sevareid remarked glumly on "how far we've drifted to the right." The *New York Times* wrote breathlessly that, with Buckley's victory, there now seemed no stopping "the ruthless night riders of the radical right," despite the stand made by Goodell, "a public official determined . . . to keep freedom from being assassinated." Buckley, the editorial went on, was a "symbol of all the primitive forces that would turn back the political clock, encourage repression and deepen the alienation now felt by the young and dispossessed." Buckley benefitted most, it concluded, from his "naked appeal to the spirit of right-wing reaction so shadowing the nation."[57]

But media hysteria mattered little to conservatives. Their man had won. As James Burnham wrote in *NR*'s lead editorial after the election, an editorial Meyer surely delighted in, Buckley's victory was "the most important thing" occurring on election day, and this had been shown especially by the "ferocity . . . of the campaign waged against him . . . by the combined assault force of the liberal media, local and national." Buckley's election, and the campaign that brought it about, Burnham continued, "did in truth bring into voice and action large sections of the American majority that has long been politically silent and passive. These are the citizens who, busy with the constructive work of the country, their homes and families, and the day-by-day round of civic and charitable duties, have kept largely aside while so much of the political structure of the nation slipped into the hands of ideologues. The nation's affairs having been brought under that guidance to a condition that dismayed these taken-for-granted citizens, they found a champion and a voice in Buckley."[58]

This sounded a great deal like what Meyer had been saying about the "producing majority." That was no accident. Conservatives had won an important victory. And Meyer had played an important, albeit behind-the-scenes, role.

THE TURMOIL OF the late 1960s sometimes brought personal pain. Meyer's relationship with his old friend and protégé Garry Wills was an excellent example. By 1970, the two men had drifted apart. They developed opposing views on almost all the major issues of the era. Wills was sympathetic to the civil rights and anti-war movements, while Meyer was highly critical of them. Wills criticized sharply the Nixon administration for being too conservative; Meyer argued that Nixon wasn't conservative enough.[59]

Finally, in 1970, Wills began writing his own syndicated newspaper column, in which he was highly critical of both mainstream conservatism and the Nixon administration. It caused a bit of a stir, since it was well known in opinion circles that he wrote for *National Review* and was reputed to be a Catholic conservative. This could no longer be ignored. Meyer decided to devote a column to it—a difficult column to write, Meyer admitted; Wills was a "former colleague" and "still a close personal friend." But in Wills's syndicated column, Meyer spotted many heresies. Wills expressed "scorn" for Nixon and "support for immediate unilateral withdrawal from Vietnam." He appeared to be "egging on the campus radicals."Wills's entire course was a "political apostasy."

Meyer tried to analyze why this had happened. First, he believed that Wills was "a sucker for the spirit and elan of revolutionary movements." Second, he failed to understand the continuing Soviet threat to American national security; hence his lack of support for the war in Vietnam. Third, Wills had lost his appreciation for capitalism and the free market and presently had nothing but contempt for Middle America and its values. "In rejecting it," Meyer concluded, "Garry Wills rejects what has made his country and his civilization great."[60]

A couple of months later, Meyer renewed the attack. By now Wills had come out with a new book, called *Nixon Agonistes,* a work that took a broad look at many of the major events of the late 1960s, along with Richard Nixon's role in them. Meyer was not impressed. He took the unusual step of reviewing the book himself and led off the book section with his analysis. He called the book "strange," arguing that it "portrays an America about which there is nothing good to be said." Wills was denigrating such important conservative values as self-reliance, individualism, and aspiration, Meyer claimed. "I have not been Mr. Nixon's warmest admirer," he went on, "but this book has raised him inestimably in my esteem. If he stands as symbol for the American tradition—and the insight of a hostile critic should be taken most seriously— then he is indeed a great blessing to the nation."[61]

And so Meyer was once again undertaking a familiar role—interpreting just what conservatism was, properly understood, and defining who truly deserved to be called a conservative. He no longer believed that Garry Wills could accurately be said to belong to the movement; Wills would have disagreed, but not other conservatives. William Rusher received a letter from Patrick Buchanan in which Buchanan commiserated with Rusher on the direction Wills had taken. Buchanan included a copy of a slashing, nasty column Wills had written on the role of Buchanan and others in the administration. "Thanks for offering to buy me a drink," Rusher replied;"after reading the kind of stuff Garry Wills has been writing lately, I could use one." Rusher went on,"I feel very badly indeed about the way Wills has turned out. . . . In any case, I hope it may console you to know that Frank Meyer, in his column . . . sorrowfully but firmly reads Garry out of the conservative movement altogether."[62]

Meyer and Wills never completely severed their ties—they had been friends for too long—but things were never the same. The 1960s had ruined another friendship.

The capstone for *National Review* during this late era—an event that summed up all *NR* had been saying about the changes America was undergoing, and which symbolized how far conservatives had come in receiving attention and respect—came late in 1970 on the occasion of *NR's* fifteenth anniversary celebration. Since this was not the tenth or twenty-fifth anniversary, it would not be heralded with great fanfare. But still, Buckley and the other senior editors planned to put out a special edition of the magazine, which Buckley wanted Burnham to edit, as well as a party.[63]

NR's fifteenth anniversary party, smallish, intimate, and fun, was held at Tavern on the Green in New York City. The theme for the *NR* special issue, after some fiddling, was refined to the question: "After liberalism, what?" Such a theme was in itself a measure of how far things had changed. *NR* conservatives now assumed that liberalism, their archenemy for so long, was dead, and that the only question was what would follow it. Moreover, instead of soliciting pieces for the magazine only from its usual stable of conservative writers, Burnham got a noted liberal academic, Charles Frankel, to submit a piece, as well as the radical, Marxist historian Eugene Genovese. Given all the changes of the late 1960s, conservatives seemed to have hit their stride, to have found some basic themes that resonated with a broad spectrum of the populace. As Buckley wrote in leading off *National Review's* special issue, it was the continuing challenge of the magazine "to argue the advantages to everyone of the rediscovery of America, the amiability of its people, the flexibility of its institutions, of the great latitude that is still left to the individual, the delight of spontaneity, and, above all, the need for superordinating the private vision over the public vision."[64]

Frank Meyer wrote one of the more impressive analyses of the entire special issue. Not surprisingly, given his political bent, his topic was the future of the Republican Party. Meyer agreed with the overall theme of the issue: liberalism, clearly, had lost its power in America. He spoke of the breakup of the old New Deal Democrat voting coalition, with union members and blue-collar workers moving to the Right, and blacks and intellectuals moving to the Left. Showing his familiarity with the political analysis of Kevin Phillips, Meyer argued that this could be a good thing for conservatives. A new social category had sprung up, a new voter, whose home was "Middle America," the "Sun Belt," "suburbia." On the other hand, it was also clear that with the growth of the radical intelligentsia and black nationalism, America was dangerously divided. The division was not, as many thought, along the lines of age (here Meyer gave a nod to social analyst Seymour Martin Lipset), but rather different social categories—worker vs. intellectual, suburbanite vs. rootless radical. And this could be dangerous. "If social order is not reasserted soon and the revolutionary threat from the Left repressed," Meyer wrote, "an anti-constitutional mood may arise on the Right out of outrage and despair." In other words, there was a real danger of dictatorship, of the destruction of democratic institutions. The U.S. could fall prey either to "revolutionaries on the Left," or in response to that threat, a "redressing emanation of total power." To prevent this, to find a solution to the present crisis, Americans needed to look to "a legitimate existing institution that can fill the intellectual role of articulation and symbolization" of the ideas and thoughts of Middle America.

This, then, was the role the Republican Party could fill, Meyer wrote. It could articulate the hopes and dreams of Middle Americans. Meyer continued to stress what other observers had been slow to grasp—that 1964 had been a crucial year. Although Barry Goldwater had been defeated, the leadership of the GOP had "shifted decisively from me-too liberals to essentially conservative hands." Richard Nixon's nomination in 1968 was due to conservative delegates and a conservative leadership. The question was: How well had Nixon done as a leader of Middle America? Meyer, articulating the mixed views of *National Review* conservatives, said that the answer was "ambiguous." The administration's rhetoric was fine, but the Nixon White House had not given conservatives enough *action*. Meyer approved of Agnew, and generally of the Supreme Court appointments Nixon had made, as also of Nixon's "holding firm against the radical defeatist campaign on the Vietnam war, however murky the actual conduct of that war." But Meyer opposed "the proposals for immensely extending the scope of welfare; the strange maneuverings on forced integration; the continuing decay of the American arms posture vis à vis the Soviet Union; the growing influence of liberal-oriented personnel in the White House staff." There seemed to be "some understanding in Nixon's mind of the hopes and fears of his broad American base." But words were not enough. The Republican Party must, Meyer concluded, "rid itself, in its pro-grammatic actions, of the remaining residues of liberalism that make its present course so uncertain . . . if the energies of Middle America are to be contained within the constitutional tradition."[65]

It was an interesting analysis, even though hindsight suggests Meyer was somewhat mistaken about the Silent Majority. For if they do not find leadership, we now know, they will not necessarily turn to authoritarianism but will instead become cynical and withdraw from politics altogether, as the declining voter participation of recent years suggests. In any case, Meyer had obviously read widely, had written well, and had set the stage for one of the more provocative pieces in the NR special issue—James Burnham's concluding essay. Burnham argued that America in 1970 was in serious trouble. It was faced with what he called a "sex/drug/pornography/incivility/self-indulgence subculture." Lib-eralism, which spawned it, badly demoralized, was basing its principles only on reason and permissiveness that, taken to an extreme, could lead to anarchy. And anarchy was exactly what was happening.

But then liberalism, said Burnham, had always to a great extent rejected authority; it had denied the authority of tradition, custom, standards. Now it faced a generation of extremist militants who took liberalism's message seriously. America today was threatened by "bombers, arsonists, wreckers, police-shoot-ers," who were really guerrillas, terrorists, and revolutionaries. The big question, Burnham believed, concerned how to restore authority. The American govern-ment no longer seemed capable of winning wars or of containing domestic violence. How can a government be authoritative but not authoritarian? Burnham suggested, provocatively, that we should examine right-wing authoritarian re-gimes around the world for clues. He contended that many of them displayed great "creativity," "creative flair," and "impressive endurance." Society must not be destroyed by the revolutionaries. Conservatives should prefer a Bismarck to a Robespierre.[66]

How could there be a major event at *National Review* without a debate? Frank Meyer, for one, had problems with some of what Burnham had said, and he aired them in short order. Meyer agreed with much in Burnham's column; he saw it as "a lengthy and impressive analysis of the contemporary decay of moral and social authority," and he agreed that the "authoritative" in society must be reestablished. Here Meyer drew on the teaching of philosopher Eric Voegelin to argue that, in the past, successful societies imposed "symbols of order" upon their people. Such needed to be done now. But he also criticized Burnham's apparent belief that the most important thing was "order," without thought as to whether that order was good or bad. In the Soviet Union, "order" existed; but it was not the order that existed in Britain or France, nor could it be justified. Beyond that, Meyer stressed that while America needed authoritativeness, it must not become authoritarian. Recent times had weakened the American constitutional order, but they had not destroyed it. Our constitutional republic contained all that was needed to hold society together; what was missing was the will to reaffirm what we had. "To lose patience with constitutional means," Meyer concluded, "to play with concepts of a sharp and simple authoritarian solution to our problems is to forget the first lesson of conservatism—that we must build on what we have inherited, on what, in the case of the American Constitution, is close to two centuries of achievement." Raw authoritarianism led only to "terror and agony." Meyer had seen communism close up; this little debate once again showed that he'd never forgotten it.[67]

Such differences aside—and maybe such differences were a strength; conservatives did not, in fact, march in lockstep—*National Review*'s fifteenth anniversary appeared to be a success. Richard Nixon had planned to make an appearance at the celebration, but he had to cancel at the last minute in order to attend a state funeral overseas. He did, however, send a telegram: "At a time when intelligent dialogue and responsible public information are more than ever the key to constructive action for the public good," his telegram read, "it is especially gratifying to applaud the fifteenth anniversary of the National Review." A few days later, James Burnham was invited to a White House state dinner. There, upon shaking the president's hand, Burnham discovered that Nixon had read his provocative concluding essay and agreed with it. The key, Nixon said to him in commending him on the article, was the attitude of a nation's "thought leaders"; should they become defeatist and demoralized, a society was in trouble. *National Review*'s words now really did reach the Oval Office.[68]

But as would soon become evident, *NR*'s honeymoon with Richard Nixon was over. Frank Meyer played a role in ending it.

Final Lessons

ONSERVATIVES' INITIAL EXCITEMENT upon the election of their ally Richard Nixon did not mean that conservatives had suddenly become united. Members of the American Right often sharply disagreed with each other in their responses to the many societal changes that occurred during the late 1960s. Furthermore, given the twists and turns of the Nixon administration, conservatives sometimes appeared rudderless, leaderless, unsure whether to support Nixon's pragmatism and—at times—abandonment of conservative principle in order to reach out to the center, or to oppose Nixon outright.

Thus, as he approached the end of his life, Frank Meyer had yet more opportunities to take part in the debates he loved, to engage in the fundamental discussions and analyses of principles and heresies that he thought essential to the development of American conservatism.

IN KEEPING WITH Meyer's emphasis on what many now called "fusionism," there was no single faction with whom he debated during this period. Instead, he seemed to take on everybody—when, that is, he believed they departed from a proper understanding of conservatism.

This frequently meant that Meyer again argued with "traditionalist" conservatives over their emphasis upon social "order," and of maintaining that order against revolutionary threat. On this question were focused many of the fiercest debates among *National Review* conservatives. An excellent example came early in 1969, when conservative sociologist Kenneth Melvin contributed a lengthy essay to *NR*. Titling his piece "Big Brother Is Dead, Too," Melvin, as did so many conservatives during these years, began with student radicalism on the campuses. Since student antics and their revolutionary philosophy threatened civilization itself, Melvin contended, society needed to reevaluate many of the themes of George Orwell, such as the fear of government as "Big Brother." Maybe such assumptions were incorrect. Instead, Melvin argued, government—most concretely, the welfare state—was inevitable and should be used to preserve the order that student revolutionaries were trying to destroy. Bureaucracy "grew because it was inescapable in the kind of society most men want—the provident kind, no less than the exploitative." Thus "social man must come to terms with social power and social efficiency—and pay due price in social conformity. . . . Whether one regards welfarism altruistically as social justice or cynically as insurance against revolution, it yields by far the better deal for all."[1]

If anything could raise Frank Meyer's ire, it was either the idea that a goal of society should be "conformity" or that the welfare state was "inevitable." Meyer's rejoinder came swiftly and was hard-hitting. Melvin's article, he grumbled, illustrated that "even in conservative circles old errors never die. . . . It would hardly seem necessary, after twenty years of intense discussion in the American conservative movement, to reiterate in these pages one of the central political axioms of that movement—that the modern state, in its massive growth, is the primary instrumentality of liberal utopianism and the greatest contemporary enemy of man's freedom and spiritual growth." Reflecting once again his deep reading in history and classic literature, Meyer agreed that, throughout history, many peoples hungered after security. But the "glory of the West" lay in the fact that "we have always raised the standard of the person against this age-old nostalgia of mass-men for slavish security. . . . It is clear, both from history and from theory: the greater the security, the closer to slavery; the firmer the self-reliance, the deeper the freedom; the deeper the freedom, the wider the human achievement." Meyer cited the frequent murmurings of the Israelites against Moses, despite the fact that he was leading them out of slavery.

But what especially bothered Meyer, as he admitted frankly in his column, was that Melvin presented his "statist prescription" cloaked as "an attack on ideology. No ideologist he, just pragmatic, down-to-earth, as offended as you or I by the posturings of revolutionary students." But in truth Melvin's argument was "economic and social determinism," a "helpless surrender to material conditions." Claiming that the welfare state was "inevitable," Meyer insisted, was quasi-Marxism, "a pattern for a society as spiritually arid as it is politically tyrannical."[2]

Melvin's article clearly diverged from *National Review*'s general position on the power of the federal government and the welfare state, and Buckley probably decided to publish it for just this reason. He knew it would stir a debate. And that it did. James Burnham soon weighed in in a special "open question" column. He had to admit, Burnham wrote, that Meyer's "excommunication" of Melvin was "stirringly pronounced." But it missed the point: "welfarism" was no longer the issue. Some "welfarist" responsibility had *always* been assumed, by all governments. True, in modern times, this responsibility had grown. But, Burnham contended, this was due to factors such as population growth, the decline of an agrarian society, and society's increasing reliance on technology. Welfarism *was* inevitable. "Or do we conclude, in the words of a World War I song, that they're all out of step but Frank?"

Burnham also jabbed at Meyer's "careless equating of Nazism, Communism, social democracy and the American system." Some political theorists argued in the past that socialism must lead to communism, but, Burnham said flatly, this was wrong; freedom could coexist with the welfare state, and the masses recognized the difference between communism and welfarism. "It in no way follows from what I have written that conservatives must simply resign themselves to any and every welfarist project and proposal," he added. "By undiscriminating resistance to *welfarism*, conservatives may have indirectly nurtured the welfare *state*.... [N]o serious politics in our time can be based on a simplistic anti-welfarist doctrine. Granted that axiom, there remains an enormous field of dispute and choice."[3]

Meyer chose not to reply. His mind was not changed; as he once wrote a friend, "I think that you cannot control Government if it gets too big and the thing to do is to keep it out of all affairs but defense, public order and justice. I have, I am afraid, no confidence in any body whatever with power, so I want to break power up into the smallest bits technologically possible."[4]

Later that same year *NR* again ran a piece from another traditionalist conservative, Canadian political scientist Donald Atwell Zoll. Zoll began his lengthy analysis from a familiar starting point: the relationship between liberalism and the extremism of the New Left. Zoll argued that liberalism was dying. It had misunderstood the New Left, failing to see its radical, revolutionary character. Liberalism demonstrated an "utter weariness with itself, [and has a] spiritual malaise that now affects its ability to move, to respond."

Little of this was objectionable to most *NR* conservatives. But Zoll went on to write that conservatives were now faced with a "terrible decision." After all, many on the Right shared "civilized values" with liberals, such as those "connected with libertarianism and legalism." Indeed, if given a choice, right-wingers "prefer the maintenance of the liberal hegemony to the . . . persecutions that a New Left revolutionary would be likely to induce." The problem, however, was that "a liberalism bent on self-immolation would sound the death-knell not only of itself, but of conservatism also." Would conservatives "elect to fight, uninhibited . . . by liberal proprieties as to method?"

This was yet another example of what the extremism and campus violence of these years had caused; it led a rather sober-sounding academic such as Zoll to believe that the government, indeed the entire civilization, was under revolutionary threat. The only question was how the coming war would be fought. Zoll conceded that he did not present conservatives with an easy choice. It might "imply common cause with the radical Right or even some variety of expediential fascism—hardly an appealing association." Ultimately, there were only two choices. One was that the coming end of liberalism could lead to the election of representatives of "moderate conservatism by voters reacting against the radicals, and against the liberals' helplessness against them." But if not, and the situation worsened, then, said Zoll, "the prize at stake is the conquest of the public authority and physical power of the state."

If this kind of brutal struggle broke out, then, Zoll held, conservatives should "acknowledge the primacy of social conservation." They must "reject both the death-wish of liberalism and its anti-authoritarian inhibitions" and "prepare to fight—whatever this may entail—against the tide of contemporary Jacobinism, candidly facing the necessity of employing techniques generally ignored or rejected by Western conservatives." These statements, he acknowledged, might "cause a certain amount of shock or dismay. But in the modern age there has been a skeleton in the conservative closet. Its name is *order*."[5]

Once again, Buckley probably published the article knowing the controversy it would arouse, and indeed hoping for it. Meyer did not disappoint. In *NR*'s very next issue he responded, with the title of his column indicating what he hoped to say: "What Kind of Order?" Again, Meyer the libertarian was speaking. He agreed readily that liberalism had lost the will to govern, and that this was proving disastrous. He even conceded that preserving order was perhaps "the outstanding political question of the day." But, on the whole, Meyer argued that Zoll's prescription seemed "to be unacceptable to the conservative spirit."

Why? For one thing, Zoll's conception of order was mistaken. "Order is not . . . the opposite of freedom and the pluralistic drives of hundreds of individuals toward meaning and value," he stressed. "It is the preservation of the condition of civility in which freedom and differing individual fulfillment becomes possible. . . . Professor Zoll is positing order for order's sake, for the physical survival of society without concern for the quality of that society." The choice Zoll presented "between revolutionary anarchy and some iron state is as false as the choice so widely promulgated in the Thirties between fascism and Communism." There was another alternative: "the vindication of the American tradition, the defense of an order based upon civility and freedom." America's existing constitutional tradition could yet save the day.[6]

A couple of months later Zoll counterattacked. He claimed that he did not want, had never wanted, repression. "The Toryism I endorse," he wrote, "is the ultimate vindication of order; as opposed to repression, the recognition of social order as resting upon an ontological and naturalistic mandate." In other words, Zoll contended that order for its own sake was society's most important value. He argued that the U.S. Constitution was flawed and not necessarily up to the challenge of contemporary radicalism. Meyerian analyses of freedom, he sniffed, should be left to "Locke, Madison, and Mill." If views like Meyer's carried the day, the most likely outcome of the current radicalism, Zoll stressed again, was the rise of a "primitive and irrational retaliation of the Right."[7]

Meyer in his response again agreed that order was important; but order for its own sake was not acceptable. Some kinds of order, some civilizations, were in fact better than others, with Western civilization leading the list. Meyer seldom spoke of religion, but here he stressed that the West, "inspired by the Incarnation," had developed "a complex symbology and rationale of the person as the ordering principle, the fount and the end of social being." And the Constitution expressed all this "in the highest political terms that human beings have yet found." Yes, it was flawed. But conservatives, Meyer emphasized, were attempting "to *restore* flawed institutions to their pristine virtue, rather than ideologically projecting an abstract concept of order based upon images of power." In sum, the challenge of "radical nihilism" was great. But Meyer stressed that "every necessary resource exists, given the will, for our constitutional republic to survive and maintain social order."[8]

Later, Meyer tried to be more specific. What exactly should be done about the radicals? In April 1970 he listed a number of steps he would take—steps which, rather shockingly, showed that his libertarianism only went so far, and that showed further how the rise of student radicalism had affected conservative thinking. Meyer proposed:

> prosecution of all organizations (and their members) that stand for revolutionary attacks upon our Constitutional institutions. Quick and decisive police action against all demonstrative assemblages attempting extra-legally to overawe political or private institutions, and the prosecution of participants under the relevant statutes for preservation of civil peace. (Our present state of civil peril may well make it necessary to ban all outdoor assemblages of a demonstrative nature, since they are avowedly directed toward overawing representative politics and thereby do not fall within the Constitutional right "peaceably to assemble and to petition the government for a redress of grievances.")[9]

It would not be long, however, before Meyer found himself arguing with his libertarian friends just as vigorously as he debated Burkean defenders of order. And in some ways, the stakes were higher.

LIBERTARIANS CONSTITUTED an increasingly vocal and sizable portion of the American conservative movement by the late 1960s. They became much more visible in organizations such as Young Americans for Freedom and the Young Republicans, and in publications such as *National Review* and the *New Guard*. Libertarians' main thrust was to maximize individual freedom and sharply curtail the power of the state. As a result, many had been uncomfortable with the military draft and America's involvement in Vietnam. And they found themselves attracted by New Left denunciations of the Vietnam War and of a stifling bureaucratic "Establishment." Was it possible for those on the Right to ally, in a principled way, with elements of the New Left?

Signs of discontent among younger, libertarian-minded members of the conservative movement had been evident for some time. In the pages of the YAF journal *New Guard,* for example, David Friedman, a graduate student at the University of Chicago and the son of conservative economist Milton Friedman, frequently criticized America's role in Vietnam in a regular column. "America has totally abandoned the non-interventionist policy recommended by George Washington, " he wrote. "The government that conducts our foreign policy is the same government that conducts our domestic policy. It is the same government that helps the poor by using urban renewal to tear down their homes and minimum wage laws to destroy their jobs. It is the same government that fights illegitimacy by bribing fathers to desert their families, and fights riots by rewarding rioters with OEO [Office of Economic Opportunity] money. Why should we expect it to fight communism any more intelligently?" After World War II, Friedman argued, it was indeed necessary for the U.S. to defend western Europe. But now America's allies could stand on their own.[10]

Meanwhile, by 1969, Karl Hess, a former Goldwater speechwriter, had become an extreme libertarian with strong ties to the New Left. Hess even went so far as to argue that anarchy equaled "opposition to the state and not advocacy of chaos. Opposition to anarchy equals support of the state."[11]

Many libertarians had always had their doubts about William F. Buckley Jr., *National Review,* and *NR's* style of conservatism. Jerome Tuccille, a libertarian political activist during this period, wrote later that Buckley "had never really turned us on that much." Tuccille thought that Buckley had attracted many individualists in the 1950s and early 1960s, when he leavened his views with a healthy dollop of "anarchistic individualism," but Tuccille believed that Buckley's anticommunism contradicted his libertarianism and allowed him to justify support for the draft, confiscatory taxation, and the curtailing of civil liberties. Many nevertheless continued to follow Buckley and to read *NR* because "there was simply no one else to turn to." Libertarians held similar beliefs about Frank Meyer and his "fusionism." For a time, many libertarians eagerly embraced Meyer's

ideas, seeing in fusion, in Tuccille's words, a "philosophical life-preserver."
Perhaps one *could* be both a libertarian and a conservative. But by the late
1960s, many became disenchanted. Tuccille saw "the inconsistency of a small
decentralized government that would be large enough to have nuclear-pow-
ered policemen in every potential hot spot in the world. The schizophrenia
inherent in the very concept of 'libertarian conservatism' was bound to erupt
in a major conflict sooner or later."[12]

Now, with the New Left's numerous shadings of anti-state and anti-
authoritarian positions, there were other places to turn. And some libertarian
conservatives began to do so, thereby sowing real dissension within the conservative movement. By the end of 1969, many libertarian factions had seceded from the national Young Americans for Freedom organization. One of
their spokesmen claimed that YAF was now dominated by "reactionaries and
bigots," and that the organization (still led by a faction friendly to *NR*) supported "statist and socialist controls over the individual's life." At the 1969
YAF convention, held in St. Louis, a libertarian delegate burned his draft card
openly on the floor of the convention hall, which led to a physical confrontation and a walkout by some three hundred libertarian YAF members. A month
later, radical libertarians held their own convention in New York City, attended by over four hundred people. Karl Hess, who by now had become so
radicalized that he completely identified with the New Left, appeared wearing a kind of khaki camouflage guerrilla army uniform, complete with combat boots. Hess called for the revolutionaries in the audience to act on their
beliefs by taking on the military-industrial complex directly by marching on
Fort Dix. Hess had written months earlier to Buckley: "you would not like
me at all, not a patriot, not a believer, no longer even deeply concerned about
the difference between *their* imperialism and ours."[13]

Frank Meyer soon became convinced that these radical libertarians were
following a disastrous path and, wearily, resolved to do something about it. Thus
in the summer of 1969 he took part in a special debate in New York City before
a YAF audience. He participated on a panel with "libertarian nationalist" Henry
Paolucci, Jerome Tuccille, and Karl Hess (who arrived sporting beads around his
neck, patched blue jeans, and a long Ulysses Grant-style beard). Meyer was the
first to speak. He sought to be gentle, but he was determined to make his point.
"He gave a fifteen minute presentation, criticizing Hess indirectly by condemn-

ing 'unprincipled alliances' with the Left," Tuccille wrote later.

> It was his position that conservatives could never join forces with the New
> Left—even on such issues as the military draft which he, too, opposed on
> principle—because the motivation of the radical Left was actually to weaken
> the U.S. military presence in Vietnam. Meyer would have preferred to see the
> Communists wiped out by a "voluntary" and "professional" strike force, but
> since it was mandatory that we win in Vietnam, conservatives must take care
> to separate their anti-draft sentiments from their position on the war. In
> other words, the draft should be repealed eventually, but not until the war
> was won.[14]

Significantly, most in the crowd appeared to support Meyer.[15]

Meyer also took aim at extreme libertarians in his column in *National Review*, trying not to be too harsh (after all, by temperament and by inclination, libertarians were his soulmates), but making firm criticisms. He frequently condemned traditionalists for leaning too much towards "authoritarianism," but now he spied the danger of a new imbalance, the tendency of "untrammeled libertarianism" toward "anarchy" and "nihilism." Anarchists and nihilists were not libertarians, nor were they conservatives; from here on Meyer would call them "libertines."

What was wrong with "libertinism"? Meyer explained that it disregards "all moral responsibility, ranges itself against the minimum needs of social order, and raises the freedom of the individual (regarded as the unbridled expression of every desire, intellectual or emotional), to the status of an absolute end." Libertines reminded Meyer of socialists or communists, for they too were "ideologues" who rejected reality. Returning to the theme of his 1962 book *In Defense of Freedom*, Meyer held that while freedom must be the highest goal of a political order, once attained the question must be: "[H]ow are men to use their freedom? The libertine answers that they should do what they want." But only in "civilizations" have men risen above savagery. Libertinism, "in its opposition to the maintenance of defenses against Communism, its puerile sympathy with the rampaging mobs of campus and ghetto . . . , is directed towards the destruction of the civilizational order which is the only real foundation in a real world for the freedom it espouses. The first victim of the mobs let loose by the weakening of civilizational restraint will be, as it has always been, freedom—for anyone, anywhere."[16]

Many libertarians were unimpressed with Meyer's analysis. Ralph Raico, a professor of history at SUNY Buffalo, wrote to *NR* in vigorous disagreement. Meyer, he wrote, was "missing the point when he rails at libertarians who see a good deal of sense in some of the attitudes and even some of the actions of the New Left." Raico went on to point to the millions of men drafted into the military and to what he saw as the injustices America was perpetrating in Vietnam. Many conservatives, he claimed, "blank out these facts by directing their attention to the Maoism of the SDS, the nihilism of the hippies, the less-than-simon-pure motivation of many of the intellectuals who support them, etc. But to the libertarian, this is beside the point."[17]

But Meyer did not back down. He suggested that those of the ideological stripe of Hess and another radical libertarian, Murray Rothbard, did not belong on *NR*'s masthead. Meyer's influence could also be seen in Buckley's writings on libertarianism. In 1971, Buckley, reacting to a spate of publicity received by Hess and Rothbard, tepidly applauded their belief that "the job of the state is, most of the time, to be seen but not heard. So what else is new?" But their "absolutization" of freedom was an old, tempting "heresy" (it is significant that Buckley used that word). "It is one thing to demonstrate that a federal program is hurting the poor people it aims to help . . . ," Buckley wrote. "It is another to shout blindly against necessary institutions, and to worship unthinkingly at the altar of Ayn Rand."[18]

The influence of Meyer's writings over the years and the libertarians' own extremism helped keep this problem small. Radical libertarianism remained a fringe movement. But it showed once again the problems that societal change caused for conservatism, and it gave Meyer an opportunity to do more teaching, to impart yet one more lesson to the Right. He was soon grappling with an even bigger problem, one that would receive national attention: the problem of Richard Nixon.

IN MANY WAYS, Richard Nixon heartily disliked domestic policy. He felt more confident dealing in foreign affairs. But Nixon did what he did always with an eye to his reelection in 1972. To that end, Nixon had several new domestic proposals in hand as 1971 dawned. Together with startling new developments in foreign policy, these initiatives would begin to turn many *National Review* conservatives decisively against Nixon.[19]

In a series of interviews and speeches given in early 1971, Nixon laid out six major proposals: strengthening environmental regulations; increasing the government's role in health insurance; a welfare reform package; a proposal on "revenue sharing"; administrative reorganization; and a so-called "expansionary budget" designed to stimulate the economy. Revenue sharing was one of the more interesting parts of Nixon's proposals. It meant sending some $5 billion back to the states as a sort of rebate, to be spent as they wished.[20]

NR conservatives struggled in responding to Nixon's proposals. Shortly after Nixon's state of the union address, the magazine's lead editorial, almost surely written by James Burnham, was remarkably cautious. It noted that "important segments of conservative opinion" had "perceptibly cooled" toward the Nixon administration in response to its more liberal domestic initiatives, and that they had been awaiting Nixon's speech with "gradually rising anger." But Burnham concluded that "careful analysis" of the address "neither confirms nor dissipates their most serious misgivings, for the political meaning of the various Nixon proposals will not be clear until certain key questions are answered." Many more details were needed. Nixon's address was "the beginning of a national conversation about long-range directions," Burnham summarized. "It can be read as anticipating the platform on which Nixon will run in 1972."[21]

Others connected to *National Review* were not as cautious. William F. Buckley Jr., who had been a staunch defender of the president, began to step up his criticisms. "Mr. Nixon has not sufficiently indulged the presumptions in favor of individual liberty," he wrote in his column in late January 1971. "When will we begin the great disestablishment of those useless agencies that clutter Washington D.C. and feed on social energy?"[22]

But not all conservatives in *NR* agreed. A measure of the confusion within the magazine became apparent when, not long after Buckley's sharp criticisms, another *NR* editorial appeared that took a far more optimistic view of Nixon. It pointed out that the president had conservative economists advising him, such as George Schultz; that the administration was reducing government regulations of natural gas prices; and that it proposed the elimination of the food stamp program. In short, the editorial argued, the Nixon administration still possessed "a strong presumption in favor of the marketplace ... [and] only angels and absolute dictators can afford not to compromise in practice."[23]

National Review would not develop a consistent position on Nixon's new initiatives until issues of defense and foreign policy came to the fore. Nothing was more important to *NR* conservatives than the maintenance of a strong U.S. national defense against the communist threat. They assumed that with Nixon the long time anticommunist in charge they had nothing to fear. But by the spring of 1971 conservatives were no longer so sure. A sensational article in *National Review* by defense analyst Charles Benson contended that the Soviet Union was quickly surpassing the United States in nuclear weapons capability. The Soviets had in recent years tripled their number of intercontinental ballistic missiles and were rapidly developing a first-strike capability—and Benson implied that the Nixon administration bore the blame for America falling behind. *NR* accompanied the article with an editorial pleading with Nixon to take such warnings seriously. "We feel that the assertion of an approaching crisis in defense strategy is supported by a sufficient body of serious, informed and responsible opinion to require an equally serious response from the relevant officials in the government: that is, the President himself," the magazine editorialized.[24]

This appeal was met with silence from the administration. Instead, evidence abounded that Nixon and his national security adviser, Henry Kissinger, were intensifying their efforts to secure some kind of arms-control treaty with the Soviet Union. And the bad news for conservatives kept on coming. Soon the news surfaced that an American table-tennis team would be allowed to visit communist China, an event which Nixon, who had long condemned any and all proposals to recognize the legitimacy of Mao Tse-tung, welcomed and followed up with an announcement that travel and trade restrictions between America and China would be eased. There were even rumors that official recognition of China would soon follow. "Do we now forget about Chinese nuclear developments?" demanded Burnham in his column. "Will the doves now point to administration policy as proving we have no need for an ABM system? . . . What will it profit us to have model relations with the Peking government if meanwhile the Peking supported revolutionary movement cuts the ground from under us?" Buckley was distressed at the country's general mood upon hearing the news. "It is quite remarkable, the general elation," he mused. "It is as though Golda Meir had suddenly eloped with Arafat, and a new state of Israbia had been promulgated." He worried about what it would all mean in the end: "The victory over the American team at ping-pong is no doubt a precursor to more important victories." A core assumption of conservatives had always been that during a Nixon presidency American national security would be safe, that the president, Buckley wrote later, "simply will not let us down. Why? Because Mr. Nixon, whatever you say about him as a practical politician, is undeniably a patriot." But "the facts of life are that Mr. Nixon is sitting in the White House while the Soviet Union is accumulating a first-strike capability."[25]

It was clear that *NR* was beginning to move toward opposition to the Nixon administration. As 1971 progressed, the magazine's quarterly editorial Agonies found the editors increasingly focusing on their position toward Nixon. In late summer 1971 the participants had a "long conversation" concerning Nixon, read the minutes of a typical Agony. "We are prepared to go in any direction." Later in the year, "the whole balance of the time" of another quarterly meeting, Buckley recorded, "was spent on various aspects of the Nixon problem."[26]

As 1971 closed, *NR* finally took a stand on Nixon, a stand quite different from the one the magazine envisioned when Nixon took office, and a stand that many around the country found surprising, given the president's conservative credentials and *NR*'s past support of him. But by then, Nixon's actions forced some on the Right, led by *National Review*, to reevaluate their position. That reevaluation came at least in part because of Frank Meyer, and it was embodied in one of the last great "principles" for which he would fight.

AT THE BEGINNING of the Nixon administration, Meyer gave Nixon every opportunity to prove himself. During Nixon's first two years in the White House, Meyer's criticisms were few, and they came in measured, gentle tones. When Nixon announced his major domestic policy proposal of 1969, the Family Assistance Plan, Meyer in his *NR* column opposed it in calm, moderate words. Meyer argued that, on the whole, FAP departed too far from conservative principle. It would be too costly, and it would not do away with bureaucrats—on the contrary, government would now be deciding what income level was desirable for families. (Meyer the ex-communist never forgot his hatred of any kind of "regimentation.") It would make welfare, and welfare dependency, much more respectable by doubling the numbers of people receiving it, thus leading to the "pauperization" of a large sector of the American public. Meyer, still immersed in his readings of ancient history, recalled that such dependency and

helplessness were among the first signs of the decline of the Roman Empire.[27]

By early 1971 Meyer had grown increasingly troubled by Nixon's course.
In January Meyer reported in his column that he had been speaking with
many "responsible conservatives around the country" concerning Nixon policies. Their mounting concern centered around two major issues. The first
was "the deteriorating strength of our military power relative to the USSR."
Nixon had made no "authoritative rebuttal" to this concern, and soon the
Soviet Union would pass the United States in nuclear research and development and might even achieve first strike missile capability.

The Right's second major difference with Nixon involved his domestic
policies, specifically his 1971 budget message. The Nixon White House, Meyer
went on, had clearly decided to "present a budget in deficit" by pushing the
"welfarist" Family Assistance Plan and national health insurance legislation, possibly costing $30 billion per year. Such plans would promote dependency by
keeping too many individuals on the dole, thus turning them into "drones" who
lived off the toil of others. National defense, of course, must be the top priority.
If it took a budget deficit to guarantee the nation's safety, then so be it. Where
Meyer differed with Nixon was that the president did not present this as the best
of flawed alternatives, but rather as a good in itself. Such issues were "disturbing"
to many "responsible people" around the country (Meyer used the word "responsible" twice, obviously to show that these were not the fears of a tiny band
of extremists, but of the conservative mainstream—Nixon's base). "It is to be
hoped," he concluded, "that cooler and more conservative counsel will prevail
before the emergence of a settled policy."[28]

But the weeks went by with no change. So Meyer remained on the attack,
trying to put pressure on Nixon from the Right. In March 1971, Meyer wrote
again on Nixon, focusing exclusively on domestic policy and basing his column
on a careful study of Nixon's state of the union message and his budget and
economic reports. Meyer's alarm was evident. Nixon, he emphasized, was placing before the nation "a program to double the welfare rolls, open the door to
socialized medicine, and finance these welfarist measures by inflationary methods."

Meyer made several points. First, he wanted to allay the fears of his many
conservative friends who worried about his "break with Nixon," as they put it.
Meyer assured them that he did not mean to "break" with the president, "nor to

minimize his firm stand in Indochina and his fine start toward improving the composition of the Supreme Court," but "to insist that conservatives, if they are to be loyal to their principles, must oppose Nixon where he is wrong." Other conservatives faulted Meyer for opposing Nixon's initiatives without putting forward proposals of his own. But, he responded, some problems, such as poverty, were simply part of the human condition and could not be "solved." Had we not spent billions in taxation and bureaucracy in the last decade on poverty? Yet little had changed.

Meyer conceded that there were things government *should* do. "Pollution is reaching heights that only government . . . can deal with," he acknowledged. But even here, Meyer preferred to see the government use tax incentives to encourage business to cut back on polluting, rather than to engage in direct government spending to combat the problem. As for the rest of Nixon's proposals, there was "little to be said." The Family Assistance Plan would add ten million persons to the welfare rolls and lead to vastly increased spending. "The real problem of welfare is to reduce it," Meyer affirmed, "and the only way to reduce it is to end once and for all the idea that welfare is a right." Revenue sharing at first seemed "deliciously attractive." But some of the money coming from it might not be spent on current federal programs but added to the existing federal budget. Instead of the federal government collecting taxes, and only then turning the money over to the states, Meyer wondered, why shouldn't that government simply relinquish some of its taxing power? "All in all," Meyer ended his column sadly, "with the President's program, we would move farther into welfarism, not away from it."[29]

More discussion among conservatives about revenue sharing followed. In February 1971, Meyer proposed to the executive board of the American Conservative Union that the ACU favor "the relinquishing to the states taxation power over such tax sources as gifts, excise, gasoline, estate, and cigarettes." He also got the board to adopt a motion that stated that "the ACU is opposed to revenue sharing in principle." And finally he urged the ACU to prepare a report "critical of the general collectivist impact of the President's annual State of the Union message taken as a whole." This motion faced some opposition, but was eventually adopted by a 6-to-3 vote.[30]

Meanwhile, within *National Review* both Meyer and William Rusher worked to educate their fellow editors about revenue sharing. Rusher in a memo urged that conservatives act on the issue "with caution." On the one hand, he continued, the Right "ought to approve of anything that turns control (and the expenditure of money certainly equals control) back to the states and localities." But much like Meyer, Rusher had major philosophical, theoretical, and practical objections to the idea. As Rusher commented to Buckley privately, "the ideological pros and cons have not been sorted out as yet. I think that conservatives (not to mention liberals) are likely to fall into a serious error if we are not careful."[31]

This was just the kind of philosophical discussion both Meyer and Rusher loved, and while both men were active in the ongoing debate within *NR*, Meyer especially got busy within the ACU on the "Nixon problem" (as Buckley called it). Later in 1971 Meyer, at an ACU board meeting, moved that the organization, in accord with other conservative groups, take "a most strong position against the proposed US-USSR SALT-ABM accord along the lines publicly proposed by the President." This was agreed to, with only one dissenting vote. He also moved that the organization immediately endorse Vice President Agnew, the one shining light for conservatives within the administration, for re-nomination by the Republican Party in 1972. This was unanimously approved.[32]

Meyer was determined to keep the pressure on Nixon, especially in his "Principles and Heresies" column. As time went on, his voice became more and more insistent. In April 1971, Meyer once again addressed the weakening U.S. defense posture vis à vis the Soviet Union. He pointed especially to the Soviet buildup of SS-9 missiles, which could move the USSR toward a first-strike capability, and to the fact that the Soviets outspent the United States on defense by some $3 billion per year. This was "scandalous," Meyer thundered, and so far the administration's response was too little, too late. Even worse, it was leading many in influential circles of opinion to "minimize" the danger. Too many placed all their hope on the upcoming SALT talks. "In this hope," Meyer wrote sadly, again drawing on his long experience with communism, "anyone with a knowledge of Soviet diplomatic activity over fifty years can give a categorical answer: the Soviets will sign no treaty of armament limitation that does not strengthen them and weaken us."

So why was Richard Nixon acting this way? This question vexed many conservatives, and Meyer took a stab at answering it. He tried to be gentle, to refrain from burning any bridges. Meyer assumed "that President Nixon, while aware of the great growth in Soviet military potential, does not seriously believe in the intention of the enemy to use his potential" against America. He noted that Nixon, in a recent interview with C.L. Sulzberger of the *New York Times,* was quoted as saying that "this war [the Vietnam War] is ending. In fact I seriously doubt we will ever have another war." Meyer believed the president was profoundly mistaken, engaging in "pious wishful thinking." History and Soviet ideology showed that the communists would indeed be willing to use their arsenal and to engage in war. Perhaps, Meyer offered, Nixon thought he could not get more money for defense from the current Congress. Nixon, however, did have alternatives: "Let him go before the people," he urged, "making dramatically clear the urgency of our needs, pulling no punches either as to the gravity of the crisis or the expenditures necessary to meet it. To do less is to yield leadership to those in the media and in the Congress who are taking us down the perilous path toward defeat."[33]

But no such address ever came. Instead, in April 1971 conservatives received another shock: American policy toward communist China was changing. How, Meyer wondered, had all this come about? The whole scenario, he wrote, struck him as having a "rich element of Gilbert and Sullivan farce" in it. First, an American table-tennis team was suddenly invited to China. It was "decorously" defeated by a Chinese team and received an audience with Zhou Enlai. In response, Nixon reduced a twenty-year-old trade embargo against China, and the press was suddenly rife with rumors of impending U.S. diplomatic recognition. "If they'd invited the Mets or the Knicks," Meyer was told by a friend, "Heaven knows what concessions would have been made."

This was a very serious issue. Nixon's turn toward China must lead, Meyer held, to the "strengthening of the economy of a sworn enemy of the United States." He understood the arguments in favor of what Nixon was doing—the balance of power, the idea that the U.S. must take advantage of the Sino-Soviet split. But to Meyer it was far more worrisome that this would add to "the euphoria in the public mood" concerning Soviet and communist Chinese "mellowing." In a recent poll, he noted that 50 percent of Americans wanted cutbacks in the U.S. defense budget.

Here Meyer returned to a theme that he'd been sounding for years: first John F. Kennedy, then Lyndon Johnson, and now Nixon had not given a "coher-

ent explanation" to the American people of how the world was still threatened "by the drive of the Soviet Union toward world domination." The United
States was fighting a war in Vietnam against the communists, yet at the same
time it sought to build bridges with communism in the Soviet Union and
China—with table tennis serving as its symbol, no less! It didn't make sense.
"The classical world knew the decisive political importance of political rhetoric," Meyer wrote, betraying both his recent historical reading and his familiarity with Richard Weaver's *Ethics of Rhetoric*. "It is the means by which the
citizens are persuaded for good or evil." The U.S. was now a victim, not of evil
rhetoric, but of something worse—the "television gimmick," or, in other words,
of nonevents, "photo ops." Events were not reality, but manufactured make-
believe. "The pollution of our political discourse," Meyer declared, "is a danger far greater than the pollution of our air and water."[34]

Meyer and *NR* were hardly extreme in their views on Richard Nixon.
Some believed that Meyer did not go nearly far enough. When he refused in his
column to formally break with Nixon, for example, one irate subscriber wrote
in to claim that this marked "the collapse of the last vestige of anti-Nixon sentiment to be found in the pages of *NR*." Another reader, writing directly to Buckley,
expressed the same view: "There are a helluva lot more of us High School Drop-
Out conservatives than of you intellectuals, Mr. Buckley, and we ain't none of us
gonna vote for Mr. Nixon no more." A number of other letters boiled down, in
the words of a harried *NR* staffer, to requests "that we openly break with Nixon
to convince him of the errors of his ways."[35]

THE BREAK FINALLY CAME at the end of July 1971. Opposition to Nixon had
continued to build throughout the conservative movement, and at the beginning of June the American Conservative Union, although it came out aggressively for the re-nomination in 1972 of Vice President Agnew, announced that
it would not endorse Nixon's reelection, at least at the moment, because
conservatives had been "bitterly disappointed" in many of his policies. Young
Americans for Freedom, meanwhile, announced that it was supporting Ronald
Reagan for president in 1972.[36]

But bad news for conservatives continued to come from the Nixon administration. First, in mid-June came Nixon's admission, in discussing the bloated
budgets submitted by his administration, that he in truth was a liberal Keynesian—

"we are all Keynesians now," were Nixon's words. Frank Meyer, in his next column, put it flatly—the Nixon White House had accepted "the liberal policy of spending and borrowing as the core of his economic program." Meyer's "uneasy doubts" concerning the administration were not his alone, he told his readers; they were the sum of what many in the "responsible conservative community" felt. But what could they do? Many of Meyer's correspondents feared that a lack of support for Nixon could elect a Democrat in 1972, and that things would consequently only get worse. They also fretted that the only alternative to Nixon was George Wallace—in other words, there was no alternative, there was no "sober political possibility" of challenging Nixon from the right.

Thus Meyer reaffirmed that conservatives should support Nixon in 1972. But there was a huge difference between pro forma backing and "enthusiastic" support, and that could spell the difference between victory and defeat in a close race. Perhaps this pressure from conservatives would make Nixon "change course." "This," Meyer concluded, "unlike some conservative dreams, is a realistic course and one with a chance for success."[37]

But at the end of July came the announcement that early in 1972 President Nixon would be traveling to Peking on a formal state visit and have an official audience with Mao Tse-tung himself. *NR* conservatives were stunned. *National Review* contended that Nixon's trip would lead inevitably to U.S. concessions to the Chinese, in order to secure some kind of agreement. They compared it to Neville Chamberlain's negotiations with Adolf Hitler in Munich in 1938. "So it is to be Peace in Our Time," wrote the editors. "We will continue to believe, Mr. President, that you are not deluding yourself. Do not seek to delude the rest of us." Meyer took exactly the same position in his column. Nixon's coming visit to China represented "a symbol of the liquidation of the anti-communist stance of the American government," he proclaimed. It signaled a U.S. retreat from Asia, leaving it primarily a Chinese area of influence. Meyer compared Nixon's trip to the 1959 visit to the U.S. of another communist dictator, Nikita Khrushchev. But at least Khrushchev had attacked Stalin in public. Mao, Meyer complained, "sits unrepentant atop the corpses of millions upon millions of his victims." This was a "tragedy." Communism had not changed. Meyer recited the familiar litany of recent communist atrocities: the Chinese Cultural Revolution, the Soviet persecution of

Jews, the support of both China and the Soviet Union for North Vietnam, the
"rape" of Czechoslovakia, the Soviet arms buildup. And, in an obvious reference to Buckley's friend Henry Kissinger, Meyer stressed that this was no
time for "Metternichean games" of playing off China against the USSR amidst
balance-of-power maneuverings. This was not the nineteenth century and
Napoleon had not been defeated. Meyer too remembered Neville
Chamberlain's 1938 visit to Hitler. Shortly thereafter came World War II. "What
will Nixon bring back," Meyer wondered, "from Beijing?"[38]

The Right was deeply shaken by Nixon's moves. An anticommunist foreign policy was one of the most important reasons for conservatives' support of
Nixon in 1968. They thought it was something on which they could always
count. Apparently, they had been mistaken. It was time to act.

And so the leadership of the movement met in late July in New York City
to decide what to do. They all came—the leaders of the American Conservative
Union, the Southern States Industrial Council, the New York State Conserva-
tive Party, the Conservative Book Club, *Human Events,* Young Americans for
Freedom, and no fewer than three representatives of *National Review*: Burnham,
Buckley, and Frank Meyer. It was a lengthy meeting, and the usual arguments
surfaced. If the group completely broke with Nixon, what next? There was no
Democrat they could support, and George Wallace was not a viable alternative.
On the other hand, if they did nothing, President Nixon would continue to take
them for granted. Unsurprisingly, given that Meyer was present, one participant
remembered that there "was much basic philosophical root-seeking conversation" and that many saw themselves engaged in a "revolutionary" act. Finally,
James Burnham came up with a compromise acceptable to all. The group would
not irrevocably break with the administration but would instead announce a
"suspension of support" for Richard Nixon. The group then drew up a formal
statement.[39]

Titled simply "A Declaration," the document appeared in most conservative journals around the country. When Richard Nixon was elected in 1968, it
read, conservatives hoped that "substantial headway" would be made to "reorient" the nation's policies in a conservative direction. That was not happening, as
witness "excessive taxation and inordinate welfarism." But the document's main
focus was on foreign policy. It applauded Nixon for resisting the pressure to
"desert" Southeast Asia, but he had lacked firmness in opposing Soviet moves in

the Middle East and West German Chancellor Willy Brandt's "Ostpolitik."
The conservative leaders charged Nixon with making overtures to China but
failing to wrest any concessions in return. And Nixon had made no effort to
call attention to the "deteriorated American military position," both conven-
tional and nuclear, which "could lead to the loss of our deterrent capability,
the satellization of friendly governments near and far." In great part, then, the
document echoed what Burnham and Meyer had been writing in *NR*. For
the single most important factor both motivating and holding together the
conservative movement was anticommunism.

The signers of the declaration stated explicitly that, at the moment, they
did not plan to seek an opponent to run against the president. However, "we
propose to keep all options open in the light of political developments in the
next months." On the other hand, they were careful to include a paragraph in
which they reaffirmed their "personal admiration" and "affection" for Richard
Nixon. "We consider," the declaration concluded, "that our defection is an act of
loyalty to the Nixon we supported in 1968."[40]

The document's emphasis on Nixon's departure from conservative principle, its focus on foreign policy, its declaration that Nixon was not firm enough
in meeting the Soviet threat—all bore Meyer's imprint. But would this statement do any good? Would it have any effect upon the Nixon administration?

The members of the "Manhattan Twelve," as the signers of the declaration
began to call themselves, grappled with these questions long and hard. Jeffrey
Bell of the ACU worried that they had been too vague, that conservatives needed
to come up with a "shopping list"—specific policies and actions that they wanted
from the administration. Most members quickly agreed, and they accordingly
began to submit proposals. Neil McCaffrey of the Conservative Book Club
urged that conservative leaders demand that the defense budget be increased by
$20 billion; that a constitutional amendment to outlaw involuntary school bus-
ing be proposed; that the FBI and federal prison budget be doubled; that the
federal budget be balanced; and that there be a mandatory death penalty for
anyone convicted of murdering any law enforcement officer.[41]

Meyer weighed in on this subject as well, and, as was now typical, he
combined his commitment to political principle with a solid dash of realism.
Meyer asserted that although some rumblings were being heard, he did not
believe that at present they had the money, or the candidate, to make a primary

threat to Nixon realistic. Conservatives could, though, make additional demands, perhaps influencing the overall debate. Meyer thus urged that their "shopping list" contain "comparatively few points. If we submit a long list, it is possible that concessions might be made on minor and inessential ones, leaving the important points unanswered." First must come a demand to strengthen the defense budget. "The fact of the matter is," Meyer emphasized, "that increases in defense appropriations of the kind that would have been satisfactory two or three years ago would be much too little today." America's military readiness had reached crisis proportions, mainly because "of the massive Soviet buildup presently going on." On defense matters, the Manhattan Twelve must "detail" their proposals: they must seek a crash program for building Minuteman and Poseidon submarines; a doubling of research and development expenditures; an increase in the production of the B-1 bomber; an expansion of the ABM program. "Such a program would undoubtedly mean a massive increase in expenditure," Meyer admitted, "but it is the only prudent course." Domestically, Meyer was less specific, but he did call for the Nixon administration to stand against "forced integration by busing," to veto a pending child care social spending bill, and to make "a full commitment to the phasing out of economic controls by July 1972." "There are many other things we disapprove of in the Administration's policies," he said in summary, "but these demands seem to me to be essential."[42]

Eventually a specific list of conservative "concerns" was drawn up and delivered by *Human Events* editor in chief Allan Ryskind to Nixon aide Charles Colson in early November 1971. The platform contained many of the things that Meyer and McCaffrey mentioned, as well as such items as a call for continued U.S. aid and air support to South Vietnam and a demand that Vice President Agnew be kept on the ticket in 1972. Colson, upon receiving the list, "appeared amiable and sympathetic with many of our recommendations," Ryskind later reported, and promised an official response soon.[43]

These same conservatives, however, differed vastly over what they should now do—and whether they were having any impact. Neil McCaffrey believed they should focus almost exclusively on defense and rearmament in the face of the Soviet buildup. "The rearmament plank," he told the other group members, "so transcends the others as to differ in kind, not just degree. If Nixon gives us *real* rearmament but nothing else, I think we would be foolhardy not to support him." Others among the twelve, angry at what they saw as the administration's poor response to them, talked again of running a conservative candidate against Nixon in the 1972 primaries. A couple of them even spoke of finding a moderate Democrat to support in the primaries and general election in 1972. There were so many whispers, and so much intrigue, that members of the group began jokingly to call themselves "The Conspiracy" and "The Dirty Dozen."[44]

The conservative leaders met again on October 21, 1971, and although there was much talk, no consensus was reached. Anthony Harrigan of the Southern States Industrial Council complained shortly after the meeting that they "haven't seriously alarmed the administration, for the reason that our unhappiness doesn't pose a political threat." And Neil McCaffrey soon informed them that he would sign no more explicitly anti–Nixon manifestoes, for these had the potential to create "ill-will for CBC and Arlington House." As for 1972, no conservative candidate would do well in the primaries against Nixon. But perhaps the group should pursue the option anyway. "It might not be a bad idea if we got mussed up a little," he wrote. "It could just lead to that soul-searching now so long overdue. . . . If we ever get to the point of agony, I hope we will [ask] . . . : did the conservative movement get in Nixon the President it deserved?"[45]

In the days and weeks following the Manhattan Twelve's "suspension of support" for Nixon, the group faced a great deal of criticism. Publicly, at least, the administration did not seem to take them seriously. "It's not the conservative politicians," said one unidentified Nixon staffer to columnist Kevin Phillips. "Barry Goldwater, Ronald Reagan and Strom Thurmond are backing the President. They're not part of this thing." Indeed, neither Goldwater nor Senator James L. Buckley associated themselves with the conservatives' declaration. "I don't believe this is going to amount to much," Goldwater was quoted as saying, "because when the chips are down, they're going to be with Nixon.... [T]he alternatives are too frightening." Nixon loyalist Allen Drury, meanwhile, sneered in his column at the Manhattan Twelve as "the pouting panjandrums of the Righteous Right . . . , the Moody Elves of the Miffed Minority." The readers of *National Review* were split on the issue. In an internal *NR* summary of reader reaction, staffer Linda Bridges found that 50 percent of reader mail supported the suspension of support, while 25 percent were in favor of it but only as a first step (they urged support for either Reagan or Wallace), and 25 percent were against it.[46]

In the end the declaration seemed to have little effect on Nixon's policies. In late August came the administration's announcement of a government-mandated wage-price freeze (the New Economic Policy, or NEP)— one of the most heavy-handed governmental intrusions into the economy that the U.S. had seen since World War II. *NR* called it "a very heavy gamble . . . with the well-being of the nation—and of more of the world than this nation." Polls, however, showed that more than 75 percent of Americans were in favor of the freeze. That, of course, did not slow down Frank Meyer one whit. In his column he averred that Nixon's moves were pushing us toward "economic isolation under a government-directed economy." What most worried Meyer was a part of Nixon's plan that received less publicity— the levying of a 10 percent tariff surcharge on imports and the devaluation of the dollar. Meyer argued that this "disastrous move" would harm Western Europe and Japan and lead to a trade war. Nixon's wage and price controls meanwhile contained "implications of a controlled economy and a controlled society." Meyer, however, believed that what ailed the United States went deeper than Nixon's latest program; rather, it concerned "an insistence upon an ever-increasing scale of welfare and natural comfort." Americans wanted low taxes, but they wanted the benefits of big government, too. To beat inflation, for example, what was needed was to cut government social spending programs and to increase taxes to pay for the ones we had. But in the early 1970s this was politically impossible. Instead, Nixon's most recent steps symbolized, to Meyer, our "withdrawal from a leading status" in the world, much as had happened to England after World War II. Whether this continued, Meyer mused, "depends upon our recovery from the disease that grips us."[47]

Various of Meyer's conservative friends and contacts protested strenuously against both his and *NR*'s growing opposition to Nixon. Some argued that, with regard to the president's economic proposals, he was simply doing what he had to do; the voters lacked the patience to wait for traditional, free-market economic policies to work. Nixon, as a politician, had to respond to their will. Meyer would have none of it. "The voters [in 1968] elected him to do something else than he is now doing," he reminded them. "His surrender to liberal concepts in domestic and foreign affairs is his responsibility, not

theirs. It can only be interpreted as a failure of nerve, not before the electorate, but before the incessant pressure of the liberal Establishment." Furthermore, Nixon, in juxtaposing his liberal policies with his conservative rhetoric, was corrupting the uses of rhetoric. Meyer in a later column carefully
analyzed Nixon's words in an October 1971 televised speech. Nixon charac-
terized 1971 as a year in which "the American competitive spirit is reborn,"
stressed the "voluntary" nature of his programs, and spoke of the "voluntary
cooperation from business and labor." This, Meyer contended, was "a dangerous program of economic statism and protectionism that is being presented
to us with a rhetoric of free enterprise and free trade," and it imperilled free
society. Here Meyer again drew on Weaver's *Ethics of Rhetoric,* which held that
"the distortion of the public language, the public rhetoric, of a society per-
verts the ethics of its leadership and erodes the foundations of free and ordered government." Nixon's abuse of rhetoric also reminded Meyer of his
old communist days, of why he became a conservative in the first place. He
found repellent the idea, which he believed was implicit within Nixon's policies, that "you are perfectly free to do what you want as long as you do what
we want you to do." Meyer would never support such hypocrisy. And he
reminded his readers yet again just why such issues were important for conservatives: "one of the first responsibilities of conservatism is to defend the
tradition, of which the maintenance of standards of public discourse is an
essential aspect, so that responsibility must be exercised without fear or favor
and not merely in a narrowly partisan way. Whether the wells are muddied
by our liberal opponents or by those with whom we have been allied, an
overwhelming duty exists to maintain the conditions of a free constitutional
society—in this case, to maintain the necessary standards of public discourse."[48]

Fortunately not everyone disagreed with *NR*'s position on Nixon. An
American Conservative Union poll of its membership in October 1971 showed
that 58 percent of them wanted to see conservative opposition to the president in the primaries. And as things stood now, 29 percent of ACU members
said they would vote for Nixon in 1972; 30 percent would not vote for him;
and 41 percent were undecided. J. Daniel Mahoney, of the New York Conservative Party, urged the Manhattan Twelve to stand firm. "The liberals," he
told the group, "have never let horror at the Republican alternative prevent

them from pressing their views on Democratic presidents. We should emulate their tactical example in dealing with Republican presidents."[49]

Mahoney touched on a very important point. Was a "suspension of support" enough? Should conservatives go further?

NIXON'S WAGE AND PRICE controls continued for months. This was big government beyond most conservatives' wildest imagination. *National Review* in an editorial perhaps tried to hint to Nixon what was coming: "Thirty-two million Americans did not elect Richard Nixon president in order that he and his merry men on the Pay Board and Price Commission could try to fix the price of toothpaste, the wages of short-order cooks and the salaries of office managers," the editors snapped. "The President's taste for the dramatic reversal is becoming something of a habit. He may find, though, that he has lost a good many of his friends a few twists and turns back."[50]

The straw that broke the camel's back was the administration's policy toward Taiwan, a nation for which the American Right had a soft spot in its heart. Conservatives saw the island, and its anticommunist government, as a bastion of strength for the Free World against the communist Chinese behemoth, and many in addition believed that the now-aging Taiwanese leader, Chiang Kai-shek, had not been well served by the West in his struggle with Mao Tse-tung many years back. But by the end of 1971, with Richard Nixon's forthcoming trip to China, U.S. diplomatic recognition sure to follow, and the communist Chinese about to enter the United Nations, the question was brewing—if it was no longer to be recognized as the legitimate government of China, would Taiwan be expelled from the UN?

Conservatives hoped that Nixon would use all his power to prevent the UN General Assembly from voting for Taiwan's ouster. They believed he could prevent the expulsion, if he so chose. But the assembly voted to remove Taiwan, and conservatives watched as UN delegates danced and cheered wildly, flaunting their anti-Americanism and adding to their humiliation. Later, a despondent Buckley, in a speech in New York City, said that the United Nations was a "derelict" that took "obscene" pleasure in humiliating both America and Taiwan. The president should reduce U.S. involvement in it. If he did not, Buckley warned, he "will have lost an opportunity for penetrating leadership."[51]

Nixon took no such action. Many on the Right had had enough. The

president's policy on Taiwan was the final indignity. For a number of conservatives, the "suspension of support" became a complete break. William Rusher
helped lead the way. He wrote a thirty-page-long impassioned memorandum
laying out the anti-Nixon case, and he circulated it to the Manhattan Twelve and
to other leaders on the Right. There should be no "barked order" from remaining Nixon loyalists, Rusher wrote, "to get back in line and shut up." They should
not be giving orders to a movement "for whose present plight they are so largely
to blame." Rusher advocated Richard Nixon's defeat in 1972, and he urged that
conservatives take the lead in seeking the president's ouster. The conservative
movement would be better off having a Democrat in the White House, who
could be "vigorously opposed by a hungry, articulate and thoroughly conservative Republican Party." Nixon's election had not been good for conservatives.
They had little influence. "It is insufficiently appreciated," Rusher wrote, "to
what a marked degree the fact that a Republican president has proposed a policy
inhibits conservative criticism of that policy."[52]

Rusher's memo hit home. Many influential activists on the Right were
ready to take action, including many of the Manhattan Twelve. Rusher and others began sounding out the one conservative politician of any stature who was
willing to consider challenging Nixon—Congressman John Ashbrook of Ohio.
Ashbrook had been in Congress for a number of years, had a solidly conservative
voting record, took a leadership role in such movement organizations as the
American Conservative Union, was a contributor to *National Review,* and was
"personally close" to many of the conservatives who had signed the anti-Nixon
"suspension of support" statement. On November 30, the Manhattan Twelve
met again in New York City to decide whether to urge Ashbrook formally to
run. It was a long and at times difficult discussion. Some in the group, including
Frank Meyer, had in the past been rather firmly opposed to any primary challenge to President Nixon from conservatives. An Ashbrook run would be a last-
minute campaign, some worried, with no organization in place. A poor Ashbrook
showing in New Hampshire might give the impression that the conservative
wing of the Republican Party was either "complacent" or, worse, "decimated."

But those favoring an Ashbrook candidacy ultimately carried the day. This
was the only way to give expression to conservative dissatisfaction. And, with
liberal Republican congressman Peter McCloskey already mounting a primary challenge to the president, conservatives could not allow the public to

think that the only choice within the Republican Party was between McCloskey and Nixon. There must be a conservative alternative. Frank Meyer went along, despite his reservations; Nixon's most recent actions were too much for him, too. As *National Review* put it, while the journal would not sponsor Ashbrook's candidacy, if he entered the race "we will of course endorse him (a longtime friend and colleague) as most closely embodying the opinions of this journal."[53]

Meanwhile, the Nixon administration took action to forestall a rival candidacy. Nixon sent Spiro Agnew to meet with Buckley and Rusher in order to urge them to keep Ashbrook out of the primaries. Rusher told a Washington reporter that "people in the White House have been raising hell with their conservative contacts, including threats, whines, and whistles." But futile though their quest may be, many conservatives did not care. Nixon had pushed them too far.[54]

Few in mainstream political and media circles appeared much impressed with Ashbrook's candidacy; some were even forecasting the end of the conservative wing of the GOP. Early in 1972, the *New York Times* editorialized: "After the Nixon Administration's record, Republican candidates can no longer inveigh against big government, budget deficits, government subsidies or Federal regulation of the economy." At this, Rusher exploded again in anger, writing furiously to Buckley that "what the Times is obviously trying to do is pin the new Nixon positions to the wall as the limiting definition of responsible conservatism. Anything to the right of these is henceforth to be regarded as mere kookery. . . . If we accept this for an instant, conservatism—at least conservatism regarded as anything other than a vagrant impulse on the part of certain members of the Nixon administration, to be consulted by the President when and if he pleases—is simply out of business now, and hereafter. The fight that *National Review* has waged—that you have waged, and I have waged—is, quite simply, over."[55]

Events continued to deepen conservative gloom. That winter Richard Nixon made his triumphant visit to Beijing. There he toasted the man many believed to be one of the greatest communist tyrants of them all, Mao Tse-tung, and affirmed a longstanding communist Chinese position—that there was only one China, and that Taiwan was part of China. There was no mention of the mutual defense treaty that the United States currently maintained with Taiwan. Buckley, who covered Nixon's trip as a member of the news media, called the final communique a "staggering capitulation. . . . [W]e have lost—irretrievably—any remaining sense of moral mission in the world." Buckley, witnessing Nixon's fulsome toast to Mao, wrote that it was "unreasonable to suppose that anywhere in history have a few dozen men congregated who have been responsible for greater human mayhem than the hosts at this gathering. . . . I would not have been surprised that night if [Nixon] had lurched into a toast of Alger Hiss."[56]

This was a difficult time for *National Review* conservatism. Rusher that spring reported to Buckley that contributions in response to their annual fund appeal were down, subscription renewals were down, and *NR* again faced a significant deficit. It was a "worrisome time," Rusher wrote, "because of the general and very evident malaise that is afflicting American conservatism these days." Conservatives had fallen out among themselves. Goldwater and Reagan, for example, remained staunchly loyal to Nixon. Goldwater and Buckley privately argued with each other over the Ashbrook candidacy. Buckley emphasized his opposition to Nixon's China trip. "I have come increasingly to believe," he told Goldwater, "that that which is accepted as truth, comes very close to being the operative truth, or at least propels the world towards the acceptance of that truth. For that reason I think Nixon's toasts to Mao, his endorsement of Chou's 5 points, his omission of Taiwan in the communique, his role as postulant add up to a 'truth' of the kind that moves nations. I note that . . . Senator Mansfield has come out for the repeal of SEATO. I fear that that is only the beginning."[57]

But privately, early in March, he told Rusher, "As things now appear to me, the Ashbrook candidacy is not amounting to very much. . . . What I fear is a dissipation of our strength. . . . Although the analysis I have made over the months has not significantly changed, I find myself emotionally undermined on the matter and consequently feel more listless on the subject of trying to get John to withdraw from California, or, barring that, clamping down on the campaign ourselves, whether by a straightforward disavowal or by simply ceasing to pay it heed."[58]

But Buckley stood firm. It helped that his mentor, James Burnham, urged that *NR*'s position remain the same. As Burnham told Buckley: "However things turn out in percentage terms, I continue to believe that [Ashbrook's] running is a necessary operation, both from the point of view of an honorable portion of the conservative constituency, and for the historical-moral record. I . . . may vote for Nixon; but if so, it will not be because he is my leader, carrying my banner. I would be . . . in an autonomous section of a pragmatic united front; and I think the Ashbrook candidacy is the way, and the only way, no matter how badly it does in quantitative terms, to symbolize the relationship publicly."[59]

Ashbrook did not do well. In New Hampshire, he only got 10 percent of the vote, coming in behind Pete McCloskey; in Florida, he only managed 11 percent; in California, he did little better. But Buckley had *NR* applaud Ashbrook's decision to enter the race, claiming that he at least limited "the Administration's leftward options." Frank Meyer, meanwhile, watched on the sidelines while the drama unfolded. He was not feeling well. But he had a significant influence on the evolution of *NR*'s stance toward Nixon, and his views unquestionably also helped inspire the Ashbrook campaign. For it was Meyer who, early in 1971, began lecturing conservatives about holding to their principles in addition to understanding political realities. It was Meyer who, very early on, gave voice to the many conservative doubts and uneasiness about Nixon. It was Meyer who wrote bluntly that conservatives must not support a candidate who was untrue to principles. And despite his doubts, it was Meyer who encouraged the idea of an Ashbrook run. Many on the Right had heeded, again, one of Frank Meyer's continuing, and in this case one of his final, lessons: that to abandon principle in exchange for political gain was to abandon everything. Conservatives had, through the Ashbrook campaign, made a statement in 1972. And it was, at least in part, this campaign that inspired the Reagan candidacy of 1976 and brought about Reagan's victory in 1980.[60]

Meanwhile, the relentlessly cynical, devious, and opportunistic political professionals and technicians operating in the Nixon White House were dedicated first and foremost to one thing only: the reelection in 1972 of Richard Nixon. The Nixon White House expected loyalty from the American Right. In return, Nixon would occasionally toss the Right a few bones.

Thus, when the Manhattan Twelve announced their "suspension of support" of the administration in the summer of 1971, Nixon and his aides were not too concerned. "We had some discussion of how to deal with that," chief of staff H.R. Haldeman later wrote in his diary. "The P[resident] is not too concerned, although he wants answers communicated to them, but he makes the point that we don't need to worry too much about the right wing nuts on this, we do need to worry about Buckley getting off the reservation, and he wanted Henry [Kissinger] to talk to Buckley." One of the few who advocated doing something concrete was Charles Colson, and even he didn't favor doing much. He wrote in a memo that perhaps a small "task force" should be created to generate ideas to bring the Right "back into line." "It seems to me," Colson continued, "that we need to make some significant gesture—not immediately and not too obviously—to the conservatives. That is what they are playing for." On the other hand, Nixon adviser John Ehrlichman dismissed the suspension of support as the unthinking reaction of "the knee-jerk right."[61]

Nixon once told Buchanan, responding to conservative attacks upon his policies: "Here we see the fundamental difference between the right-wing extremists and the left-wing extremists. The right-wingers would rather lose than give up one iota as far as principle is concerned. The left wing's primary motivation is power." To many distressed conservatives, that seemed too often to be Nixon's primary motivation as well. Nixon did not, meanwhile, apparently worry too much about Ashbrook. In January 1972, he chuckled to Haldeman about "poor old Ashbrook and McCloskey, up there trekking through the snows of New Hampshire"; and, in the wake of his trip to China, one item on Nixon's agenda was to "review again the need of following up with the conservatives." But his policies did not change.[62]

NIXON'S APOSTASY WAS surely one of the greatest disappointments of Meyer's last years. And yet there was more to being a conservative than merely influencing national policy, important as that could be. There was also a conservative movement to be strengthened, organizations to be staffed, decisions to be made, and contacts to be maintained. In these ways, Frank Meyer continued to be an "activist" in every sense of the word. Meyer was, for starters, the official coordinator of the American Conservative Union's "Advisory Assembly," which gave him "operational responsibility for all activities of the ACU in the 'intellectual area.'" It was Meyer's job to maintain the ACU's contacts with as many conservative writers and intellectuals as possible, and to see to it that the organization contributed to the battle of political ideas in general. In 1971 Meyer sought out experts who could analyze and report on, from a conservative perspective, such problems as air pollution, the proposed education voucher system, and American military preparedness. He then edited the reports. Later that year, he edited ACU reports on the first three years of the Nixon administration and on the consumer activist Ralph Nader.[63]

Meyer was also active within the New York State Conservative Party, appearing at its major functions and advising party leaders Kieran O'Doherty and J. Daniel Mahoney. He lent his expertise to the top leadership of Young Americans for Freedom as well, speaking at its national conference in St. Louis in 1969 and appearing as one of the featured speakers at the reunion marking the tenth anniversary of the founding of YAF, held in September 1970 at the Buckley family home in Sharon, Connecticut. Almost all who played a role in the organization's beginning were there, and all had maintained contact, in one way or another, with their mentor Frank Meyer. Hence there was "amazement" (and no doubt amusement), reported one observer, "that Frank Meyer should be scheduled to speak at 9 A.M., an almost universal in-joke." And when a huge conservative awards dinner was held in Washington, D.C., in February 1971, attended by over six hundred people, Meyer was there, laughing and joking with other activists like Robert Bauman and Thomas Winter, and listening to the main speaker of the evening, Senator James Buckley.[64]

Meyer also continued to edit and publish the *Exchange,* his little newsletter of ideas, trends, and communications that was sent out three or four times a year to the small band of conservative scholars active in the United States. He opened it to the penetrating insights of libertarian author and analyst Thomas Szasz, used it as a forum for debate about computer technology, and allowed the young R. Emmett Tyrrell to seek support for his projected conservative collegiate magazine, the future *American Spectator.* The *Exchange* could serve a political purpose, too; Meyer used it to encourage his faculty colleagues from around the nation to report on how the battles against the anti-war movement and the counterculture were progressing, as well as to follow the progress of the radicals in infiltrating such academic organizations as the Modern Language Association.[65]

And you never knew just what all these connections could bring. Helped along at least a little by the *Exchange,* Tyrrell's magazine became a reality, and one of his first acts was to hire a Washington correspondent—a young, bespectacled, conservative but iconoclastic young man named George Will. Will was not afraid in his column to skewer conservatives as well as liberals. This sometimes raised hackles, especially Meyer's. Tyrrell later wrote that after nearly every Will column came the call from Woodstock, which would "burn my ears over one or another of the heresies [Will] had allegedly committed." Still, Meyer recognized Will's talent, and eventually Will joined the long list of Meyer's telephone friends.[66]

Meyer gained a larger stage, too. In May 1971, Harvard University held a symposium on the Evolution of American Conservatism, to be conducted at the Institute of Politics at the Kennedy School of Government. It seemed that everyone of note was there—the symposium was chaired by David Brudnoy, and participants included Ernest van den Haag, *Human Events* editor Thomas Winter Jr., YAF's J. Alan MacKay, the New York Conservative Party's Leo Kesselring, Russell Kirk, M. Stanton Evans, Anthony Harrigan, Murray Rothbard—and of course Frank Meyer. Later that summer, Meyer lectured at the Intercollegiate Studies Institute's week-long summer school, along with fellow intellectual luminaries van den Haag, Will Herberg, Leo Strauss, Ludwig von Mises, Eric Voegelin, Stephen Tonsor, and Gerhart Niemeyer. Whenever and wherever prominent, well-known figures in the American conservative movement gathered, Frank Meyer was sure to be there.[67]

BUT MEYER INFLUENCED the conservative movement even when he simply stayed home. For he continued to be very active in Woodstock in these last years, running *NR*'s book section, maintaining all his contacts through the magic of the telephone, and having as many young conservatives as possible visit him. For example, Meyer spent a good deal of time poring over one of the most socially and politically important books of the late 1960s, Nathan Glazer and Daniel Patrick Moynihan's *Beyond the Melting Pot,* devoting an entire column to it. He also daily perused the *New York Times,* the *New York Daily News,* an airmail edition of the *London Times,* and literally dozens of magazines and periodicals. Elsie was an avid reader, too, though she focused especially on books having to do with Africa, an interest she'd developed while teaching geography to her two boys.[68]

Another of Meyer's passions in these last years was poetry and drama. He liked nothing better than to read Shakespeare plays aloud with willing visitors, playfully fighting over who would get to read the best parts, then all shouting their lines at the top of their lungs. He had also developed a more specialized interest—"heroic" British and American poems and ballads. He decided to collect and edit them, and his collection, *Breathes There the Man: Heroic Ballads and Poems of the English-Speaking Peoples,* was published in 1973, shortly after Meyer's death. Its purpose was both aesthetic and political. Meyer dedicated the book to "the American soldiers who fell in Indochina," and its purpose, as he wrote in its introduction, was to "fill a gap created by the aesthetic prejudices of these times—to bring together in a single volume outstanding examples of heroic and patriotic poetry in the English language. As a lover of such verse, I have searched high and low and found no such collection published in the last fifty years." This was an era, Meyer continued, when "heroism and patriotism have gone out of fashion," when "most of the received poetry of the century has been difficult, abstruse, and more or less obscure," and when "makers of heroic and patriotic verse have been condemned as mere writers of jingles." This book was designed to show that such "jingles" were valuable and could stand on their own. They were "affirmations of the nobility of the human spirit, of courage and devotion." And, undoubtedly thinking of the many delightful nights he had spent with his many friends, Meyer had one special suggestion for his readers: "Read these poems aloud. They are made, like the poetry of the Ancients, to be spoken, not read on the silent page. They will, I predict, make the blood run and the heart beat faster."[69]

The book contained some of the great English poets, such as Tennyson, Shakespeare, Macaulay, Browning, and A. E. Housman. It included Scottish poets, including Sir Walter Scott and Robert Burns. And it held the work of great American writers and poets like Longfellow, Emerson, Bret Harte, William Cullen Bryant, Francis Scott Key, Julia Ward Howe, John Greenleaf Whittier, Stephen Vincent Benét, and Walt Whitman. This book was not Frank Meyer's alone. He was aided immensely by his wife and a few friends. Elsie wrote later that, although Meyer had for years thought about such an anthology, "its accomplishment was greatly assisted through his association with Jared Lobdell. Early in their acquaintance they discovered their mutual love of heroic and patriotic verse and chanted, say, stanzas of 'Lepanto,' 'The Revenge,' or 'Horatius' at each other across the dinner table or during the long nights of conversations at Woodstock."[70]

One of Meyer's main nonpolitical passions, meanwhile, was chess. He loved the game, as did his two sons. Meyer was only, as he once said, a "duffer tournament player," but by the early 1970s both of his boys were ranked as masters. The three Meyer men traveled to the occasional tournament and faced off against each other in grand matches at home. It seems only natural that chess—with its intricate strategy, and its demands on discipline and concentration and intellectual rigor—was embraced by Meyer.[71]

He also continued to work hard at editing his beloved "Books, Arts and Manners" section, as always allowing his writers a great deal of freedom but editing where necessary in order to keep articles and reviews within *NR*'s political and aesthetic boundaries. Occasionally in these later years Meyer had some difficulty with *NR*'s film reviewer. "I had to send him back his last column because of certain political editorializing implicit in it," he told a friend. "It was not only of the wrong kind, but in any case it was out of place in a movie review. He says I misunderstood him and that he wants to rewrite—so we shall see."[72]

Friends and acquaintances continued to visit him and to stay for a long night of food, drink, and conversation. He especially encouraged younger conservatives to come so that he might learn from them—and so that he might impart to them his wisdom. R. Emmett Tyrrell and William Kristol, a future top aide to Vice President Dan Quayle and founder of the *Weekly Standard,* both stayed overnight with the Meyers in the late summer of 1969. Their visit was full and eventful, yet typical. They arrived not long after the huge rock music festival held in Woodstock, and hence they found Meyer "still smarting from the influx of idiots. . . . [T]he Vandals had ravaged the town, potheads squatted on every street corner, and Bob Dylan had become his closest neighbor, about a mile down the mountain." The three discussed many other things as well: John Lindsay, Ted Kennedy and Chappaquiddick, Libya, China, America's black population. Kristol at the time still considered himself a liberal, and said so; Meyer loved a good challenge, and so, as Tyrrell wrote later, "a lively seminar commenced, and Professor Meyer amiably albeit rigorously discoursed on subjects ranging from the Israeli struggle for survival to the Russian presence in the Indian Ocean and from the founding of *National Review* to Bill Buckley's karate lessons." As for the state of things in 1969, Tyrrell found Meyer "unhappy with Nixon, distressed over the universities . . . , and unrepentant in his

hawkish prescriptions for Vietnam." More than anything, though, Tyrrell was
struck by his "deep erudition, broad yet incisive views, and unfailing confidence. . . . In fact, confidence is as important an element in Mr. Meyer's work
as is his brilliant intellect." As always with his guests, Meyer arose from his
bed to greet them at "breakfast" at 4 P.M., and remained with them until 8 A.M.
the following morning, "examining hundreds of books and periodicals from
all over the world, methodically calling any embattled point on the globe,"
and conversing with his friends throughout. No, Meyer had not changed over
the years.[73]

Tyrrell and Kristol also conducted during that late summer evening a wide-
ranging, lengthy interview with Meyer for Tyrrell's magazine. The interview is
significant both for the insight it gives into Frank Meyer's state of mind as he
approached the end of his life, and because, whatever his eccentricities, Meyer
was an excellent example of the conservative "mainstream," as he titled his last
book. Indeed, it is easy to note the many continuities between Meyer's political
conservatism of the late 1960s and early 1970s, and that of our own age. As
Tyrrell put it at the time, Meyer was "a distinguished spokesman for modern
conservatism. . . . For his wide erudition, incessant intelligence and intense faith,
Professor Meyer's remarks command special consideration."[74]

Meyer and his interviewers spent much time discussing the New Left and
the state of the universities (the latter a continuing worry). Meyer opined that
the New Left was "fundamentally anarchistic and nihilistic," and held within it
"organized sections" of "communists of various kinds—orthodox, Trotskyite,
Maoist, Castroite, who I strongly suspect but can't prove are gaining a good deal
of influence there." Its overall tendency was nihilism, "one of utter negativity," a
throwback to "the older nineteenth-century anarchism." Meyer dismissively referred to a common New Left phrase of the day, "creative disorder." "As though
by destroying," he barked, "somehow suddenly something good could come of
it. In point of fact, however, this is not the kind of social movement that can ever
be more than destructive." What had contributed to the growth of the New
Left? Tyrrell wondered. The Vietnam War had something to do with it, Meyer
replied, specifically, the draft—"Or shall we say," he added, foreshadowing conservative anger at President Clinton in the 1990s, "the selfishness and self-
centeredness of a large number of moderate students have made the draft issue
one on which the New Left is able to get wide support over and beyond their

own ranks." But the main culprit in the corruption of the young, Meyer believed, was liberalism. It had dominated the universities for the last fifty years, and now its effects had come to "full fruition." Liberalism, Meyer said—as so often in his column—"can give people nothing. The liberals do not teach people the tradition of Western civilization, they do not give them anything to hold onto. There is no will to govern on the part of liberal leadership, there's no will to teach on the part of liberal teachers. Into this void anyone who has any determined position can step, and that's why the New Left has gotten the following it has."

On foreign policy, Meyer remained a traditional conservative anticommunist, and thus advocated what today would appear to be a strong interventionist stance. But his views were more nuanced than some perceived. Meyer still spoke in 1969 of "world communism . . . [or] that communism which is directed by the second major military power in the world, the Soviet Union, and which dominates all the communist countries except Yugoslavia and China." Tyrrell, quite aware of how controversial Meyer's views were by then, pressed him on these points, asking doubtfully whether, for example, North Vietnam fit into Meyer's bipolar conception. Yes, "fundamentally," he responded. "All of North Vietnam's aid, 90 percent of it, comes from the Soviet Union," Meyer went on. "The Vietnam War would be over tomorrow if the Soviet Union decided it wanted it to be, as it has fundamental control there." China, on the other hand, still in the midst of the turmoil of the Cultural Revolution, was "in chaos and doesn't count. Rule China out. It is in this sense unimportant. It is not China but the Soviet Union who is moving toward world domination." Tyrrell, still skeptical, went on: "A nation like China which has historically been in competition with Russia—you actually believe that these people can come together in the brotherhood of communism? Under Moscow's leadership?" Meyer did not back down. It wasn't a question of "brotherhood," he said, it was "a matter of where the strength rests. The strength will in the foreseeable future rest in the Soviet Union which is industrially and militarily infinitely more advanced than China." Furthermore, Meyer explained, when speaking of world domination or "conquest . . . we don't speak in terms of every inch of the earth's surface. We speak in terms of control of the three main centers of power of the world—the Soviet Union, Western Europe, and the United States."

Tyrrell then turned to Eastern Europe. "It certainly seems that Russian communism is losing its influence in Eastern Europe," he ventured. "And this shows perhaps our policy of tolerance has been judicious." "I would hardly say the Soviet Union has lost influence in Czechoslovakia," Meyer answered, refer-ring to the Soviet invasion in 1968. Then, speaking more broadly, he explained that conservative philosophy in foreign policy need not be, and should not be, always internationalist, a view held by the followers of Patrick Buchanan and many in the Republican Party today.

> I have no interest, and I think the U.S. should have no interest, in how any other people govern themselves. I would be, if there were not an armed enterprise determined on our destruction, an isolationist. I do not think that the United States has the right or the duty to interfere in the world for any other purpose than our own national interest. I don't think it's our concern how people govern themselves. But I think it is very definitely our concern when there exists a world power . . . as a combination of a secular atheistic church with an army, deeply, fundamentally and ideologically determined to conquer the world. And when we are part of that world, I am determined that [the Soviet Union] must be destroyed if the U.S. is to survive, and if Western civilization is to survive.

Returning to the theme of young people and education, Meyer re-vealed a typical conservative fondness for small, traditional, faith-based insti-tutions that focused on a classical liberal arts education in the Western tradi-tion, seen today in such institutions as Hillsdale College and the University of Dallas. To Meyer, the ideal university was one "determined to teach the West-ern tradition, man to man, faculty member to student, on the basis of a strict, disciplined curriculum . . . which should limit itself to language, literature, philosophy, mathematics and science." One of the things that most angered him about New Left radicals was that they wished "to turn the university from a place in which people retire from the world for a few years to prepare themselves for it, into some replica of the world in which all the nefarious, nervous confusion of the world is repeated." Tyrrell, now playing devil's ad-vocate, asked: What about "relevance"? Why shouldn't universities teach, for example, how to do away with poverty in Harlem? "Because there is no such thing as a human discipline of eliminating poverty in Harlem," Meyer an-swered. "Universities do not exist to solve problems. They exist to create better human beings. Human beings are created best outside of the hurly-burly of the world, in isolation, where they can be taught how to think and write and speak and read, and where they can be taught the tradition of their civilization with which they will then be armed to go out and solve problems. The moment it becomes a problem-solving institution it ceases to be a university." But students were now so "idealistic," Tyrrell pressed. Didn't this give them a better chance to learn in school how to solve problems? No, Meyer said. "No problems are ever solved by idealism. Problems of a social character are solved by wisdom, which may contain a modicum of idealism, but which is fundamentally a knowledge of reality, a knowledge of what is possible and what is not possible and how to go about doing it."

What did Meyer think were the biggest problems facing America as the country entered the 1970s? Did he think "poverty" was an important issue, as many intellectuals claimed? Meyer agreed that "pockets of poverty" remained in the United States, but, like many libertarian conservatives today, he argued that the further development, through free markets, of "affluence" could greatly reduce the remaining areas of poverty. Private institutions and private charities could also do their share. The big problems, Meyer contended, were "the breakdown of ethics, the problem of the breakdown of morality, problems of the breakdown of understanding, the breakdown of the universities. But these are not, unfortunately, the problems about which people are worried in your generation." Meyer then summarized the greatest challenges facing America: "One is defense against the world-conquering impetus of Soviet Communism, and the other is the restoration of order in our society." Few conservatives in 1969 would have disagreed with him.[75]

IN THE SUMMER OF 1956, Whittaker Chambers, in musing to Ralph de Toledano about the state of American conservatism, wrote, "If I had to raise a slogan for the Right, it would be: Study. We must go to school; we do not know enough.... The liberal Left puts up a wondrous facade of knowledge. An informed Right should be able to cut it to shreds, but to do so, it is necessary to know. I am more and more impressed by Frank Meyer, who, if he does not know as much as he seems to, makes a wonderful fist of it."[76]

By the end of 1971, many on the Right had indeed studied, and Frank Meyer was there to provide some of the curriculum and to make sure that many would come, in Chambers's words, to "know." A number of people, both within and outside of the conservatve movement, had come to recognize him for his accomplishments. Sidney Hook, still in these years an outspoken liberal, recognized Meyer's book *The Moulding of Communists* as one of the best works available for understanding the technical workings of the American Communist Party. Meanwhile, when the Young Americans for Freedom in 1970 wanted to publish a pamphlet explaining conservatism to younger people, they featured Meyer's essay titled "Freedom, Tradition, Conservatism," written back in 1960. This was not surprising, since in a poll taken of YAF members in 1970 fully 72 percent of those surveyed cited Meyer, along with William F. Buckley Jr. and Russell Kirk, as one of their "intellectual leaders." When Buckley put together his anthology of twentieth-century conservative thought, published in 1970, he included another Meyer essay, this one from *What Is Conservatism?,* which explored the ideas uniting the Right. As Jared Lobdell put it, in an otherwise admiring profile of Buckley, praise for *NR's* editor in chief "does not mean that what he says is always centrally important to the development of this conservative movement. For philosophical guidance, one looks instead, in Mr. Buckley's words, to 'mission control' in Woodstock." Or, to sum up in the conservative historian Peter Witonski's words, in Meyer, "the major conservative political spokesmen of the past decade, Barry Goldwater, Ronald Reagan, Spiro Agnew, found an intellectual advocate. Not only did Meyer's ideas filter down into their collective rhetoric; his philosophy reflected, intellectually, the positions they defended in the arena of practical politics. . . . [I]n his concern for the conservative *movement,* Meyer has been unique. More than any other conservative thinker, he reflects the aspirations of the conservative rank-and-file."[77]

Not everyone agreed with Meyer. He was not universally loved. His views, and the vehemence with which he held them, could still lead to fearful rows at *National Review's* quarterly editorial Agonies, when, as managing editor Priscilla Buckley described it, ideological debates grew hot, and *NR's* editors accused each other of "insufficiently deimmanentizing the eschaton" in their columns. But, as always, the managing editor tried to inject calm with soothing words, words which Meyer, for one, increasingly came to appreciate. "Priscilla, you are the grease in our crankcase!" Meyer once exclaimed. "Epitaph-stuff!" she later said, grinning. But still, even the editor in chief, who had great love and respect for Meyer, at times chafed under his ideological guidance. Buckley dealt with this by teasing him. For instance, in his review of Meyer's last book, *The Conservative Mainstream,* he wrote that Meyer was "the house theologian, who looks darkly at any trace of heresy on the horizon, and is trained to spot the signs of it days and weeks before the lesser meteorologists feel there is any reason at all to cease romping about the maypole, come inside, and blast away. Oh, how aggravating that can be, especially for those who believe that a little creative heresy is good for the system—to feel that gyroscopic tug which reminds us that whatever the splendor of our lift-off, ground control over there in Woodstock is guiding us all the way, and if we would land safely, we had better leave the leash connected."

But Buckley, in the same review, put his finger on something that most conservatives who came into contact with Meyer soon grasped: that, no matter how irritating Meyer sometimes was, everyone respected him. Over the years "the old man has held his ground, and enough years have gone by to encourage a feeling towards him which lies somewhere between admiration and reverence. Granted that doesn't make him any less exasperating, or his adamance any less appalling." Yet Buckley had to admit that "little by little his profound attachment and profound understanding of the conservative position in America will get under more and more skins, even as, looking back, it is doubtful that anyone who has worked with him would say that he is untouched either by Meyer's intelligence, or by the intensity of his faith."[78]

FRANK MEYER'S FINAL COLUMN ran in the issue of *National Review* dated December 3, 1971. In it, he returned once again to the theme of communism, the Soviet threat, and American foreign policy. This was fitting, given how much of his life had been determined by his involvement with communism and his subsequent reaction against it. What attracted Meyer's attention in late 1971, however, were two apparently unrelated events: President Nixon's imposition of a 10 percent import surcharge, and, in Congress, the forging of a liberal-conservative voting coalition in the United States Senate that led to the defeat of an administration foreign aid bill. The two sides came to their positions in different ways. Conservatives were angry over Nixon's refusal to fight harder against the expulsion of Taiwan from the United Nations; liberals opposed the president's continuation of the Vietnam War. The defeat of the foreign aid bill, combined with congressional calls to reduce the number of U.S. troops stationed in Europe, led some to believe that America was returning to "isolationism." Was it? Meyer wondered. His answer was no. No one was calling for a full, total American retreat from the world. The U.S. must continue to be a force in world affairs. Rather, Meyer argued, the dividing line between supposed isolationists and their opponents mainly "reflected differences of opinion not as to whether America should be involved in world affairs, but how it should be involved."

The real question, Meyer continued, was over whether the liberals' view of foreign policy should prevail, with its "predilection for international organizations at the expense of American interests," or, as some conservatives argued, whether U.S. foreign policy should "be based on American interests and be deeply involved in world politics only when those interests are threatened by a foreign power." Meyer supported the latter view, but stressed that in this time and place American policy must remain interventionist in order to counter the Soviet threat, which was the "stark underlying reality" of the world situation. Many intellectuals and media members persisted in "obscuring" this reality. Over the last twenty-five years "resistance to communism has been only mildly and apologetically asserted," Meyer wrote, "while great emphasis has been laid upon one-world utopianism, exporting democracy, and generally acting as social worker to the whole world." The reaction against interventionism was a response to such doubletalk, and President Nixon made this "confusion" worse with his rhetoric of détente, with the "sickening spectacle" of the "hoopla" over the admittance of communist China to the UN, and with the SALT talks proceeding in the face of the U.S. "armaments deficit" relative to the Soviet Union. What was really at stake, Meyer concluded, was not "isolationism"; rather, it was "whether we face up to the sheer threat to our survival, whether our leaders make clear the danger of Communism and the need to refurbish our armaments before it is too late."[79]

This was Meyer's parting shot in the anticommunist struggle, for he was now forced to turn his attention to a far more personal, and final, struggle.

Legacy

B Y THE EARLY MONTHS OF 1972 it had become clear that Frank Meyer
was dying. He began to feel unwell in the fall of 1971; he had pain in his
stomach and chest, lost his appetite, began losing weight, and had little
energy. In December he entered the hospital for a round of tests and a thorough
examination. But it took a maddeningly long time for his doctors to get the test
results, and meanwhile his health continued to decline. His many friends grew
increasingly worried. "I am sorry to report," James Burnham wrote Buckley in
February 1972,

> I get the impression that Frank is in bad shape. There has not been much
> change in his condition as he describes it, but the more he has told me about
> it the more it sounds to me like the fairly typical development of a systemic
> cancer. He told me a day or two [ago], for example, about how he had been
> steadily losing weight over the past year, and how food more or less nauseated
> him so that he is eating mostly fortified eggnogs, and how his energy seems to
> be drained. I hope my apprehensions are wrong, and they of course may well
> be—they may be mostly an automatic inference from the knowledge of his
> heavy smoking history.[1]

The final results came in March. There was some faint hope that perhaps
Meyer had something treatable—tuberculosis, perhaps. Meyer himself was pre-

pared for the worst. The day before the test results came in, he was on the phone with one of his *NR* reviewers, the historian John Greenway. Meyer told him, almost in passing, that he expected to be told, the next day, that he had inoperable cancer. Greenway wrote later that he was "astonished" that someone could continue to carry on his professional duties with such an awful possibility hanging over his head. On the following day the news came: cancer, too extensive to operate on. There was little more the doctors could do. Meyer made his decision: he would return home, to his beloved Woodstock, to die. He arrived on March 11.[2]

His last few weeks were difficult. The pain soon became so great that he was confined to bed. He was relieved somewhat by medication, but mostly by his wife Elsie, who sat with him, hour after hour, holding his hand. When he finally, mercifully, passed away on April 1, 1972, Meyer's son, Gene, phoned Buckley to tell him the news. An emotional Buckley could only say what was in his heart, that Gene's father "was a great man." He quickly hung up the phone, too devastated to say more. Meyer's funeral was held a few days later on a cold, gray April day on the Meyers' Woodstock property. It was "the saddest funeral I have ever attended," wrote one of his close friends. Indeed, as another friend said at the gravesite, "The old warrior is gone." But his funeral also testified to how far Meyer's cherished conservative movement had come. Literally hundreds of his friends and associates were there, many of them young conservatives, all of whom had felt his influence. President Nixon sent a telegram of condolence. Congressman (and Republican presidential candidate) John Ashbrook attended, as did Senator James Buckley. And although it was indeed a sad day, Meyer's many friends were cheered by one thought: that, before he died, Frank Meyer, the long time agnostic, had become a Catholic. And therein lay a story.[3]

MEYER'S VIEWS ON RELIGION had always been complicated. His family was Jewish; but once Meyer became a communist around 1930, he accepted its atheism, abandoning his Jewish roots. He never returned to them. When Meyer became a conservative in the 1950s he seemed slowly to edge closer and closer to a belief in God, specifically to Christianity. But he never fully embraced it. He of course enjoyed discussing it with his friends (there was virtually nothing that Meyer would not or could not discuss). He was especially eager to debate the pros and cons of the positions taken by the Catholic Church; and, occasionally, he and an acquaintance would demonstrate their interest in Catholic history by, for fun, tunelessly intoning ancient Gregorian chants. He told friends that he believed in the doctrine of God's Incarnation in Christ, and that he himself proclaimed and championed the works and the ideas of a historical God. There need be no contradiction between this and individualism. After all, why not try to further the rights of, and opportunities for, man? Had not God created man, had He not created individuals, in order for them to administer His civilization?[4]

But, at the same time, Meyer resisted calling himself a Christian. His mind told him that God existed in history, and shaped it. But his heart was the heart of an individualist, and it led him to the belief that man's present and future were to be chosen by men, not God. He worried that in joining a church an individual might somehow lose some of his freedom, that it might open the door to coercion and regimentation (as communism had done so many years before). He might think about joining the Catholic Church, he once told Buckley, "if only he could figure out a way of taking the collectivism out of the church." This, one of Meyer's friends once put it, was his great "inner debate." No one could discuss the nature of man and society, as Meyer so often did, and completely ignore the question of God. Meyer, in struggling with such ultimate questions, was not sure exactly where he stood.

Meyer did know that he disagreed with religious fundamentalists and absolutists who launched "Jeremiah-like diatribes against literate and analytical civilization," who saw "the analytic as the work of the devil," as he once put it in a book review. Technology, he argued, did not mean the end of civilization. How we *used* it was what was important. He disliked the "Manichean" view of some religious thinkers that decried everything man had done in the world. But then what *was* Meyer's view of Christianity? If validating man as an individual ought to be the primary end of the political realm, as he argued in *In Defense of Freedom,* was not Meyer in fact criticizing religious associations? In that book, while discussing the role of the individual, he addressed the question of religion in a little-noticed footnote, and allowed his uncertainty concerning religion to come out into the open. He had, Meyer admitted, intentionally "omitted from this discussion what is the most important of the associations related to the inculcation of virtue: the association for the worship of God, the church. Questions are involved here that go much deeper than the political or the social; and I am not personally able, at this point in my life, to speak with certainty on these questions." Meyer, however, was sure about some things:

> That no civilization can come into being or develop without being in-formed by one kind or another of relationship between the men who make it up and God, I am certain; that Christianity, which informs Western civili-zation, is the highest and deepest relationship between the men who make it up and God, I am certain; that Christianity, which informs Western civiliza-tion, is the highest and deepest relationship to the Divine that men can attain, I am also certain; but I am not able to say that any single institutional church is the bearer of God's spirit on earth. And this makes it impossible for me to discuss the Church in the terms of this book. . . . [T]he association of human beings for the worship of God, the church, is, of all human associa-tions, the most important and the most directly related to the inculcation of virtue. But still it is individual persons in that association who, with the sustenance of God's grace, themselves as persons are virtuous or not, incul-cate virtue or fail to do so.[5]

Frank Meyer would not yet declare himself a Christian or formally join any organized church. As his friend L. Brent Bozell later wrote, "[H]e was too humble before the consequences of choice, too heartstrong before its gran-deur, to bend the knee falsely." But it was an issue that Meyer wrestled with occasionally, and which bothered him; it was the "great anxiety" for him and his friends in his later life.[6]

Yet Meyer never pushed religion away completely. The great debate never ended. A number of factors kept pulling him back to God. As age creeps in, and health begins to fail, it is only natural to begin thinking about ultimate ques-tions, about "first things," and to worry about the fate of the soul. Furthermore, finally accepting and embracing Christianity only seemed to make sense, given Meyer's other premises. Since he wished to vindicate the ideas, values, and tradi-tions of the West, surely he could not exclude God and Christianity. Meyer had also always had a principled, indeed a religious, objection to utilitarianism, the idea that justice is found in the greatest good for the greatest number. Meyer believed this led to individuals being left behind, to control and regimentation in the name of "the greater good." The teachings of Christ seemed to voice the same objection.

And then, finally, came the word early in 1972: Meyer had inoperable lung cancer. When he returned home from the hospital that March, he had less than one month to live. And so he began thinking hard, and talking to others in depth, about finally joining the church—the Catholic Church, to which he had always been drawn. He had some long talks with Monsignor Eugene Clark, of New York City, a kind of unofficial religious adviser to the New York State Conservative Party. But even now, with death looming, Meyer put off being baptized as a Catholic. Not yet. For one thing, as he told Buckley a bit later, he did not find the Church's position on suicide convincing. "Frank was not going to give up arguing merely to expedite death," Buckley later wrote.[7]

Whittaker Chambers once wrote to a friend that conservatism "is truly this ... [:] the chain of grace, the evidence of things unseen, working out, in the world, in chains of succession and authority. Too many who suppose themselves conservatives have forgotten, or never knew, that the chain of the spirit alone has binding force, and that the mere chain of authority with which the other is no longer interlinked, binds only to kill." Perhaps Frank Meyer came to realize this too, in his final hours. On the afternoon of April 1, Meyer told Monsignor Clark and Elsie that he was ready; that he accepted God and Christ, the "chain of grace" and "the evidence of things unseen"; and that he wished to be received into full communion with the Catholic Church. Meyer prayed aloud; and then he was baptized. "I am a Catholic," he told Elsie. His last great debate was over. Meyer appeared visibly to relax. It was his last day on earth. Six short hours after finally acknowledging belief in the Incarnation and the Resurrection, Frank Meyer died.[8]

The following day was Easter Sunday.

MEYER'S DEATH HAD a powerful effect on conservatives, both young and old. Younger conservatives, such as *National Review* editorial assistant C.H. Simonds and Agnew speechwriter John Coyne, remembered the long nights of conversation in Woodstock, which went hand in hand with Meyer's ability to teach. They would sorely miss him. James Burnham, with whom Meyer clashed so often for nearly twenty years, had a deep respect for him. Frank Meyer was, first and foremost, an anticommunist, Burnham wrote in the wake of Meyer's death; for the man from Woodstock, "any idea of ultimate convergence be-

tween Western civilization and communism, of a true and permanent de-
tente, is an illusion." Meyer's other fundamental belief was that, in this conflict between communism and the West, "faith and freedom, in the freedom
of each individual human being, is our indispensable armor." Such thinking
was not popular in today's "ping-pong era," Burnham observed. "But Frank
was never one to confuse truth with popularity."[9]

Shortly after Meyer's death, the tributes from conservatives began to pour
in. Peter Witonski called Meyer conservatism's "greatest teacher." The economist
Henry Hazlitt said he would be "irreplaceable." Meyer's old friend, Suzanne La
Follette, who had known him since the days of the *Freeman,* grieved over his
loss. The young George Will, who would become one of the most famous and
recognized conservative columnists and writers of the 1980s and 1990s, called
Meyer "one of the very best of men." Elsie Meyer received letters of condolence
from both President Nixon and Vice President Agnew. Indeed, in January 1973,
nine months after Meyer's death, William F. Buckley Jr. wrote in his annual fund
appeal letter that "the death of Frank Meyer cast a pall which will never dissi-
pate." Buckley's only condolence was that other young writers, "affected by
Frank Meyer, are coming into their own" and carrying on his legacy.[10]

What *was* the legacy of Frank Meyer? What had his life, his ideas, really
meant? How significant had his life and his writings been? Since his death, this
has been a matter of some debate, both outside and within the conservative
movement. Some conservatives have used Meyer's memory to plead for unity
among the sometimes disparate elements of the Right. Senator James Buckley,
for example, in a speech before the Conservative Political Action Conference in
January 1974, said, before quoting some of Meyer's writings on the things that
libertarians and traditionalists held in common, that it was "the late, beloved and
unforgettable Frank Meyer who best summed up why we have to present a
common front against the great heresies that dominate our times. . . . [He] understood the necessity for conservative unity." On the other hand, in 1986,
Republican senator John P. East made the rather dubious claim that the key
to understanding Meyer was "to appreciate fully that the Christian faith is the
summum bonum of his thinking, and all other ideas flow from that fact and are
corollaries to it," that the essential Meyer was "a Christian theorist." But there
were also traditionalist, religious conservatives such as Craig Schiller, a former
aide to Senator Buckley, who in the mid-1970s complained that Meyer's

fusionism was merely a pragmatic, somewhat artificial way of holding the diverse elements of conservatism together; he argued that Meyer's thinking was "a philosophy that could lend credibility to the Blaine-McKinley-Hoover Republicanism of the 1868–1932 period." Some libertarians, meanwhile, have expressed deep disagreement with Meyer. Justin Raimondo has claimed that Meyer's theory of fusion is "phony," designed mainly to "purge" the conservative movement of libertarians. Murray Rothbard added, in discussing Meyer, that "it is almost impossible to agitate for the State to kill Communists throughout the world without adopting statism at the root of one's social philosophy."[11]

Nor have historians, journalists, or political analysts and philosophers always looked favorably upon Meyer, or the anticommunist cause in general, to which he was so devoted. The historian Edward Pessen, in a lengthy denunciation of the anticommunism prevalent in America during the Cold War, never once mentioned Frank Meyer or *NR,* and claimed that anticommunists "regularly violated the law, flouted the Constitution, and offended elementary standards of fairness, decency, and morality in their zeal to demonstrate the depth of their hostility to communist subversion." The journalist Michael Lind, who once worked at *National Review* and has since disavowed the conservative movement, argues that true conservatism is dead, that the movement is now effectively controlled by the "radical right," and that the conservatism traditionally espoused by Buckley and those who built *NR* "will be viewed by historians as nothing more than the icebreaker for a resurgent radical right" of authoritarian religious conservatives and those who pathologically hated Bill Clinton. Conservatism today, according to Lind, has no unifying philosophy. Frank Meyer once "concocted" a philosophy for the "Buckleyites," but his fusionism did not remove the fundamental differences between libertarians and traditionalists; it merely papered them over. Meyer's fusionism was not the beginning of a debate, of the building of an intellectual tradition. Rather, it was the end. Serious discussion within the conservative movement stopped. "The glaring contradiction between social conservatism and radical, destabilizing capitalism had not been resolved," Lind concluded, "but conservatives pretended it had been."[12]

But although some are ignorant of Meyer's work, and others disagree with his philosophy and positions, there remains an overwhelming amount of testi-

mony, from conservatives and others, of the continuing importance and relevance of Meyer and his legacy. Conservative publisher Henry Regnery would
beg to differ with Lind about whether "debate" continued within conservative
circles after Meyer's theory of fusionism was proposed. In fact, the debate
never ended. It was only beginning. When Regnery published Meyer's book
In Defense of Freedom in 1962, it led to an intense debate and exchange of views
among intellectuals on the Right, Regnery recalled, "to Meyer's intense pleasure." Meyer "enjoyed a fight," Regnery continued, "and was equally skillful
in defending his position and seeking out weak points in that of his adversary.
But he could also be most persuasive." Regnery believed that *In Defense of
Freedom* "became one of the landmark books in the development of the conservative movement."[13]

Others agree on Meyer's importance within conservatism. The libertarian
conservative economist Milton Friedman, responding to libertarian concerns
about *National Review*-style conservatism, was quoted recently as saying, "Buckley's
not a libertarian. But he's also not a socialist. And if you look at the political
scene, his *National Review* has had a tremendous influence in providing a base for
collaboration between the libertarians on the one side and the free-market
conservatives on the other. That was epitomized in its most obvious form by
Frank Meyer when he was with *National Review.* They've helped that coalition
to form and hold together and have influence." Richard Viguerie, so important in building the conservative movement in the late 1970s and 1980s through
the use of direct mail and his espousal of social conservatism, has said that
Meyer influenced the movement as one of its primary "philosophers." David
Brudnoy, a leading conservative author and talk-radio host in the New England area for years, listed Meyer as his most significant "mentor," the man
who "helped me see a way to reconcile traditional conservatism with pro-
grammatic libertarianism." The political scientist Sara Diamond has argued
that Meyer's fusionism "facilitated the eventual mobilization of system-sup-
portive outsiders within policymaking processes." The historian William C.
Berman, in analyzing the growth of conservatism in America from the 1960s
through the 1990s, noted that "a sophisticated thinker like Frank Meyer fused
their antistatist ideology and moral traditionalism with a militant anticommunism. Thus, when Senator Barry Goldwater made his bid for the presidency
in 1964, he operated from a conservative 'vital center,' which reflected Meyer's

ideological construct of the fifties." Prominent so-called "paleoconservative" authors Paul Gottfried and Thomas Fleming, despite serious differences with Meyer, agree that he helped create a conservative "vital center," that he "constructed the edifice of ideas that would accommodate various conservative positions." Conservative historian Lee Edwards has written that fusionism served as the "effective synthesis" of conservatism until the collapse of communism in 1991. And R. Emmett Tyrrell believes that both Meyer and James Burnham, especially through their work at *National Review,* "inspired closely-reasoned thought and political action." Since their deaths, they have had no successors. Yet their legacy—most particularly Meyer's philosophical legacy—must endure, Tyrrell argues, or the consequences for conservatives will be severe: "[T]he American conservative's task is to preserve ordered liberty. For many years there have been conservatives and libertarians of a cantankerous turn of mind who have made this difficult task more difficult still by slamming the claims of virtue into the claims of liberty or vice-versa. Theirs is a parlor game best played by those who are not really serious about participating in politics. Frank Meyer set them straight four decades ago. Liberty cannot endure in an atmosphere of license, and virtue is not virtue without the opportunity to choose it."

And finally, the historian Richard Gid Powers, writing about the cherished anticommunist cause of Frank Meyer and the rest of the conservatives clustered around *National Review,* makes a brilliant case for why Meyer, and indeed all who dedicated much of their lives to opposing communism, should be honored:

> Anticommunism was made up of men and women who had come to know a great deal about communism, and who believed that what they were doing was urgent and important. For many of them, trying to tell what they saw as the appalling truth about communism consumed their lives. Some anticommunists built careers around fighting communism; others sacrificed careers. As a consequence of their struggle to persuade the rest of the country to share their alarm about the danger of communism, they left behind books, magazine articles, petitions, and letters that constitute the record of America's collision with a political ideology and movement that at one time threatened to take the world by storm. That record is an essential part of the drama of twentieth-century American history, and without it, that history is incomplete.[14]

That history would also be incomplete without mentioning the important role *National Review* has played in the growth of conservatism in America since 1945, and Meyer's part in it. Probably the conservative speechwriter Peggy Noonan, who served for several years in the Reagan White House, was typical. In the late 1960s, at the time a dedicated liberal, she started reading *NR,* "and it sang to me. They saw it the way I was seeing it: America is essentially good, the [Vietnam] war is being fought for serious and valid reasons, the answer to every social ill is not necessarily a social program, when you let a government get too big you threaten your own liberties—and God is real as a rock. I was moved, and more. It assuaged a kind of loneliness. Later I found that half the people in the Reagan administration had as their first conservative friend that little magazine." When the author Samuel G. Freedman wrote about some of the typical conservative voters and party activists who had helped create the Republican electoral sweep of 1994, he held that "these men, and the intellectual legitimacy they embodied, descended ultimately from William F. Buckley Jr. and the *National Review.* The man and the magazine did for conservative ideology what F. Clifton White and the Draft Goldwater movement had done for conservative organization—prepared it to dominate the Republican Party."

And everyone connected with the magazine knew the important role that Frank Meyer played in the founding, building, and strengthening of *NR,* and the part he therefore also played in helping conservatism dominate the GOP. As Buckley wrote to *National Review's* subscribers in 1978, fully six years after Meyer's death, "When we have a specially well-executed cover, or an adroitly illustrated essay, or a book section that teems with energy and intelligence and wit, or a superlatively explicated analysis by Jim Burnham, or a lyrical autobiographical account from a refugee from the Soviet Union, there is a shared satisfaction. The late Frank Meyer might have frowned at the heresy that a collective endeavor could bring in such satisfaction, but we'd have soothed him by reminding him that the Philadelphia Convention was a collective undertaking, and also—if he got obstinate, which he probably would have gotten—that he shared that pride."[15]

In September 1954, Whittaker Chambers told Ralph de Toledano that it all "seems to me to illustrate much that is wrong with the Right; people popping out like rabbits; no common consultation; no possibility of getting six Right wingers around one table at one time; or, if you could, little possibility of finding common ground. The Left is not really particularly strong or clever. But the Right is a trampling herd. So the game goes to the Left by default. . . . Is it really too much to ask that 20 (or even 10) conservative intellectuals should meet and see, at the very least, whether there would be any point in their ever meeting again?"[16]

By the time of Frank Meyer's death, there *was* consultation among conservatives, there *were* meetings, common ground *had* been found—put another way, there was a conservative movement. And Frank Meyer had a great deal to do with the creation, the slow building, and the establishment of a permanent infrastructure of ideas and organizations for that movement. The question at the time of his death was: How well would that movement continue after the loss of one of its founders? And what would be the future of the causes Meyer had so passionately believed in? What about the struggle against communism? Meyer's friend Jameson G. Campaigne mused sadly at Meyer's funeral that he had died "not knowing the outcome of the earthly struggle between Evil and those whose heritage has conscripted them to the standard of the Good, the True and the Beautiful. . . . [He was] gone before the earthly struggle between Communism and the West was resolved." Campaigne believed that those influenced by Meyer "will eventually have to be the makers of that victory. The responsibility for this victory is an acutely felt obligation for many of them, what 'the conservative movement' is all about." Eliseo Vivas, for his part, told the young conservatives he met at Meyer's funeral: "You young fellows won't have Frank around to give you orders any more. You are going to have to start giving them yourselves."[17]

But thanks to Meyer's teachings, many of those young people were ready for action in the years ahead. There were young men like John Coyne, an intern at *National Review* in the late 1960s, a member of Spiro Agnew's staff in Washington from 1971 to 1974, and after he left Washington a keen observer of political events and an occasional contributor to *NR* in the 1980s and 1990s. He too was a disciple of Frank Meyer, with vivid memories of late-night phone calls demanding an overdue review, of the long conversations late into the night in Woodstock, of the influence of Meyer's thought. Coyne wrote that *In Defense of Freedom* "probably had more to do with converting members of my generation to conservatism than any other single work." Meyer "was a teacher, especially effective at calming and guiding the younger, often hot-headed members of the American Right." He "had a way of coaxing the best out of you, so that at the end of the 'evening' [at Woodstock], when the sun came up, you felt you never before had been quite so brilliant." The atmosphere at the Meyer home was "exhilarating, intellectual. But it was a joyous intellectuality that springs from pure love of ideas." Meyer, Coyne concluded, will be "the voice we'll always be able to hear in our minds encouraging us to give our very best."[18]

Meyer's influence lives on within American conservatism. What of his causes? The Soviet Union is no more. Marxism is a largely discredited ideology. The number of communist states in the world has dwindled to a pitiful few. Yet Meyer's ideas remain. As for the conservative movement, it achieved perhaps its greatest triumphs in 1980 and 1984, when it elected one of its own, Ronald Reagan, twice to the presidency. Meyer's influence and ideas existed within that administration, too. As President Reagan himself said, in a speech to the Conservative Political Action Conference on March 20, 1981:

> It's especially hard to believe that it was only a decade ago, on a cold April day on a small hill in upstate New York, that another of these great thinkers, Frank Meyer, was buried. He'd made the awful journey that so many others had. He pulled himself from the clutches of "The God That Failed," and then in his writing fashioned a vigorous new synthesis of traditional and libertarian thought—a synthesis that is today recognized by many as modern conservatism. It was Frank Meyer who reminded us that the robust individualism of the American experience was part of the deeper current of Western learning and culture. He pointed out that a respect for law, an appreciation for tradition, and regard for the social consensus that gives stability to our public and private institutions, these civilized ideas must still motivate us even as we seek a new economic prosperity based on reducing government interference in this marketplace.[19]

NOT LONG AFTER Meyer's death, Jameson Campaigne wrote: "What of the rest of us? Has Frank Meyer transmitted his toughness of character along with his wisdom to the many who traveled to sit in front of the fireplace at Woodstock?" Conservatives have accomplished much since 1972. What they accomplish in future years may continue to depend on the answer to that question—whether they stand, as Frank Meyer always urged, "in defense of freedom."[20]

Notes

PREFACE (Pages xi-xiv)
1. George H. Nash, *The Conservative Intellectual Movement in America Since 1945* (Wilmington, Del.: Intercollegiate Studies Institute, 1996 edition), ix.

CHAPTER 1 (Pages 1-18)
1. Interview with Eugene Meyer, January 18, 1994 (by telephone); interview with John Meyer, February 12, 1994 (by telephone). See also "Frank S. Meyer: RIP," *NR* 24 (April 28, 1972): 471; Garry Wills, *Confessions of a Conservative* (Garden City, N.Y.: Doubleday and Co., 1979), 39 ff; Tracy F. Munsil, "The Moulding of a Conservative: The Political Thought of Frank Meyer" (master's thesis, Arizona State University, 1989), 3–4.
2. Ibid; see also George Nash, *The Conservative Intellectual Movement in America Since 1945,* 87–88; John B. Judis, *William F. Buckley Jr.: Patron Saint of the Conservatives* (New York: Simon and Schuster, 1988), 146–47.
3. See Lewis Perry, *Intellectual Life in America: A History* (New York: Franklin Watts, 1984), 342 ff.; Paul Carter, *Revolt Against Destiny: An Intellectual History of the United States* (New York: Columbia University Press, 1989), 216–20.
4. Quoted in Paul Johnson, *Modern Times: The World from the Twenties to the Nineties* (New York: HarperCollins, 1991), 248.
5. Frank Meyer, "The Scope of Soviet Activity in the U.S.," *Hearings Before the Subcommittee to Investigate the Internal Security Act and Other Security Laws,* U.S. Senate, 85th Congress, 1st session (Washington, D.C.: U.S. Government Printing Office, 1957), 3577 ff.; interview with John Meyer, February 12, 1994 (by telephone); Peter Witonski, "The Political Philosopher," *National Review* 24 (April 28, 1972): 467–68.
6. Meyer, "Scope of Soviet Activity in the U.S.," U.S. Senate Hearings, 3579; see also Frank S. Meyer, *The Moulding of Communists: The Training of the Communist Cadre* (New York: Harcourt,

Brace and Co., 1961), 91.

7. Arthur Koestler, in *The God That Failed,* ed. Richard Crossman (Salem, N.H.: Ayer Publishers, 1949), 23; interview with John Meyer, February 12, 1994 (by telephone). Nearly every historian of American communism, as well as most ex-Communists, emphasizes the impact of the Great Depression and the heightened impact that Marxist ideology had on vulnerable individuals. See, for example, Irving Howe and Lewis Coser, *The American Communist Party: A Critical History* (Boston: Beacon Press, 1957), 280 ff.; Harvey Klehr, *The Heyday of American Communism: The Depression Decade* (New York: Basic Books, 1984), 78–79; George Charney, *A Long Journey* (Chicago: Quadrangle Books, 1968), 22–24; John Gates, *The Story of an American Communist* (New York: Thomas Nelson and Sons, 1958), 14–18; Granville Hicks, *Where We Came Out* (New York: Viking Press, 1954), 27–42; and Perry, *Intellectual Life in America,* 342.

8. William Henry Beveridge, *The London School of Economics and Its Problems, 1919–1937* (London: George Allen and Unwin Ltd., 1960), 43–44.

9. Meyer, "Scope of Soviet Activity in the U.S.," U.S. Senate Hearings, 3579 ff.

10. Ibid.; see also Nash, *American Conservative Intellectual Movement,* 87–88, and Wills, *Confessions of a Conservative,* 43 ff. It is significant that, according to Wills, Meyer in later life retained a deep interest and respect for things British.

11. Meyer, "Scope of Soviet Activity in the U.S.," U.S. Senate Hearings, 3579 ff.; Nash, *American Conservative Intellectual Movement,* 97–98; Frank Meyer, testimony in *U.S. v. Eugene Dennis et al.* Volume VI, U.S. Court of Appeals for the Second Circuit (New York: Adams Press, 1950), 4507–8; Judis, *William F. Buckley Jr.,* 146–47.

12. Saul Bellow, "Writers, Intellectuals, Politics: Mainly Reminiscence," *National Interest* 9, no. 31 (Spring 1993): 124–34; see also Guenter Lewy, *The Cause That Failed: Communism in American Political Life* (New York: Oxford University Press, 1990); Klehr, *Heyday of American Communism,* 79 ff.; Howe and Coser, *American Communist Party,* 280 ff.

13. Edward Shils, in John H. Bunzel, *Political Passages: Journeys of Change Through Two Decades, 1968-1988* (New York: Free Press, 1988), 2–13.

14. Meyer, "Scope of Soviet Activity in the U.S.," U.S. Senate Hearings, 3582; Frank Meyer, "Communist Training Operations," *Hearings Before the Committee on Un-American Activities.* U.S. House of Representatives, 86th Congress, 1st session (Washington, D.C.: U.S. Government Printing Office, 1959), 1007 ff.

15. See Klehr, *Heyday of American Communism,* 154–61; Howe and Coser, *American Communist Party,* 216–20; C. H. Simonds, "At Home," *NR* 24 (April 28, 1972): 468–69.

16. See Maurice Isserman, *Which Side Were You On? The American Communist Party During the Second World War* (Middletown, Conn.: Wesleyan University Press, 1982), 51–71; see also Charney, *Long Journey,* 115 ff.

17. See Charney, *Long Journey,* 123 ff.; Howe and Coser, *American Communist Party,* 280 ff.; Isserman, *Which Side Were You On?;* Harvey Klehr and John Earl Haynes, *The American Communist Movement: Storming Heaven Itself* (New York: Twayne, 1992), 93.

18. Meyer, *Moulding of Communists,* 128; indeed, by now he had almost completely broken with his family. Meyer's son John recalled that the only member of Meyer's side of the family that he ever saw in person was his great aunt Amelia (interview with John Meyer, February 12, 1994).

19. Meyer, *Moulding of Communists,* 81–84.

20. Ibid., 16–45; see also Richard Wright's description of Party trials in Crossman, ed., *The God That Failed,* 150–61.

21. See Howe and Coser, *American Communist Party,* 199 ff.; Hicks, *Where We Came Out,* 43–

44; Charney, *Long Journey,* 22–30.

22. Frank Meyer, "The Unrepentant Left," *Freeman* 4 (June 14, 1954), 677–8; Meyer, "Communist Training Operations," U.S. House of Representatives Hearings, 1016–17.

23. Meyer, *Moulding of Communists,* 54, 90–91; see also Koestler, in Crossman, ed., *The God That Failed,* 65–66.

24. Interview with Eugene Meyer, January 18, 1994 (by telephone); interview with John Meyer, February 12, 1994 (by telephone); see also C. H. Simonds, "At Home," 468; see also Wills, *Confessions of a Conservative,* 41.

25. See Isserman, *Which Side Were You On?* 104 ff.

26. Meyer, "Scope of Soviet Activity in the U.S.," U.S. Senate Hearings, 3599; William A. Rusher to the author, November 30, 1991 (in the author's possession).

27. Meyer, "Scope of Soviet Activity in the U.S.," U.S. Senate Hearings, 3600.

28. Ibid., 3601; see also Priscilla L. Buckley to the author, December 29, 1992 (in the author's possession).

29. Edward Shils, in Bunzel, *Political Passages,* 13; Frank Meyer, "The Gray Menace," *Freeman* 2 (June 30, 1952): 671–72.

30. Priscilla L. Buckley to the author, December 29, 1992 (in the author's possession).

31. Meyer, quoted in Isserman, *Which Side Were You On?* 153–56.

32. Ibid., 185 ff.

33. Meyer, "Scope of Soviet Activity in the U.S.," U.S. Senate Hearings, 3608; Meyer, testimony in *U.S. v. Eugene Dennis et al.,* 4516.

34. See Charney, *Long Journey,* 137–38; Howe and Coser, *American Communist Party,* 300 ff.; Meyer, "Scope of Soviet Activity in the U.S.," U.S. Senate Hearings, 3608.

35. Meyer, *Moulding of Communists,* pp. 130-131. 155; Frank Meyer, "The Unrepentant Left," 672; Wills, *Confessions of a Conservative,* 42; interview with Eugene Meyer, January 18, 1994 (by telephone).

36. Meyer, testimony in *U.S. v. Eugene Dennis et al.,* 4524–25, 4528.

37. Meyer, "Scope of Soviet Activity in the U.S.," U.S. Senate Hearings, 3609.

38. Eliseo Vivas, "RIP: In Brief," *NR* 24 (April 28, 1972), 473–74.

CHAPTER 2 (Pages 19-34)

1. Interview with John Meyer, February 12, 1994 (by telephone).

2. See Whittaker Chambers, *Witness* (New York: Random House, 1952); Priscilla L. Buckley to the author, January 5, 1993; Patricia B. Bozell to the author, June 22, 1993 (in the author's possession).

3. Priscilla L. Buckley to the author, January 5, 1993; Patricia B. Bozell to the author, June 22, 1993; Wills, *Confessions of a Conservative,* 43; interview with John Meyer, February 12, 1994 (by telephone).

4. Interview with John Meyer, February 12, 1994 (by telephone). See also Priscilla Buckley to the author, ibid.; and Patricia B. Bozell to the author, ibid.

5. Meyer, "Communist Training Operations," U.S. House of Representatives Hearings, 1014.

6. Friedrich von Hayek, *The Road to Serfdom* (Chicago: University of Chicago Press, 1944).

7. See Frank Meyer, "Champion of Freedom," *NR* 8 (May 7, 1960): 304–5; Wills, *Confessions of a Conservative,* 43 ff.; Nash, *American Conservative Intellectual Movement,* 87.

8. See Richard M. Weaver, *Ideas Have Consequences* (Chicago: University of Chicago Press, 1948); Frank Meyer, "Richard M. Weaver: An Appreciation," *Modern Age* 14 (Summer–Fall 1970), 243–48.

9. Wills, *Confessions of a Conservative,* pp. 41, 43 ff.; see also Travis Bogard and Jackson R. Bryer, eds., *Selected Letters of Eugene O'Neill* (New Haven: Yale University Press, 1988), 588.

10. For an excellent summary of, and provocative interpretation of, the origins of the Cold War, see Johnson, *Modern Times,* 432–505.

11. Meyer, "The Scope of Soviet Activity in the U.S.," U.S. Senate Hearings, 3610; interview with John Meyer, February 12, 1994 (by telephone); Nash, *American Conservative Intellectual Movement,* 87–88; Priscilla L. Buckley to the author, January 5, 1993.

12. Earl Browder, in Gates, *Story of an American Communist,* pp. viii–ix, 5; Charney, *Long Journey,* 221.

13. Frank Meyer, "Hard Going," *NR* 2 (July 11, 1956): 20; see also Frank Meyer, "Retreat from Relativism," *NR* 1 (December 14, 1956): 24–25; Frank Meyer, "Sunday-Supplement Moralist," *NR* 2 (July 4, 1956): 27.

14. To see the *Freeman's* and the *American Mercury's* move rightward, see (for example) James Burnham, "Editor Meets Senator: Mr. Wechsler Goes to Washington," *Freeman* 3 (June 15, 1953): 662 ff.; "The Case Against Adlai Stevenson," *American Mercury* 75 (October 1952): 16 ff. On the "new conservatism," see Gertrude Himmelfarb, "The Prophets of the New Conservatism: What Curbs for Presumptuous Democratic Man?" *Commentary* 9 (January 1950): 78–86; Russell Kirk, *The Conservative Mind* (Chicago: Henry Regnery, 1953); Nash, *American Conservative Intellectual Movement,* 88 ff.

15. Ralph de Toledano to the author, December 7, 1993 (in the author's possession).

16. Ibid.

17. Ibid.

18. Ralph de Toledano to the author, November 22, 1993 (in the author's possession). For examples of Meyer's published work in the ea 1950s,0s, see Meyer, "The Gray Menace," 671–72; Frank Meyer, "Cliches and Shibboleths," *American Mercury* 75 (November 1952): 108–10; Frank Meyer, "Books in Review," *American Mercury* 76 (May 1953): 68–78. The *Mercury* was at this time under the editorship of Robert Clements. Toledano was on its editorial advisory board.

19. Meyer, "Cliches and Shibboleths," 108–10.

20. Frank Meyer, "He Adds Little to Philosophy," *Freeman* 5 (May 1955): 486; Meyer, "The Unrepentant Left," 677–78; "Books in Review," *American Mercury* 77 (July 1953): 137–44.

21. Frank Meyer, "The Rotten Apple in Our Schools," *Freeman* 5 (September 1954): 100–102; see also Frank Meyer, "Education For What?" *Freeman* 4 (February 22, 1954): 388–89; Wills, *Confessions of a Conservative,* 43 ff.

22. Frank Meyer, "The Real UNESCO," *Freeman* 5 (March 1955): 378–80; "Books in Review," *American Mercury* 76 (May 1953): 68–78; "The Booby-Trap of Internationalism," *American Mercury* 78 (April 1954): 85–88.

23. Meyer, "The Booby-Trap of Internationalism," 87–88.

24. Meyer, "Books in Review," *American Mercury* 76 (May 1953): 68–78; "Books in Review," *American Mercury* 76 (June 1953): 135–44.

25. Frank Meyer, "Books in Review," *American Mercury* 76 (March–April 1953): 119–28; "Books in Review," *American Mercury* 76 (June 1953): 135–44; "Books in Review," *American Mercury* 77 (August 1953): 137–44.

26. Meyer, "Books in Review," *American Mercury* 76, 119–28; Frank Meyer, "Where Is Eisenhower Going?" *American Mercury* 78 (March 1954): 123–26.

27. William F. Buckley Jr., "A Dilemma of Conservatism," *Freeman* 5 (August 1954): 51–52; see also William S. Schlamm, "But It Is Not 1940," *Freeman* 5 (November 1954): 169–71.

28. Meyer, "Books in Review," *American Mercury* 76 (May 1953): 76–77; see also Peter Viereck, *Shame and Glory of the Intellectuals: Babbitt Jr. vs. the Rediscovery of Values* (Boston: Beacon Press, 1953); Nash, *American Conservative Intellectual Movement,* 124 ff. Largely because of this and subsequent Meyer attacks, Viereck would never become a part of the *NR* circle.

29. See Nash, *American Conservative Intellectual Movement,* 69 ff.; Frank Chodorov to Robert J. Needles, July 13, 1955. Yale University Archives, Buckley Papers, Box 3.

30. Underlining in the original.

31. Frank Meyer, "Collectivism Rebaptized," *Freeman* 5 (July 1955): 559–62.

32. Robert J. Needles to Frank Chodorov, July 8, 1955. Buckley Papers, Box 3.

33. See Chodorov to Needles, July 13, 1955. Buckley Papers, Box 3.

34. Frank Meyer to William F. Buckley Jr., July 10, 1955. Buckley Papers, Box 3; see also Buckley to the author, August 16, 1993 (in the author's possession).

CHAPTER 3 (Pages 35-48)

1. Ralph de Toledano to the author, December 11, 1993 (in the author's possession).

2. Ralph de Toledano to the author, December 11, 1993; See Judis, *William F. Buckley Jr.,* 17–131; Nash, *American Conservative Intellectual Movement,* 133-135; William A. Rusher, *The Rise of the Right* (New York: William Morrow, 1984), 37–46; Kevin Smant, *How Great the Triumph: James Burnham, Anticommunism, and the Conservative Movement* (Lanham, Md.: University Press of America, 1992), 65–66; see *National Review* masthead in the magazine's first issue, in *NR* 1 (November 19, 1955): 3.

3. "The Magazine's Credenda," *NR* 1 (November 19, 1955): 4.

4. On the policy differences among *NR* editors, see James Burnham, "The Problem of No. 1," *NR* 2 (October 17, 1956): 10; Burnham, "Should Conservatives Vote for Eisenhower-Nixon? Yes," *NR* 2 (October 20, 1956): 13 ff.; William Schlamm, "Should Conservatives Vote for Eisenhower-Nixon? No," ibid., 13 ff.; James Burnham, "Liberation: What Next?" *NR* 3 (January 19, 1957): 60 ff.; William Schlamm, "Neutralization: What Next?" ibid.: 81; Frank Meyer, "New Ideas or Old Truth?" *NR* 3 (February 2, 1957): 108; see also Judis, *William F. Buckley Jr.,* 149; and also see Buckley to Burnham, n.d. (1957?). Hoover Institution Archives, James Burnham Collection, Box 1.

5. Buckley to Burnham, July 31, 1957. Yale University Archives, Buckley Papers, Box 2.

6. Priscilla L. Buckley to the author, August 9, 1993 (in the author's possession).

7. Burnham to Buckley, July 15, 1958. Buckley Papers, Box 5.

8. Meyer to Rusher, August 8, 1961. Buckley Papers, Box 14; see also Meyer to Buckley, November 18, 1957. Buckley Papers, Box 2.

9. Buckley to Meyer, December 23, 1957. Buckley Papers, Box 8; Buckley to Meyer, August 20, 1957. Buckley Papers, Box 2.

10. Buckley to Meyer, December 12, 1960. Buckley Papers, Box 10; Buckley to Meyer, January 29, 1960. Buckley Papers, Box 10; Buckley to Meyer, November 15, 1957. Buckley Papers, Box 2.

11. Frank Meyer, "Norman Mailer's Culture Hero," *NR* 4 (July 27, 1957): 113; see also the following by Frank Meyer: "Simulacrum of Freud," *NR* 1 (February 22, 1956): 25–26; "The Wrong Alarm," *NR* 2 (August 1, 1956): 22; "Reviewed in Brief," *NR* 3 (April 20, 1957): 385.

12. Frank Meyer, "The Revolt Against Congress," *NR* 2 (May 30, 1956): 9–10; see also Frank Meyer, "Freedom, Virtue, and Government," *NR* 4 (October 12, 1957): 329; on the views of other conservatives, see for example James Burnham, *Congress and the American Tradition*

(Chicago: Henry Regnery, 1959), or the many *NR* editorials in favor of the Bricker Amendment.

13. Frank Meyer, "In the Great Tradition," *NR* 3 (June 1, 1957): 527–28.

14. Frank Meyer, "The Constitutional Crisis," *NR* 4 (October 26, 1957): 378.

15. Meyer, "In the Great Tradition," 527–28.

16. Frank Meyer, "The Times Finds Another Nice Communist," *NR* 4 (July 6, 1957): 41; Frank Meyer, "Of Khrushchev, Stalin, and Sitting Ducks," *NR* 2 (July 11, 1956): 16; Frank Meyer, "Saved by the U-2," *NR* 8 (June 4, 1960): 365.

17. Meyer, "Of Khrushchev, Stalin, and Sitting Ducks," 16; "Moral Coexistence," *NR* 8 (April 23, 1960): 267.

18. Frank Meyer, "Of Betrayal and Shame," *NR* 3 (April 27, 1957): 408–9; "An American Tragedy," *NR* 2 (December 8, 1956): 12; "The Ethics of Mr. Eisenhower's Rhetoric," *NR* 3 (February 9, 1957): 137.

19. See James Burnham, "Sighting the Target," *NR* 2 (December 29, 1956): 12.

20. Meyer, "New Ideas or Old Truth?" 107–8.

21. See Frank Meyer, "Nature of the Enemy," *NR* 3 (March 23, 1957): 283.

22. Frank Meyer, "The Meaning of McCarthyism," *NR* 5 (June 14, 1958): 565; see also Frank Meyer, "McCarthy's Unforfeited Word," *NR* 3 (June 8, 1957): 548.

23. Frank Meyer, "What Price a Patch of Sand?" *NR* 6 (January 31, 1959): 494.

24. Frank Meyer, "They Cry 'Peace, Peace' When There Is No Peace," *NR* 7 (October 10, 1959): 391; on *NR*'s activities, see Judis, *William F. Buckley Jr.*, 175–78, and Rusher, *Rise of the Right,* 37 ff.

25. Frank Meyer, "The Relativist 'Re-Evaluates' Evil," *NR* 3 (May 4, 1957): 429.

26. Frank Meyer, "Dilemmas of Foreign Policy," *NR* 5 (March 29, 1958): 303–4; see also Judis, *William F. Buckley Jr.*, 174–75.

27. Frank Meyer, "The Concept of Fortress America," *NR* 5 (April 26, 1958): 400.

CHAPTER 4   (Pages 49–66)

1. Russell Kirk, "Mill's 'On Liberty' Reconsidered," *NR* 1 (January 25, 1956): 23–24.

2. Frank Meyer, "In Defense of John Stuart Mill," *NR* 1 (March 28, 1956): 23–24.

3. Frank Meyer, "Conservatives in Pursuit of Truth," *NR* 2 (June 6, 1956): 16.

4. Ernest van den Haag, "Must Conservatives Repudiate Keynes? No," *NR* 8 (June 4, 1960): 361–64.

5. Frank Meyer, "Why Conservatives Reject Keynes," *NR* 9 (July 30, 1960): 52–53.

6. Underlining from the original.

7. Frank Meyer, "The Roots of Libertarian Conservatism," *NR* 5 (April 6, 1957): 331 ff.; see also Frank Meyer, "A Political Law of Parity," *NR* 6 (January 17, 1959): 462.

8. Frank Meyer, "Success and Failure in the Modern World," *NR* 7 (August 15, 1959): 277; see also Frank Meyer, "Politics and Responsibility," *NR* 1 (April 4, 1956): 20–21.

9. Frank Meyer, "Symptoms of a Mass Delusion," *NR* 1 (February 8, 1956): 23–24; Judis, *William F. Buckley Jr.*, 161 ff.

10. See Frank Meyer, "The Politics of 'The Impossible,'" *NR* 7 (November 7, 1959): 459; Frank Meyer, "On What Ball?" *NR* 5 (January 4, 1958): 17; Frank Meyer, "What Time Is It?" *NR* 6 (September 13, 1958): 180.

11. Ralph de Toledano, *Lament for a Generation* (New York: Farrar, Straus, and Giroux, 1960), 175–77.

12. Whittaker Chambers, *Odyssey of a Friend: Letters to William F. Buckley Jr., 1954–1961,*

edited with notes by William F. Buckley Jr. (Washington, D.C.: Regnery Gateway, 1987), 231; see also Judis, *William F. Buckley Jr.,* 159–60.

13. Chambers, *Odyssey of a Friend,* 217–18.

14. See, for example, Burnham to Buckley, October 23, 1957, a long memo on *NR*'s recent articles, along with ideas on how the magazine could come up with more capital. Buckley Papers, Box 2.

15. Burnham to Buckley, November 24, 1957. Buckley Papers, Box 2.

16. Meyer to Buckley, April 22, 1960. Buckley Papers, Box 10.

17. Elsie Meyer to Buckley, December 4, 1959. Buckley Papers, Box 8.

18. Burnham to Buckley, n.d. Hoover Institution Archives, James Burnham Collection, Box 1.

19. See Priscilla Buckley, "Notes on a Fifth Birthday," *NR* 9 (November 19, 1960): 307 ff.

20. See Wills, *Confessions of a Conservative,* 20 ff. and 38–48.

21. On the Babcock Agency and Meyer's involvement, see Buckley to the Editors, March 14, 1960. Buckley Papers, Box 10; see also Meyer to the Editors, May 10, 1960. Buckley Papers, Box 10.

22. Meyer to Russell Kirk, December 13, 1962. Russell Kirk Papers, Clarke Historical Library, Central Michigan University.

23. Meyer to Kirk, August 5, 1959. Russell Kirk Papers.

24. See Meyer to Buckley, May 20, 1958. Buckley Papers, Box 5; and Meyer, "Richard M. Weaver: An Appreciation," 243–48.

25. Priscilla Buckley to the author, August 26, 1993 (in the author's possession).

26. Meyer to Buckley, May 20, 1958. Buckley Papers, Box 5.

27. Meyer to Buckley, April 22, 1960. Buckley Papers, Box 10.

28. Frank Meyer, "'Slippage' and the Theory of the Lesser Evil," *NR* 6 (March 13, 1959): 556; Frank Meyer, "The President and 'The True Believer,'" *NR* 1 (May 2, 1956): 15.

29. Frank Meyer, "The Politics of 'The Impossible' II," *NR* 7 (December 19, 1959): 555.

30. Frank Meyer, "A Man of Principle," *NR* 8 (April 23, 1960): 268–70; on the book's authorship, see Patricia B. Bozell to the author, December 11, 1993 (in the author's possession). Patrick Buchanan, in his introduction to the latest Regnery edition of the book, also refers to Bozell's authorship.

31. Frank Meyer, "New Men or Whole Men?" *NR* 9 (August 27, 1960): 116.

32. Meyer to the Editors, May 10, 1960. Buckley Papers, Box 10.

33. See Buckley to the Editors, September 19, 1960. Buckley Papers, Box 2; see also Buckley to the Editors, August 10, 1960. Buckley Papers, Box 10; Patricia B. Bozell to the author, January 4, 2001 (in the author's possession).

34. See "*National Review* and the 1960 Elections," *NR* 9 (October 22, 1960): 233–34.

35. Buckley to Burnham, October 11, 1960. Buckley Papers, Box 10.

36. Frank Meyer, "Only Four Years to 1964," *NR* 9 (December 3, 1960): 344.

37. "Notes on a Fifth Birthday," *NR* 9 (December 17, 1960): 441 ff.; see also Judis, *William F. Buckley Jr.,* 179–80.

CHAPTER 5 (Pages 67-92)

1. Quoted in George Brown Tindall and David E. Shi, *America: A Narrative History,* 3rd edition (New York: W. W. Norton, 1992), 1334.

2. Tindall and Shi, *America: A Narrative History,* 1338–1341; see also David Burner, *John F.*

Kennedy and a New Generation (Boston: Little, Brown, 1988); and Michael R. Beschloss, *The Crisis Years: Kennedy and Khrushchev, 1960–63* (New York: HarperCollins, 1991).

3. Frank Meyer, "Which Way for JFK?" *NR* 10 (February 11, 1961): 81.

4. Frank Meyer, "Khrushchev, Mao, and Orthodoxy," *NR* 14 (April 9, 1963): 280; see also Frank Meyer, "Heads We Lose, Tails They Win," *NR* 10 (March 11, 1961): 148.

5. Frank Meyer, "*Commonweal* Puts the West in Its Place," *NR* 11 (October 7, 1961): 239. Underlining from the original.

6. Frank Meyer, "The Myth of 'The People's Revolution'," *NR* 11 (July 29, 1961): 53.

7. Tindall and Shi, *America: A Narrative History,* 1341–43; see also Beschloss, *Crisis Years,* 64 ff.

8. Frank Meyer, "Kennedy, Cuba, and the Voters," *NR* 13 (November 6, 1962): 352.

9. Hans J. Morgenthau and Frank Meyer, in "To the Editor," *NR* 11 (December 2, 1961): 391–93.

10. Frank Meyer, "Just War in the Nuclear Age," *NR* 14 (February 12, 1963): 105 ff.

11. Quoted in Frank Meyer, "What Does Kennedy Mean?" *NR* 15 (July 16, 1963): 18.

12. Meyer, "What Does Kennedy Mean?" 18; and Frank Meyer, "The Khrushchev-Kennedy Treaty," *NR* 15 (August 13, 1963): 107.

13. Meyer to Buckley, January 25, 1963. Buckley Papers, Box 26.

14. Meyer to Buckley, April 23, 1961. Buckley Papers, Box 14; and Meyer to Buckley, May 7, 1961. Buckley Papers, Box 14.

15. Meyer to Buckley, May 21, 1961. Buckley Papers, Box 14. See also Meyer to Buckley, June 4, 1961. Buckley Papers, Box 14.

16. Meyer to Buckley, August 15, 1961. Buckley Papers, Box 14.

17. Meyer, to The Editors, June 18, 1963. Buckley Papers, Box 26; Meyer to Buckley, February 27, 1963. Buckley Papers, Box 26.

18. For typical *National Review* editorials, see "The Mindless Way," *NR* 8 (March 26, 1960): 189–90; "The Week," *NR* 8 (May 21, 1960): 316; "Adlai Stevenson Unfurls His Umbrella," *NR* 8 (June 4, 1960): 349–50; "Neutral and Neutralist," *NR* 10 (January 28, 1961): 39–40; "Gone Goa," *NR* 11 (December 30, 1961): 439–40; "The Collaborators," *NR* 13 (July 17, 1962): 8–9. Nor did *NR* always shy away from recommending specific military steps. Early in 1961, it suggested an American military blockade of Cuba, in order to increase the pressure on Fidel Castro. See "Yanqui Sí," *NR* 10 (January 14, 1961): 7.

19. Interview with John Meyer (by telephone), April 1, 1995; interview (by telephone) with Eugene Meyer, March 20, 1995; see also Richard de Mille to the author, January 4, 1995.

20. Meyer, *Moulding of Communists,* 3.

21. Ibid., 9–69 ff.

22. Ibid., 65–66.

23. Ibid., 66, 71; underlining in the original.

24. Ibid., 107, 155.

25. All quotes from previous three paragraphs from ibid., 170–71.

26. "The Moulding of Communists," *Human Events* 18 (March 24, 1961): 187; Gerhart Niemeyer, "The Bending of Human Souls," *NR* 10 (January 28, 1961): 53–54; see also Thomas Molnar, "Cadre Training," *Commonweal* 73 (February 3, 1961): 490–91; Anthony T. Bouscaren, in *Annals of the American Academy of Social Sciences* 338 (November 1961): 147; Willard Edwards, in *Chicago Sunday Tribune* (January 22, 1961): 6.

27. From an advertisement for the book in *National Review.* See *NR* 10 (April 22, 1961): 256.

28. Gene M. Lyons, in *American Political Science Review* 55 (September 1961): 622; Alexander Dallin, in *New York Times Book Review* (January 8, 1961): 3.

29. See Michael Kramer and Sam Roberts, *"I Never Wanted to Be Vice-President of Anything!" An*

Investigative Biography of Nelson Rockefeller (New York: Basic Books, 1976), 8–11, 215, 230–235, 240; Joseph E. Persico, *The Imperial Rockefeller: A Biography of Nelson A. Rockefeller* (New York: Simon and Schuster, 1982), 59 ff.

30. J. Daniel Mahoney, *Actions Speak Louder* (New Rochelle, N.Y.: Arlington House Publishers, 1968), 23 ff.

31. Telephone interview with the Honorable Judge J. Daniel Mahoney, January 7, 1994. In 1958, both Mahoney and Meyer were helping *NR* senior editor L. Brent Bozell in his ultimately unsuccessful run for the Maryland state senate.

32. See "Statement of Principles of the New York Conservative Party," in Mahoney, *Actions Speak Louder,* 378–79.

33. Telephone interview with the Honorable Judge J. Daniel Mahoney, January 7, 1994.

34. See Mahoney, *Actions Speak Louder,* 53–54 ff.

35. See E. Merritt, "To the Editor," *NR* 13 (November 20, 1962): 407; Mahoney, *Actions Speak Louder,* 103–4.

36. Mahoney, *Actions Speak Louder,* 125 ff. and 143 ff.

37. Ibid., 167 ff.

38. See William F. Rickenbacker to the Editors, May 22, 1962. Buckley Papers, Box 20; for more on Burnham's general outlook on this subject, see Smant, *How Great the Triumph: James Burnham, Anticommunism, and the Conservative Movement,* 72–76.

39. William A. Rusher to the author, April 20, 1995 (in the author's possession).

40. Rickenbacker to the Editors, May 22, 1962. Buckley Papers, Box 20.

41. Meyer, "New York Conservatives and the Two-Party System," *NR* 12 (July 3, 1962): 486.

42. Buckley to the Editors, August 21, 1962. Buckley Papers, Box 20; for more on Buckley's general attitude toward this subject, see Judis, *William F. Buckley Jr.,* 188, 193–200.

43. See Mahoney, *Actions Speak Louder,* 28–29; note also that Buckley was the featured speaker at the Conservative Party's annual dinner in 1964. See his speech, reprinted in ibid., 392–96.

44. Telephone interview with the Honorable Judge J. Daniel Mahoney, January 7, 1994.

45. See M. Catherine Babcock Agency Inc. brochure, 1961. Included in papers of Richard C. de Mille, now in the author's possession; and see Babcock Agency advertisement, in *NR* 14 (March 26, 1963): 252.

46. Rusher, *Rise of the Right,* 114–15.

47. Meyer to Richard de Mille, June 4, 1961. From the Meyer–de Mille correspondence, now in the author's possession courtesy of Mr. de Mille.

48. Telephone interview with Daniel Kelly, September 30, 1994. Kelly was a graduate student at the University of Wisconsin in 1961–62, and met Meyer twice when he lectured in Madison at the behest of the Wisconsin Conservative Club.

49. Meyer to Buckley, February 27, 1963. Buckley Papers, Box 26.

50. Meyer to Buckley, March 1, 1962. Buckley Papers, Box 20.

51. See Frank S. Meyer, "By Way of Explanation," *The Exchange* 1 (1962): 1–2; Milton Friedman, "Tentative," in the above, 2 ff. *The Exchange* was not sent to libraries or to newsstands; it is not widely available. (The author got his copies courtesy of Mr. Richard de Mille, a longtime friend of the Meyers and fellow conservative.)

52. See Meyer, in *The Exchange* 2 (December 1962), 1–2; Meyer to Richard Ware, June 4, 1962. Buckley Papers, Box 20; Buckley to Meyer, December 21, 1962. Buckley Papers, Box 20.

53. See, for example, Hugh Kenner, "Propositions on Fellowships, the Academy, and the Climate of Opinion," *The Exchange* 3 (March 1963): 1–3; Stephen Tonsor, "The New Ameri-

can History," *The Exchange* 4 (June 1963): 3–4; Garry Wills, "The Status of the Student," *The Exchange* (April 1964): 1–3; Peter Witonski, "UNESCO's Social Science Journal," *The Exchange* 14 (October 1965): 1–2; Nils Erit Broden, "The Philosophical and Metaphysical Implications of Berkeley," *The Exchange* 14 (October 1965): 3–5

54. Meyer to Buckley, March 17, 1963. Buckley Papers, Box 26; Meyer to de Mille, June 30, 1963. In de Mille–Meyer correspondence, in the author's possession.

55. "The Sharon Statement," in *NR* 11 (September 24, 1960): 173; Marvin Liebman, *Coming Out Conservative: An Autobiography* (San Francisco: Chronicle Books, 1992), 150–51.

56. Meyer to Buckley, March 1, 1962. Buckley Papers, Box 20. Bruce was a Republican who represented the Indianapolis area. Meyer's reference to "kiver to kiver" was apparently an attempt to mimic Bruce's Indiana accent.

CHAPTER 6 (Pages 93–110)

1. See Chambers to Buckley, December 1, 1958, and Chambers to Buckley, August 6, 1954, in William F. Buckley Jr., *Odyssey of a Friend: Whittaker Chambers' Letters to William F. Buckley Jr., 1954–1961* (Washington, D.C.: Regnery Gateway edition, 1987), 45, 218–19.

2. Burnham to Buckley, March 11, 1962. Buckley Papers, Box 20. Burnham to Buckley, March 17, 1962, ibid; for the internal conflicts within YAF, see Rusher, *Rise of the Right,* 81–82.

3. Frank Meyer, "Hope for the 60s," *NR* 10 (January 14, 1961): 19.

4. Frank Meyer, "The Liberal Veto," *NR* 12 (February 27, 1962): 131.

5. Meyer to Buckley, September 3, 1961. Buckley Papers, Box 14. Underlining from the original.

6. Frank Meyer, "The Conservative Movement: Growing Pains," *NR* 10 (May 6, 1961): 281.

7. Frank Meyer, "The Twisted Tree of Liberty," *NR* 12 (January 16, 1962): 25–26; see also Meyer, "The Conservative Movement: Growing Pains," ibid.

8. See Patrick Allitt, *Catholic Intellectuals and Conservative Politics in America, 1950–1985* (Ithaca, New York: Cornell University Press, 1993), 21–22, 97–98.

9. L. Brent Bozell, "Freedom or Virtue?" *NR* 13 (September 11, 1962): 181 ff.

10. Frank Meyer, "Why Freedom," *NR* 13 (September 25, 1962): 223–25.

11. "To the Editor: Freedom or Virtue?" *NR* 13 (October 9, 1962): 283; Patricia B. Bozell to the author, April 1, 1995 (in the author's possession); Meyer to Buckley, January 25, 1963. Buckley Papers, Box 26. And in fact, the debate would continue later in 1963, with a new participant: William F. Rickenbacker. See Rickenbacker, "Freedom, Virtue, and the State," *NR* 15 (September 10, 1963): 191 ff. Rickenbacker's position is very close to Meyer's.

12. Frank S. Meyer, *In Defense of Freedom: A Conservative Credo* (Chicago: Henry Regnery Co., 1962), 1, 3.

13. Meyer, *In Defense of Freedom,* 6–7.

14. Ibid., 21–22.

15. Ibid., 52.

16. Ibid., 62–63.

17. Ibid., 69–70.

18. Ibid., 98–99.

19. Ibid., 133, 136–37.

20. Ibid., 146.

21. Ibid., 147 ff.; Meyer may here have laid the groundwork for the idea of "family values," so popular now with American conservatives.

22. Ibid., 154–55.

23. Ibid., 155.

24. Ibid., 169–70.

25. Ibid., 170.

26. Ibid., 171–72.

27. Stanley Parry, "The Faces of Freedom," *Modern Age* 8 (Spring 1964): 208–10.

28. Richard M. Weaver, "Anatomy of Freedom," *NR* 13 (December 4, 1962): 443–44; Willmoore Kendall, *The Conservative Affirmation* (Chicago: Henry Regnery, 1963), 4–5.

29. Edwin J. Feulner Jr., "Kirk in Washington," *NR* 46 (June 13, 1994): 56–57; see also Henry Regnery, "A Conservative Mind," *NR* 46 (June 13, 1994): 56; William F. Buckley Jr., "Russell Kirk, At Work and Play," *NR* 46 (June 13, 1994): 60–61; Richard de Mille to the author, January 3, 1995.

30. Quoted in Nash, *American Conservative Intellectual Movement,* 377 n. 91; see also George Panichas, "Russell Kirk as Man of Letters," *Intercollegiate Review* 30, no. 1 (Fall 1994): 7–17.

31. Russell Kirk, "An Ideologue of Liberty," *Sewanee Review* 72 (April/June 1964), 349–50.

32. Telephone interview with John Meyer, April 1, 1995. "Credo" is a Latin verb meaning "to believe."

33. Chambers to Buckley, January 12, 1960, in Buckley, *Odyssey of a Friend,* 281–84; Weaver, "Anatomy of Freedom," 444; Murray Rothbard, "Conservatism and Freedom: A Libertarian Comment," *Modern Age* 5 (Spring 1961): 217–20; Nash, *American Conservative Intellectual Movement,* 385 n. 119.

34. See Nash, *American Conservative Intellectual Movement,* 161–165.

35. Meyer to Buckley, September 3, 1961. Buckley Papers, Box 14.

36. Meyer to Buckley, February 21, 1963. Buckley Papers, Box 26.

CHAPTER 7 (Pages 111-126)

1. Louis Hartz, *The Liberal Tradition in America: An Interpretation of American Political Thought Since the Revolution* (New York: Harcourt, Brace and World, Inc., 1955), 15 ff.

2. M. Morton Auerbach, *The Conservative Illusion* (New York: Columbia University Press, 1959), VII.

3. Auerbach, *Conservative Illusion,* 1, 39.

4. Auerbach, *Conservative Illusion,* 202, 237.

5. Clinton Rossiter, *Conservatism in America: The Thankless Persuasion* (New York: Vintage Books edition, 1962), 12, 27, 40.

6. Richard Hofstadter, *The Paranoid Style in American Politics and Other Essays* (New York: Alfred A. Knopf, 1966), xii, 35 ff.; Rudolf Heberle, in *American Sociological Review* 21 (August 1956): 516–17; James MacGregor Burns, "Psychology of the Radical Right," *Saturday Review* 48 (December 25, 1965): 37–38; Daniel Bell, ed., *The Radical Right* (Garden City, N.Y.: Anchor Books, 1964), 2, 41, 156.

7. See "Lion of Conservatism," *Newsweek* 61 (May 13, 1963): 94–95; "Angry Voice on the Right," *Time* 76 (October 31, 1960): 54; "Thunder on the Right," *Time* 79 (February 16, 1962): 47–48; "Spokesman for Conservatism," *Time* 84 (July 10, 1964): 74.

8. Peter Viereck, in Bell, ed., *Radical Right,* 203–4; Massimo Salvadori, "The Future Is in the Past," *Saturday Review* 42 (October 10, 1959): 42 ff.

9. Daniel Bell, "The National Style and the Radical Right," *Partisan Review* 29 (Fall 1962): 519–34.

10. Dwight Macdonald, "Scrambled Eggheads on the Right: Mr. Buckley's New Weekly,"

Commentary 21 (April 1956): 367–73; John Fischer, "Why Is the Conservative Voice So Hoarse?" *Harper's* 212 (March 1956): 17–22. Interestingly, there soon came a reply to Macdonald's article in *Commentary*'s "Letters to the Editor" section, from libertarian Murray Rothbard. In challenging Macdonald's view that *NR* was vulgar and simple-minded, Rothbard wrote: "I will pit the intellectuality and literateness of Frank Meyer . . . against a dozen assorted Dwight Macdonalds. . . . [L]et him turn to Meyer's column. After he finishes, perhaps he will be able to recognize a truly consistent, civilized voice." (Murray Rothbard, "The National Review," *Commentary* 21 [June 1956]: 584–85.)

11. James Epstein, in *The New York Review of Books* 2 (June 11, 1964): 12 ff; Margaret L. Coit, "A Partisan Review of Democracy," *Saturday Review* (March 28, 1964): 38–39.

12. Irving Brant, "Why Do They Get Away With It?" *New Republic* 146 (June 4, 1962): 17–20; Brant, "The Anti-Communist Hoax," 15–18.

13. Margaret L. Coit, "View From the Right," *Saturday Review* 46 (April 27, 1963): 35 ff.; James Reichley, "The New Conservatives Last Gasp," *New Republic* 141 (October 19, 1959): 27.

14. William F. Buckley Jr., "An Evening with Jack Paar," *NR* 12 (March 27, 1962): 205 ff.; see also Judis, *William F. Buckley Jr.*, 203–5.

15. Quoted in Michael Wreszin, *A Rebel in Defense of Tradition: The Life and Politics of Dwight Macdonald* (New York: Basic Books, 1993), 275; see also Robert Graham, "William Buckley's Review," *America* 98 (October 19, 1957): 61; "Spokesman for Conservatism," *Time* 84 (July 10, 1964): 74; "Thunder on the Right," *Time* 79 (February 16, 1962): 47–48; "Lion of Conservatism," *Newsweek* 61 (May 13, 1963): 94–95; Richard Hofstadter, *The Paranoid Style in American Politics*, 41–65, 82–83.

16. R. H. S. Crossman, "Radicals on the Right," *Partisan Review* 31 (Fall 1964): 555–65.

17. See "Some Comments on Senator Goldwater," *Partisan Review* 31 (Fall 1964): 584–608.

18. Emmett John Hughes, "Goldwaterism," *Newsweek* 64 (July 27, 1964): 17; foreign press reports quoted in Emmett John Hughes, "The View from Defeat," *Newsweek* 63 (June 15, 1964): 20–21; and in "Can Anyone Stop Goldwater?" *Newsweek* 63 (June 15, 1964): 23; Walter Lippmann, "The Republican Agony," *Newsweek* 63 (June 22, 1964): 19.

19. Quoted in Judis, *William F. Buckley Jr.*, 229; quoted in Michael Barone, *Our Country: The Shaping of America from Roosevelt to Reagan* (New York: Free Press, 1990), 279.

20. Quoted in Arthur Schlesinger Jr., *A Thousand Days: John F. Kennedy in the White House* (Boston: Houghton Mifflin, 1965), 18, 702; Kenneth P. O'Donnell and David F. Powers, *Johnny, We Hardly Knew Ye: Memories of John Fitzgerald Kennedy* (Boston: Little, Brown, 1970), 213, 384–85; Theodore C. Sorensen, *Kennedy* (New York: Harper and Row, 1965), 334–35.

21. See Schlesinger, *Thousand Days*, 752–53, 1018.

22. See John Andrew, *The Other Side of the Sixties: Young Americans for Freedom and the Rise of Conservative Politics*, chapter 8, pp. 1–23 of an unpublished manuscript in the author's possession. Cited with the permission of John Andrew.

23. Jack Valenti, *A Very Human President* (New York: W.W. Norton, 1975), 146–47; Richard N. Goodwin, *Remembering America: A Voice from the Sixties* (Boston: Little, Brown, 1988), 303; Eric F. Goldman, *The Tragedy of Lyndon Johnson* (New York: Alfred A. Knopf, 1969), 191.

24. Doris Kearns, *Lyndon Johnson and the American Dream* (New York: Harper and Row, 1976), 154 ff., 207.

25. William Rusher, *The Rise of the Right* (New York: National Review Publishers edition, 1993), 83.

26. See William A. Rusher to the author, May 18, 1994 (in the author's possession); William A.

Rusher, *Rise of the Right,* 89; Buckley to James Burnham, July 25, 1963. Buckley Papers, Box 26; Buckley to the Editors, March 5, 1964. Buckley Papers, Box 30.

27. William F. Rickenbacker, *The Fourth House: Collected Essays by William F. Rickenbacker* (New York: Walker and Co., 1971), xix–xx.

28. Buckley to Burnham, September 1, 1959. Buckley Papers, Box 8.

29. ". . . And the New Republic," *NR* 12 (June 19, 1962): 435.

30. Meyer to Buckley, June 4, 1959. Buckley Papers, Box 8; Buckley to Meyer, June 26, 1959. Buckley Papers, Box 8; Buckley to Burnham, March 7, 1958. Buckley Papers, Box 5; Burnham to Buckley, February 16, 1964. Buckley Papers, Box 30.

31. William F. Buckley Jr. to the Editors and Staff, June 9, 1964. Buckley Papers, Box 30.

32. Meyer to Buckley, March 17, 1963. Buckley Papers, Box 26; Meyer to Buckley, February 15, 1963. Buckley Papers, Box 26.

33. Kenneth Crawford, "Buckleyism Forever?" *Newsweek* 66 (November 15, 1965): 49.

CHAPTER 8 (Pages 127-156)

1. See, for example, Judis, *William F. Buckley Jr.,* 183–84, 221; Nash, *American Conservative Intellectual Movement,* 253–95; Rusher, *Rise of the Right,* 117–30.

2. Rusher, *Rise of the Right,* 50–51.

3. Burnham to Buckley, March 11, 1962. Buckley Papers, Box 20.

4. Burnham to Buckley, October 12, 1963. Buckley Papers, Box 26.

5. Buckley to the Editors, August 25, 1965. Buckley Papers, Box 35; Buckley to All Concerned, February 18, 1963. Buckley Papers, Box 26.

6. William F. Rickenbacker to the Editors, November 3, 1965. Buckley Papers, Box 35. "*Hunc nunc, vacca fusca,*" translated, means "How now, brown cow?" Burnham to Buckley, February 15, 1961. Buckley Papers, Box 14; on election bets, see William A. Rusher to the Editors, December 14, 1962. Buckley Papers, Box 20; or Buckley to the Editors, January 5, 1964. Buckley Papers, Box 30.

7. William A. Rusher to the author, September 4, 1993 (in the author's possession); interview (by telephone) with John Meyer, April 1, 1995.

8. Meyer to Buckley, February 8, 1964. Buckley Papers, Box 30.

9. See John Gregory Dunne to Meyer, February 22, 1964; Meyer to Dunne, February 25, 1964; Meyer to Buckley, February 27, 1964. Buckley Papers, Box 30.

10. Meyer to Buckley, February 27, 1963. Buckley Papers, Box 26.

11. Meyer to Buckley, February 27, 1963; Buckley to Meyer, March 8, 1963. Buckley Papers, Box 26.

12. Guy Davenport to the author, January 27, 1994 (in the author's possession).

13. It should be stressed that this committee did not include Senator McCarthy as a member. McCarthy in 1953 and 1954 had chaired the U.S. Senate's Government Operations Committee, and also served on the Permanent Investigations Subcommittee. But he had no involvement with the Internal Security Subcommittee; Rusher had little contact with him.

14. See Judis, *William F. Buckley Jr.,* 156–57; Rusher, *Rise of the Right,* 9–20, 38–39; William F. Buckley Jr., *Happy Days Were Here Again: Reflections of a Libertarian Journalist* (New York: Random House, 1993), 412–15.

15. See William F. Buckley Jr., "Introduction," in Rickenbacker, *The Fourth House: Collected Essays,* v–xiii; Judis, *William F. Buckley Jr.,* 212–13.

16. See Smant, *How Great the Triumph;* John P. Diggins, *Up from Communism: Conservative*

Odysseys in American Intellectual History (New York: Harper and Row, 1975); Judis, *William F. Buckley Jr.*, 121–24; telephone interview with John Meyer, April 1, 1995.

17. Judis, *William F. Buckley Jr.*, 147–48, 172–73; Priscilla Buckley, "James Burnham 1905–1987," *NR* 39 (September 11, 1987): 53–54.

18. William A. Rusher to the author, September 4, 1993 (in the author's possession).

19. William F. Rickenbacker to the author, August 25, 1993 (in the author's possession). The negotiations between the Meyer-Rickenbacker-Rusher faction and Buckley were rather intricate, with some trickery involved. "Our maneuver may amuse you," Rickenbacker remembered. "We wanted quarterly conferences. We knew that Bill would whittle our demand down to semiannual conferences. So we came out for *monthly* conferences, knowing full well that Bill would die if he had to go through that "agony" so often and would probably try to fall back to merely the quarterly conference. That's exactly how he negotiated, and we got what we wanted while he thought he had headed us off at the pass." (Rickenbacker to the author, ibid.)

20. See William A. Rusher to the author, September 4, 1993; Priscilla Buckley to the author, August 26, 1993 (both in the author's possession).

21. Priscilla Buckley to the author, August 26, 1993; Rickenbacker to the author, August 25, 1993 (both in the author's possession).

22. Rusher to the author, September 4, 1993 (in the author's possession).

23. William F. Buckley Jr. to the author, April 19, 1995; Rusher to the author, September 4, 1993; Priscilla Buckley to the author, August 26, 1993 (all in the author's possession).

24. Burnham to Buckley, March 3, 1963. Buckley Papers, Box 26.

25. Ralph de Toledano to the author, December 2, 1993 (in the author's possession).

26. Meyer to Buckley, February 21, 1963. Buckley Papers, Box 26.

27. See Barry Goldwater with Jack Casserly, *Goldwater* (New York: Doubleday, 1988), 32–55, 110–11, 118–24; Judis, *William F. Buckley Jr.*, 221–22.

28. See Goldwater and Casserly, *Goldwater*, 142–43. It appears that, in attempting to make contacts and gain possible allies among conservatives, Rockefeller may have attempted to meet with Frank Meyer. Meyer, in a letter to Buckley in March 1963, mentions that coming up soon on his schedule was a "meeting with Rockefeller" which "Kissinger" had arranged, and that Meyer would later tell how it went. Unfortunately there is no evidence proving that such a meeting actually took place, or if it did, what occurred. Rockefeller did meet with a Young Americans for Freedom delegation in the spring of 1963, and it may be that Meyer was accompanying them. See Meyer to Buckley, March 3, 1963. Buckley Papers, Box 26; and Rusher to the author, March 19, 1995 (in the author's possession).

29. "Goldwater and the Race Issue," *NR* 15 (July 30, 1963): 45 ff.; telephone interview with J. Daniel Mahoney, April 1, 1995; Goldwater and Casserly, *Goldwater*, 142–43.

30. Frank Meyer, "Conservatism and the Goldwater Consensus," *NR* 15 (November 5, 1963): 386 ff.; see also Frank Meyer, "And Still . . . Goldwater Can Win," *NR* 15 (December 17, 1963): 528.

31. Frank Meyer, "President Johnson and the Tides of Ideology," *NR* 16 (January 14, 1964): 23 ff.

32. Burnham to Buckley, July 20, 1963; Buckley to Burnham, July 25, 1963. Buckley Papers, Box 26; see also Judis, *William F. Buckley Jr.*, 221–25.

33. Meyer to Buckley, February 27, 1963. Buckley Papers, Box 26.

34. See "*NR* and Goldwater," *NR* 16 (January 14, 1964): 9; Judis, *William F. Buckley Jr.*, 225–26.

35. Meyer to the Editors, January 4, 1964. Buckley Papers, Box 30.

36. Priscilla Buckley to the author, March 22, 1995 (in the author's possession); see also Buckley to the Editors, January 5, 1964. Buckley Papers, Box 30.

37. Burnham to Buckley, February 16, 1964; Burnham to Buckley, February 27, 1964. Buckley Papers, Box 30.

38. Burnham to the Editors, February 23, 1964. Buckley Papers, Box 30.

39. William F. Rickenbacker to the Editors, March 2, 1964; Meyer to the Editors, February 23, 1964. Buckley Papers, Box 30.

40. Buckley to the Editors, March 5, 1964. Buckley Papers, Box 30. Underlining from the original.

41. "What New Hampshire Said," *NR* 16 (March 24, 1964): 218–20.

42. See Goldwater and Casserly, *Goldwater,* 147–48; Judis, *William F. Buckley Jr.,* 222–24; "Reflections on California," *NR* 16 (June 16, 1964): 477–78.

43. Frank Meyer, "When the Chips Are Down," *NR* 16 (April 21, 1964): 319.

44. Frank Meyer, "Goldwater: The Home Stretch," *NR* 16 (June 2, 1964): 447.

45. See Judis, *William F. Buckley Jr.,* 227–29.

46. Judis, *William F. Buckley Jr.,* 227–29; Rusher, *Rise of the Right,* 118–19.

47. Meyer to the Editors, July 6, 1964. Buckley Papers, Box 30. "WAR" refers to Rusher.

48. Interview (by telephone) with Eugene Meyer, March 22, 1995.

49. Frank Meyer, "The Republican Platform," *NR* 16 (June 30, 1964): 535.

50. Frank Meyer, "A New Political Map of America," *NR* 16 (August 11, 1964): 687.

51. William F. Buckley Jr., "The Vile Campaign," *NR* 16 (October 6, 1964): 853–56, 858; Nash, *American Conservative Intellectual Movement,* 274; Rusher, *Rise of the Right,* 121–22.

52. Frank Meyer, "What Consensus?" *NR* 16 (October 20, 1964): 912.

53. Richard de Mille to Frank Meyer, October 13, 1964. From the private collection of Mr. de Mille (in the author's possession); Priscilla Buckley to the Editors, October 1, 1964. Buckley Papers, Box 30.

54. Arlene Croce to the Editors, November 17, 1964. Buckley Papers, Box 30.

55. Frank Meyer, "What Next for Conservatives?" *NR* 16 (December 1, 1964): 1057. Interestingly, in this column Meyer sounded much very much like his nemesis, James Burnham. In this same issue of *NR,* Burnham wrote that what conservatives most needed to do was "the translation of conservative ideas and values into a practical, political program viable in relation to the given realities and persuasive to widening sections of the citizenry." (James Burnham, "Must Conservatives Be Republicans?" *NR* 16 [December 1, 1964]: 1052.)

56. Frank Meyer, "Conservative Strategy Now," *NR* 16 (December 29, 1964): 1145.

57. Frank Meyer, "Richard Cornuelle and the Third Sector," *NR* 17 (February 9, 1965): 103; Cornuelle's ideas also won praise from William F. Buckley Jr., and even from the leftist Saul Alinsky. See Nash, *American Conservative Intellectual Movement,* 266-67. Meyer made many of these same points in an article he contributed to a book of essays edited by Kenyon College political scientist Robert Goldwin, which was published this same year. See Meyer, "Conservatism," in *Left, Right and Center: Essays on Liberalism and Conservatism in the United States,* ed. Robert Goldwin (Chicago: Rand McNally, 1965), 1–16.

58. Frank Meyer, "Is Social Security a Sacred Cow?" *NR* 17 (June 1, 1965): 463.

59. Frank S. Meyer, ed., *What Is Conservatism?* (New York: Holt, Rinehart, and Winston), 3–4.

60. Frank Meyer, "Freedom, Tradition, Conservatism," in Meyer, ed., *What Is Conservatism?* 19–20.

61. Frank Meyer, "Conclusion," in Meyer, ed., *What Is Conservatism?* 191–204.

62. Frank Meyer, "Introduction," in Meyer, ed., *What Is Conservatism?* 3.

63. Meyer to the Editors, January 17, 1962. Buckley Papers, Box 20.

64. See Nash, *American Conservative Intellectual Movement,* 317–319; M. Stanton Evans, "The Committee Man," in "RIP: Frank S. Meyer," *NR* 24 (April 28, 1972): 471–72; Rusher, *Rise of the Right,* 133–34. Meyer and Rusher, however, still had no luck in persuading Buckley and *National Review* to give more formal support to such political ventures. After yet another argumentative editorial Agony in early 1965, it was decided that "we shall not give exorbitant publicity to the ACU until it proves itself" (see Buckley to the Editors, January 7, 1965. Buckley Papers, Box 35).

65. Frank Meyer, "For the Editors," *NR* 17 (November 30, 1965): 1123; Rusher to the author, March 19, 1995 (in the author's possession).

CHAPTER 9 (Pages 157-176)

1. William A. Rusher to L. Brent Bozell, September 28, 1961. Buckley Papers, Box 14.

2. Rusher, *Rise of the Right,* 40 ff.; H.W. Brands, *The Devil We Knew: Americans and the Cold War* (New York: Oxford University Press, 1993), 97–98; Irving Brant, "The Anti-Communist Hoax: Who Are the Right Wing's Real Enemies?" *New Republic* 146 (May 28, 1962): 15–18.

3. "The Ultras," *Time* 78 (December 8, 1961): 22–23; Brands, *The Devil We Knew,* 98; "The Americanists," *Time* 77 (March 10, 1961): 21–22; "Beware the Comsymps," *Time* 77 (April 24, 1961): 20; Allan Westin, "The John Birch Society: 'Radical Right' and 'Extreme Left' in the Political Context of Post World War II," in Bell, ed., *Radical Right,* 239–68.

4. See Judis, *William F. Buckley Jr.,* 193–96.

5. Judis, *William F. Buckley Jr.,* 193–94.

6. Interview (by telephone) with J. Daniel Mahoney, March 20, 1995; William F. Rickenbacker to the author, May 12, 1994 (in the author's possession).

7. See Goldwater and Casserly, *Goldwater,* 126–27.

8. See "Beware the Comsymps," *Time* 77 (April 24, 1961): 20; "Thunder Against the Right," *Time* 78 (November 24, 1961): 11–12; "The Ultras," *Time* 78 (December 8, 1961): 22–23.

9. Judis, *William F. Buckley Jr.,* 195; Buckley, *Odyssey of a Friend,* 244.

10. William Rusher to the author, May 18, 1994 (in the author's possession); Rusher to Buckley, quoted in Judis, *William F. Buckley Jr.,* 196.

11. Meyer to Buckley, February 14, 1961. Buckley Papers, Box 14.

12. Meyer to Buckley, March 26, 1961. Buckley Papers, Box 14.

13. William F. Buckley Jr., "The Uproar," *NR* 10 (April 22, 1961): 241–43; see also Judis, *William F. Buckley Jr.,* 196.

14. Richard de Mille to Frank Meyer, May 29, 1961; Meyer to de Mille, June 4, 1961. From the private correspondence of Mr. de Mille, in the author's possession; Rusher to Bozell, September 28, 1961. Buckley Papers, Box 14; Judis, *William F. Buckley Jr.,* 197.

15. Meyer to Buckley, April 23, 1961. Buckley Papers, Box 14.

16. Rusher to Buckley, September 14, 1961. Buckley Papers, Box 14. It is not merely a coincidence that, less than a month later, Rusher attended the first secret meeting of conservative Republican insiders that would eventually become the Draft Goldwater Committee.

17. Meyer, "The Conservative Movement: Growing Pains," 281.

18. Meyer to Buckley, September 3, 1961. Buckley Papers, Box 14.

19. See "The Question of Robert Welch," *NR* 12 (February 13, 1962): 83–84.

20. See Rusher, *Rise of the Right,* 81–82; Judis, *William F. Buckley Jr.,* 198–99.

21. Priscilla Buckley to the author, May 3, 1994 (in the author's possession); Judis, *William F.*

Buckley Jr., 198–99.

22. Judis, *William F. Buckley Jr.,* 198–99; Patricia B. Bozell to the author, April 1, 1995 (in the author's possession).

23. Meyer to the Editors, January 17, 1962. Buckley Papers, Box 20.

24. "The Question of Robert Welch," *NR* 12 (February 13, 1962): 83–88.

25. "Thunder on the Right," *Time* 79 (February 16, 1962): 47–48; Buckley to Burnham, March 7, 1962; Judis, *William F. Buckley Jr.,* 199–200; Burnham to Buckley, March 11, 1962. Buckley Papers, Box 20.

26. Priscilla Buckley to the author, May 3, 1994 (in the author's possession); Judis, *William F. Buckley Jr.,* 199–200; "To the Editor: The Question of Robert Welch," *NR* 12 (February 27, 1962): 140 ff.

27. Meyer to the Editors, February 4, 1962. Buckley Papers, Box 20; see also William Rusher to the Editors, January 30, 1962. Buckley Papers, Box 20.

28. Frank Meyer, "What Is Under the Bed?" *NR* 12 (April 10, 1962): 244.

29. Meyer to Buckley, March 1, 1962. Buckley Papers, Box 20.

30. Burnham to Buckley, July 20, 1963. Buckley Papers, Box 26.

31. Buckley to Burnham, July 25, 1963. Buckley Papers, Box 26.

32. See "The John Birch Society and the Conservative Movement: The Background," *NR* 17 (October 19, 1965): 914–16.

33. Ibid., 914–16; Judis, *William F. Buckley Jr.,* 246–47.

34. Buckley to the Editors, August 25, 1965. Buckley Papers, Box 35; Judis, *William F. Buckley Jr.,* 246–47.

35. Rusher to the Editors, August 26, 1965. Buckley Papers, Box 35.

36. See Rusher to the Editors, October 1, 1965; Rusher to the Editors, October 6, 1965; Buckley to the Editors, October 1, 1965. Buckley Papers, Box 35.

37. See William F. Buckley Jr., "The Birch Society: August 1965," and "More on the Birch Society"; and James Burnham, "Get US Out!" in "The John Birch Society and the Conservative Movement," *NR* 17 (October 19, 1965): 916, 917, 925.

38. Meyer to Buckley, January 2, 1965. Buckley Papers, Box 35.

39. Frank Meyer, "The Birch Malady," in "The John Birch Society and the Conservative Movement," *NR* 17 (October 19, 1965): 919–20.

40. William Rusher to the author, May 15, 1990 (in the author's possession); Judis, *William F. Buckley Jr.,* 246–47, 274 ff.

41. Telephone interview with J. Daniel Mahoney, March 20, 1995.

CHAPTER 10 (Pages 177-202)

1. See Robert A. Goldberg, *Barry Goldwater* (New Haven: Yale University Press, 1995), 234–35; Alonzo Hamby, *Liberalism and Its Challengers: From FDR to Bush* (New York: Oxford University Press, second edition, 1992), 259; David Halberstam, *The Best and the Brightest* (New York: Random House, 1969), 103.

2. Allen Guttmann, *The Conservative Tradition in America* (New York: Oxford University Press, 1967), 161; "Fascism and Harvard," *NR* 19 (April 4, 1967): 337–38; George F. Gilder and Bruce K. Chapman, *The Party That Lost Its Head* (New York: Alfred A. Knopf, 1966), 27. Ironically, by the 1970s Gilder moved to the right in his thinking and became an *NR* contributor.

3. "For the Record," *NR* 17 (September 7, 1965): 788; "For the Record," *NR* 17 (October 5, 1965): 892; Johnson's speech quoted in Allen J. Matusow, *The Unraveling of America: A History*

of Liberalism in the 1960s (New York: Harper and Row, 1984), 153.

4. See Mary C. Brennan, "Conservatism in the Sixties: The Development of the American Political Right, 1960–1968" (Ph.D. dissertation, Miami University, Oxford, Ohio, 1988), 195 n. 126; M. Stanton Evans, *The Future of Conservatism: From Taft to Reagan and Beyond* (New York: Holt, Rinehart and Winston, 1968), 18.

5. "New York and the GOP," *NR* 17 (November 16, 1965): 1014–15; William F. Buckley Jr., "Platform, Anyone?" *NR* 18 (May 17, 1966): 455; William A. Rusher to the Editors, December 8, 1966. Buckley Papers, Box 43.

6. Priscilla Buckley to the author, October 22, 1996 (in the author's possession); William Rusher to the Editors, November 2, 1964. Buckley Papers, Box 30.

7. William Rusher to the Editors, May 22, 1967. Buckley Papers, Box 43; Rusher to the author, November 1, 1996 (in the author's possession).

8. See Donald Bruce to William Rusher, April 6, 1965; Meyer to ACU Directors, September 11, 1965; Meyer to John M. Ashbrook, September 25, 1965. Rusher Papers (Washington, D.C.: Library of Congress), Box 132, Folder 6; Meyer to Ashbrook, July 11, 1968. Rusher Papers, Box 132, Folder 10.

9. See Judis, *William F. Buckley Jr.,* 238; Mahoney, *Actions Speak Louder,* 327; Richard H. McDonnell, "A History of the Conservative Party of New York State, 1962–1972" (Ph.D. dissertation, Pennsylvania State University, 1975), 82, 96.

10. See Meyer to Buckley, February 2, 1968. Buckley Papers, Box 50; Nash, *American Conservative Intellectual Movement,* 169; Brad Miner, *The Concise Conservative Encyclopedia* (New York: The Free Press, 1996), 156–57.

11. See R. Emmett Tyrrell, *The Conservative Crack-Up* (New York: Simon and Schuster, 1992), 50 ff.

12. Lee Edwards, "The Other Sixties: A Flag-Waver's Memoir," *Policy Review* 46 (Fall 1988): 58 ff.

13. See "YAF Roundup," *New Guard* 5 (May 1965): 22; "Around and About," *New Guard* 7 (March 1967): 24; "Summer School—for Leaders," *New Guard* 6 (September 1966): 6–10.

14. William Rusher to the author, November 1, 1996 (in the author's possession); see also Lou Cannon, *Reagan* (New York: G. P. Putnam's Sons, 1982): 164; William F. Buckley Jr., "A Relaxing View of Ronald Reagan," in William F. Buckley Jr., *The Jeweler's Eye* (New York: G. P. Putnam's Sons, 1968), 94 ff.

15. See Lee Edwards, *Reagan: A Political Biography* (San Diego: Viewpoint Books, 1967), 93–94.

16. William F. Buckley Jr., "How Is Ronald Reagan Doing?" *NR* 18 (January 11, 1966): 17; F. Clifton White and William J. Gill, *Why Reagan Won: A Narrative History of the Conservative Movement 1964–1981* (Chicago: Regnery Gateway, 1981), 82–83.

17. Buckley, "A Relaxing View of Ronald Reagan," 96; William Rusher to the author, June 21, 1997 (in the author's possession).

18. Frank Meyer, "The Importance of Reagan," *NR* 18 (December 27, 1966): 1315.

19. See Meyer to Buckley, March 1, 1962. Buckley Papers, Box 20; Meyer, "Heads We Lose, Tails They Win," 148; Patricia B. Bozell to the author, April 1, 1995 (in the author's possession).

20. Meyer to Buckley, February 8, 1964. Buckley Papers, Box 30.

21. Elsie Meyer to Buckley, December 4, 1959. Buckley Papers, Box 8; Elsie Meyer, "Anatomy of a Smear," *New Guard* 5 (February 1965), 10.

22. Interview (by telephone) with John Meyer, February 12, 1994; interview (by telephone) with Eugene Meyer, March 20, 1995.

23. Richard de Mille to the author, January 4, 1995 (in the author's possession); Wills, *Confessions of a Conservative,* 42.

24. Frank Meyer, "Books in Brief," *NR* 12 (May 22, 1962): 380; interview (by telephone) with Eugene Meyer, March 20, 1995; interview (by telephone) with John Meyer, April 1, 1995.

25. Neil McCaffrey to the author, August 26, 1993 (in the author's possession).

26. Edwin Feulner, "Foreword," in Frank S. Meyer, *The President's Essay: Freedom, Tradition, Conservatism* (Wilmington, Del: Intercollegiate Studies Institute reprint, 1991), 6–7. William F. Buckley Jr. estimated that there were 20,000 books in the Meyer home. William Rusher also remembers that the house was "dominated by a collection of enormous quantities of bookshelves, in room after room. There were books, books, books—just everywhere." Rusher to the author, September 4, 1993 (in the author's possession).

27. Carol Buckley, *At the Still Point: A Memoir* (New York: Simon and Schuster, 1996), 156–57.

28. See Meyer to Buckley, February 15, 1963. Buckley Papers, Box 26; Meyer to Buckley, February 21, 1963. Buckley Papers, Box 26; Meyer to Buckley, January 21, 1965. Buckley Papers, Box 35; Meyer to Buckley, April 10, 1968. Buckley Papers, Box 49.

29. Russell Kirk, *The Sword of Imagination: Memoirs of a Half-Century of Literary Conflict* (Grand Rapids, Mich.: William B. Eerdmans, 1995), 188; Meyer to Buckley, January 21, 1965. Buckley Papers, Box 35; Buckley to Meyer, February 2, 1965. Buckley Papers, Box 35.

30. Neal Freeman to the Editors, May 3, 1965. Buckley Papers, Box 35.

31. Meyer to Buckley, September 3, 1961. Buckley Papers, Box 14.

32. Arlene Croce to the Editors, November 7, 1966; Meyer to the Editors, November 14, 1966; Buckley to Those Concerned, January 5, 1967. Buckley Papers, Box 43; Priscilla Buckley to the author, June 6, 1997 (in the author's possession). The compromise, as Buckley summarized it in the minutes of the Agony, was: "We will eliminate the capital L when we write the word liberal. However, when we use liberal to mean what it meant in the 19th century, we will use some qualifying phrase in order to make that meaning clear."

33. Frank S. Meyer, *The Conservative Mainstream* (New Rochelle: Arlington House, 1969), 13.

34. Frank S. Meyer, "Western Civilization: The Problem of Political Freedom," in Meyer, *Conservative Mainstream,* 411–26.

35. Frank Meyer, "Books in Brief," *NR* 17 (June 15, 1965): 520.

36. William F. Buckley Jr., "To The Editor," *NR* 17 (July 27, 1965): 661.

37. Frank Meyer, "Lincoln Without Rhetoric," *NR* 17 (August 24, 1965): 725.

38. Harry Jaffa, "Lincoln and the Cause of Freedom," *NR* 17 (September 21, 1965): 827 ff.

39. Buckley to the Editors, April 1, 1965. Buckley Papers, Box 35; on the continuing debate over Lincoln, see for example M. E. Bradford, *Remembering Who We Are: Observations of a Southern Conservative* (Athens: University of Georgia Press, 1985), or Harry Jaffa, *Conditions of Freedom: Essays in Political Philosophy* (Baltimore: The Johns Hopkins University Press, 1975).

40. Frank Meyer, "Anything Goes," *NR* 18 (June 28, 1966): 629; Buckley, *Jeweler's Eye,* 44.

41. Frank Meyer, "The Draft," *NR* 18 (August 9, 1966): 785.

42. See "Summer School—for Leaders," *New Guard* 6 (September 1966): 6–10; Frank Meyer, "The Twisted Tree of Liberty," *New Guard* 8 (January 1968): 9–10; R. Emmett Tyrrell, "Reviews," *The Alternative* 2, no. 3 (October–November 1968): 9 ff.

43. Frank Meyer, "The Right and Duty of Self-Defense," *NR* 18 (May 17, 1966): 471.

44. Neil McCaffrey, "To The Editor," *NR* 18 (June 28, 1966): 602; Dorothy Rea to the Editors, October 31, 1966. Buckley Papers, Box 39. It is interesting that the 1990s has seen an increase in "gated" private housing developments, and private businesses and other en-

terprises hiring their own security details, as Meyer predicted; see John J. DiIulio Jr., "A More Gated Union," *The Weekly Standard* 2, no. 42 (July 7, 1997): 13–15.

45. See Godfrey Hodgson, *America in Our Time* (New York: Vintage Books, 1978), 325; Matusow, *Unraveling of America,* 291.

46. Frank Meyer, "The LSD Syndrome," *NR* 19 (March 21, 1967): 301. Meyer was not wrong in worrying about libertarian conservatives possibly using drugs. David Brudnoy, for example, a conservative activist of libertarian bent, who would eventually be an *NR* contributor, has admitted that he used drugs during this period. See David Brudnoy, *Life Is Not a Rehearsal: A Memoir* (New York: Doubleday, 1997).

47. See Meyer, "The LSD Syndrome," 301; Frank Meyer, "The Medium is the Medium," *NR* 19 (April 18, 1967): 419.

48. Frank Meyer to the Editors, May 23, 1966. Buckley Papers, Box 39.

CHAPTER 11   (Pages 203–218)

1. "Utopia and Civil Rights," *NR* 4 (August 3, 1957): 126–28; "Has Congress Abdicated?" *NR* 4 (June 29, 1957): 5; "The Right to Destroy a Right," *NR* 4 (July 6, 1957): 31; Richard M. Weaver, "Integration Is Communization," *NR* 4 (July 13, 1957): 67–68.

2. "Why the South Must Prevail," *NR* 4 (August 24, 1957): 148–49.

3. L. Brent Bozell, "Mr. Bozell Dissents from the Views Expressed in the Editorial 'Why the South Must Prevail,'" *NR* 4 (September 7, 1957): 209.

4. "The Court Views Its Handiwork," *NR* 4 (September 21, 1957): 244–45; L. Brent Bozell, "Governor Faubus Clouds the Issue," *NR* 4 (September 21, 1957): 248 ff.; "The Lie to Mr. Eisenhower," *NR* 4 (October 5, 1957): 292–93.

5. "Let Us Try, At Least, to Understand," *NR* 10 (June 3, 1961): 338; "The Week," *NR* 8 (March 12, 1960): 156.

6. William Rusher to K. B. Walker, July 5, 1961. Quoted in John A. Andrew, *The Other Side of the Sixties: Young Americans for Freedom and the Rise of Conservative Politics* (New Brunswick: Rutgers University Press, 1997), 132; "The Week," *NR* 13 (October 9, 1962): 251; William F. Buckley Jr., "The Mess in Mississippi—An Afterword," *NR* 13 (October 23, 1962): 304.

7. "The Week," *NR* 14 (January 29, 1963): 52; "To the Editor," *NR* 13 (November 6, 1962): 363.

8. "The Week," *NR* 14 (April 23, 1963): 305; William F. Buckley Jr., "Birmingham and After," *NR* 14 (May 21, 1963): 397.

9. "Goldwater and the Race Question," *NR* 15 (July 30, 1963): 45–48; James Jackson Kilpatrick, "Civil Rights and Legal Wrongs," *NR* 15 (September 24, 1963): 231 ff.; "When the Plaints Go Marching In," *NR* 15 (August 27, 1963): 140.

10. Garry Wills, "What Color Is God?" *NR* 14 (May 21, 1963): 408 ff.; "Doomed Revolution," *NR Bulletin* 16, no. 7 (February 18, 1964): 1. The editorial is unsigned, but Burnham almost always wrote the lead editorial for the *Bulletin,* and he was noted for his "sociological" interest in the civil rights movement. See Buckley to the author, April 1, 1995 (in the author's possession).

11. William F. Buckley Jr., "The Issue at Selma," *NR* 17 (March 9, 1965): 183; "The Selma Campaign," *NR* 17 (March 23, 1965): 227–28.

12. "Government Unlimited," *NR* 17 (August 24, 1965): 712 ff.

13. See Farber, *The Age of Great Dreams,* 111–15, 206; Matusow, *Unraveling of America,* 214–15, 368.

14. "Chaos in LA," *NR Bulletin* 17, no. 25 (August 31, 1965): 1.

15. William F. Buckley Jr., "Time for a Hiatus?" *NR* 18 (October 18, 1966): 1035; "The End of Dr. King?" *NR Bulletin* 19, no. 34 (August 29, 1967): 1.

16. "King-Talk," *NR* 19 (April 18, 1967): 395–96; William F. Buckley Jr., "The Protest," *NR* 19 (May 2, 1967): 470; Buckley, "King-Sized Riot in Newark," 142–44; "Are the Rioters Racists?" 144–46; "The Little Clouds," 151–53; "The End of Martin Luther King," 140–42, all in *Jeweler's Eye*.

17. Frank Meyer, "The Negro Revolution," *NR* 14 (June 18, 1963): 496. Emphasis from the original.

18. Frank Meyer, "The Violence of Nonviolence," *NR* 17 (April 20, 1965): 327.

19. Frank Meyer, "The Negro Revolution—A New Phase," *NR* 18 (October 4, 1966): 998.

20. Frank Meyer, "The Heredity-Environment Problem," *NR* 19 (October 3, 1967): 1065; interview with John Meyer (by telephone), April 1, 1995.

21. Frank Meyer, "Showdown with Insurrection," *NR* 20 (January 16, 1968): 36.

22. Frank Meyer, "Liberalism Run Riot," *NR* 20 (March 26, 1968): 283; Frank Meyer, in response to R. D. Sommers, "Suppress Dr. King?" *NR* 20 (February 13, 1968): 112. The Bush administration in 1992 argued in terms very similar to Meyer when it blamed the 1992 Los Angeles riots on Great Society social programs.

23. William Rusher to the author, March 19, 1995 (in the author's possession); Edwards, "The Other Sixties," 62.

24. Edwards, "The Other Sixties," 62; Buckley to the author, April 1, 1995 (in the author's possession).

25. Rusher to the author, March 19, 1995 (in the author's possession).

26. Meyer to the Editors, June 17, 1966. Buckley Papers, Box 43; Buckley to the author, April 1, 1995 (in the author's possession).

CHAPTER 12 (Pages 219-232)

1. See George C. Herring, *America's Longest War: The United States, 1950–1975* (Philadelphia: Temple University Press, 1986); Guenter Lewy, *America in Vietnam* (New York: Oxford University Press, 1978); Stanley Karnow, *Vietnam: A History* (New York: Viking Press, 1983); George Donelson Moss, *Vietnam: An American Ordeal* (Englewood Cliffs, N.J.: Prentice-Hall, 1990).

2. See Irwin Unger, *The Movement: A History of the American New Left, 1959–1972* (New York: Dodd, Mead and Company, 1974); John P. Diggins, *The Rise and Fall of the American Left* (New York: W. W. Norton, 1990); Todd Gitlin, *The Sixties: Years of Hope, Days of Rage* (New York: Bantam Books, 1987).

3. Gitlin, *Years of Hope, Days of Rage*, 185; John Morton Blum, *Years of Discord: American Politics and Society, 1961–1974* (New York: W.W. Norton, 1991), 271; Matusow, *Unraveling of America*, 329; Hodgson, *America in Our Time*, 351.

4. Terry H. Anderson, *The Movement and the Sixties* (New York: Oxford University Press, 1995), 235; Ronald Radosh, *Divided They Fell: The Demise of the Democratic Party, 1964–1996* (New York: The Free Press, 1996), 92; Kim McQuaid, *The Anxious Years: America in the Vietnam-Watergate Era* (New York: Basic Books, 1989), 130; David Horowitz, *Radical Son: A Journey Through Our Times* (New York: The Free Press, 1997), 392.

5. "The Debate Takes Shape," *NR* 17 (March 9, 1965): 178; "The Peace Corps," *NR* 17 (May 4, 1965): 358; William F. Buckley Jr., "Needed: Another Investigation," *NR* 18 (September 6, 1966): 875; "Will Johnson Do It? And Can He Take It?" *NR* 17 (May 4, 1965): 355–57; James Burnham, "Can Democracy Work?" *NR* 19 (May 16, 1967): 510.

6. Frank Meyer, "The Communist Party and the New Left," *NR* 20 (February 27, 1968): 191.

7. Meyer to the Editors, January 28, 1966. Buckley Papers, Box 39.

8. William Rusher to the Editors, January 31, 1966. Buckley Papers, Box 39.

9. "Will Johnson Do It? And Can He Take It?" 355–57; "Blinkers," *NR* 18 (June 28, 1966): 713–14; James Burnham, "The Other Vietnams," *NR* 19 (May 2, 1967): 465; James Burnham, "McNamara's Non-War," *NR* 19 (September 19, 1967): 1012–14.

10. "More Men or New Thinking?" *NR* 19 (July 25, 1967): 779; James Burnham, "What Is the President Waiting For?" *NR* 18 (June 28, 1966): 612.

11. Priscilla Buckley to the author, October 22, 1996 (in the author's possession); William Rusher to the Editors, August 22, 1967. Buckley Papers, Box 43.

12. See James Burnham to William F. Buckley Jr., February 12, 1965. Buckley Papers, Box 35; Buckley to the Editors, May 25, 1966. Buckley Papers, Box 39; "The Week," *NR* 17 (November 30, 1965): 1059–60; Chris Simonds to the Editors, n.d. (1968?). Buckley Papers, Box 49; William Rusher to the author, November 1, 1996 (in the author's possession).

13. Meyer to the Editors, February 8, 1964. Buckley Papers, Box 30; Meyer, *Conservative Mainstream,* 308; Meyer, "The McNamara Policy: Road to Disaster," *NR* 19 (August 8, 1967): 856.

14. Frank Meyer, "Reflections on Vietnam," *NR* 18 (February 22, 1966): 162.

15. See Terry Dietz, *Republicans and Vietnam, 1961–1968* (Westport, Conn.: Greenwood Press, 1986), 91–92, 100–1, 121.

16. Frank Meyer, "Vietnam—The Republican Performance," *NR* 18 (April 5, 1966): 316.

17. Frank Meyer, "Republican Bug-Out," *NR* 19 (October 31, 1967): 1208.

18. See "Involuntary Servitude in America," 3–4; David Franke, "Conscription in a Free Society," 4–7; Barry Goldwater, "End the Draft," 10; Russell Kirk, "Our Archaic Draft," 11; all in *New Guard* 7 (May 1967).

19. James Burnham, "The Antidraft Movement," *NR* 19 (June 13, 1967): 629.

20. Frank Meyer, "The Council for a Volunteer Military," *NR* 19 (July 11, 1967): 749.

21. R. Emmett Tyrrell, "The Alternative Interviews an American Gothic: William F. Buckley Jr.," *The Alternative* 1, no. 6 (May–June 1968): 5–8.

22. Michael H. Hunt, *Lyndon Johnson's War: America's Cold War Crusade in Vietnam, 1945–1968* (New York: Hill and Wang, 1996), 99; Brian VanDeMark, *Into the Quagmire: Lyndon Johnson and the Escalation of the Vietnam War* (New York: Oxford University Press, 1991), 25.

23. Irving Bernstein, *Guns or Butter: The Presidency of Lyndon Johnson* (New York: Oxford University Press, 1996), 337; VanDeMark, *Into the Quagmire,* 60, 67, 76, 108, 136.

CHAPTER 13   (Pages 233-262)

1. William F. Buckley Jr., "Vietnam and Partisan Politics," *NR* 20 (February 27, 1968): 206.

2. James Burnham, "Time for Some Answers," *NR* 20 (March 26, 1968): 282.

3. Frank Meyer, "Ten Days in April," *NR* 20 (May 7, 1968): 453.

4. Buckley to the Editors, April 29, 1968. Buckley Papers, Box 49; James Burnham, "Just Shut Your Eyes," *NR* 20 (May 21, 1968): 487.

5. Gitlin, *Years of Hope, Days of Rage,* 307; John C. Meyer, "What Happened at Columbia (And Why)," *New Guard* 8 (September 1968): 14–17.

6. R. Emmett Tyrrell, "The Demise of the Politics of Emptiness," *New Guard* 8 (September 1968): 18–19; "Freedom Forum," *New Guard* 9 (March 1969): 8; Tyrrell, *Conservative Crack-Up,* 37.

7. Frank Meyer, "When Governors Cease to Govern," *NR* 20 (June 4, 1968): 554.

8. "The Week," *NR* 20 (June 18, 1968): 588.

9. "Anything Goes," *NR* 20 (June 18, 1968): 592–93.

10. Frank Meyer, "The Right of the People to Bear Arms," *NR* 20 (July 2, 1968): 657.

11. "The Unhappy Warrior," *NR* 20 (September 10, 1968), 889 ff.

12. Priscilla Buckley to the author, June 6, 1997 (in the author's possession); Wills, *Confessions of a Conservative,* 78.

13. Garry Wills, "Convention in the Streets," *NR* 20 (September 24, 1968): 952–59.

14. See Wills, *Confessions of a Conservative,* 78; James Burnham, "Care and Feeding of Riots," *NR* 20 (September 24, 1968): 951.

15. Frank Meyer, "Richard Daley and the Will to Govern," *NR* 20 (October 8, 1968): 1015; Hodgson, *America in Our Time,* 373.

16. See Richard Nixon, *RN: The Memoirs of Richard Nixon* (New York: Grosset and Dunlap, 1978), 257, 654; Theodore H. White, *The Making of the President 1968* (New York: Atheneum, 1969), 127, 254; Tom Wicker, *One of Us: Richard Nixon and the American Dream* (New York: Random House, 1991), 411.

17. White, *Making of the President 1968,* 127 ff.; John Ehrlichman, *Witness to Power: The Nixon Years* (New York: Simon and Schuster, 1982), 29, 163.

18. Goldberg, *Barry Goldwater,* 234–35; Chester Lewis et al., *An American Melodrama: The Presidential Campaign of 1968* (New York: The Viking Press, 1969), 256; William F. Buckley Jr. to the author, November 18, 1996 (in the author's possession); Rusher, *Rise of the Right,* 144–45.

19. William Rusher to the Editors, October 26, 1965. Buckley Papers, Box 35; Kirk, *Sword of Imagination,* 400; Nick Thimmesch, *The Condition of Republicanism* (New York: W.W. Norton, 1968), 91; Rusher, *Rise of the Right,* 145–47.

20. Goldberg, *Barry Goldwater,* 251; Meyer to Buckley, September 3, 1961. Buckley Papers, Box 14; Meyer to Buckley, March 12, 1961. Buckley Papers, Box 14.

21. Frank Meyer, "Thinking Aloud About 1968," *NR* 19 (June 13, 1967), 640.

22. Frank Meyer, "Conservatism and Republican Candidates," *NR* 19 (December 12, 1967): 385.

23. Judis, *William F. Buckley Jr.,* 279–81; William Rusher to the author, June 21, 1997 (in the author's possession); William F. Buckley Jr., "The Lesson of Mr. Romney," *NR* 20 (March 20, 1968): 310.

24. William A. Rusher, "Reflections on the Rise of the Right: The Keynote Address at the Conference on American Conservatism, Princeton University, May 3, 1996." (Claremont, California: The Claremont Institute for the Study of Statesmanship and Political Philosophy, 1996), 8; see also Rusher, *Rise of the Right,* 144 ff.

25. William Rusher to the Editors, January 3, 1967. Buckley Papers, Box 43.

26. Rusher to the Editors, July 10, 1967; Buckley to the Editors, November 7, 1967. Buckley Papers, Box 43; Frank Meyer to the Editors, May 25, 1968. Buckley Papers, Box 50; see also Rusher, *Rise of the Right,* 148–51; and Rusher to the author, June 21, 1997 (in the author's possession). Rusher notes that Buckley, once he could see that Reagan quite possibly would in fact run for the presidency, lost his doubts about Reagan's qualifications for the office, stating "serenely" by early 1968 that he'd "changed his mind" about Reagan's image as an actor harming his presidential hopes; which may have added to the felt need to be neutral between Nixon and Reagan.

27. Rusher to the Editors, May 22, 1968. Buckley Papers, Box 50; Rusher to the Editors, August 12, 1968. Buckley Papers, Box 49; Rusher to the author, June 21, 1997 (in the author's possession).

28. Frank Meyer, "Why I Am for Reagan," in Meyer, *Conservative Mainstream,* 294–99. Originally published in the May 11, 1968 edition of the *New Republic.*

29. On Strom Thurmond's (and other conservatives') fear of Rockefeller, see F. Clifton White
with Jerome Tuccille, *Politics as a Noble Calling* (Ottawa, Ill.: Jameson Books, 1994), 173–81;
Rusher to the author, June 21, 1997 (in the author's possession).

30. Meyer to Buckley, March 9, 1968. Buckley Papers, Box 50.

31. Meyer to Buckley, March 21, 1968; see also Rusher to the Editors, May 22, 1968.
Buckley Papers, Box 50.

32. Meyer to the Editors, May 25, 1968. Buckley Papers, Box 50.

33. "Nixon," *NR* 20 (June 4, 1968): 533–34.

34. Frank Meyer, "What Is at Issue in 1968," *NR* 20 (July 30, 1968): 751.

35. Rusher to the Editors, August 12, 1968. Buckley Papers, Box 49; see also Rusher, *Rise of
the Right,* 153–61.

36. Frank Meyer, "A Conservative Convention," *NR* 20 (August 27, 1968): 859; see also
White, *Making of the President 1968,* 254 ff.

37. See Michael Kazin, *The Populist Persuasion: An American History* (New York: Basic Books,
1995); Dan T. Carter, *The Politics of Rage: George Wallace, the Origins of the New Conservatism,
and the Transformation of American Politics* (New York: Simon and Schuster, 1995); Jody Carlson,
*George C. Wallace and the Politics of Powerlessness: The Wallace Campaigns for the Presidency,
1964–1976* (New Brunswick: Transaction Books, 1981).

38. On Wallace's extremist ties, see Carter, *Politics of Rage,* 295–98; Carlson, *George C. Wallace
and the Politics of Powerlessness,* 76.

39. Priscilla Buckley to the author, October 22, 1996 (in the author's possession); Buckley to
the Editors, May 17, 1967. Buckley Papers, Box 43; "The Week," *NR* 19 (November 14,
1967): 1244.

40. Frank Meyer, "The Populism of George Wallace," *NR* 19 (May 16, 1967): 527. Interestingly, Meyer's interpretation of Wallace as populist is largely supported by most historical
scholarship today on Wallace. See Kazin, *Populist Persuasion,* 237–42.

41. See Judis, *William F. Buckley Jr.,* 283–87, 295; William F. Buckley Jr., "A Look at George
Wallace," in *The Governor Listeth: A Book of Inspired Political Revelations* (New York: G. P.
Putnam's Sons, 1970), 57–61; Buckley, "What George Wallace Means to Me," *Look* 32
(October 29, 1968): 101 ff.; John Ashbrook, "And Anyway Is Wallace a Conservative?" *NR*
20 (October 22, 1968): 1048–49; Barry Goldwater, "Don't Waste a Vote on Wallace," *NR* 20
(October 22, 1968): 1060 ff.

42. See "Letters," *NR* 19 (May 30, 1967): 550; later, after another *NR* editorial salvo against
Wallace, pro-Wallace mail again flooded in—"all of it mad at us," reported a staffer, "and
almost all of it taking exception to our phrase 'racist-minded demagogue.'" See Chris
Simonds to the Editors, n.d. (1968?). Buckley Papers, Box 49.

43. "Nixon for Prez," *NR* 20 (November 5, 1968): 1097–98.

44. Frank Meyer, "The Mandate of 1968," *NR* 20 (November 19, 1968): 1170; see also
Rusher, *Rise of the Right,* 161.

45. McCarthy to Arendt, 1952, in Carol Brightman, ed., *Between Friends: The Correspondence of
Hannah Arendt and Mary McCarthy 1949–1975* (New York: Harcourt, 1995), 11–12.

46. See William Rusher to the author, November 1, 1996 (in the author's possession); *The
Challenge for Responsible Conservatives* (Republican State Central Committee of Washington: 1966); Lee W. Huebner and Thomas E. Petri, eds., *The Ripon Papers 1963–1968* (Washington, D.C.: The National Press, 1968), 28, 227; Thimmesch, *Condition of Republicanism,*
31; Stephen Hess and David S. Broder, *The Republican Establishment: The Present and Future of*

the GOP (New York: Harper and Row, 1967), 80–83.

47. See "Notes and Asides," *NR* 18 (November 1, 1966): 1090; "For the Record," *NR* 20 (May 7, 1968): 468; "Notes and Asides," *NR* 20 (August 27, 1968): 843; "Notes and Asides," *NR* 20 (August 13, 1968): 790.

48. See McDonnell, "A History of the Conservative Party of New York State, 1962–1972," 82, 96, 129; "Intrigue in New York," *NR* 20 (September 24, 1968): 948–49.

49. See "The Sniper," *Time* 90 (November 3, 1967): 70 ff.; Hess and Broder, *Republican Establishment,* 78.

CHAPTER 14 (Pages 263-294)

1. See Judis, *William F. Buckley Jr.,* 298–99.

2. See Judis, *William F. Buckley Jr.,* 300–4; J. Anthony Lukas, *Nightmare: The Underside of the Nixon Years* (New York: Penguin, 1988), 30–31.

3. See, for example, William A. Rusher to William F. Buckley Jr., February 12, 1969. Rusher Papers, Box 121, Folder 2; Rusher to Patrick J. Buchanan, March 10, 1969. Rusher Papers, Box 13, Folder 4; Buchanan to Rusher, October 31, 1969, Box 13, Folder 4; Rusher to Buckley, September 28, 1971. Rusher Papers, Box 121, Folder 4.

4. See Rusher to Buckley, March 4, 1969; Buckley to Rusher, March 11, 1969. Rusher Papers, Box 121, Folder 2.

5. Rusher to Buckley, June 30, 1969. Rusher Papers, Box 121, Folder 2.

6. Frank Meyer, "Curtains for John Lindsay?" *NR* 21 (April 22, 1969): 383.

7. "The Campaign Ahead," *NR* 21 (July 1, 1969): 628; Frank Meyer, "As New York Goes . . . ?" *NR* 21 (July 29, 1969): 751.

8. See Rusher to Buckley, October 5, 1960. Rusher Papers, Box 121, Folder 2; "Nixon at the Six-Month Mark," *NR* 21 (July 29, 1969): 734–35; William F. Buckley Jr., *Inveighing We Will Go* (New York: G. P. Putnam's Sons, 1972), 33.

9. "What Is Nixon's Policy?" *NR* 21 (February 25, 1969): 158 ff.

10. See "Vietnam: The Political Crunch," *NR* 21 (November 4, 1969): 1100–1101; "Now Is the Time for All Good Men to Come to the Aid of Their President," *NR* 22 (May 19, 1970): 500–501.

11. "Deeper and Deeper Still," *NR* 22 (March 24, 1970): 292 ff.

12. See the following by James Burnham: "Richard de Nixon, Gaullist?" *NR* 21 (April 22, 1969): 382; "Stripped Down," *NR* 22 (July 28, 1970): 786; and "The Case of the Mountain Climbers," *NR* 22 (March 10, 1970): 248.

13. See "What Now in Vietnam?" *NR* 21 (May 6, 1969): 418–21; "The Sands Are Running," *NR* 21 (July 29, 1969): 736–37; and "The Commander-in-Chief Reports to the Nation," *NR* 21 (November 18, 1969): 1153–54.

14. See James Jackson Kilpatrick, "Report Card for Richard Nixon," *NR* 21 (June 3, 1969): 532 ff.; and "Nixonology: Centrism," *NR* 22 (December 29, 1970): 1383.

15. See Robert E. Bauman to William F. Buckley Jr., September 4, 1969. Rusher Papers, Box 121, Folder 2; Linda Bridges to the Editors, June 17, 1969; Bridges to the Editors, August 11, 1969. Buckley Papers, Box 61.

16. See Buckley to Bauman, October 6, 1969. Rusher Papers, Box 121, Folder 2; Rusher, *Rise of the Right,* 167.

17. See "Barbarism Without Virtue," *NR* 21 (January 14, 1969): 16–17; "Who Shall Be Master in the House?" *NR* 21 (May 6, 1969): 423–24; William F. Buckley Jr., "An Evening with the Kids," *NR* 21 (May 20, 1969): 507; Buckley, "Commencement Dilemma," *NR* 21 (July

1, 1969): 663.

18. See "The Week," *NR* 22 (March 10, 1970): 238; "The Week," *NR* 22 (March 24, 1970): 290; "Can American Education Survive One More Year Like the One We Have Just Been Through?" *NR* 22 (June 30, 1970): 722–28; William F. Buckley Jr., "Dear Diary," *NR* 22 (July 14, 1970): 748; Stephen F. Ambrose, *Nixon: The Triumph of a Politician, 1962–1972* (New York: Simon and Schuster, 1989), 350–52.

19. See "The Week," *NR* 21 (July 15, 1969): 678; "Scare City," *NR* 21 (December 2, 1969): 1206–7; "Week of the Bombs," *NR* 22 (March 10, 1970): 245–46; "Coincidences," *NR* 22 (March 24, 1970): 296; "Radicals: Ilse Koch Section," *NR* 22 (April 21, 1970): 394–96; Adam Garfinkle, *Telltale Hearts: The Origins and Impact of the Vietnam Antiwar Movement* (New York: St. Martin's Press, 1995), 195–96.

20. See "For the Record," *NR* 21 (October 21, 1969): 1040; "The Persecution and Assassination of the Black Panther Party as Directed by Guess Who," *NR* 21 (December 30, 1969): 1306–7; "The Time for Words Is Over," *NR* 22 (May 5, 1970): 448; "For the Record," *NR* 22 (January 13, 1970): 4; Garfinkle, *Telltale Hearts,* 184; Gitlin, *Years of Hope, Days of Rage,* 256.

21. See William Rusher, "Memo on the New Left," *NR* 21 (August 12, 1969): 803 ff.; "Containment and Counterattack: Hayakawa at the Bridge," *NR* 21 (March 11, 1969): 215–16; "Radicals: Ilse Koch Section," *NR* 22 (April 22, 1970): 396.

22. Quoted in Frank Meyer, "The Revolution Eats Its Parents," *NR* 21 (June 3, 1969): 541.

23. Ibid.

24. Frank Meyer, "Apotheosis of the Crybaby," *NR* 21 (July 1, 1969): 646.

25. Frank Meyer, "Counterculture or Anticulture?" *NR* 22 (November 3, 1970): 1165.

26. Frank Meyer, "Reaping the Whirlwind," *NR* 22 (January 27, 1970): 89.

27. Frank Meyer, "Oct. 15, 1969, vs. Nov. 5, 1968," *NR* 21 (November 4, 1969): 1117.

28. Frank Meyer, "The Real Constitutional Crisis," *NR* 22 (June 2, 1970): 571; Meyer, "Mass Intimidation," *NR* 23 (June 1, 1970): 594.

29. James Burnham, "Party to Movement," *NR* 22 (September 22, 1970): 993.

30. "Where We Are," *NR* 22 (June 2, 1970): 549.

31. Ronald Reagan, "The Key Is Understanding," in *Seeds of Anarchy: A Study of Campus Radicalism,* ed. Frederick Wilhelmsen (Dallas: Argus Academic Press, 1969). 17; KL to the Editors, November 7, 1969. Buckley Papers, Box 61.

32. William F. Buckley Jr. speech text, "Reflections on Current Disorders." Rusher Papers, Box 121, Folder 3; Buckley, "Reflections on Violence," *NR* 22 (October 6, 1970): 1072–73.

33. Rusher to Buckley, Janurary 7, 1970. Rusher Papers, Box 121, Folder 3.

34. Tom McSloy, in "Notes and Asides," *NR* 22 (April 7, 1970): 347–48.

35. See William F. Buckley Jr. to Priscilla Buckley and Frank Meyer, February 9, 1970. Buckley Papers, Box 165, Folder 1080.

36. Frank Meyer, "Comment from Frank S. Meyer," *NR* 22 (April 7, 1970): 348–49.

37. See Buckley to the Editors, February 24, 1970. Rusher Papers, Box 121, Folder 3; Rusher to the Editors, April 10, 1970. Rusher Papers, Box 121, Folder 3; Tom McSloy, in "Notes and Asides," *NR* 22 (June 2, 1970): 554.

38. On Simonds's column, see C. H. Simonds, "Playing It Straight," *NR* 23 (January 12, 1971): 35; and "Settling Down," *NR* 23 (February 9, 1971): 145. See also William F. Buckley Jr., "The Old Man in the Back of the Room," *NR* 21 (March 25, 1969): 287–88.

39. See Jules Witcover, *White Knight: The Rise of Spiro Agnew* (New York: Random House, 1972), 1–173 (on Agnew's early life), and especially 174–78 for his move towards conserva-

tism; and Theo Lippman, *Spiro Agnew's America* (New York: W. W. Norton, 1972), 154–55.

40. See Rusher, *Rise of the Right,* 170; Rusher to Agnew, December 16, 1969; Rusher to Agnew, February 16, 1970; Rusher to Agnew, July 28, 1970; Rusher to Agnew, December 15, 1970. Rusher Papers, Box 6, Folder 6.

41. Quoted in the following by William F. Buckley Jr.: "Mr. Agnew and the Demonstrators," *NR* 21 (November 18, 1969): 1182; "Agnew Comes Through," *NR* 21 (November 18, 1969): 1183; and "Agnew on TV," *NR* 21 (December 2, 1969): 1235.

42. See Patrick Buchanan to Rusher, November 13, 1969. Rusher Papers, Box 13, Folder 4; Rusher to Agnew, February 16, 1970. Rusher Papers, Box 6, Folder 6. "The Mob and the Media," *NR* 21 (December 2, 1969): 1204.

43. Buckley, "Mr. Agnew and the Demonstrators," 1182; Buckley to Priscilla Buckley, James Burnham, William Rusher, February 19, 1970. Rusher Papers, Box 121, Folder 3.

44. Frank Meyer, "Storm Over Agnew," *NR* 21 (December 2, 1969): 1220; see also Meyer's "Apotheosis of the Crybaby," 646; "Oct. 15, 1969, vs. Nov. 5, 1968," 1117; and "The Real Constitutional Crisis," 571.

45. Burnham to Buckley, March 6, 1970. Buckley Papers, Box 165.

46. See Buckley's "Agnew Comes Through," 1183; "Agnew on TV," 1235; "Notes and Asides," *NR* 22 (December 29, 1970): 1390; and Rusher to Agnew, December 15, 1970. Rusher Papers, Box 6, Folder 6.

47. See John R. Coyne Jr., *The Impudent Snobs: Agnew vs. the Intellectual Establishment* (New Rochelle, N.Y.: Arlington House, 1972); H. R. Haldeman, *The Haldeman Diaries: Inside the Nixon White House* (New York: G. P. Putnam's Sons, 1994), 107.

48. See Rusher, *Rise of the Right,* 173–74 ff.; Judis, *William F. Buckley Jr.,* 311–16.

49. Rusher, *Rise of the Right,* 173; Rusher to Jim Buckley, Dan Mahoney, Clif White, April 8, 1970. Rusher Papers, Box 169, Folder 3.

50. See "The Conservative Party of New York State Seventh Anniversary Dinner Program, October 13, 1969." Rusher Papers, Box 147, Folder 6; Myron Waldman, "James L. Buckley: Consistently Conservative," *Newsday* (October 2, 1971): 4A–5A. Rusher Papers, Box 13, Folder 5.

51. See Arnold Steinberg to Rusher, June 8, 1970. Rusher Papers, Box 169, Folder 3; Randall C. Teague to James Buckley, April 20, 1970. Rusher Papers, Box 169, Folder 3; Rusher to Tony Dolan, September 8, 1970. Rusher Papers, Box 169, Folder 4; Richard Reeves, "Buckley Ready to Oppose Nixon on SST and Welfare," n.d., not referenced [December 1970?]. Rusher Papers, Box 13, Folder 5.

52. See "Confidential Memorandum: Subject—Prospects for Buckley Victory in N.Y. Senate Race," May 20, 1970. Rusher Papers, Box 169, Folder 3; J. Daniel Mahoney to James Buckley, F. Clifton White, David Jones, July 3, 1970. Rusher Papers, Box 169, Folder 4.

53. See "The First Hurrah?" *NR* 22 (June 16, 1970): 601–2; "And in New York . . . ," *NR* 22 (July 28, 1970): 772–73; "Onward and Upward," *NR* 22 (August 11, 1970): 827–28; "For the Record," *NR* 22 (September 22, 1970): 976; "Republicans and Hard Hats," *NR* 22 (September 22, 1970): 989.

54. See William F. Buckley Jr. to John Tower, July 29, 1970. Rusher Papers, Box 169, Folder 3; Patrick J. Buchanan to Rusher, July 23, 1970. Rusher Papers, Box 169, Folder 3; and Haldeman, *Diaries,* 191–92.

55. Rusher, *Rise of the Right,* 174–75; Haldeman, *Diaries,* 207.

56. See James Jackson Kilpatrick, "Hi There! Your Next Senator . . . ," *NR* 22 (November 5, 1970): 1154–58.

57. "The Week," *NR* 22 (November 17, 1970): 1196; James Burnham, "Something New Is

Added," *NR* 22 (November 17, 1970): 1198–99.

58. Burnham, "Something New Is Added," 1199.

59. See for example Patrick Allitt, *Catholic Intellectuals and Conservative Politics in America, 1950–1985* (Ithaca, N.Y.: Cornell University Press, 1993), 243–44.

60. Frank Meyer, "The Course of Garry Wills," *NR* 22 (July 28, 1970): 791.

61. Frank Meyer, "Attack on Middle America," *NR* 22 (October 20, 1970): 1112–13.

62. Rusher to Buchanan, July 21, 1970. Rusher Papers, Box 13, Folder 4.

63. See Buckley to Burnham, February 9, 1970. Rusher Papers, Box 121, Folder 3; Burnham to Buckley, February 6, 1970. Buckley Papers, Box 165.

64. See Burnham to the Editors, June 29, 1970. Buckley Papers, Box 165; William F. Buckley Jr., "In the Beginning . . . ," *NR* 22 (December 1, 1970): 1263–65.

65. Frank Meyer, "The Future of the Republican Party," *NR* 22 (December 1, 1970): 1271–73.

66. James Burnham, "Notes on Authority, Morality, Power," *NR* 22 (December 1, 1970): 1283–89.

67. Frank Meyer, "Authoritative or Authoritarianism?" *NR* 22 (December 29, 1970): 1246.

68. See "The Week," *NR* 22 (December 1, 1970): 1246; William F. Buckley Jr., 1973 Fund Appeal Letter to all *NR* subscribers. Rusher Papers, Box 121, Folder 5.

CHAPTER 15   (Pages 295-336)

1. See Kenneth Melvin, "Big Brother Is Dead, Too," *NR* 21 (February 11, 1969): 114–118.

2. Frank Meyer, "Brave New World," *NR* 21 (February 25, 1969): 180.

3. James Burnham, "The Welfare Non-Issue," *NR* 21 (March 11, 1969): 222.

4. Frank Meyer to Richard de Mille, October 6, 1964. From the private collection of Mr. de Mille (in the author's possession).

5. Donald Atwell Zoll, "Shall We Let America Die?" *NR* 21 (December 16, 1969): 1261–63.

6. Frank Meyer, "What Kind of Order?" *NR* 21 (December 30, 1969): 1327.

7. Donald Atwell Zoll and Frank Meyer, "In Re Professor Zoll: I—Order and Freedom," *NR* 22 (March 24, 1970): 311.

8. Meyer, "In Re Professor Zoll: I," 311.

9. Frank Meyer, "In Re Professor Zoll: II—Defense of the Republic," *NR* 22 (April 7, 1970): 362.

10. David Friedman, "Mekong or Rio Grande," *New Guard* 8 (May 1968): 15.

11. Karl Hess, "In Defense of Hess," *New Guard* 9 (April 1969): 15–16.

12. Jerome Tuccille, *It Usually Begins with Ayn Rand* (New York: Stein and Day, 1971), 46–47, 77–78.

13. See "The Week," *NR* 21 (December 2, 1969): 1202; Tuccille, *It Usually Begins with Ayn Rand*, 104, 115–25; Hess to Buckley, January 18, 1969. Buckley Papers, Box 61.

14. Tuccille, *It Usually Begins with Ayn Rand*, 85–87.

15. Tuccille, *It Usually Begins with Ayn Rand*, 87.

16. Frank Meyer, "Libertarianism or Libertinism?" *NR* 21 (September 9, 1969): 910.

17. Ralph Raico, "Did Meyer Take Liberties?" in "Letters," *NR* 21 (November 4, 1969): 1094–95.

18. See Rusher to Buckley, March 11, 1969. Rusher Papers, Box 121, Folder 5; William F. Buckley Jr., "The Right-Radicals," *NR* 23 (February 9, 1971): 162.

19. On Nixon's general attitude towards domestic policy, see Ambrose, *Nixon: The Triumph of a Politician*, 431–32.

20. Ambrose, *Nixon: The Triumph of a Politician,* 432.

21. "State of the Union," *NR* 23 (February 9, 1971): 124.

22. William F. Buckley Jr., "The Right-Radicals," *NR* 23 (February 9, 1971): 162.

23. "Are the Elephant and the Donkey Twins?" *NR* 23 (March 23, 1971): 303–4.

24. See Charles Benson, "Deterrence Through Defense," *NR* 23 (March 9, 1971): 257 ff.; "Mr. President, Sir . . . ," *NR* 23 (March 9, 1971): 240.

25. See James Burnham, "Who Watches the Watchman?" *NR* 23 (October 8, 1971): 1105; Burnham "Whose Serve?" *NR* 23 (May 4, 1971); William F. Buckley Jr., "The New China," *NR* 23 (May 4, 1971): 497; Buckley, "The Patience of Mr. Nixon," *NR* 23 (June 15, 1971): 669.

26. See Buckley to the Editors, September 6, 1971; Buckley to the Editors, November 30, 1971. Rusher Papers, Box 121, Folder 4; Rusher to Buckley, January 21, 1972. Rusher Papers, Box 121, Folder 5.

27. Frank Meyer, "Tory Men and Whig Measures," *NR* 21 (October 7, 1969): 1013.

28. Frank Meyer, "Mr. Nixon's Course," *NR* 23 (January 26, 1971): 86.

29. Frank Meyer, "Nixon's Domestic Program," *NR* 23 (March 9, 1971): 262.

30. See Minutes of the Meeting of the Executive Board of the American Conservative Union, February 5, 1971. Rusher Papers, Box 134, Folder 3.

31. See Rusher to the Editors, February 3, 1971; Rusher to Buckley, February 3, 1971. Rusher Papers, Box 121, Folder 4.

32. See Minutes of the Meeting of the Executive Board of the American Conservative Union, May 23, 1971. Rusher Papers, Box 134, Folder 3; Rusher to Buckley, February 24, 1971. Rusher Papers, Box 121, Folder 4.

33. Frank Meyer, "The Defense Crisis," *NR* 23 (April 6, 1971): 372.

34. Frank Meyer, "Let a Hundred Flowers Bloom," *NR* 23 (May 4, 1971): 482.

35. See Linda Bridges to the Editors, July 2, 1971; Bridges to the Editors, ibid.; Bridges to the Editors, July 16, 1971. Buckley Papers, Box 1065, Folder 1084.

36. See "For the Record," *NR* 23 (June 15, 1971): 620.

37. Frank Meyer, "Uneasy Doubts About Nixon," *NR* 23 (June 29, 1971): 706.

38. "The Twain Shall Meet," *NR* 23 (August 10, 1971): 845–47; Frank Meyer, "Peace in Our Time," *NR* 23 (August 10, 1971): 873.

39. See Judis, *William F. Buckley Jr.,* 329; Rusher, *Rise of the Right,* 178.

40. "A Declaration," *NR* 23 (August 10, 1971): 842.

41. Jeffrey Bell to the Manhattan 12, September 16, 1971; Neil McCaffrey to the Manhattan 12, September 20, 1971. Rusher Papers, Nixon-Richard-Conservatives' Suspension of Support File, 1971–1972.

42. Meyer to the Manhattan Twelve, October 16, 1971. Rusher Papers, Nixon-Richard-Conservatives' Suspension of Support File, 1971–1972.

43. See "Foreign Policy Planks/Domestic Policy Planks," n.d.; Allan Ryskind to William Rusher, November 2, 1971. Rusher Papers, Nixon-Richard-Conservatives' Suspension of Support File, 1971–1972;

44. See Neil McCaffrey to the Manhattan Twelve, October 22, 1971; William Rusher to Jerry Harkins, November 5, 1971. Rusher Papers, Nixon-Richard-Conservatives' Suspension of Support File, 1971–1972.

45. Anthony Harrigan to the Manhattan Twelve, November 4, 1971; Neil McCaffrey to the Manhattan Twelve, December 1, 1971. Rusher Papers, Nixon-Richard-Conservatives' Suspension of Support File, 1971–1972.

46. "Echoes and Re-Echoes," *NR* 28 (August 24, 1971): 908–9; Allen Drury, "Richard and

the Elves," *New York Post* (September 29, 1971), in Rusher Papers, Nixon-Richard-Conservatives' Suspension of Support File, 1971–1972; Linda Bridges to the Editors, August 24, 1971. Buckley Papers, Box 165, Folder 1084. "The people who reject it mostly do so on the grounds that, although Nixon is by no means the best we could hope for, our lack of support for him will only make it easier for Kennedy or Muskie . . . to win," Bridges reported. "A few have said that Nixon hasn't been doing so badly, and why don't we quit whining and sulking."

47. "For the Record," *NR* 23 (September 10, 1971): 960; "Richard Nixon's NEP," *NR* 23 (September 10, 1971): 969; Frank Meyer, "Down the Primrose Path," *NR* 23 (September 10, 1971): 994.

48. Frank Meyer, "The Voter or the Politician," *NR* 23 (October 8, 1971): 1120; Frank Meyer, "The Rhetoric of Phase II," *NR* 23 (November 5, 1971): 1240.

49. See "For the Record," *NR* 23 (November 5, 1971): 1208; J. Daniel Mahoney to the Manhattan Twelve, September 30, 1971. Rusher Papers, Nixon-Richard-Conservatives' Suspension of Support File, 1971–1972.

50. See "Rat, for Love of Country," *NR* 23 (December 31, 1971): 1451–52; . .Whose Pill?" *NR* 23 (December 17, 1971): 1391–92.

51. William F. Buckley Jr., "The End of the United Nations," *NR* 23 (November 19, 1971): 1300 ff.

52. See William A. Rusher to Those Concerned, November 23, 1971. Rusher Papers, Nixon-Richard-Conservatives' Suspension of Support File, 1971–1972. The day after the UN expelled Taiwan, Rusher summed up his feelings far more succinctly. He telephoned an increasingly beleaguered Patrick Buchanan at the White House. "I am just phoning," Rusher snapped, "to say goodbye." (See Rusher, *Rise of the Right,* 180.)

53. See The Editors, "In Re New Hampshire," *NR* 23 (December 31, 1971): 1449.

54. See "Letter from Washington," *NR* 23 (December 31, 1971): 1451; Witcover, *White Knight: The Rise of Spiro Agnew,* 436 ff.; Charles A. Moser, *Promise and Hope: The Ashbrook Presidential Campaign of 1972* (Washington, D.C.: Free Congress Research and Education Foundation, 1985), 10–12.

55. See "The Ashbrook Candidacy," *NR* 24 (January 21, 1972): 18 ff.; Rusher to Buckley, February 9, 1972. Rusher Papers, Box 121, Folder 5.

56. See William F. Buckley Jr., "Veni, Vidi, Victus," *NR* 24 (March 17, 1972): 258 ff.; Buckley, "Richard Nixon's Long March," ibid., 264 ff.

57. See Rusher to Buckley, March 14, 1972; Goldwater to Buckley, March 13, 1972; Buckley to Goldwater, March 24, 1972. Rusher Papers, Box 121, Folder 5.

58. Buckley to Rusher, March 7, 1972. Rusher Papers, Box 121, Folder 5.

59. Burnham to Buckley, February 7, 1972. Buckley Papers, Box 166, Folder 1093.

60. See "The Week," *NR* 24 (March 31, 1972): 310; "Primary Notes," *NR* 24 (March 31, 1972): 316 ff.; Moser, *Promise and Hope,* 35.

61. See Joan Hoff, *Nixon Reconsidered* (New York: Basic Books, 1994), 112; Ambrose, *Nixon: The Triumph of a Politician,* 444; Haldeman, *Diaries,* 332; Bruce Oudes, ed., *From The President: Richard Nixon's Secret Files* (New York: Harper and Row, 1989), 306–7; Richard Whalen, *Catch the Falling Flag: A Republican's Challenge to His Party* (Boston: Houghton Mifflin, 1972), 267–68.

62. See Oudes, *From The President,* 343, 474–76; Haldeman, *Diaries,* 368, 397, 423.

63. See Minutes of the Special Meeting of the Board of Directors of the American Conservative Union, March 2, 1966. Rusher Papers, Box 134, Folder 2; Minutes of the Meeting of the Board of Directors of the American Conservative Union, February 5, 1971; Minutes of

the Meeting of the Board of Directors of the American Conservative Union, May 23, 1971. Rusher Papers, Box 134, Folder 3.

64. See "The Conservative Party of New York State Seventh Anniversary Dinner Program," October 13, 1969. Rusher Papers, Box 147, Folder 6; Gregory Schneider, *Cadres for Conservatism: Young Americans for Freedom and the Rise of the Contemporary Right* (New York: New York University Press, 1999), 212; Jerome Tuccille, *Radical Libertarianism: A New Political Alternative* (New York: Harper and Row, 1971), 125; C. S. Horn, "Reunion in Sharon," *NR* 22 (October 6, 1970): 1056–57; "Over 600 Attend Conservative Awards Dinner," *Human Events* 31 (February 20, 1971): 12.

65. See "Reactions: The Cybernetic Monster," *The Exchange,* no. 18 (October 1966): 1–3; Thomas Szasz, "Involuntary Mental Hospitalization: A Crime Against Humanity," *The Exchange,* no. 25 (December 1967): 1–4; Frank Meyer, "Editorial Note," *The Exchange,* no. 26 (May 1968): 3; "Trends: Straws in the Wind," *The Exchange,* no. 32 (November 1969): 1–2; R. E. Tyrrell, "Projected Collegiate Magazine," *The Exchange,* no. 34 (April 1970): 2.

66. See Tyrrell, *Conservative Crack-Up,* 194–95.

67. See "The Week," *NR* 23 (June 1, 1971): 570–71.

68. See Frank Meyer, "The Negro Dilemma," *NR* 22 (August 25, 1970): 898; Meyer to Buckley, March 24, 1971. Buckley Papers, Box 165, Folder 1083; "Books in Brief," *NR* 23 (June 15, 1971): 663.

69. Elsie Meyer, "Introduction," in *Breathes There the Man: Heroic Ballads and Poems of the English-Speaking Peoples,* ed. Frank S. Meyer (LaSalle, Ill.: Open Court, 1973), 1–2.

70. Meyer, "Introduction," in Meyer, ed., *Breathes There the Man,* 2 ff.

71. See Meyer to A. M. Rosenthal, June 10, 1971. Buckley Papers, Box 165, Folder 1084. In explaining his and his sons' love of chess, Meyer was pleading with Rosenthal for the *Times* to give more coverage to the world chess championships.

72. Meyer to Richard de Mille, June 17, 1970. From the private collection of Mr. de Mille. In the author's possession.

73. R. Emmett Tyrrell, "Reviews," *The Alternative* 3, no. 3 (November–December 1969), 6–7.

74. R. Emmett Tyrrell, "Frank S. Meyer: An Interview," *The Alternative* 3, no. 1 (August–September 1969): 3 ff.

75. Ibid.

76. Chambers to de Toledano, July 9, 1956, in *Notes from the Underground: The Whittaker Chambers–Ralph de Toledano Letters, 1949–1960,* ed. Ralph de Toledano (Washington, D.C.: Regnery Publishing Co., Inc., 1997), 279.

77. See Edward S. Shapiro, ed., *Letters of Sidney Hook: Democracy, Communism, and the Cold War* (Armonk, N.Y.: M. E. Sharpe, 1995), 273; "Conservatism for the New Generation," (Washington, D.C.: Young Americans for Freedom pamphlet, 1970); Tuccille, *Radical Libertarianism,* 59; William F. Buckley Jr., ed., *Did You Ever See a Dream Walking? American Conservative Thought in the Twentieth Century* (Indianapolis and New York: Bobbs-Merrill, 1970), 75–92; Jared Lobdell, "Save General Ceremony: A Portrait of WFB," *The Alternative* 4 (December 1971), 31–32; Peter Witonski, ed., *The Wisdom of Conservatism,* vol. I (New Rochelle, N.Y.: Arlington House, 1971), 37; see also Peter Witonski, "The Conservative Consensus," *NR* 22 (December 1, 1970): 1304–7.

78. Buckley, "The Old Man in the Back of the Room," 287–88.

79. Frank Meyer, "Isolationism?" *NR* 23 (December 3, 1971): 1356.

CHAPTER 16   (Pages 337–348)

1. Burnham to Buckley, January 23, 1972. Buckley Papers, Box 166, Folder 1094; William F. Buckley Jr., "RIP: Frank S. Meyer," *NR* 24 (April 28, 1972): 466–67.

2. "Letters," *NR* 24 (May 26, 1972): 559; Buckley, "RIP: Frank S. Meyer," 466.

3. Buckley, "RIP: Frank S. Meyer," 466–67; Priscilla Buckley, ibid, 475; James G. Campaigne, "Frank Meyer, RIP," *The Alternative* 5, no. 9 (September 1972): 31–32.

4. See "Letters," *NR* 24 (May 26, 1972): 559; L. Brent Bozell, "RIP: Frank S. Meyer," NR 24 (April 28, 1972), p. 473.

5. Frank S. Meyer, *In Defense of Freedom and Related Essays* (Indianapolis: Liberty Fund edition, 1996), 146–47 n.; see also Richard de Mille to Elsie Meyer, April 21, 1972 (in the author's possession); Meyer, "Design for an Electronic Utopia," *NR* 23 (February 23, 1971): 208–9; L. Brent Bozell, "RIP: Frank S. Meyer," 473; Buckley, "RIP: Frank S. Meyer," 466.

6. L. Brent Bozell, "RIP: Frank S. Meyer," 473.

7. See Richard de Mille to Elsie Meyer, April 21, 1972 (in the author's possession); Witonski, "Frank S. Meyer," 467; Buckley, "RIP: Frank S. Meyer," 466–67.

8. Buckley, "RIP: Frank S. Meyer," 466–67; L. Brent Bozell, "RIP: Frank S. Meyer," 473; Chambers to de Toledano, March 17, 1954, in de Toledano, *Notes from the Underground,* 63.

9. See Simonds, "At Home," *NR* 24 (April 26, 1972): 468–69; James Burnham, "RIP: Frank S. Meyer: The Anti-Communist," ibid, 470–71; John R. Coyne Jr., "The Voice We'll Always Hear in Our Minds," *The Alternative* 5 (September 1972): 32–33.

10. See Witonski, "Frank S. Meyer," 467–68; "Letters," *NR* 24 (May 12, 1972): 494; "Notes and Asides," *NR* 24 (May 12, 1972): 505; William F. Buckley Jr. 1973 Fund Appeal Letter to Subscribers of *National Review.* Rusher Papers, Box 121, Folder 5.

11. See text of speech by Senator James L. Buckley to the Conservative Political Action Conference, January 26, 1974. Rusher Papers, Box 13, Folder 6; John P. East, *The American Conservative Movement: The Philosophical Founders* (Chicago: Regnery Books, 1986), 71, 102; Craig Schiller, *The (Guilty) Conscience of a Conservative* (New Rochelle, N.Y.: Arlington House, 1978), 51–54; Justin Raimondo, *Reclaiming the American Right: The Lost Legacy of the Conservative Movement* (Burlingame, Calif.: Center for Libertarian Studies, 1993), 61–62; Walter Block and Llewellyn Rockwell, eds., *Man, Economy and Liberty: Essays in Honor of Murray Rothbard* (Auburn: The Ludwig von Mises Institute, 1988), 368.

12. See Edward Pessen, *Losing Our Souls: The American Experience in the Cold War* (Chicago: Ivan R. Dee, 1993), 144; Michael Lind, *Up from Conservatism: Why the Right Is Wrong for America* (New York: The Free Press, 1996), 14–15, 53–54.

13. Henry Regnery, *Memoirs of a Dissident Publisher* (New York: Harcourt Brace Jovanovich, 1979), 189–90.

14. Richard Gid Powers, *Not Without Honor: The History of American Anticommunism* (New York: The Free Press, 1995), 426–27; see also Brian Doherty, "Best of Both Worlds: Interview with Milton Friedman," *Reason Online* (http://www.deltanet.com/Reason/9506/FRIEDMAN.jun.html), January 4, 1997; Robert Whitaker, ed., *The New Right Papers* (New York: St. Martin's Press, 1981), 28; Brudnoy, *Life Is Not a Rehearsal: A Memoir,* 145; Sara Diamond, *Roads to Dominion: Right-Wing Movements and Political Power in the United States* (New York: The Guilford Press, 1995), 30–31; William C. Berman, *America's Right Turn: From Nixon to Bush* (Baltimore: The Johns Hopkins University Press, 1994), 2; Paul Gottfried and Thomas Fleming, *The Conservative Movement* (Boston: Twayne, 1988), 17–18; Lee Edwards, *The Conservative Revolution: The Movement That Remade America* (New York: The Free Press, 1999), 108; Tyrrell, *Conservative Crack-Up,* 91, 280–81.

15. William F. Buckley Jr., Winter 1978 Fund Appeal Letter. Rusher Papers, Box 121, Folder ll; Peggy Noonan, *What I Saw at the Revolution: A Political Life in the Reagan Era* (New York: Fawcett, 1990), 14–15; Samuel G. Freedman, *The Inheritance: How Three Families and America Moved from Roosevelt to Reagan and Beyond* (New York: Simon and Schuster), 338–39.

16. Chambers to de Toledano, September 25, 1954, in de Toledano, ed., *Notes from the Underground,* 177.

17. James G. Campaigne, "Frank S. Meyer, RIP," *The Alternative* 5, no. 9 (September 1972): 31–32.

18. Coyne, "The Voice We'll Always Hear in Our Minds," 32–33.

19. Ronald Reagan, "Remarks at the Conservative Political Action Conference Dinner," *Public Papers of the Presidents of the United States: Ronald Reagan, 1981: January 20 to December 31, 1981* (Washington, D.C.: U.S. Government Printing Office, 1982), 275–79.

20. Campaigne, "Frank S. Meyer, RIP," 32.

Index